Dukes, Ramsey
What I did in my holidays - Essays on Black
Magic, Satanism, Devil Worship and other niceties
ISBN 0-904311-20-1

First edition, 1998, published in collaboration with The
Mouse That Spins (TMTS) by:
Mandrake of Oxford
PO Box 250
OXFORD OX1 1AP (UK)
http://www.mandrake.uk.net/

Second printing, 2010, print on demand.
Copyright © 2010 The Mouse That Spins (TMTS)

Cover illustration: "Inverse alternation" by Austin Osman Spare, 1953

ISBN 978-0-904311-25-9

IN MEMORY OF ERM
whose kind bequest made possible the publication of these essays

Hewas a lifelong pacifist. In so far as this book, and the following
title, have a strongly pacific message, we would like to offer them as
a tribute to his memory. Insofar as they equally preach a rediscovery
of joy in combat, we would wish for his forbearance.

WHAT I DID
IN MY HOLIDAYS

ESSAYS ON BLACK MAGIC, SATANISM,
DEVIL WORSHIP AND OTHER NICETIES

BY RAMSEY DUKES

THE MOUSE THAT SPINS

CONTENTS

CONTENTS

PREFACE

This book is the third volume of collected essays by Ramsey Dukes. The second volume (Blast Your Way To Megabuck$ With My SECRET Sex Power Formula and other reflections upon the spiritual path) was published by Revelations 23 in 1993, and the first volume (Uncle Ramsey's BUMPER Book of Magick Spells and other essays on science and magic) may be published at some future date - the first shall be last because its content was generated before the author had a computer and so it still has to be keyed in. The essays in it are also even more dated and embarrassing.

This volume contains all the essays and shorter pieces written since his book "Words Made Flesh", ie since about 1986. As a collection set in approximate chronological sequence, it has no deliberate theme or structure other than its reflection of the author's concerns during these years. Bearing this in mind, however, a definite thread can be detected: it is an exploration of humanity's demons and the right way to relate to them.

This theme was highly relevant when the collection was assembled in the early 90s, but delays in publishing meant that many of these essays are a bit dated. For example, who now wants to read a sensible reduction by analysis of Satanic abuse hysteria? At the height of 80s media frenzy on the subject, it seemed a radical and interesting contribution - but now it preaches to the converted.

Perhaps the material should have been cut and edited to bring it up to date? The Mouse That Spins decided that the window of publishing opportunity opened by a small inheritance was too fleeting to allow any further delay - even if it would have meant a better book. So readers are invited to approach this rag bag of essays in the spirit of the jumble sale hunter-warrior. Thus I hope everyone will come away with some items of interest and value.

So why the word 'niceties' in the sub-title?

It was originally chosen intuitively: the juxtaposition of that word with the topics black magic, devil worship and satanism bore the droll charm of a mid afternoon tea party at Hellgate Hall. Yet the author did feel some obligation to research the word in anticipation of possible dissent.

According to the Oxford English Dictionary 'nicety' began its recorded life in Chaucerian times meaning 'folly, stupidity'. From there it came to mean 'wanton conduct', 'licentiousness' and 'lust' as well as 'sloth' and 'idleness'. By the fifteenth century it was referring to 'excessive refinement or elegance in dress or living' and that evolved over the next three centuries to mean 'delicacy of feeling' or 'fastidiousness'. In the nineteenth century it took on the more familiar meaning of 'precision', 'accuracy' or 'refinement'. And now it is generally taken to mean 'a minute or subtle point of detail'.

The fact that a single word could evolve from base stupidity to the heights of refinement is somehow utterly in keeping with the spirit of this collection of essays. Hence its place in the title.

There is space on this page, and there are people I wish to thank.

First and foremost Carl, who did so much work on this volume without enjoying the fruits of completion. At times of postponement I could have murdered you - but the occasion never really presented itself, so you live to witness my enormous gratitude and this book offered as some tribute to your labour and your craft.

Something of the same applies to Mal - and Jake is another who laboured without satisfaction. Thank you both and thanks to Mogg who stepped in later.

Collected old material and locating past reviews was sometimes a daunting task - I am very grateful for the help of Phil, Ray, Ian and Ingrid, Caroline, Caroline, Matthew, John, Louise, Julian, Catherine, Joel and the Cambridge University Library. Many of you may also have contributed unwittingly to the inspiration of these essays, thanks for that and thanks to others who pointed the way - especially Sonia, Pete, Robert, Sally and members of the extended family of He Who Channels my words.

In the final stages there was one supreme source of inspiration and resolve with which to complete this task. I lay this volume at the feet of My Lady Of The Laughing Waters.

O

ARTIFICIAL INTELLIGENCE & SOCIETY

*This article is the odd one out in this collection as it was written for a
'respectable' journal in an attempt to get someone interested in my book
Words Made Flesh. That's why it's got an abstract and all the other academic trimmings.*

Abstract
   This article looks at the broadest implications of public acceptance of AI.
   A distinction is drawn between "conscious" belief in a technology, and
   "organic" belief where the technology is incorporated into an unconscious world model. The extent to which we feel threatened by AI's
   apparent denial of "spirit" is considered, along with a discussion of how
   people react to this threat. It is proposed that organic acceptance of AI
   models would lead to a rebirth of popular spiritual concepts as paradoxical as the "New Age" ideas that have their roots in the theories of
   physics. Finally the relevance of this speculation is discussed in terms of
   how it could impinge upon public acceptability of AI technology.

Keywords: Artificial intelligence, social attitudes, concepts of "mind", computer modelling.

The editorial to the very first issue of AI & Society begins
with the words "Until recently, artificial intelligence was
predominantly an academic area of study". Key phrases
which follow include "..this journal will introduce some
new questions", "..aims to widen the debate" and "..a strongly inter-
disciplinary journal".
   Now this sort of "leading edge" can be a mine-field for the intrepid layman: a mine-field patrolled by defensive academics eager to
make sure that "inter-" is not given too much emphasis at the expense
of "-disciplinary" - their deepest nightmare is an invasion by enthusiastic cranks. Speaking as an enthusiastic crank myself, rest assured
that I have no plans to colonise this territory; and there is no reason
why less informed contributions should be a threat, just as long as
everyone recognises that their value is more likely to lie in the questions raised than in any ill-informed conclusions which may be
drawn!

My immediate interest in AI lies not in detailed problems of implementation, nor even in broader questions of its possible effects on the work-place, but rather in its widest implications for mankind. How might it influence public beliefs and attitudes.

LEVELS OF BELIEF

In looking at something as irrational as public belief, we expect to find paradoxes. I don't mean mysterious paradoxes, simply the sort of psychological quirk that makes, for example, deep feelings of inferiority often manifest themselves as an arrogant, overbearing personality. It is sometimes easier to predict that an individual will have extreme opinions on a particular topic, than it is to predict which extreme the individual will fly to.

I recognise two levels of belief. There is the rational, conscious level: when you "know" something is true because you have heard it on good authority. Then there is the "organic" level: when you "feel" something is true because it has been incorporated into an inner, semi-unconscious, model of the world you live in. Beliefs on these two levels can be at odds with each other, as I will illustrate below.

The first paradox is that public belief at the organic level can simultaneously both lag behind technological or scientific advance and also run ahead of it.

Consider as an example the spread of ideas about relativity and quantum physics. In the earliest days such notions were cranky, then they became acceptable to the scientific community. In the second half of this century, given the publicity of the atom bomb, there could be few people who had not heard about these theories: indeed, by the 1960s they became part of our school science syllabus. As such the general public "knew" the theories must be true, and yet basic attitudes made it clear that at the organic level the world model was still very much that of Victorian absolute mechanism (plus a smattering of divine intervention). What interests me is this: in recent manifestations like the "New Age" movement in America, are we seeing the first signs of some elementary relativistic and quantum ideas having become organic beliefs for a significant body of the population? Note that the significance is not so much in the individual New Age beliefs - there have always been a few occultists on the fringes of science - but in the fact that the movement is becoming so influential.

4

If a new-ager honestly interprets his/her experiences as "communication from other dimensions", it reveals that the inner model of reality has extended beyond Victorian materialism, towards more recent ideas. But it also shows how this individual's organic belief has jumped ahead of science to assume "other dimensions" containing communicating intelligences. This is an example of how organic belief can be both behind and yet ahead of science: because the inner model has its roots in primitive, magical levels of the unconscious, it tends to be slow to adapt to the latest theories, but when it does so it is likely to absorb them uncritically - maybe taking in some of the science's wilder speculations along the way.

I believe that such shifts in public attitude can feed back into problems of implementing new technology, and it is unwise to ignore them. If one does not accept the concept of organic belief, one can explain such public attitudes in terms of "misinformation", or by arguing that fear of nuclear war has created an insecurity which drives people to seek mystical panaceas. But, if this was the whole explanation, one would expect that the recent more peaceful political climate, together with the spread of information on modern physics, would combine to de-fuse the New Age movement: whereas I would predict that an increasing acceptance of ideas about relativity and quantum uncertainty at the organic belief level would lead rather to the movement's spread.

THE RELEVANCE TO AI

If it has taken more than 80 years for the new physics to work its way into public attitudes, then it might seem absurdly premature to start considering the possible effects of AI in this area. But there is an important distinction here: atomic physics is very much an "ivory tower" discipline. The number of people with direct experience of its working is negligible, instead we hear about it from teachers, books and television documentaries. AI, on the other hand, is set to invade our offices, shops and even our homes. People who have never seen a particle accelerator will become familiar with remarkably intelligent-seeming devices. And again: perhaps the significant factor in popular acceptance of the new physics has been the comparatively recent phenomenon of the television documentary; in that case we can soon expect a similar popular exposure to the more exciting advances in

5

AI. For such reasons it will surely take far less than 80 years before a significant proportion of the population has incorporated AI into its unconscious model of the world?

As an illustration of the person who has accepted AI at the conscious level but not yet integrated it into organic belief, I would suggest the layman who vigorously argues that "we are just computers" but who, when asked if he would have any sense of guilt when switching off a computer, dismisses the question as a trivial red herring. Such a person accepts at the rational level that there is no absolute unbridgable gulf between a brain and a computer, but reveals an unconscious contempt for computers as "mere machines". If his conscious beliefs had become organic, he would at least recognise the question of possible responsibility.

The chances are that such a layman will be found engaged in heated argument with another who asserts that "AI is nonsense" and that computers will never show any intelligence. I suspect that this second character is one who has jumped ahead to a partial assimilation of the computer model of the brain into his unconscious beliefs, but tainted with the belief that computers are stupid machines. The resultant is a fear that we are, therefore, just stupid machines. This unconscious fear is so threatening that the conscious attitude is a neurotic denial of any validity in AI in order to keep the unwelcome unconscious assumptions at bay.

What would be the likely effect on society if those two characters, plus the majority of the public, evolve to incorporate into their world model the combined idea that firstly there is no theoretical limit to the intelligence - nay, wisdom even - of computers, and that secondly the brain is itself a type of computer?

This is an idea whose exploration formed the basis of a book I wrote in 1985. The book was written largely for the benefit of those who feel threatened by the concept of artificial intelligence, and so I had to address myself to the problem of writing an interesting, even convincing, argument for those defensive readers who refused to allow themselves to believe in the basic idea. So I began by considering reasons for such resistance, and how best to deal with it.

RESISTANCE TO AI

I do not deny that there are many diverse reasons why people resist the idea of AI, ranging from fear of losing their jobs to fear of nuclear catastrophe through machine error, but I choose to concentrate on one reason that is very basic - indeed it may well lie at the root of many more practical-seeming objections raised by opponents. The reason is that people do not welcome the notion that everything they call "mind" could be generated by a brain that is a computer: we do not want to be machines.

I suggested above that a person with an unconscious fear of being a machine might reveal it in a conscious refusal to believe in AI. This was the first problem in my book: how to write interestingly for people who refuse to believe in the subject matter. The solution adopted was the use of fiction to illustrate the ideas.

If I had begun by asking "is the brain a computer?", many of the people I wanted to speak to would have responded with such a negative reaction that it would make it hard for them to accept the arguments that followed. Instead I might begin by telling a story of another world where a scientist builds a super computer that is capable of modelling human thought, and then exploring the idea in the story. If the exploration leads to some interesting and intriguing ideas which seem to have a bearing on our own world, then I have paved the way for a worthwhile discussion of artificial intelligence and our world. Instead of presenting AI as an outside "real possibility", I present it in a fictional story - ie an inner model in the reader's imagination. Such a model is no threat, for the reader can get to know it by "playing with" it. (Furthermore, for the purposes of the book, I later pointed out what I had done, as an example of modelling a world.)

Return now to the suggestion "we do not want to be machines", and imagine that I have written two science fiction short stories. The first is about the totally computerised Stock Exchange of the future: suddenly there is an emergency when dealing has to be suspended and a team of psychologists, economists, theologians and AI experts have to be shipped in to argue with the central computer because it has gone through a spiritual crisis, become a born-again Christian, and is now concerned about the role it is being asked to play. The second story is about a day in the life of a man in a future society who receives a note in the post announcing that his commercial pilot's licence has been revoked for next month because the regular computer analysis run by the Safety Executive has shown that he is almost certain to suffer a marital crisis that month and would not therefore be in a fit psychological state to fly.

Do these stories sound disturbing? Imagine further that we try them out on a large section of the population, and I predict that the tendency would be to see the first story as amusing, while the second would sound rather more threatening. This despite the fact that the first story is of a major world crisis precipitated by a computer, while the second is about human lives actually being protected by a computer. The point is, I suggest, that in the first story the financial computer proves that it is rather more lovable than one expected, because it betrays human weakness; but in the second story the human is shown to be predictable in a way that only machines are supposed to be, and the human is thereby reduced in value.

"Computers are only human" - that's quite a nice idea. Whereas "humans are only computers" is nasty. This asymmetry is similar to that which causes books like "The Human Zoo" which describe human behaviour in animal terms to be seen as controversial, and books like "Watership Down" which describe animal behaviour in human terms to be seen as totally charming.

What does this asymmetry tell us about the reason why we do not want to be machines or animals?

A major component in this reluctance is surely that AI seems like the last link in that chain of reductionism which leads back to the earliest distinction between animate and inanimate matter. We understand that there was a time when there was no distinction between "inner" and "outer", that "mind" or "spirit" was assumed to underlie all phenomena so that storms had spirits, trees and rivers had spirits, even mountains and rocks had spirits as had humans. Then we learned to distinguish inanimate matter like rocks and rivers from living matter - only the latter had spirit. Then we learned that plants did not have spirit, they were just complex chemical structures - a plant no longer turned towards the sun because it "loved" the sun, but because of the retarded growth of cells in direct sunlight. Then we learn that animals do not have spirit, they too are complex organic mechanisms.

So eventually we learnt that only humans have, as a matter of definition and observation, something we call "spirit". However the process of reductionism has a certain momentum, and the same arguments that banished spirit from the animal world can be applied to banish spirit from humanity. Spirit itself rebels against such banishment: however, the belief in the possibility of artificial intelligence provides the last link in this chain, because it suggests that even our most sublime mystical experiences might be an "illusion" begotten of the movements of matter.

This "chain of reductionism" is surely one strong reason for resistance to AI - it threatens to squeeze out of us that spirit which has already been squeezed out the rest of the universe. And yet this threat is not a real threat: it is only spirit that chooses to interpret it as a threat. Far from killing spirit in us, the ultimate artificial intelligence would be more likely to put spirit back into nature. This is because, if we can finally accept that there is no uncrossable qualitative abyss between our highest human spirit and the workings of a complex computer, then we can begin to see the elements of what we call "spirit" in the workings of simpler computers. But every physical event is a simple computer - even a free particle in space has computational ability (it will compute the resultant of a number of forces acting on it) and a memory (in the form of momentum) - and so the vestiges of spirit exist in every event. Now a field of grass, or the fluidic network of interactions in a river, add up to extremely complex information systems, containing an awful lot of those vestiges of spirit. So we will once again feel free to say that a flower turns toward the sun because it "loves" the sun, bearing in mind that the chemical reactions involved in the flower's love are not inseparably distinct from the chemical reactions behind human love: we will of course understand that the flower's experience of love may be utterly alien and incomparable with our experience of love, but that is something that intelligent primitives probably knew all along by simple observation.

What I am saying is this: if we define "spirit", or "mind" or "soul" or whatever in empirical terms as something we observe, then its existence is not threatened by artificial intelligence: on the contrary, it is set to return to its omnipresent place in nature - a rebirth of animism (or of pantheism if we see the universe as a one giant computational system).

Spirit is only threatened if, instead of defining it by observation, we define it in such purely logical terms as "that which transcends matter or mechanism". This is the viewpoint that sees mechanism as a sub-world within a greater world of spirit; which sees "the known and understood" as an island in an ocean of "the unknown and transcendent". Spirit is then that which lies beyond the mechanistic bit. The "squeezing out" process described above has amounted to an extending of the known, mechanical world so that parts (like animal consciousness) which were previously considered mysterious have now become annexed as part of the known mechanical world. The fear here is that extending of the island of knowledge is causing a drying up of the ocean: it is feared that one day we shall find that there is nothing outside the known and understood. There will be no spirit, for all will be understood in rational, explicable terms.

The fear this engenders is what I call "spiritual claustrophobia" in my book, and I consider it to be an interesting idea. If we take the extreme rationalist viewpoint - that there is no transcendent spirit and that the whole universe is no more than the ordering of matter by physical laws - then we can marvel at the wonderful diversity of phenomena engendered within this universe. But one of the most philosophically intriguing things engendered by this mechanistic universe is the concept of a world of spirit which transcends the universe itself. In other words the motions of matter have modelled, in man's brain, a reality greater than the reality of matter itself. When mankind "dreamed up" the idea of a spirit world, the universe transcended itself and gave itself room to move about and "breath"!

Spiritual claustrophobia is the fear of finding that there is no longer any spare room, there is nothing outside matter. When the new ager is told that those "messages from other dimensions" are actually messages from untapped portions of his own brain, then he feels disappointed. Even if they remain very good and very wise messages, they have lost value. His world has been made smaller, it has fewer dimensions.

Is an explorer someone who expands our horizons by making new discoveries, or is he someone who narrows our horizons by eliminating possibilities? When I was born there was still the possibility of active life on Mars and at least some remains of life on the Moon. Subsequent discovery has reduced those possibilities to zero. In past centuries the mechanistic universe had modelled, in our minds, a spirit-filled world of limitless wonder: it is now learning that such a world has no reality, there is nothing but itself. The claustrophobia we feel is the claustrophobia of reality itself - of a universe that dreamed of something greater, and is now awakening to face its own limitations and aloneness.

To summarise this section: behind the rather dismissive statement "it hurts people's pride to be seen as computers" I see justification for a profound sense of loss, on two counts.

Firstly, if we define "spirit" and all its attendant phenomena like "purpose", "desire", "love" etc in terms of our own subjective observation, then the computer model of the brain seems like the last step in the process which has already eliminated all those concepts from Nature. In answer to that fear I propose that the computer model could equally serve to justify quite the opposite conclusion: that the motions which we experience as "love", "purpose" etc are in their rudimentary forms co-extensive with all material existence.

Secondly, if we instead define spirit as something that transcends the known material world, then the computer model of the brain leaves us with very little room for transcendence. Once mystical experiences have been "explained" in material terms by computer simulation, then what use is any concept of "higher worlds"? I suggest that this sense of spiritual claustrophobia is very profound, because it has roots in the philosophical conundrum of a material world which has managed to develop a model of itself which transcends its own reality.

However, the fact is that the idea of machines behaving like humans (by becoming mysterious and unpredictable) is generally less threatening than the idea of humans behaving like machines. So this fact serves to suggest that spiritual claustrophobia (the fear of losing the unknown) is the greater threat of the two. So the greater part of my book "Words Made Flesh - Artificial Intelligence, Humanity and the Cosmos" is concerned with a possible solution to this very problem.

FREEING THE SPIRIT

The solution to the problem of spiritual claustrophobia that I suggest is a very simple one - so much so that half the book is concerned with the exploration of the profound and far-reaching consequences of an idea that is too easily ignored for its own obviousness.

The solution I suggest is that the growing public belief that it is possible to model a universe in a computer will lead to a belief that the universe we presently experience is itself an "illusion" created by the ordering of information in some "higher" universe.

Note that this belief, as in the examples suggested earlier, will very possibly run ahead of the actual technology. The sort of scenario I envisage is of a computer generated soap opera with sophisticated graphics which look like a real tv image of human actors. If the actual characters in this drama were themselves computer generated, it would give the program an interesting advantage: it would allow fans to 'phone in direct to the computer between episodes and talk to their favourite characters. If the characterisation was getting anywhere near able to pass the Turin test, it would be like being able to 'phone up "JR" and argue him into behaving better in the next episode. The advantage being that the computer, unlike any human actor, could handle simultaneous calls from thousands of fans by duplicating the programs as needed.

Experiences like this, even at a crude stage, would foster a public belief in "computer worlds" with self conscious, intelligent inhabitants who believe in their world just as much as we believe in our world.

Once this belief became organic it would become increasingly difficult to believe that there could be two distinct types of reality - indistinguishable to their respective inhabitants - one of which is "real" and the other is an "illusion" formed by ordered flow of information. The same principle of economy (Occam's razor) that makes it hard to believe in psychic phenomena once a valid scientific explanation has been given, and the same statistical instinct that makes it hard to believe that in all of this vast universe our planet alone has intelligent life, will together conspire to create a public belief in the idea that this universe must be in some sense an illusion created within a greater world beyond our senses.

Although the understanding of this view of our reality will be totally new, it is of course an idea utterly in keeping with centuries of traditional religious or mystical thinking. This will make the idea all the more infectious and attractive - one reason why public belief may well run far ahead of the actual technology of computer modelling. In the book I explore the possibilities at length, and show how many traditional ideas about spirit and reality will indeed be very much at home in an information universe.

In the final pangs of spiritual claustrophobia, the public will suddenly find the prison walls falling away to reveal a vast new universe of possibilities beyond the all-too-known world. So, paradoxically, the intelligent computer which threatens us with spiritual claustrophobia will provide its own remedy in time - "like curing like", as in some ancient medical traditions.

AI AND COMPUTER MODELLING

That, basically, is the solution suggested in my book, a book that was written before the advent of "AI & Society", and a book written for a general reader rather than for readers of this journal.

Because my field of enquiry concerned popular attitudes to AI, rather than academic theories or technological realities, I would not have chosen to target the book specifically for readers of this journal. In particular I can see that my terminology has been much too broad: I use the term "artificial intelligence" liberally whereas the actual argument in the last section is based far more on computer modelling than on AI proper.

The reason I did not clarify these terms in my book was that I felt the distinction to be at present simply an academic and technical convenience - a definition of boundaries to narrow a field of enquiry rather than the recognition of any absolute boundary. Myself I do not see how any intelligence could approximate to a human intelligence if it did not contain an approximately human model of reality within its software (indeed, self awareness or consciousness would seem to have its roots in the feedback cycle due to an image of self existing within that inner model - and free will is an illusion born of the chaos inherent in such real feedback loops). Conversely, I feel that computer modelling will never be universally useful until the models are able to contain intelligent human minds within them - an economic model of Britain should incorporate some measure of the personality of the Chancellor of the Exchequer, for example. So, in my somewhat futuristic view, I do admit to having lumped together AI and computer modelling in a way that might seem insensitive to present conventions.

CONCLUSION

In looking so far ahead, my discussion may have ranged beyond the usual boundaries of AI & Society; but I will argue that, just once in a while, it is worth stepping back and examining such speculations. I would also suggest that it is, in fact, mostly what I don't know about AI that has made me especially qualified to discuss the way that others like myself might react to its greater influence in our lives.

Although, by analogy, the "new ager's" conceptions of quantum physics might seem not only irrelevant but positively irritating to those working at the "leading edge" of the nuclear industry, nevertheless the broad impact of those conceptions should not always be ignored. Readers of, let us imagine, "Nuclear Physics & Society" might feel that a discussion of "new-age" philosophy had no place at all in their journal... but what if the spread of that philosophy went hand in hand with public resistance to nuclear energy? Some openness towards recognising the possible consequences might prove helpful.

Similarly, although my speculations about public belief have little relevance to most day-to-day AI developments, they might have a bearing upon the technology's future acceptability.

For example: at what point might we need to draw the line between "keeping computers in their place" by giving them recognisably machine-like voices (even when we have the technology to modulate those voices in a more human manner), and making them seem more "lovably human" as in my discussion of the sci-fi stories above? A socially acceptable answer to this problem would need to allow for the sort of considerations covered in this article.

In face of naive and ill-informed objections to AI, or any other technological advance, it is tempting to dismiss the opposition as ill-educated cranks and to imagine that the technology will eventually prove itself by its own usefulness to society. But belief moves in mysterious ways and I am suggesting that even public acceptance of the principle of AI could have unexpected consequences.

Public acceptance of the "new physics" does indeed seem to be engendering a new religious impulse, and this New Age religion is tending to take sides against the exploitation of the nuclear power by mankind. So what might be the consequences of a religion inspired by an extended view of artificial intelligence - a sort of "cybernetic universe"?

It is far from clear whether such a religion would turn out to favour the exploitation of AI, or to consider it taboo. It would be ironical if the success of AI research were to result in a parliamentary decree that the human creation of intelligence constitutes a blasphemy against The Great Program.

Those concerned with the impact of AI on society may ignore this possibility at their own peril.

BIBLIOGRAPHY

Dukes R. (1988) *Words Made Flesh - Artificial Intelligence, Humanity and the Cosmos.* TMTS, Winchester.

LETTER TO CHAOS

For the sake of completeness this letter to Chaos 8 is included. The reference to BBOMPSpells is "Uncle Ramsey's Bumper Book Of Magick Spells" which will be published for the first time in Volume 1 of these collected essays.

Dear Joel,

Thanks for Chaos 7, and for drawing my attention to the correspondence on suicide.

You ask if I would like to add to it. Reading carefully, I reckon that you and Hakim have between you penetrated very much to the heart of what I had to say and there is little that I could add. However, there is no harm in hearing things rephrased, and it would be a pleasure to contribute to the debate.

I think you have still got the original, so I cannot check this, but am pretty sure that the last page(s) of BBOMSpells described the following incident: A young man drives to a corporation refuse tip, finds a secluded spot in the piles of junk and sits there. He then contemplates his whole life, going on to consider all the magnificent, fortunate things which *might* just happen to him in the future. This is continued until he is sitting there like a king, with a great pageant of glittering possibilities parading before him in the rubbish. He then takes out a polythene bag and places it over his head, snuggling down into the heap so that his body will never be discovered. He closes the back tightly around his neck and the world swims around him in his pangs of asphyxiation. Then suddenly he rips off the bag, gulps in lungfuls of air, rebuilds reality, and climbs out of the heap. Finally he goes dancing into the city.

I hope I'm right about the story, but anyway know I wrote something like that somewhere and it is relevant to your debate because I can still recall what it meant to me sixteen years ago.

The young man had gone through three initiations (or 'crossed three abysses'): 1) accepting the Total Magic Act. 2) rejecting the TMA in favour of the Total Art Death. 3) rejecting the TAD in favour of Life.

Beginning from the individual's sense of powerlessness in society, the first initiation is a realisation of one's own power, provided you are prepared to give *all* (the key being the preparedness, not the actual giving). Contemplating the TMA, the individual realises that The Great Dictator now lives in terror, knowing that every extra soldier he recruits to the Palace Guard will increase the chances of one of those soldiers having a deeply repressed psychopathic streak which would turn him into a crazed assassin under the strain of responsibility: nor can he feel safe behind his electrified fence if he believes that wave upon wave of people might hurl themselves onto that fence until it collapses under the weight of their corpses.. The TMA takes power away from the Great Dictator and gives it back to the individual - whether he uses it or not.

The TAD transcends this state because it reveals how you are still in slavery: by becoming a Freedom Fighter (say) you have gained power over the Dictator, but have you not in fact become slave to the concept of Freedom? Traditional tales of pacts with the Devil include those where the individual manages to trick the Devil at the last minute: there is Maggie Thatcher cowering at the end of your rifle barrel (you have got her alone in a quiet place, you have fixed the perfect alibi) as your figure tightens on the trigger she composes herself and prepares to become the Great Martyr for the Conservative Cause; but you stop, lower the rifle, open it and unload it, saying 'actually I value this bullet rather more than your trivial and ineffective existence'. To plan the perfect assassination, then not to do it: is this a cop out, or is it the ultimate display of contempt?

Provided that you have passed the last initiation, the TAD is an act of defiance against the universe itself: it says that you KNOW your vast potential, but are prepared to chuck it all away by choosing the humblest, feeblest cop-out suicide imaginable.

The young man in the story does not complete his TAD: is that because he didn't have the guts to go through with it? Or is it a sign of an even higher act of defiance against existence - a refusal even to end it?

We need not know the answer. Only by getting right inside his head at that cuspal point of decision can one know exactly why he did/didn't do it. Even from that position one cannot be sure of an answer: perhaps he does not know himself? In trying to judge someone who has taken an initiation beyond ours, we have to fall back on studying his subsequent behaviour. Not 'is it better?', because we may not even be able to comprehend his motives now, but simply 'is it different?'. The young man arrived at the rubbish tip driving a Lea-Francis saloon, he left it on foot, dancing. This suggests an achievement of some higher state, or it could simply symbolise the casting off of the physical body.

I never decided the answer: he kept his secret. Death is taboo in our society, but it is also a Great Initiator: you can succumb to it, woo it, play with it, or reject it. Those who never dare even contemplate it are in no position to judge those who approach more closely. Consider a samurai who opts for hara-kiri but, instead of choosing the traditional form, decides to transcend it by challenging an enemy to combat and, by feigning lack of skill, allows himself to be killed; perhaps that samurai believes he has struck a blow against the tyranny of the Code of Honour, but this victory is his own personal secret carried to the grave. In the eyes of the world he has shown himself to be an inferior samurai. In magical terms he has given great energy to a revolutionary idea which is now released into the group unconscious; in materialist terms he has sold his life and his honour for a fleeting sensation of (unshared) triumph.

I have dwelt on the high initiations, but what of the genuine pitiful suicide who simply starts from a position of misery and decides to opt out? I take comfort from the establishment horror of such acts: surely you might expect them to encourage it? after all it rids society of one more snivelling and ineffective failure and surely that can do nothing but good to the year's productivity figures? Despite such obvious advantages, society reacts in horror to the suicide, and that alone is enough to give the act a certain dignity: one more soul has escaped the system, slipped through the net.

Hakim suggests that I harbour 'romantic notions about the idea... some sneaking suspicion that it could make a difference'. He is right. But I would defend my position by saying that these romantic notions are ones I believe I have chosen to harbour in order to resist the tyranny of that 'Sensibleness' which says 'you may talk about suicide, but you are too sensible to do it because you know it is an ineffective waste of time'.

Romance does have the merit of scaring Good Sense shitless. Even if one sees oneself as a helpless pawn in a game between the gods of Romance and Sense, one can at least improve the game by keeping them guessing right up to the last minute.

That is why I never wanted to know whether the end of my story was a cop-out or a triumph.

Yours in Chaos...

2

SATANISM FOR TODAY

First published in Chaos International, under Hugo l'Estrange's name.
Shock horror! What is Ramsey Dukes doing, claiming to be a satanist?
The fact is that this piece was ghost written for Hugo l'Estrange by
Ramsey Dukes. The result is a little too indecent for the latter, and far too
decent for the former - so I decided to put it in the Ramsey Dukes collection
rather than Hugo's "Hellgate Chronicles".

It arose from the publicity given to satanism by the hilarious "Satan
Sting" trial of 1986. In particular it was the Guardian which had the dis-
tinction of being the only newspaper to write a fairly sensible article on the
subject, so Hugo decided that they should be offered the chance to publish an
article by a genuine satanist. Alas, even with the gentle touch of Ramsey
Dukes the result proved too steamy for what turned out to be their religious
columns.

So blame this one on confused channelling.

There is a problem in trying to present the satanist's case. It is that as soon as I write anything that sounds at all reasonable, or agreeable, or even endearing, my words are liable to be dismissed as 'not real Satanism'. Why? 'Because Satanism is totally evil'.

There is an analogy: a strong case could be made to prove that President Reagan is not a Christian: he is not meek and mild, he shows no sign of turning the other cheek, nor of renouncing worldly wealth... on the other hand *he* considers himself to be a Christian, and his supporters would largely agree. So, at the practical level of this article, I go along with his belief.

In return I do not expect, when I show signs of flagging from my heavy round of blasphemy and blood sacrifice, to be told that I am therefore not a 'real Satanist'. Let him who is without merit throw the first raspberry.

The subject of Satanism is surrounded with veils of illusion. Removing those veils one by one, we do seem to approach a more credible core. The first veil is the idea, held by Christian fanatics and popular journalists, that the only alternative to science or religion is a thing called 'black magic'.

The second veil embodies the more useful notion that there is also something called 'white magic'. White magic is magic employed for purposes of good, black magic is magic employed for purposes of evil. Anyone of open mind who has experience of white magicians will surely agree that we are moving in the direction of truth, relative to the last veil.

The third veil defines a continuum between these poles: arguing that there are many shades of magic, depending upon the practitioner's purity of intent and relative selflessness. Satanism is the embodiment of the extreme black end of this 'spectrum'. Sometimes this continuum is seen as a slippery slope leading down to Satanism, analogous to the view that the political left is a slippery slope which plunges unavoidably into ultimate communism.

The last idea is a reasonable day-to-day belief (whether in its magical or political form). With it one can win friends and influence people, write acceptable articles, earn a living... But it has its limitations for the experienced magician who will, one day, wake up and ask 'who the hell actually does magic for the purposes of evil?'

The only people likely to dedicate themselves to absolute evil would be the odd artist or pimply adolescent going through a decadent crisis. Far from seeing that minority as a Great Cosmic Threat, I feel quite affectionate towards them, love them for their fleeting efforts to add a little colour to our lives. If black magic really is a tool of absolute evil, it can be neither prevalent or dangerous.

Removing the next veil we recognise that pure evil is virtually impotent. All really dangerous and vicious acts are dedicated not to pure evil, but to over-refined notions of good. If Adolf Hitler had initially announced a movement dedicated to pure evil, or even to providing an outlet for man's common nastiness, he would have remained a harmless crank. Instead the exoteric aims were to revive Germany, to create a new 'order', and to be safe from the evils of communism - all very good, and all very similar to the aims of present day government.

So black magic, if it is indeed a powerful and dangerous alternative to white magic, must mean something other than magic done for evil purposes.

Removing the next veil we see a different polarity, one that really does reflect a vital distinction. Although there are few who openly admit to black magic, those who do, and those most likely to be labelled 'black' by knowledgeable persons, are not so much those people working *for* evil, as those who work *with* evil. The whitest magicians are extremely unwilling to do anything but banish demons and evil forces, while black magicians will acknowledge, respect and even risk the dangers of working with such forces.

I will give a psychological example. A university student has a nervous breakdown, is torn apart by inner violence. He is directed to the psychiatrist who banishes this demon with the 'sword of analysis'. This is white magic: it frees the student to return to his work, get a good degree, and carve a successful career. After twenty years of success, however, there is a lingering malaise. He feels poisonously guilty, because nothing obvious is actually wrong - it is all just a little pointless. He now goes to a different more expensive type of analyst, who reveals that the demon banished was in fact a valid part of his make-up, and when it departed it took life's magic with it. The task now is a dangerous one, it is to make an inner journey to renew contact with that now deeply incarcerated demon, and attempt to assimilate or redeem it in order to restore the fullness of life. This is black magick (perhaps that's why it costs more!)

Don't say it must be white magic because the purpose is good: to approach such demons as a righteous crusader is unwise, just as (presumably) the lion tamer is not one who sets out to destroy a lion's basic nature. The aim is better called 'wholeness' than 'good'.

White magic does an excellent job but, in these terms, it does not do the whole job. Those who risk the mucky bits left over can call themselves black magicians, but not in public.

Psychological examples don't suit everyone, so I'll balance it with a simplified political one. Someone organises an atrocity to express their anger. The horror of this act catches the imagination of a slightly bored public and it is named 'terrorism'. Publicity validates the act, and in a few years you have a movement. This process is called 'evocation' of a demon, the demon of terrorism.

The demon begins to feed on the social equivalent of psychic energy, but it remains out there rather than a real danger. Then comes a new development: people in *no real danger* begin to feel threatened, and personally involved in the 'fight' against terrorism. This is called 'possession by' the demon, because these people will forget that a demon is a discarnate entity, and direct their attack against a (typically) human target. Bombs are dropped on the Libyan people in an attempt to destroy an abstract principle. The demon which causes men to express violence by politically aimed violence, is now exultantly pulling the trigger; those who most loudly oppose 'terrorism' have become terrorists, and denounce as weak those with stronger and more resistant minds!

The white magician would banish an evil demon, the black would make a pact with it. Be warned, accounts of black magic pacts can cause offence.

A relationship is made with the demon, a sort of understanding, but less the analytical 'banishing' approach of white magic. Appreciate what fun the initial plans of a terrorist attack could be. Then consider how often early IRA bombs were defused harmlessly after a warning phone call - a procedure seldom adopted by legal governments who underestimate the power of imagined explosions and prefer to kill outright. When an IRA nail bomb first exploded in London, it was heralded as a sign that the terrorists were 'worse than animals'; yet the US Government used plastic shrapnel in Vietnam because it was too easy to separate metal fragments from human flesh. It begins to look as if terrorism is more gentlemanly than the governments it opposes. And the vast majority of British have suffered more under Thatcherism than from the sum total of terrorist activity. Sympathy for the Devil does not mean identity with the Devil: there is even a sense in which the very horrors of black magic make it safer than white magic.

What happens next is not predictable, for black magic is more anarchic than white. One simply acts from one's new-found perspective. Outwardly one might act the same as the non-magician: one might bomb Libya. However (and this is where the rationalist abandons us in ridicule and despair) the magician believes that, however similar the outward act, the long-term result will be different. One's aim will be truer, because it will be a human rather than a demonic finger on the trigger.

Satanism, as the extreme of black magic, calls for a relationship with one's ultimate demon. This is likely to be a more general and personal evil than terrorism, but our Christian establishment is helpful in defining such devils. For example consider a nice, hard-working teenager who never rebels. He develops a horrid repulsion for the loud, brazen bullies who lay all the best girls and then, a few years later, get all the best-paid jobs. To him, Satan is the lord of the world, the flesh and aggression. This possession is confirmed when, as an adult, he finds himself madly in love with another man's wife: the other man is painfully nice and his wife is a compellingly brazen slut who made all the running. If he is lucky he awakens to the fact that it is himself that he is hurting; exaggerated guilt comes from identifying with the suffering husband. He begins to notice how the husband is passively exacerbating the situation; the realisation that the husband and he are both onto the same kick (possessed by the same devil) is the time for magic. White magic would end the affair, while the Satanist might consider flaunting his sexual triumph before the simpering wimp. This apparently callous act would pay homage to a shared demon through which the Satanist would know how the other person felt: if a hopeless case, the wimp's life would at least be elevated into the sweet masochism of a cosmic tragedy; if not, the crisis could awaken him to freedom. In either case adultery takes on new pleasures, for one has learned how to relate to humans as well as to demons.

In these examples I have not managed to define precisely the nature of the relationship with Satan. To expect that in a short article would be unrealistic: what is the precise nature of any religious devotion? Nor have I dwelt on the precise ritual forms and prayers, but rather on the principles. The former are so varied and personal that they would only obscure the basic argument. It is also too easy to read one's prejudices into the details of other peoples' religion; the Holy Communion shows ample evidence of being a cannibalistic cult if you look for that evidence.

Nor have I dwelt on blood sacrifice. This is partly due to squeamishness: some day I must do it for my own salvation. Satanic blood sacrifices are sporadic rather than performed on the grand scale.

Personally, though I recognise the need, I feel that the need for large-scale human sacrifice is more the mark of an old and weary religion. There is little doubt that Christian fervour in Ulster is nourished by spilt blood, and that the major human sacrifice at Jonestown has done its job of reversing the decline in church attendance in the USA. Satanism has not been reduced to such extremes.

As a traditional Satanist I despise the Christian Church, but am untypical in that I respect its origins. Christianity and communism are the religions of the underdog: as such they both perform wonders when kept in their place by persecution. But as soon as such religions rise to institutional power they turn extremely nasty.

The world becomes a wonderfully civilised place when you embrace Satan: for years you have been believing the world 'needs Christian principles because without them men would revert to savagery', then one day you reject those principles and find, like the humanists, that you do not revert to savagery! Then you realise that anyone who holds such beliefs about mankind has got something pretty nasty pulling the strings at the back of his mind. Having discovered how nice you yourself really are, you want to invite that nastiness to the dance...

To return to the problem with which this article began: the world of Satan is 'The World'. So I make my judgement not on spiritual principle but on worldly effects. The person who spends an hour each Sunday in church likes to be considered a Christian even if he spends the other six days being greedy, arrogant, vicious, aggressive and lustful. The Satanist who performs monthly rites which would make *The News of the World* curl up and turn yellow, would similarly like to consider himself a Satanist and would like to be forgiven the other days when he lapses into a twinkle-eyed philanthropist.

One drawback of the Christian despisal of the world and the flesh, is that more extreme Christians feel free to exert correspondingly extreme pressures on the body and property of those whose souls they wish to save. So please do not publish my address.

3

EXPLORING SPARE'S MAGIC

*First published in "Austin Osman Spare - The Divine Draughtsman"
exhibition catalogue.*

*This was one of three articles on Spare commissioned for the London
exhibition in 1987. This was a great thrill, because it suggested that I was
considered to be an expert on Spare. That is also a daunting thought, as I
see myself only as one who has been impregnated by his ideas (and born,
maybe, a bonny child as a result). The act was performed by artificial
insemination (via his books) and I never learnt much about the donor.
Honestly, m'lud.*

INTRODUCTION

The Book of Pleasure describes Spare's magical system and
its philosophical basis. In it he introduces an ultimate
called "Kia" (analogous to the "Tao", the Cabalistic
"Unmanifest", or Jung's "Pleroma") from which all manifestation stems via a process of refraction through the principle of
duality: we perceive, for example, black and white because they are
manifest as a polarised pair, in the Kia they exist only in potential,
being undistinguished and so unmanifest. It is clear from elsewhere
in his writing that Spare was acquainted with Boehme's tract On the
Supersensual Life, where the disciple asks the master how he can
come to know the supersensual life and is told "when thou canst
throw thyself into THAT, where no creature dwelleth, though it be
but for a moment..."

As humans we are caught up in dualities, divided against ourselves and ever seeking completion by living in desire, our universe
being fragmented by our beliefs. Spare advocates a turning back to
Kia and the end of all belief, denying all the dualities by his "neither
neither": think of a manifestation, eg "white"; not white implies
black; neither white nor black implies what? say grey; neither black,
white nor grey implies what? ... and so on until our imagination is
exhausted and consciousness teeters on the brink of the void - as in
the Buddhist "not this, not that" meditation. Thus we get to know the
Kia, and Freedom.

To practice Spare's magic one must disentangle a conscious desire
from one's web of conscious and semi-conscious beliefs, distilling the

essence of that desire into a simple sigil with no conscious associations, then carrying that sigil back into the Kia by exhausting oneself and collapsing into what he describes as "the death posture" - a
total flop-out with no consciousness other than the awareness of the
sigil, until that too fades. For greatest effect this should be done at a
time of despair or disappointment, when some other desire has been
thwarted and there is a pool of frustrated libido - "free belief" he calls
it - to fuel the operation.

Such a bare description of his magic doesn't do it great justice. It
is best to read his original works together with the commentaries listed at the end of this essay. Rather than repeat existing material, this
essay suggests some further ideas for research.

THE BIRTH OF AN AEON

In 1904 Austin Spare wrote - or rather created - his first book, which
was published in 1905 as Earth Inferno: 'created' because this book
contains more images than words, and half the words in it are themselves quotation from other sources. The result is pretty incompre-
hensible - even with hindsight.

In the wake of *fin de siècle* decadence, was this incomprehensibil-
ity just a deliberate attempt by a trendy young artist to create an aura
of mystery and glamour? Reading Earth Inferno I have the impression of someone who has passed through despair to receive a glimpse
of mystical truth, and who is now struggling to portray that realisation. It looks like a revelation which fails to communicate (to me) the
essence of what the artist experienced. The fact that nine years later
he is still earnestly trying to explain his discovery, and with slightly
greater success, in his Book of Pleasure does confirm a genuine desire
to teach rather than mystify.

In that case, what is Spare trying to communicate? Nothing less
than an entire philosophy of life and magic; but one so simple yet so
difficult to grasp that it is perhaps best approached by comparison
and contrast with other better known systems. I begin with some
comparisons.

CROWLEY AND SPARE

The opening words of Earth Inferno are a picture caption (dated
1904) which ends with a prophecy: "Hail! The convention of the age

is nearing its limit/And with it the resurrection of the Primitive Woman". So Spare is announcing some sort of turning point in history. In that same year Aleister Crowley received his Book of the Law which announced the birth of a new age. Interestingly one element of this revelation is a celebration of the "scarlet woman" - a female archetype unchained and reminiscent of Spare's "primitive woman". This element is even more clearly present in the work of Dion Fortune. In 1904 she too was writing her first book: as a young girl she was finding inspiration for her schoolgirl poetry on the coast near Weston Super Mare, an inspiration which many years later blossomed in the book "The Sea Priestess", set in that place and concerned with a magical operation to liberate society from the Victorian straight-jacket and announce a new female archetype - the priestly woman of power.

These coincidences suggest that Spare might have 'tuned into' what one would call, depending on one's own beliefs, a ferment of ideas, a new current of thought, the spirit of the times, or the birth of a new aeon. There is other evidence of this surge of revolutionary thinking around 1904: this was the year when Jung became drawn to Freud and his concept of the unconscious; it was the birth year of another explorer of the unconscious - Salvador Dali; it was the time of Steiner's disenchantment with theosophy which lead to the birth of anthroposophy. Other works completed in 1904 to be published in 1905 include Einstein's special theory of relativity, and his paper on the photoelectric effect which won him the Nobel Prize in 1921 and which provided the first strong evidence to support the newly formulated quantum theory.

All in all 1904 was a most interesting year, and this was put most clearly by Crowley when he announced it as the year of the birth of a new aeon. So let us begin by comparing Spare's revelations with Crowley's.

Disappointingly there is no obvious comparison between Crowley's Book of the Law and Spare's Earth Inferno - one the work of a writer, the other the work of an artist. The nearest thing to the Book of the Law written by Spare is the first part of his later Focus of Life. It consists of three chapters of aphorisms dictated by three different beings - Kia, Zos and Ikkah - which first appear in Earth Inferno, and it therefore demands comparison with the Book of the

Law which also consists of three chapters dictated by three beings. As the last words from Kia are "I - infinite space" it is natural to identify Kia with Nuit and to try to see parallels in the two texts.

The only obvious parallels are in Spare's second chapter which contains some pretty Thelemic utterances, such as:

"The mighty are righteous for their morals are arbitrary";

"Judge without mercy, all this weakness is thy self abuse";

"There is only one sin - suffering";

"... be surely what thou wilt" (an interesting comparison with "do what thou wilt");

"Fear nothing - strike at the highest" ... and so on.

The Focus of Life was, however, written after Spare had been in contact with Crowley, so these similarities may well be due to Spare knowing the Book of the Law; but remember that he had by then rejected Crowley, so any influence would not be slavish imitation but rather ideas chosen because they were in accord with his own vision.

The conclusion I'm suggesting is that one way to view Spare's magic is as his own interpretation of a new current which entered the group mind around 1904. He was seeing one facet of the whole; Crowley, Einstein, Jung, Fortune and probably many others were to pick up other facets of it. Each tried to explain what they saw: some like Crowley provided very full accounts, others like Einstein provided very detailed accounts of smaller parts of the whole. Spare was trying to give a full account, an entire philosophy of existence but did not communicate it very clearly. So we can understand his work better if we allow other people's ideas to cast light on it.

The first difference between Crowley and Spare that strikes me is that Spare's writing provides a simple, coherent theory where Crowley provides a detailed technology. It is possible to read Spare carefully and come up with the response "yes, but what are you supposed to *do*?" - there is little practical instruction. Crowley, on the other hand, has provided an enormous corpus of ritual and other practices, more than any person could ever master in a lifetime, but there are times when one is hard to put to find one coherent theory behind all these practices - he went through his Golden Dawn phase, his Buddhist phase, his Thelemic phase and so on. By way of analogy you could compare Spare's writing to Einstein's - it may be hard to understand, but behind it lies a very simple model of reality. To obtain great energy, according to Einstein, it is only necessary to split the atom; to obtain a desire, says Spare, it is only necessary to remove it to the unconscious, organic level and consciously forget it. But in practice the simple splitting of an atom requires a vast investment in technology; similarly, most people cannot follow Spare's simple instructions unless they have previously done a lot of self development along the lines of, say, Crowley's magical technology (there may be some with innate magical sense, but most of us are still adrift on a sea of beliefs and desires). So one approach to Spare is to use his world-view to help clear one's mind of a surfeit of gods, while actually practicing Thelemic techniques to strengthen one for Spare's magical methods.

I like the contrast between Crowley's "do what thou wilt" and Spare's "be what thou wilt" because it illustrates my feelings that Crowley and Spare represent, as it were, the yang and yin of the new aeon. Though Crowley recognises that existence is pure joy, his magic reflects the will to power where Spare's reflects the will to pleasure. There is much of taoism in Spare's writings. Paradoxically, however, although female forms abound in his art, "the feminine" plays little part in his apparently misogynist writings. It is the spirit of his ideas which is so yin - as if the Feminine was working at the unconscious level in Spare whereas the Masculine was driving Crowley's unconscious.

One example of the "yin" nature of Spare's system is his emphasis on the importance of forgetting. In his system you have a desire, you devise an apparently meaningless sigil to encapsulate that desire, you exhaust yourself in a frenzy of activity until the only object remaining in consciousness is the sigil, you hold on to it until it has become charged with "free belief", then you must do all you can subsequently to forget the original desire - for conscious desiring will impede the realisation of the sigil. This is the difficult bit. It is also rather puzzling because we find a big divide here in magical theory: those systems which emphasise the "not desiring" (eg Spare, taoism, zen) and those which advocate inflaming oneself with desire - as in Crowley's instructions for devotion to a deity, or as in the "self help" systems which demand a constant affirmation of one's objectives (I recall seeing an American lady doing Swedish drill while chanting "I *must*, I *must*, I *must* increase my *bust*"). Both these extremes have a ring of truth, how can they be reconciled? It is not enough just to split the operation in two and say one needs to inflame oneself before it, and forget after - in traditional conjurations of the Holy Guardian Angel one goes on inflaming until success happens.

THE INNER AND THE OUTER

One possible explanation is that the distinction may reflect the difference between introversion and extroversion. The extrovert is positive to the outside world, and negative to the inner world. When the extrovert attempts "inner" work he finds it a crazy place like Alice's looking glass world - you have to metaphorically walk backwards in order to move forwards. The introvert is much more at home in his inner world, but is more likely to be perplexed by the outer world: here the introvert finds that he has so often to go backwards in order to move forward. The introvert feels desire as such a vivid tangible force - perhaps more tangible than the actual object of desire - that the desire really does serve to block and render him impotent; thus the introvert is more often driven to using paradoxical methods in the outer world. This is in keeping with Eysenck's idea of the extrovert as someone who needs greater stimulation to be effective, while the introvert needs to avoid over-stimulation. If an extrovert wants his record in the charts he should plug it like crazy, but if the introvert wants to do the same he would do better to try to get the record banned! If the extrovert wants to become successful he should hang up "I'm the greatest" posters and constantly affirm his desire, while the introvert would do better to blow his desire on a sigil and then try so hard to fail that he eventually becomes an underground cult figure. Thus it seems that the magic of taoism and Spare is magic for introverts, while the out and invocatory stuff is better suited to the extrovert.

This is, of course, a gross oversimplification: no-one is pure extrovert or introvert; we are a mixture and so need to blend our magics. But it does suggest a useful concept to experiment with, and a possible answer to the problem that magic so often fails when the operator is too personally involved: if you wish to practice magic in a situation which seems very extroverted and "other" (like healing an unknown person at a distance), then you would well to "inflame yourself with prayer". But if the matter is one which involves you very personally, then you would do better to follow Spare's approach. Or perhaps the introvert would use Spare's magic to operate on the outside world, and Crowley's magic for inner working; while the extrovert needs Crowley's magic for the outer and Spare's on the inner? In either case, of course, the long-term object is to grow out of this slavery of the concept of intro/extroversion and start living!

MAGIC AND THE MAN

Another interesting point is the distinction between the magic and the man. Anyone studying Spare's magic books would expect the writer to be a sort of ascetic zen master: "simplicity I hold most precious" he writes. He advocates simplicity, asceticism: "Bed, a hard surface; clothes of camel hair; diet, sour milk and the roots of the earth. All morality and love of women should be ignored." He rants against ritual magicians and all their parade and paraphernalia, but later in life he painted an altar piece for Grant's Nuit Isis Lodge and was prepared to do work for Gerald Gardner as described in Grant's Images and Oracles.

One answer is that many years had passed since his books were written - the man had changed. Another is that perhaps Spare was primarily just a channel for his magical ideas: someone to whom they were revealed but who never succeeded in fully realising them. Perhaps he too had difficulty in practising what he preached, being a man ahead of his time? His final chapter of the Book of Pleasure contains these words: "I... am impervious in purity (of self-love) - but I dare not claim its service! I am in eternal want of realisation... An opinionist, I fear to advocate an argument, or compromise myself by believing my own doctrines as such..." and so on.

The Austin Spare described by Kenneth Grant in his Images and Oracles sounds much more like a tribal shaman than a zen master. Some people have asked "which is the true Spare?" Grant actually knew Spare in his later years, so it is reasonable to assume that Spare was as he describes at that time, and we hear of Spare co-operating with ritual magicians, using such elaborations as an "earthenware virgin" for sex magic, and muttering incantations as part of his procedure - elements which play no part in the pure system as described in the Book of Pleasure.

So do we conclude that he was a changed man? That he had degenerated (or even advanced?) from the pure system he described to a form of shamanistic sorcery? Personally I prefer to accept Grant's overall view of him as a master shaman, and believe that through his innate skills he obtained an early vision of a new system of magic, a magic for the coming age. Rather than debating as to which was the true Spare, we should therefore look to him as a prophet rather than a perfect practitioner of his own system, and we should instead concentrate on developing the technology of that system for ourselves and for future generations. Is this not basically what the new school of magic known as "chaos magic" is all about?

CONCLUSION

If 1904 was indeed a revolutionary year, it is reasonable to ask if there are any astrological phenomena to support this. The most obvious one to strike me is the entry of Uranus (planet of upheaval) into Capricorn (sign of structures).

Once before since its discovery Uranus had entered Capricorn, in about 1820. This was the year when Oersted demonstrated the link between electricity and magnetism - a revelation which was to have a profound effect on conventional ideas of physical reality.

Although I'm not aware of any great occult crisis at that time, James Webb (in The Flight from Reason) did choose 1820 to mark the beginning of what he called "the Age of the Irrational". I suspect that the new electromagnetic theories of the time inspired the "etheric" occult terminology of the last century, just as Einstein's theories inspire the occultists of this century to talk of "other dimensions". But if the entry of Uranus into Capricorn was less significant in 1820, could it mean we are looking at a minor cycle which had exaggerated impact in 1904 because of an impending Aquarian age, or the transition to Crowley's "Aeon of Horus"?

Anyway, in late 1987 we are now at the end of the final or "twelfth house" phase of this Uranus in Capricorn cycle, making it a very suitable time for a major exhibition and re-evaluation of Spare's work before Uranus enters Capricorn again next February.

Is the convention of the age once more reaching its limit? And will 1988 be as fruitful as 1904 was?

Books by Austin Osman Spare

Earth Inferno
A Book Of Satyrs
The Book Of Pleasure (Self Love)
The Focus of Life
The Anathema Of Zos

Published posthumously
A Book of Automatic Drawings
Axiomata & The Witches' Sabbath
Arena of Anon
The Collected Works of Austin Osman Spare

Books about Spare

Images & Oracles of Austin Osman Spare - Kenneth Grant
The Early Works of Austin Osman Spare - William Wallace
The Later Works of Austin Osman Spare - William Wallace

NOTE
Mine own introductory essay, Spare Parts, which was published in
the second edition of the Collected Works, will eventually be re-pub-
lished in Volume 1 of these essays - 'Uncle Ramsey's Bumper Book
of Magick Spells, and other essays on science and magic'.

THE LAW IS FOR ALL... SOD THE LAW!

Reflections on thelemic morality.

I wrote this piece as my contribution for a proposed OTO magazine which I was supposed to be producing. Alas, the problems of raising finance and editing a magazine were too much for me, but it was later published in The Equinox, and in German translation in Anubis.

I still feel the ideas in it are important and timely - as religious fundamentalism once more attempts to crawl forth from the sewers.

Arild Stromsvag took me up about my opening remarks on the OTO. He wrote "I have always regarded Liber Al as an 'icon'... This may not be an accurate term for it, but what I meant was that the text is as it is and it is not a text to be revised or at all tampered with. (See what happened to the Bible.) It is in this capacity that I interpret the acceptance of Liber Al."

His "see what happened to the Bible" explained the point to me. In that sense I do accept the Book of the Law as it is. When I say I wish to change it I do not mean I would like to make changes and then announce the altered version to be what Crowley really received, or even what he "really meant". I am happy that the original should be preserved as base camp or reference point, and recognised for what it is. My concern is that I would like to change it to reflect mine own exploration, to create "The Book of My Law". I hope that some others will like parts of my version, but would not want to impose it. Least of all would I pretend that my law was The Law.

As an idealist I like to believe that there will be a convergence of each individual's law towards some common values.

As a romantic I hope that the convergence is not a finite process.

As a cynic I suspect that the common law to which we all converge will prove a strange attractor. Sod's Law... not God's Law.

I have always objected to the clause in the preliminary application to the OTO which asks the applicant to say that they accept the Book of the Law and do not wish to change it.

A clause like that is a sure way of putting off those fiery souls whose nature is to want to make changes; and those very people could be pretty useful in an order intended to usher in a new aeon. The only reason I eventually succumbed was because I was growing old and jaded: my fiery idealism had been muted by the realisation that most people don't take signatures and promises as seriously as I used to. Sign on, sign on, harvest moon.

The problem was the words "not want to". Wanting to make changes is my nature, so I am being asked to deny my instinct at source. This is not the same as learning to master an instinct: if the clause had instead said "however much I might wish to change the Book of the Law, I am prepared to hold it sacrosanct for the greater good of the order" then I would have no argument with it. It then becomes a question for the individual applicant to weigh up the priorities and decide.

However, the irritation of that clause set me thinking about my attitude to Liber Al and, in the terms of the rest of this essay, that is no bad thing. You could even argue that it is sufficient justification for preserving that clause. I hope you don't.

ATTITUDES TO AL

So what is my attitude to Liber Al? Quite honestly there is a lot that I don't like in it. There is a lot that many thelemites don't like if they are truthful. Though it is interesting to note that the younger ones have much less trouble than their older brethren: I do not think this is because of any special thelemic quality inherent in youth, so much as the simple fact that each successive generation is becoming more firmly rooted in what is still a very new aeon.

It is interesting to see how people face up to these "nasty" bits - the elitism and violence which Crowley himself found so hard to come to terms with.

An obvious starting point is the "symbolic" interpretation. This is the one which argues that when the Book asks you to stamp down on the weak and helpless it is obviously not asking you to go out and kick cripples, it is rather giving a moral instruction to have no mercy with your own inner weakness, to be firm rather than indulgent (as so many people are) with your own personal foibles.

This sort of analysis is an excellent exercise, and I would never discourage anyone from spending some time meditating on Liber Al - or any scriptural text for that matter - in just this way. But if that is all there is to it, then I am disappointed in Aiwass: for this is a very old-aeon approach to scripture. Very valid, very worthwhile, by no means obsolete, but simply not adequate for a culture that has lived through a scientific revolution - a culture that has learned to demand precision and clarity (not that it always gets it!). A new aeon scripture, I believe, must be somehow objectively or outwardly testable or interpretable: it cannot rest entirely on subjective reinterpretation.

This criterion is met by the second approach, which is to draw a distinction between the "prescriptive" and the "descriptive" passages in Liber Al. When it says "do what thou wilt" it is giving an instruction that is meant to be obeyed; but when it says "I peck at the eyes of Jesus" there is no suggestion that thelemites must waste time going round churches defacing crucifixes; instead it is simply a description of the sort of thing that Horus does. Seen in this light, most of the nasty bits are actually a pretty honest description of the world as it is, and perhaps a healthy reminder to those who try too hard to insist that "all is love and sweetness and light". Too much evil has disguised itself in the sheep's clothing of official Christianity: it was not loving forgiveness or chastity that brought Thatcher to power, it was the fact that she was prepared to send soldiers to be mutilated and killed. Her policy of treading on the weak and uplifting the strong is the policy that has kept her in power. Read Liber Al in this light, and you have to admit that there is much truth in it.

But "is this interpretation good enough?" I again ask; and again I do not think it is sufficient. After all, the nasty bits are often worded as commands: looking at it again with a post-scientific eye, is Aiwass so stupid that he cannot make it clear when he is giving moral instruction and when he is merely prophesying? Furthermore, in a book as short as Al, what justification is there for filling so much of it with mere descriptions of nasty things that we can see happening anyway? Prophesy may be impressive, but the greater value in a scripture lies in the direction or inspiration it gives us. (I almost wrote "lies in the instructions it contains", but later I will argue that a scripture can do something more than give instructions.)

Having outlined two ways to defend the Book of the Law, let us look again at the criticisms that can be made of it.

The first critic is one I have no time for: it is the person who opens Liber Al, picks out a sentence like "Kill and torture; spare not; be upon them!" and says "anyone who has anything to do with a book that says that must be a sadistic fascist". Taking statements out of context says nothing: one can find a host of vicious statements in the Bible, and an equal number of contradictory calls for love and understanding. I have never seen any moral progress being made by people who simply hurl quotations at each other.

The next critic I do have some sympathy with: this is the person who says "I have read the book thoroughly, and find a lot that I don't like. I admit that you should not only take a scripture at face value, and that some of the nasty bits can be interpreted symbolically; but I am still not impressed. The overall spirit of the book is not at all what I would expect of a god to whom I should wish to aspire."

There is a big difference here: the first just looks at a few words and draws sweeping conclusions about a whole movement; the second makes a genuine effort to look behind the literal facade and "tune in to" the spirit of the message. That is surely the difference between an unsympathetic and a sympathetic critic - but does it mark the end point of critical development?

I suggest not. I suggest that there is a more modern approach which does not yet have universal recognition: it is to look not at the scripture so much as at the effect it has.

We see these three stages in a sociological context, for example the debate about video nasties: first those people who follow the letter and want art to be restricted by rigid formulae of acceptability; then there are those who recognise artistic licence, but feel that the spirit of video nasties is so vile that they cannot be anything but a bad influence; then there are those who point out the psychological complications, arguing that possibly their very nastiness could be a cathartic outlet for instincts which would otherwise turn violent. Trying to resolve this matter on the social level is not easy: if you find that ninety percent of rapists watch video nasties, you still do not know whether the nasties actually encouraged them, or merely sublimated their desire to commit even more rape. It should be easier to tackle the problem at the personal level: if you want to know whether video nasties are bad for you, then watch them and monitor the effects on yourself. Do you feel more or less aggressive after seeing them? Is that aggression more or less likely now to be expressed outwardly? Is the long-term effect one of making you a less moral person than you were before you watched it?

This is the approach I now propose for judging a scripture: not to judge it by its literal content, nor even to judge it by the effect you assume it might have upon "the man in the street", but rather to test it in the laboratory of your own life and ask "am I a worse person for having been exposed to this scripture?".

The first approach is to naively take it at face value alone. The second is all too often a question of projecting your worst fears onto society, for instance by saying "if this book was available to the general public it would mean a complete moral breakdown" while overlooking the fact that one's own exposure to the book had quite the opposite effect.

In this scriptural context note that the first approach is based on the idea that God thinks you are totally naive; that you will do exactly what God says, so God has to make sure that his commands are exactly what you should do. The second approach is based on a more sophisticated notion that God now recognises that we can think for ourselves, so God can give more general and open-ended guidelines and leave us to work out the implications in every conceivable situation. But the third approach goes further: it assumes that we are ourselves mysterious and open-ended beings who can act independently, and who are just as likely to defy scripture as to obey it. The third approach says "how can you be so sure that reading the Book of the Law might not actually make me into a more gentle and loving person?".

CROWLEY'S THREE AEONS

This essay has progressed: we began by looking at ways to explain away the nasty bits in Liber Al, now we are considering positive moral approaches to it. The development in these three approaches to scripture seems to relate to Crowley's description of the three aeons: Isis, Osiris and Horus.

The age of Isis was the matriarchal age of the mother goddesses. Though we tend nowadays to look back nostalgically to the lighter side of the Goddess, he suggests that the dark side of the Goddess played a bigger social role - why otherwise would it have been necessary to progress to the patriarchal aeon of Osiris? So a predominant characteristic of these early religions was that they laid down an absolute law like an immutable karma or fate. We see this type of religion in those primitive societies still living in the aeon of Isis, it is also seen in the Old Testament. Although Jehovah is considered male (for decency's sake in the aeon of Osiris) his personality is more like that of Binah than of any of the male sephiroth. And we find in the Old Testament pages and pages of absolute commandments - most of which are extremely down to earth and practical.

The aeon of Osiris marked a new type of deity, typified by Jesus and Dionysus. These male gods were much less like great immutable cosmic forces, much more like super-humans. These gods were capable of dying on our behalf - they would never make statements like "I the Lord thy God am a jealous god". Instead of dictating commandments, these gods give simple guidelines like "love thy neighbour" and expect us to have the gumption to work out the practical implications for ourselves. These gods do not say "do exactly what I command", instead they want us to try to model ourselves on them, to be forever asking ourselves "what would Jesus do if he was in this situation". Morality in the aeon of Osiris is not a question of obeying precise law, it is a question of living up to an ideal - "the imitation of Christ".

But now, according to Crowley, we are entering the third aeon, the aeon of Horus. So presumably we can expect a new face of deity and a new type of morality. What will it be?

It is helpful to consider the fact that all three ages are ever-present with us: primitive tribal societies still dwell in the aeon of Isis, contemporary religions like Judaism still have their roots in that aeon, though I am sure that enlightened Jews in fact interpret their religion now in Osirian terms. Conversely there are many followers of Osirian religions like Christianity and Islam who are naive enough to interpret these religions in the fundamentalist spirit of the aeon of Isis - following the letter rather than the spirit of the law. I would describe these people as "living in the aeon of Isis" whatever they may call their religion.

What we witness in society we also witness in the microcosm of the individual: for we are all born into the aeon of Isis. As infants we look up to Mother, and her word is absolute. Whatever high principles we may now have about the correct way to bring up a child, the realistic fact is that most commands to a tiny toddler have to be pretty absolute - "don't touch that", "don't put that in your mouth" - and there simply is not time to engage in lengthy explanations on every occasion. But a child soon learns to think and soon requires a different sort of discipline. You do still sometimes have to give direct commands to a nine year old, but you will also be making appeals to its better nature by saying things like "Mummy will be very unhappy if you do that", or "think of the people who don't have any money to buy sweets". Whereas in the first age you were an absolute authority, now you try to teach by setting an example, so the child looks upon its parents as ideal role models - just as the Osirian gods present themselves to us.

But what happens next? What happens when the teenage boy finds he is now bigger and stronger than his father, when the teenage girl realises that her mother too can fall in and out of love? There is a natural tendency for the parent to feel threatened, and to attempt to revert to the absolute commands of the infant stage, while the adolescent will begin to see that the parents are not so perfect after all. This is the time to realise one's own independence, leave home and grow up.

This, I suggest, is what entering the aeon of Horus is all about. And this is why the two earlier ways of judging the Book of the Law are not sufficient. Nobody in their right mind would accept it as literal commandment as one would have done in the aeon of Isis. Nor is it even correct to interpret it as one has learnt to interpret scripture in the aeon of Osiris, ie by attempting to get into the spirit of the book and model oneself on the God behind it. Instead we should stand on our own feet and recognise that, unlike the Osirian gods, Horus is a bit of a bastard, and not at all an ideal model for humanity. He in his turn does not expect us to meekly follow his aggressive ways: he expects us to do our own will. And this is the key to accepting the Book of the Law *in its own terms*.

IN SEARCH OF OUR TRUE WILLS

According to Crowley, "do what thou wilt" is the fundamental law of the new aeon. Although not everyone agrees with his idea of a "new aeon", and not everyone accepts the phrase "do what thou wilt", his basic idea is very much in keeping with the evolving moral attitudes of this century - attitudes which have been influenced by other new aeon ideas (relativity, psychology, Nietzsche etc) rather than being directly attributed to Thelema.

First it implies that we must look within ourselves for god or truth. This is not as extreme as the humanist who denies that there is any god without - it is simply that those outer authorities have been relegated to a different role. Jung does not deny the existence of gods as heroic and exemplary archetypes, he simply warns that they can be dangerous models for us, and that we do better to turn to our own "inner star" (Septem Sermones Ad Mortuos).

Having turned our back on the absoluteness of the gods, we must also turn our back on the absolute frames of reference of Newtonian physics. If we are to follow our own imperfect perceptions in search of our own true wills, then it will mean constantly having to revise our ideas as we progress. There is no longer a pillar of smoke before us by day, and a pillar of fire by night. Yesterday we thought we were doing our will, today we realise that we were wrong: we have matured. Tomorrow we may well realise that we were still wrong today. This is terribly difficult: how can an imperfect instrument (ie ourselves) guide us toward the perfection of doing our true wills? (Note that the True Will is not "perfect" in any absolute sense, but it is perfect or complete within itself).

The answer to this question may lie a long way ahead - after all this is still but the opening breath of the new aeon - but a mathematical analogy may prove helpful, because it will give us a visual image of the way we might progress. The analogy is to compare a moral dilemma with a mathematical equation.

The first moral approach described is like the most basic form of mathematical equation, a simple statement of identity, for example:

$$x = 3$$

Here there is no dilemma, no thinking to be done, the equation is the solution. This is equivalent to the commands of the aeon of Isis: you do not have to struggle to find their inner meaning, you must simply obey them.

The next type of equation is the linear equation which can be solved with more or less effort, for example:

$3x+1 = 5x -3$ *subtract 3x*
$1 = 2x-3$ *add 3*
$4 = 2x$ *divide by 2*
$x = 2$

The comparison here is with the morality of the aeon of Osiris: you are not given a precise command to be mechanically obeyed, instead you are given the knowledge that the dilemma does have just one absolute solution (God), and that it is your task to find that solution using a few basic, general rules (eg "love thy neighbour").

In these terms the moral approach of the aeon of Horus is more like solving nonlinear equations, for example:

$$x^3 - 2x^2 + 1 = 0$$

Such equations cannot normally be solved by the simple rules of linear equations, they do not always have a real solution, they may well have more than one solution. Facing moral dilemmas in the aeon of Horus, we can no longer rely on the fact that there is one absolute correct answer out there waiting to be discovered: there may be no answer, or there may be several answers, each equally correct but each totally different. Several techniques have been devised to tackle such equations, but I will focus on one type of solution that is popular because it lends itself to computer programming: it is the iterative approach.

Here is an example of the most basic iterative technique. We begin by rearranging the equation so that it looks superficially like the first type of equation (the simple aeon of Isis commandment), for example:

$x = 2 - 1/x^2$ *check if you like - it's the same equation rearranged*

Then you make a sensible guess at a solution, knowing of course that it is very unlikely to be the "true" solution.

Try $x = 2$, and put it in the right hand side of the equation: $2-1/4$, which gives a new value $x = 1.75$.

Again, we do not expect this to be the "true" solution, but we again put it in the right hand side as a value of x, to get a new value x = 1.673. Insert this in the right hand side to get a third value for x.

And so on. At each stage what we do is try a solution, study how well it works, and from the result we deduce another solution. At the same time we are remembering our earlier "solutions" and comparing

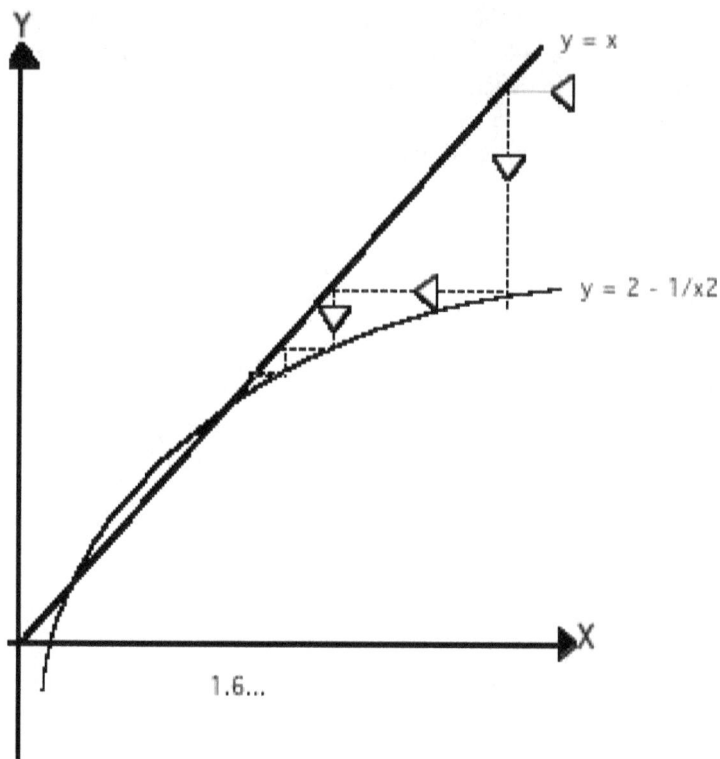

them: if they seem to be getting closer and closer (ie if they seem to be "converging"), then we continue the process. If they are not converging, we go back to the first step and try a totally new guess at the solution.

The illustration shows this graphically. The solutions to the equation are where the straight line crosses the curve, what we are doing is zigzagging in toward a solution.

To recap: in the aeon of Isis morality is easy (just as well, because this aeon dates back to a time when survival took most of our energy, and we could not afford to waste time pondering moral dilemmas!) - you hear what the Goddess says, and you obey it or suffer.

The aeon of Osiris makes it much more difficult. God now expects us to think for ourselves: instead of precise commands he gives general cosmic rules and asks us to work out the answers for ourselves. We now see God not as a detached force of nature, but as a caring, super-human; so the answer to any moral dilemma tends to be one of "what would God do in this situation? and how closely can a poor imperfect person like myself match up to that ideal?"

Whereas in the aeon of Osiris God is perfect, an ideal to be aspired to, as we enter the aeon of Horus we learn that there is no absolute perfection, all is relative, gods can be bastards. We are like adolescents who discover that their parents are not the ideals they once believed. After the high standards of the aeon of Osiris we may over-react: we may read the Horus chapter in Liber Al and say "this cannot be the word of God! it is utter blasphemy!"; or else we may be more realistic and say "yes, this is what Horus is like, and I can see it all around me. However, it is not a model which is right for mankind's survival". In either case, whether as an immature outburst or as a mature decision, the adolescent makes his break with the parents and prepares to stand on his own two feet.

For in the aeon of Horus we can no longer rely on an absolute guideline from without, we cannot even be sure there really is an answer. All we can do is to trust in ourselves, and make a stand for ourselves, knowing that it is but a temporary expedient. Life becomes an ongoing scientific experiment as we set up a hypothesis, test it against "reality", revise it and test again - each time using our memory to judge whether our overall movement is converging towards a point which we will call our "true will", or whether we are going off the rails and must make a fresh start.

What I propose is not something easy. It is no easier than the transition which has already taken place between the aeon of Isis and the aeon of Osiris.

Beware in particular of any "new aeon pride" which makes us think that we are now above anyone else's law because we are superior mature beings who accept the aeon of Horus. That is like the adolescent who, having left home, thinks he can now do what the hell he likes - society will soon hit back. In terms of the aeon we are still just taking our first steps, and it is important to remember that all 3 aeons are ever-present around us. I have already explained that direct commands will always have their place when bringing up infants - a mother busy cooking cannot stop to give her toddler a lecture on the dangers of fire every time it reaches for the oven door, however much she believes in the Osirian ideal of teaching children to think for themselves. The aeons of Isis and Osiris remain with us as stages which children must pass through, and they are also present in the form of other cultures on our globe, more or less primitive societies who are working out their own culture at their own pace.

Unfortunately, they are also all three present in our own adult population. There are some people who are not only not ready for the aeon of Horus, they are not even ready for the aeon of Osiris. These are the "fundamentalists" of whom I will write more later: people who cannot even bring themselves to live the spirit of Christ's message, but who still insist on turning back to the old testament for dogmatic rules by which to live their lives. Because these people are so distasteful, I repeat my warning against new aeon pride: every one of us, however much we embrace the new morality, will have our lapses. There will be times when we will feel so confused that we will need a guru or hero to give us some guidance; there will even be times of great despair when we will want nothing more than a strong person to tell us what to do. That is only human: to deny the fact is to run the risk of falling blindly into those very traps.

Rather than an arrogant assumption that we thelemites are the new "chosen ones" we would do better to understand the opposition that we face.

The first, and most understandable objection to thelemic morality that we should consider is the person who feels helpless in face of it. This is the person who says "but it means we cannot take any stand: we cannot even oppose Adolph Hitler because how can we be sure that he was not doing his own true will?".

What is this person doing wrong? He is right insofar as he accepts that we cannot be absolutely sure of anything, but he has instinctively slipped into old aeon ways by making that very uncertainty into a new absolute: he is not looking at the world as it is, he is speculating about what the true will of Adolph Hitler (a third party) might possibly be, rather than getting on with his own true will.

Note that the first step in solving the third type of equation began by rearranging it to look superficially like the first type (x = something): this is what I mean by taking a stand, you lay down your own commandment as a temporary measure. So, instead of pondering endlessly about whether, say, the holocaust might not in the long term mark a positive turning point in world Judaism, you look into your own feelings. If you are repulsed you then say to yourself "whatever my true will may eventually turn out to be, at present I find this man Hitler and his ideas repulsive, and I will do all I can to oppose him." In terms of action then, the only difference between yourself and a "fundamentalist" anti-Nazi is that you know that you have accepted personal responsibility for your own actions (abstract "right" is not on your side), and you are always prepared to revise your decision if the contrary evidence begins to become overwhelming. If the aeon of Osiris was the one where mankind was taught to think for itself, then the aeon of Horus could be the one where mankind is taught to feel for itself - using the word "feel" in the Jungian sense as the emotional value sense which tells you whether something is right or wrong.

This "taking stands" is just a technique that we adopt, a technique which takes into account our aeon of Isis inheritance. Future moral techniques will no doubt transcend the need to take stands - perhaps the morality of Maat will have as its starting point an instant intuitive recognition of our true wills? Maat is, after all, the Goddess of Truth.

I have a lot of sympathy with the above-described feeling of helplessness: I also feel a lot of sympathy for the Christian or humanist who cannot stomach the Book of the Law because he does not like its "spirit". This Osirian type of judgement is, after all, the way we still try to judge a work of art. We do not, as one would in the aeon of Isis, say "that cannot be poetry because it does not rhyme or scan", instead we try to enter into the spirit of the work of art in order to see whether we dig it or not. Perhaps, in the aeon of Horus, art criticism will become more akin to the "scientific" way to judge a scripture suggested earlier in this essay: looking at the effect the work of art has on the world, rather than at the work itself.

I believe it is important that we should have some sympathy for, and not try to lose all contact with, that Osirian approach. The more urgent threat lies not with these people, but with the people still living in the age of Isis: the fundamentalists who would damn the Book of the Law on the basis of the statements it contains. In the next part of this essay I will explain why I consider these people to be so dangerous.

FUNDAMENTALISM - MORE "MENTAL" THAN "FUN"

An example of someone who proclaims himself Christian but seems to me to be living in the aeon of Isis, is the Manchester Chief of Police - the one who announced that AIDS was a divine punishment on those perverts who had been wallowing in a "sewer of their own filth", or something to that effect. More recently he advocated the castration of sexual offenders.

When you actually hear him speak he sounds like a balanced, humane sort of person with firm views - the sort that you would ideally expect to run a police force. Yet he makes these statements, and claims that it is God who is using him as a mouthpiece. He is entitled to his own private opinions, the trouble with someone in his position expressing such opinions is that it makes people angry, divides the public and polarises opinion in a way that tends to destabilise society. His honest expressions of his private opinions are, in their divisive effect on society, comparable with acts of terrorism.

When asked how he can claim to be a mouthpiece of God, he explains that these revelations have come to him in such a way that he is utterly sure that they are divine in origin. Is he lying? That seems unlikely. Is he a deluded maniac? He does not speak like one. So is he in fact in communication with God?

I believe he is, for we must remember that we are now in the aeon of Horus. Five hundred years ago you could be pretty certain that the voice of God was the voice of some form of Osirian deity - eg Christ. Now you will be more likely to contact Horus. Certainly the effect of the messages coming from this police chief is much more what we would expect from Horus than from Christ. If you ask Christ how to punish sexual offenders you are more likely to be told something thought-provoking like "let him who is without sin cast the first stone"; but if you ask Horus he is more likely to say "castrate the buggers" - and he did!

This is surely the style of most of the present day people who claim to speak directly for God? For example the American fundamentalist Christians who want to "nuke the Ruskies" - a command utterly appropriate to the writer of the third chapter of the Book of the Law. As Gerald Suster points out in "The Legacy of the Beast", the Koran forbids torture and yet we find the Ayatollah Khomenei in his capacity as God's spokesman eagerly advocating Liber Al III verse 18.

Note a distinction here: these vicious demands do not come to us from the "New Age" channels, those who claim that a (as opposed to "the") deity, extra-terrestrial, or spiritual being is contacting them. The New Age channels tend to be the mouthpieces of humbler gods than the Lord of the Aeon, and most of their messages still sound pretty Osirian. It is those who speak for *the* God who sound like Horus. He is, after all, *the* God of this aeon.

This is an idea which can come as a shock to thelemites: the idea that they do not have a monopoly of Horus, that anyone who aspires to communicate with God will now tend to make a Horus contact - and that includes those bloody fundamentalists. But study what the fundamentalists are saying and doing, and ask yourself which describes them better: the Gospel of St John, or the third chapter of Liber Al. Then you see them in their true colours.

The danger of the fundamentalists is this: whereas they are making a Horus contact, their moral maturity is that of the aeon of Isis. This means that they are prepared to do exactly what Horus tells them to do - vicious stuff. If the rather more advanced Christians - the "real" ones who are living in the aeon of Osiris - made the same contact they would recognise that they were being asked to do some very unChristian things and they would be suspicious. They would try to interpret these commands symbolically, and if that did not work they would find the spirit of the messages so abhorrent that they would either decide it was the voice of Satan, or else very likely have a nervous breakdown and revert to the slavish fundamentalist position under the power of Horus. Remember that we are talking about fundamentalists who have been brought up to the letter of monotheistic Osirian religions, who therefore believe there is only one god. So when Horus appears in shining light they do not stop to question which god is speaking to them - they "know" it can only be Jesus, or Jehovah, or Allah, or whichever is their One God. Christians do have a loophole in Satan, but as long as they only allow him second-rate status, people like that Manchester police chief will be so awed by the divine presence that they will insist that it can only be "God" who has spoken.

Both groups would be making the right contact, but could not handle it because they would have no idea of thelemic morality - the moral approach for the aeon of Horus. If Horus comes to you in a fiery vision and orders you to go forth and castrate sex offenders, then you have every right to refuse - if you think it is not your true will to castrate people.

Remember that the aeon of Horus marks the point when mankind must grow up, and turn away from the parents. There is actually danger now in continuing to do God's will - it is the danger of losing sight of our own wills. We may over-react like repressed teenagers, casting aside Liber Al and screaming that Horus is a bastard and we will have nothing to do with him. Or we may listen respectfully to his violent views and choose to differ in detail. In either case it is better to do that than either to obey him outright (the Isis aeon approach to a God) or to act tough and macho in an attempt to live up to him as a role model (the Osirian aeon approach).

What will happen to those fundamentalists who slavishly take up the sword under the orders of a being whom they unquestioningly assume to be Allah or Christ, but who is in fact Horus? Given the might of the Lord of the Aeon, they may well enjoy considerable material success. But I pity them in the long run - for gods like Horus have a habit of despising their slaves just as much as they respect their most valiant opponents. There must have been a parallel problem two thousand years ago, for Jesus advised "No man putteth new wine into old bottles; else the new wine will burst the bottles, and be spilled, and the bottles shall perish." Perhaps that was the fate of those Gnostic sects like the Cainites who interpreted the new libertarian spirit as a licence to total amorality

It is a curious thing how the gods seem to respect those who resist them - provided the resistance is more than just a childish rebellion or tantrum. Have you ever attempted to be celibate for a lengthy period of time? and have you noticed how the demon of lust grows ever more exquisite in the favours it offers? My God, those mediaeval monks must have had the most mind-blowing sexual phantasies, if that's what all those succubi were about! To me this is the biggest dilemma of the permissive society: how to get back the wild excitement of "forbidden fruit" without in any way letting the bloody moralising prudes have the satisfaction of knowing that they were partly in the right (because they actually held the key to the hottest, wildest sex).

Resisting the sex demon brings out the best in him. The same is true of other gods. However hard they fight back, you sense that they respect you for standing up to them. Uniting yourself to a deity by devotion is fine as a project, but as a way of life it can be very dangerous. If you do it to a deity like Horus he may drag you through hell until you pull yourself together and walk out. I am not advocating the defiance of the angry infant, nor the defiance of the insecure child, but I am saying that mankind is now an adolescent finding its own inner strength. The only way to progress is to stand up against the gods and say "no!". In another two thousand years time we will be returning home as adults and as equals, because we will fully realise something which we are only just beginning to sense: that we too are gods. And then our old gods will surely welcome us home.

DIVIDE AND RULESVILLE

Earlier I warned of "new aeon pride". Let's forget morality for the moment and talk tactics: the temptation to see oneself as a thelemite, and to dismiss everything else under the blanket term "old aeon", is sheer bad tactics, because it unites everyone else into a unified enemy against a tiny handful of us. It is better tactics to divide the opposition by analysis.

I have described the aeons of Isis, Osiris and Horus. I have described those who consider themselves to be worshipping an Osirian deity, but reveal their moral maturity to be that of the earlier aeon. Personally I find the born-again Christian fundamentalists so repulsive that I feel sorely tempted to adopt an unselective anti-Christian stance: this could be dangerous, because it will only serve to alienate the true Osirian Christians who could otherwise help

51

oppose the fundamentalist loonies. Christianity is already divided, there is no point in uniting it against a common enemy - namely us.

In our local paper there was an anti-gay correspondence recently, and among the nominally "Christian" voices were two distinct camps (no pun intended). The first were those who said that homosexuality is the sin most abhorrent to God, quoting passages from the old testament and St Paul, and that decent Christians must fight and pray for its extermination. The second group said that homosexuals were very misguided people, and that Christians must try to help them and must pray for their redemption. Although I personally consider both groups to be equally misguided, I see a big difference in their attitudes: the second lot are what I consider to be "true Christians" while the first lot are living in the aeon of Isis and only need a word from Horus to send them on a "queer bashing" pogrom - mistaking the sin for the sinner, as the second lot would say.

I have met a third type of Christian, ones who have more sense than to waste time writing protest letters to local papers. These ones have a moral stance very much like the one I suggest for the aeon of Horus: they speak of Christ as an "inner reality", treat him very much as a personal guide, and have a truly relativistic sense of morality as an iterative path towards some inner truth. I consider them to be people who are remaining loyal to an old aeon religion but who are interpreting it in a new aeon manner (sometimes getting thoroughly screwed up as a result!).

Because of the immediate danger I sense in the present rash of fundamentalist lunacy, it seems to me bad tactics to unite christendom by lumping all those three types together. We might, if the worst came to the worst, need the help of the last two types in order to restrain the fundamentalists.

WHAT'S "NEW" ABOUT "AGE"?

That leaves one more category to consider: what about those who embrace the new aeon, but whose moral approach is more like that of the aeon of Osiris? I refer to the New Age people.

Personally I am a bit of a sucker for quartz crystals and loving vibes, but some of my colleagues fulminate against New Agers as enemies of Thelema. On reflection I do see a danger, which I will try to explain.

In the local paper correspondence mentioned above, it was clear that the "real" Christians tended to quote Christ when they quoted the Bible, whereas the red-neck, knee-jerk fundamentalists will quote the Old Testament or St Paul to support their madness.

In Thundersqueak I considered the interesting case of St Paul. He began his life as Saul and, in the early chapters of the Acts of the Apostles, we hear how he was a pillar of the old order who hated the revolutionary Christian doctrines and persecuted the disciples like a mad dog. Then, on the road to Damascus, God plays a trump card by blinding him and ordering him to lay off, saying "you can't beat us, so join us". To cut a long story short, he becomes the leader of the movement he once detested. What, I wondered, happened to the old anger? This man had been an embodiment of the rigid Old Order and its dogmatism, how can he so easily slip into the libertarian, loving ways of Christianity? Whether he did it consciously or not, the answer is obvious: he brought with him his Old Order values and superimposed them onto the new aeon. Just about all of the anti-women, anti-life, anti-fun aspects of official Christianity in the last two thousand years have been the legacy of St Paul, not of Christ.

What I would like to consider is this: was this infecting of the new Christian aeon with the diseases of the old aeon a one-off cock up to be blamed on a single sick-minded individual, or is it a general tendency against which we must guard?

"New Age" sounds very close to "New Aeon", and there are points of comparison between the beliefs and practices of New Agers and thelemites. The most obvious difference that hits me is the New Agers' denial of anything except happiness, peace and love.

St Paul made Christianity politically acceptable by keeping its non-fat solids but incorporating the old familiar intolerance into the formula: that must have been mighty re-assuring to a world threatened by political instability and the later fall of the Roman empire. Perhaps the New Agers are making the new aeon saleable by incorporating the old familiar Christian values into the formula - very re-assuring to a world living under the shadow of nuclear or ecological catastrophe. Perhaps they are making it all look nice by dressing Horus in the sheep's clothing of Jesus, and forgetting about the smell? New Age preachers are great when they dwell on the positives - pretty flowers and the one-ness of creation - but the odd moments when they refer to negatives, like "violent elements in society", I notice a subtle undercurrent of hysteria which suggests they have slipped out of their depth.

This reminds me uneasily of the Nazis. Because the Nazi has become the symbol of total evil people are inclined to assume that Hitler's regime was a sort of cess pit into which the dregs of society poured: it is convenient to forget that the SS was meant to be a high minded force of elite supermen. It was extremely difficult to get into the SS: it was "where it was at" in the sense that it attracted the sort of best educated "cream" of youthful society who would nowadays be looking for top jobs in the City. It was not created to provide sadistic gratification, but to create a "new order". Surely the great paradox of the SS was that there were all these refined people in it, dressed in beautiful clothing and savouring the finest wines as they listened to music by their best composers - at the same time as human beings were being vivisected in their cellars? You could even argue that the most intense cruelties of the regime were not so much those inflicted in brutality, as those experiments on humans carried out in the name of scientific research.

The analogy I see with those New Agers who deny any but the purest motives, is that they might in the future be sitting in their wholemeal temples vibrating love to the sound of tinkling bells while in the basement those who oppose them will undergoing a process of "cleansing" which will involve starvation to purify their physical vehicles, sensory deprivation to free their engrams, strobe lighting to evoke their alpha waves, and... oh no! don't even suggest it!.... endless tapes of New Age music to elevate their vibrations. The subtlety of the point I am making is that those techniques most useful to New Age spirituality - fasting, isolation tanking, sensory overload, controlled use of psychedelic agents, biofeedback etc - are precisely the techniques that have been developed by the most sophisticated torture technologists. It all depends upon the individual's motive as he enters these areas: if he willingly submits to them in the name of enlightenment, then it is spiritual advancement; but if he is forced to undergo them, it becomes torture. Those who deny anything but Love would find it easy to forget the latter possibility when it came to converting "the underprivileged".

When I read about those awful born-again loonies with their vast power and international broadcast networks, I am re-assured to think that the New Age people are also doing well. It is good to know there is some opposition, and that so called "Satan" can also make money. But perhaps my friends are right in seeing the New Agers as dangerous allies. Perhaps late historians of the aeon of Horus will look back on their aeon and see an early thelemic impulse that was never realised because it was infected in its cradle by old aeon values for commercial expediency - just as the infant Christianity was infected with intolerance for political expediency.

Or perhaps instead everyone in the world will read this essay and become ever so, ever so moral...

CONCLUSION

As a final point, I am reminded of a discussion program about gnosticism that I saw recently on the television. In it some notable divine described the gnostic idea of personal salvation, or something, and dismissed it with the words "of course, that's a very dangerous idea". The very phrase which was meant to put me off, in fact excited my interest - for I feel that we now *need* dangerous ideas.

Biologically we have inherited terrific physical and psychological resources for coping with danger of all sorts, but civilised life no longer provides challenges to our survival. A few are still lucky or persistent enough to seek out danger in the wilds, but the "Rambo" archetype in men's souls gets little opportunity for healthy exercise otherwise - too often it finds expression in urban violence.

In a crowded world should not the adventurer turn to other dimensions? That is the where the new frontier lies. How many have really returned whole and enriched from the drug experience? Perhaps we need a few more decades limbering up on easy tasks like landing men on Mars before society is ready to face the bigger challenges like heroin addiction? What we need now is dangerous ideas to test our mettle, not the safe and easy philosophies which offered mankind consolation while wolves howled around his puny townships. How many are ready for this challenge?

Do what thou wilt shall be the whole of the Law. So sod the Law.

FOREWORD TO 'LEAVES OF YGGDRASIL'

*First published in Leaves of Yggdrasil, by Freya Aswynn. Although writ-
ten as a foreword to another book, I'm including it because it does stand up
as an essay in its own right.*

This is a book about an ancient alphabet - it is also a book about magic.

It is easy to pay lip service to the general idea that there is power in words and sounds, but it is also easy to sympathise with Crowley's early objection to the Golden Dawn: that it promised to teach him the secrets of the universe, but all he was given was the Hebrew alphabet. We are only beginning to rediscover the possibility that an alphabet might be a "secret of the universe", that information could be more fundamental than matter or energy.

If you are new to the runes, or to any other alphabet for that matter, you may be attracted by a certain magic and mystery in the very forms of the letters. After you have studied them a little that magic can either take root and inspire you, as it did to the author of this book, or it can evaporate with familiarity and leave you with a sense of anticlimax and a yearning to explore elsewhere for that elusive magic. If you are prone to thinking "how can an alphabet be any more than just an alphabet?" it would be worth exploring the magical power of language in your imagination before starting this book.

Begin by considering what life might have been like when reading and writing were the preserve of the educated few. Most people would live without maps, without recipe books, without herbals, without calenders, without memo-pads, without road signs... This feat of memory would nowadays seem prodigious. It is hard for us to imagine that people used to know their tribal history by heart, could recite the Old Testament or sing their myths. Widespread literacy makes all this unnecessary: the familiarity of writing has released vast mental capacity by making so much memory redundant - what has happened to all that power?

Now go back further, and imagine a time when the written lan-
guage was so new that most people didn't even know of its existence. Imagine that you are a runner, and that there is a crisis in the land. A wise man has summoned you, given you a tablet of clay and instruc-

tions to run to a neighbouring land and present this tablet to your king. For some reason beyond your comprehension you are told to guard this tablet with your life, and to hand it over intact. When you arrive exhausted at your destination, the king takes this tablet in his hands, gazes at it in silent contemplation for a while, then proceeds to fire questions at you. To your astonishment his questions reveal a knowledge of the crisis which has happened several days running distant. By some extraordinary magic this little clay tablet seems to have spoken to the king, conveying knowledge of distant places, telling him that support is needed... Is it surprising that writing was early associated with magic?

Now go back even further, and imagine yourself as a hominid without any language. Suddenly your group is under attack, and you react like an animal, rushing at your attackers, perhaps clutching a stone as a primitive weapon. In your exertion and excitement you bellow and grunt, and you notice that your attackers are also making noises... but there is something odd about the way they do it. Their grunts and bellows have an eerie purposefulness which seems to link to their extraordinary fighting skill: your attacker suddenly and inexplicably retreats, making a babbling noise; you instinctively chase him and find yourself surrounded by attackers who seem to have a single mind. You are in fear and utter awe because you are witnessing something completely beyond comprehension: the use of speech to direct battle tactics. Animal survival is being transformed into the "art of war".

These simple and highly selective examples are meant to make just one general point: that from the very earliest times language and writing would have been associated with mystery and magic of the most awesome kind. The earlier such associations are made, the more deeply they will be imbedded in the group mind, or "collective unconsciousness". So when you feel an initial twinge of excitement at the idea of an ancient alphabet, you are experiencing a genuine link with the magical realm. What you must now do is to continue your studies in a way that will strengthen that link, before the sword of conscious analysis can sever the link by persuading you it is "nothing but an obsolete alphabet". Fundamental concepts of language are deeply linked to magical power in our minds, that is why it is possible to use ancient alphabets as a key or tap to magical power - provided you can strike the right balance between academic objectivity and subjective participation. A good example of this balance is found in this text of Freya's.

I remember my first acquaintance with Freya in the early eighties - I'd been told that I must meet this amazing Dutch occultist who didn't speak perfect English, but was able to fill in any gaps with fluent swear-words. This book testifies that she has come a long way since discovering the runes! Freya always was a controversial figure, and in writing about the runes she has chosen a controversial subject.

As she explains in her historical chapter, the runes are intimately linked with Norse mythology, a pantheon which was driven under-ground by Christianity, and it has remained underground for cen-turies. Another way of saying this is that Christ banished the Norse gods into hell. Another way of saying it is that these ancient gods have been driven down into the collective unconscious and aban-doned. The effect of doing this is similar to the effect you would get if you drove your cats, dogs and other domestic animals back into the jungle: when you set out to rediscover them several generations later, you find that they have reverted to the wild, grown feral and fierce. But their essential nature remains unchanged - a cat is still a cat, with all its potential.

Something like this has happened to the Norse gods. The first attempts to re-contact them this century had drastic results. Jung, in his essay on Wotan first published in 1936 describes how the "old god of storm and frenzy, the long quiescent Wotan" is awakening "like an extinct volcano, to a new activity, in a civilised country that had long supposed to have outgrown the middle ages". He describes how the "youth movement" had sacrificed sheep to this old god, and how the same spirit was now stirring in the Nazi movement. Perhaps we should compare the resulting havoc in Germany to what would hap-pen if the people who chased their cats into the wild were to enter the jungle several years later and say "oh look, there's our Kitty! Do let's take her back home".

Half a century later there is still something awesome and wild about the Norse gods. For some people that is reason enough to have nothing to do with them. Other people, like the worst of the Nazis, are so fascinated by this aspect that they become obsessed by it - like people who bait wild creatures because they are intoxicated by their bestiality, but with no respect for their basic nature. Other people, like Freya, can look beyond the rough surface and see the essential nature of a pantheon every bit as complete and noble as any other. To approach the gods in this manner is to bring them the gift of our civilisation.

Crowley described three ages of religion. In the aeon of Isis, the age of the great mother goddesses, the gods were primal forces of nature with little concern for humanity. As with Jehovah, you obeyed or perished. In the aeon of Osiris we meet a new type of god, much more human. Typically these were male gods who actually cared for mankind and suffered on our behalf. Christ, Dionysus and Wotan were examples of this type - gods who did not expect mankind to bow before the letter of the law so much as to act on the spirit of the law, gods who set an example for humanity to follow. Now we enter the aeon of Horus, and we will begin to learn that the gods are not perfect after all: as Freya explains in her chapter on "The Northern Tradition In Perspective", the gods themselves evolve and change. Now it is our task neither to obey the gods slavishly (as one should in the aeon of Isis) nor to try to model ourselves on their example (as one should in the aeon of Osiris) but rather to begin to stand up to them as equals. God became Man for our edification, now Mankind must realise our own divinity that the gods may become civilised. Fundamentalism or slavish belief has no future: the person who struggles with Horus because his true will happens to be that of a pacifist will eventually earn from Horus greater respect than the person who treads on the weak "because it says so in the Book of the Law".

There is something compelling about the return of wild gods from the underworld. It is perfectly natural to be fascinated by their primitive power, because it is the essence of the underworld itself. What is wrong is to become drunk on that power, just as it is wrong to banish that power by trivialising the gods. There may be danger in the runes, but this is a time when we need dangerous ideas - we need to turn inward to find challenge. What we must learn is to relate from a position of strength: communing with the gods without destroying their essential nature. This is how the Norse pantheon may return in splendour, to take its place beside the other gods without on the one hand becoming just another commercial novelty, or on the other hand driving us to mutual destruction.

To achieve this we need a balance between the power of ecstatic identification with the runes, and the safety of academic analysis. I believe that Freya's approach sets a good example in this respect.

I know little about history, mythology, or the runes, and I offer no guarantee of the truth of Freya's data. But that is just how she would want it to be, for everything in this book must be tested in the reader's own experience. There is a basic honesty here that one can respect: Freya makes no pretence about being privy to "ancient traditions" or "exclusive brotherhoods": this book is the work of someone who has studied the literature, and has lived with the runes.

Enjoy this stimulating book in this spirit: and if you should come to disagree with anything in it, well and good. For I know that Freya herself thrives on controversy - and no living tradition can be a static entity.

6

PAROXYSMS OF MAGIC

First published in Nox. When reading this piece over I remembered some more thoughts about the OTTO and its vital contribution to civilisation, which I have added as an appendix.

Recently I drew a comparison between two systems of ideas arising at the same moment in history (1904): Einstein's theories of space-time relativity, and Austin Spare's theories which I described as "a relativity of belief". It was interesting that the year of the writing of the Book of the Law, ie the first year of Crowley's New Aeon, should have been the time when traditional ideas of "the absolute" came under attack on these two fronts.

Einstein undermined the idea of absolute position. So such questions as "does the sun go round the earth or the earth go round the sun" were demoted from being questions about absolute truth to questions about human choice. The answer is that from an everyday perspective it is easiest to think of the sun as circling the earth: it allows us to go on using such handy expressions as "sun rise" and "sun set". But in a scientific framework it is much simpler to work with the idea of the earth circling the sun - because the equations are easier.

Austin Spare extended this idea to suggest that all beliefs have this arbitrary quality: your beliefs shape the world you inhabit, so choose your beliefs with care.

Because I saw this idea as very basic to magic, the nature of belief has been a recurring theme in mine own ideas. In SSOTBME I pointed out that the question "do you *really* believe in spirits", which is typical of the non-magician, is not very interesting to the magician. The latter is more likely to argue as Crowley did that "I perform certain actions and certain results follow"; and, as with the scientists' heliocentric equations, the spirits often provide a neater model of the phenomena than any psychological or coincidental theory of magic.

We all recognise the power of absolute belief - fanaticism can move mountains - but we see that it is a power which tends to rule the believer. Magic is more concerned with ruling over power than being ruled by it. The struggle is perhaps to "beef up" our carefully chosen beliefs by making the unconscious accept them as absolute, but without handing over control in the process.

It is because of this confusion about belief - the heavy associations which linger with the word - that I have wondered about finding an alternative or replacement concept. Instead of "believing in" some idea, might we not "delight in" it? or "rejoice in" it? Or perhaps it is better to kidnap a dated phrase and say "instead of believing in ideas I am going to dig them". So the answer to "do you really believe in spirits?" becomes "no, but I really dig them!"

This "digging" principle was in a sense the serious message behind the "Manifesto of the OTTO" published in Arrow number 21. This manifesto was a send up of "heavy heavy" New Aeon occultism, but also a justification of it. It began with the plea:

"What happened to the occult loonies, the hairy mega-thelemites of the late sixties? Where are they now?

"When was the last time you attended a festival thronging with bordello witches, warlocks with long beards and flowing cloaks, all heavy with ankhs, pentagrams and all the trappings of kitschcraft? When were you last greeted in the streets of London with cries of 'Do what thou wilt'?

"Over-the-top occultism is dead. Long live over-the-top occultism!"

The general theme of the argument was "When occultism dissociated itself from the worst excesses of Dennis Wheatley, it castrated itself; for the worst excesses of Dennis Wheatley are where it's at."

The manifesto ended:

"The OTTO is the order that makes the Typhonian OTO look like the Mother's Union; makes the Age of Maat sound like the whisper of a politely restrained fart at a Conservative Ladies luncheon gathering; makes Chaos Magic feel like a slightly limp cucumber sandwich remaining on a plate at the end of an exceptionally dull vicarage teaparty.

"So put on your cloaks, tattoo yourselves with sigils, vibrate names of power at the Cafe Royale, fill braziers with incense, wave kitsch swords... Exceed! Exceed! But ever unto Me!"

The idea behind the OTTO is this. In our early days, when we first become acquainted with the occult, it is often an awe-inspiring thing. After reading "The Devil Rides Out" we see an advert for the

Sorcerer's Apprentice in Exchange & Mart and send off in trepidation for a catalogue of amazing incenses and weird paraphernalia to read by torchlight beneath the bedclothes with chattering teeth - expecting hell-fire to blast us at any moment. A few years later we have worked our way through WE Butler, Dion Fortune and plucked up courage to read Crowley and are ready to argue the psychological validity of magical technique with anyone. What we have gained is wisdom and understanding. What we have lost is that old gut-wrenching excitement.

We know enough to steer clear of the ego-tripping loony with the piercing gaze and long black cloak. We see through his act and congratulate ourselves. But we overlook the fact that a good act can be a delight, a piece of street theatre, an art-form, an invocation in its own right.

The OTTO message is this: now we have grown up enough that we no longer are in awe of the charlatan, it means we are now free to delight in the charlatan - to *dig* the charlatan.

Now we are mature enough to realise there aren't any ancient brotherhoods with secrets passed down from time immemorial, we are now free to *dig* those brotherhoods who put on a good act of being just that.

Now we know that all that paraphernalia is just trappings with no value other than surface appearance, let us therefore maximise that residual value by making the surface appearance utterly mind-blowing!

When the 70s occultist says "there's no point in using a silver censer when a coffee tin serves just as well", the OTTO initiate replies "there's no point in using a coffee tin when a 800 year old human skull looted from the ruins of a Mexican temple serves just as well".

The excitement of the OTTO is the excitement of overdoing it, and I suggest that this approach has something to offer us now. Let's consider an example of its application.

A typical problem of a hard core magic group is getting things to happen on time: after all the excitement of planning a really staggering ritual, when it comes to the day no-one turns up on time, and then they all sit around chatting and smoking dope for a few hours before anything happens. If the master of rituals gets stroppy and says that late arrivals will be fined or excommunicated, then everyone protests that he is on an ego power trip - and quotations like "let there be no difference made...", "every number is infinite" and "do what thou wilt" start flying around.

Now the OTTO approach might be as follows: the master or mistress of ritual, with eyes blazing and flecks of foam at the mouth, would scream "at the first stroke of midnight the door of the temple will be *nailed shut*, and the ritual will commence!" Instead of rebelling at this apparent power trip, the brethren of the OTTO say "Wow! *nailed shut*! That's really over the top! We dig it!" And the ritual happens on time.

Paroxysms of delight can indeed be magical. They are an expression of the affirmation that pierces clouds of doubt. I can become so entranced by the loopiest of New Age festivals that I can even end up digging the high prices...

In a sense I see the OTTO as spiritual heirs to the Fabulous Furry Phreak Brothers. Was not much of the "magic of the sixties" a product of people's willingness to cast aside doubt and indulge in paroxysms of delight? Some ageing hippies still insist that the Pentagon really did levitate when they surrounded it with linked hands...

In the terminology of Crowley's essay on the subject, perhaps the Hunchback (?) has now had a long enough innings, and it is time to reinstate the Soldier (!).

And now at last we are fortunate enough to have once more a real incentive to encourage our actions. When the brethren of the OTTO find their enthusiasm for blood sacrifices and desecrated churchyards to be on the wane, they have learnt to sit in a circle, link hands, breath slowly and deeply, and meditate on the image of an apoplectic Geoffrey Dickens.

SHOCK OTTO CULT PROBE SENSATION
An Appendix to the Above

The above account of the OTTO does, I hope, justify its existence to the individual occultist in need of "spiritual mustard". What I have not yet done is explain the OTTO's vital contribution to society.

The popular press often reports accounts of sinister black magic groups engaged in animal sacrifices, sex and drug orgies, and the drinking of human blood etc. It would be easy to assume that the press are very gullible, but if you ask the writers of these articles you find that they are simply written to make money, because "the public like reading articles on black magic cults". Now, for those of us who have the needs of the common man at heart, and who have also been in the occult scene long enough to realise that the number of serious occult groups engaged in the sort of practices described is negligible, or even non-existent, this is tragic.

Here is a public crying out for black mass cult sensations, and here is a devoted press being forced against their highest principles to invent stories to fill this need, while those best qualified to remedy the situation - ie the occultists - are doing absolutely nothing about it. Even the blatant Satanic groups turn out to be frightfully high-minded when you really look into them. Thus the OTTO was founded to fill this crucial role.

The OTTO heartily endorses the use of group sex (the kinkier the better), drugs, animal sacrifices (though it prefers human sacrifices), devil worship and the drinking of blood as a way of improving rituals. Under the motto "never knowingly undersold" the OTTO promises that, should anyone report any other group making use of vile practices unknown to the brethren of the OTTO, then those very practices will be promptly written into the next official OTTO ritual to ensure the maintenance of their absolute rock bottom standards.

For example: one is often warned against groups who will initiate members by post, without any screening but at a high price. The OTTO will do this for anyone upon surrender of one or more gold credit cards. As an OTTO initiator I hereby pronounce that everyone who reads this article is automatically an OTTO Neophyte - and you all now owe me £666 each for the privilege (please send cheques c/o the publisher).

It has, however been pointed out that there is a problem in Britain, where a recent court case convicted an artist who had shocked members of the public. There has also been the threat of an extended law of blasphemy. It has apparently become illegal to shock people in Britain. This is shocking. It is a denial of mankind's basic rights, it is an act of mental cruelty. It is a repetition of the governmental error of the 60s when so many people were removed from their interactive slum environments and abandoned in isolationist tower blocks - cut off from the weather of human intercourse and sensorily deprived.

It must be clear that people need shocks. They crave them. Try this simple test: print two identical journals, one having the headline "Britain today - a report" and the other "Britain today - shock report", and see which sells the better. Any journalist or publisher will tell you that people will pay to be shocked - a government which denies this need is no better than the torturer who inflicts sensory deprivation on its victims.

That was the basic social problem of the 60s: so many people couldn't stand the sudden innocence. They could not live without their sense of sin and have since had to re-discover morality so that they could once more experience the shocks needed to keep them alive. Such people can hardly get going in the morning till they've had their tabloid-full of shock horror.

The worst recent example of this craving for shock must be the Victorians. As well as severe moralities they even had special electrical machines to give themselves shocks - I know because my big brother had one and he tried it out on me when I was a child - and they had weird water cures which went beyond the cold bath. In Great Malvern the Victorian search for shock went so far that they used to pay to stand on a metal grating in swimming costume and have several hundred gallons of icy water released over them in one go.

More sensitive members of the OTTO, like myself, find it hard to sympathise with this public craving for ever more shock. We are constantly being stunned by such things as the fluttering of butterfly wings, whole worlds in grains of sand, and the vibrations from candles and quartz crystals, so why should we need coarse stimulants like morality to sharpen our tastes?

We do however recognise the wishes of the majority, and are always prepared to commit ourselves selflessly to acts of public outrage as and when required.

Exceed! Exceed! But ever unto me!

7

TURDS MADE FRESH
A Response to Some Feedback on Words Made Flesh

The sense of bitterness that I felt when I wrote this article has been resolved - see later essay on Writing and Publishing. I was always hoping someone else would take up the Johnstone's Paradox idea and give it a whirl, so I could get on with something new.

Words Made Flesh was written to clear my mind of a topic that had been buzzing around in it for many years, and which was making it hard to get on with new projects. So the last thing I want is to spend any more time following it up. Although I could see many further avenues to explore, in the book I left them as more or less obscure suggestions for others to investigate if they thought them worthwhile - hoping thereby to enrich the reading experience. But the result is that some friends have come back to me with observations and reservations - and I want to respond. Although as an author my mind has moved onto fresh pastures, as a publisher I feel a certain obligation to provide such "after sales service" to repay their thoughtfulness. Hence this essay which looks at two points: overloaded memory, and hierarchies and freedom.

OVERLOADED MEMORY

"If our universe is a program running in a computer..." asked my friend, and I pointed out that Johnstone's Paradox does not demand that the meta-universe contains anything that we might recognise by the word "computer", but merely that it should be able to order its information in some manner.

"Sure, I don't mean a 'computer' as we know it, but let's just call the information processing mechanism by that word - however un-computerlike it might actually be. Then the information making up our universe takes up a certain large amount of memory. But what happens if we, in this universe, now build a computer (like Macroc in the story) to model our universe? If we create an identical universe in the computer, it will demand an equal amount of memory as the original..." at which point I reminded him that it is explained in the story that we will never be able to model our own identical universe on account of quantum uncertainty.

"That is true, but it does not effect my argument, because all I am talking about is that we model a universe as complex as ours, and so one which demands about the same amount of memory. This would mean that the memory needs of the 'computer' in the meta-universe has now doubled, because it now contains two universes, one running as a sub-program of the other. If the denizens of this inner universe now themselves create another computer universe we have three nested universes... and so on. The memory requirement of the original computer would eventually exceed any finite bounds. This is a paradox within your paradox".

This was an interesting observation, and I feel that the answer to it lies in two of the topics mentioned in the book: data compression and the relationship between entropy and information. The second point was only hinted at, so let's enlarge on it.

In the story a universe was modelled within a huge computer called Macroc, and it was explained that the timescale within this universe would change relative to time in the outer universe: it would apparently slow down as the calculations became more complex and the inner universe built up structures. The point that I wanted to leave open here was the relationship between information in one universe and entropy in the other.

The much quoted law of thermodynamics describes a universe where total "disorder", as entropy, is always increasing. Now the important point in my theory is that less information is required to describe an ordered state than a disordered state. It is not easy to give a real life example that is realistic, because all phenomena are so complex; but imagine the amount of information required to totally describe a piece of perfect crystal, compared to the information required to describe the same material once it is in a molten state. All the atoms are the same in both cases, but in the first case their positions can be precisely described by defining a three-dimensional array, and this can be done by a simple formula. In the second case, however, the molecules are "randomly" scattered (subject to certain space-filling limitations) which means that each individual position and motion of zillions of molecules would have to be described. This is an enormous increase in the memory requirement.

Imagine then that we have this super-computer chip into which we have programmed a universe. This chip would be an "island" of highly ordered matter, because not only has the matter in it been ordered into a computer chip, but the particles of that matter have been further aligned (by programming) into describing a universe. So let us imagine that we are worried about the memory load on the meta-universe, and we decide to eliminate this inner universe in order to reduce the overall memory. Let us imagine that we take the drastic action of crushing the super-computer chip, or dissolving it in acid. Now, instead of an island of ordered matter, we have a random mass of molecules. Instead of reducing the memory load in the meta universe, we have greatly increased it by creating disorder in place of order.

This suggests then that creating a universe within another universe, far from demanding more memory, actually economises on memory. But beware of this idea. This is only true in a localised sense: each time you program an inner universe you create an island of lower information by reducing entropy locally. However, for all I know, the effort of creating that local island of low entropy might well create more entropy in a global sense as you burn up calories and the computer generates heat.

All I want to put across in this explanation is this. When we build a big computer and program it full of wisdom, it is obviously tempting to feel that we have somehow generated more information. Although this may be true in an inner sense - we have generated information within the "universe" of the program's discourse, just as a financial spreadsheet program generates information within a firm's accountancy statistics - it is not true in real terms, because ordering all that information has amounted to an overall economising on information.

(If entropy is always tending to increase, however, you could argue that on a global level we have increased information, simply because everything we do increases the universe's entropy. In this sense, the final objection my friend made still stands. There has to be a limit to the nesting of universes, not for any paradoxical reasons, but simply because the meta-universe must eventually run down according to this entropic law).

Having shown how building a computer economises on information in a local sense, I need to explain how the information "saved" can be enough to describe something as complex as another universe. This is where the data compression bit comes in. But before we get onto that I would like to point out why I consider the idea of information in a meta-universe to be more useful and satisfactory than the idea of entropy.

The trouble with accepting the idea of entropy psychologically is that it only seems to describe a lifeless mechanical world running to its end, and it doesn't feel right to living organisms like us which are involved in locally reducing entropy and building up ordered structures. Increasing entropy is not, as an idea, fundamental to our nature. So, when I described that the inner universe would seem to run slower (relative to the outer universe) as it grew more complex, I was making two points at once. Firstly the one already covered: the memory load on the computer increases in direct proportion to the entropy of its inner universe, because chaos demands more description than order. But the other reason it slows down is a consequence of the many localised increases of order: as the universe evolves complexity (eg in the form of life) the equations grow more complex, and this also slows down the computer.

Now, just as sheer memory load is related to what is experienced in the inner world as "entropy", so is complexity of programming related to what is experienced in the inner world as "meaning". So this model of existence brings together two ideas which suffer when divorced from each other: entropy and meaning. Instead of a law which simply says that entropy is always increasing, I suggest a law which says that in any universe entropy and meaning are always increasing with time. Turn this around and it suggests that "time" has two separate meanings which are connected by this law. Firstly there is objective time which is experienced by mechanical systems: objective time equals increase in entropy and is experienced by a mechanism as a rate of increase. Subjective time is experienced by living systems: subjective time equals increase in meaning and is experienced as a rate of increase. These two "times" are distinct, yet they are closely related because they are two manifestations of the working out of one program: objective time is a measure of the information generated, and subjective time is a measure of the complexity generated.

Insofar as the increase in information is the result of complexity (that is, insofar as the apparent randomness of high entropy is the result of highly complex interactions which are ultimately causal), these two times are two ways of measuring the same thing: thus we will always experience entropy increasing, when we know how to look for it.

Sorry about that diversion. Back to data compression. I dealt with this at some length in the book, explaining how our apparently complex existences could actually be made up of the interplay of really basic archetypal patterns, and that the illusion of "separateness" or identity that we feel is a trick to save us from seeing the fundamental simplicity of existence. The example I gave is of the teenager in love: totally involved in the belief that he or she is the first person ever to have loved like this, while the rest of the world says "oh it's just a teenage crush". So throughout life we identify passionately with an ego which may, in the final analysis, be no more (or less) complex than our natal horoscope.

This idea, though simple, is such a big one to grasp that I am happy to work a bit more on it. The problem is this: how could the little ordered island created when we build a finite computer ever save enough information to allow us to describe something as vast as a universe? It's incredible. But there is a topic being discussed recently which I believe can help us to see just how information can be compressed: it is the mathematics of fractals as described in "The Beauty of Fractals" by Peitgen and Richter. As there has been a television program and a number of popular articles on the subject, I will not attempt to explain and will assume the reader knows what I'm talking about in the following paragraphs.

The Mandlebrot set is an entity of extraordinary complexity when experienced. It is infinite, and it is infinitely complex. Given a powerful graphics computer anyone could spend the rest of their life mapping that set without even scratching the surface, as they say. This complexity is how the set is experienced from within, as you explore it on a screen. On the other hand it is terribly simple mathematically, and the whole thing can be described from without in one paragraph. Programming a Mandlebrot set is almost child's play - the only complicated thing is writing the graphics bit so that it can be experienced on screen. It only takes a few lines of programming and yet it is infinitely complex... and so as complex as our universe.

Why does this infinite set not overload a computer's memory as soon as input? The answer is that it is only held in memory in its compressed mathematical form. An extended description is only needed when we call up a bit of the set to examine on the screen. When we decide to explore another region by calling up another screen full, then the information about the first region's appearance is erased unless we deliberately ask the computer to store it. You see, the whole Mandlebrot set is there in the computer in mathematical form, but it only manifests on the screen in little chunks as and when the person at the keyboard decides to explore a certain region at a certain magnification.

Does this not suggest a resolution of the philosophical debate between those who say that objects in our universe are only real when experienced, and those who say they are real always? Does the tree in the quadrangle cease to exist when no-one is looking at (or touching, smelling or hearing) it? The problem with his attractive idea is that we have never had a credible model to explain how so complex a phenomenon as a tree could vanish and reappear. But those who work with fractal sets will begin to see how this could happen: every time they decide to explore a certain region of the Mandlebrot set, there it is on the screen just as if it had been stored as such in the computer memory (ok, it still takes a bit of time to be generated, because our computers are still slow, and we are not part of them); and yet they know that as soon as they clear the screen all that intricate detail now exists only in another sense, in a potential sense, as a mathematical program. This mechanism would be a supreme piece of data compression in a programmed universe: there would no need to store in memory the precise data about the positions of every molecule on the far side of the Moon, it would all be stored as equations which would produce that information only when a human or other "sentient program" entered the region. The presence of consciousness in any area causes (or even, perhaps, is caused by) the unfolding of information from its latent, programmed state into its manifest, observable state in that area.

If it seems like a big jump to go from one precisely defined set, the Mandlebrot set, to something as complicated as a real four-dimensional universe with living beings in it, then I would mention some work that helps to bridge that gap. It stems from the problem of storing visual images: anyone who compares the capacity of data storage and video storage will realise that it is terribly uneconomical to store pictures, there is simply so much information to handle. That is why researchers are looking into ways to compress this data. One approach is to record only the changes: if we have a film sequence which shows a motionless flower garden with a bird flying through it, why repeat the image of the garden on every frame when you could store that information once for all the frames and simply record the bird as a smaller moving image to be superimposed on the big, unchanging image of the garden? That was just an example, while another recent development is more relevant to my argument: it is to approximate to a photograph of a real scene by summing a fractal series, in a way analogous to the Fourier analysis which approximates to any immensely complex wave-form by summing a series of sine waves. Apparently you can replace a photo of a landscape by a finite series of fractal equations appropriate to the resolution of the original series. Instead of having to store a vast amount of bits of graphic information, you only store a smaller number of equations from which the picture can be generated - and this process is already showing good results.

This shows how we can begin to grasp the possibility that a universe, which is experienced by its denizens as something infinitely rich and complex, might in fact be generated from a finite set of equations contained within a surprisingly small information structure. Perhaps the complex, shifting harmonics of the world horoscope are indeed a total description of our reality for anyone who has the mechanism to unfold that description?

I use the word "unfold" with reference to another book read since writing Words Made Flesh: "Unfolding Meaning - a weekend of dialogue with David Bohm". This book I found hard to understand, because it is a symposium with many voices, but I did get a gist of Professor Bohm's idea of "unfolding from an implicate order", and it seems to me to parallel what I am here describing. If this is a correct perception, then I would suggest that work with computer models will make it much easier for future generations to have a gut feeling for Bohm's "implicate order", because they will have seen rich and complex universes like the Mandlebrot set being unfolded from simple equations on their computer screens.

To sum up: although Johnstone's Paradox in no way depends on computer models as we know them, it helps to understand it if we consider just how much information might be generated from a few equations. In particular, to an entity that was part of that same information structure, the universe described might seem infinitely complex and vast. We are on the brink of realising just how much can be contained in very little. A universe in a grain of sand.

HIERARCHIES AND FREEDOM

Another friend objected to my idea of a meta-universe, whose ordered information generates this our universe, because he saw it in a strictly hierarchical sense: that the "higher" universe was "superior" and it contained in an absolute sense the justification or explanation of the lower universe. Therefore he felt that Johnstone's Paradox reduced the value of this universe by postulating another universe of greater value - a regression to obsolete notions of an external God to which we must all be subject.

I get the point, but do not feel that it need hold. It is true that I may have used the term "hierarchy" and "higher" in my book, but I meant it in a mathematical sense where the distinction between "set" and "superset" is not seen as a value judgement. When I use the term "hierarchy" I meant it in the loose sense of "nested universes", rather than the strict sense of government of the less sacred by the more sacred.

As an illustration of nested universes you might consider life on this planet. It can be argued that life is a phenomenon generated by chemical interactions. So the universe of chemical interactions is a meta-universe which generates the life we experience. But those chemical reactions are generated by the interactions of individual atoms: so the universe of atoms is a meta-universe which generates all those chemical reactions. But the behaviour of atoms can be analysed in terms of the movement of fundamental particles and quantum mechanics: so these are a meta-universe which generates atomic phenomena. Now most people end their description at that point, but what Johnstone's Paradox postulates is that the universe of particles and quantum mechanics is itself generated by the interactions of strings of data in a universe of information.

The reason we have not yet "experienced" those strings in the same way that we have managed (through high technology) to experience, say, atomic or particle movements, is because each step to the next universe takes us further from direct experience and into more subtle realms. A string of data when experienced from an "inner" universe is a most curious object: it has only one dimension (as a string of data) and yet contains several dimensions of meaning. For example: a mathematical definition of a five dimensional space is a one dimensional string of letters (translate it into morse code if you insist on visible one-dimensionality) describing something which can be explored as five dimensions; similarly, the one dimensional groove of a mono gramophone record can unfold in the listener's mind to the many dimensions of a symphony orchestra. How many dimensions of meaning are contained in the data strings which describe our universe? According to the traditional cabala there are ten dimensions lying behind us, the same number as postulated by modern astrology: but this may be no more than an intuitive estimate in the first case, and a reflection of the "state-of-the-art" in the second case.

If you have followed this progression of nested universes, you will see the sense in which I do not ascribe greater value to the "higher" universes. To me the fact that you could in theory ultimately describe my behaviour in terms of atomic physics does not surrender any of my value to the universe of atomic physics. The philosophy which we occultists describe as "materialism", is the philosophy which does indeed remove value from our universe and see it as "subservient" to the world of atomic explanations. You can criticise such materialists for making precisely the same mistake that they accused the religious people of making: rather than seeing the full value and richness of the universe we experience, they are shifting that value to a postulated "higher plane" where everything has its explanation and so its meaning. The religious person says this world is an illusion, only God is real; the materialist says everything we experience, including God, is just a chemical reaction in the brain.

Now, I can accept that the knowledge of atomic physics does not reduce the value of my existence, instead it increases its value by adding another level of interpretation (you see, I view the nested universes subjectively from my standpoint and see the world of atoms as a sub-universe of meaning, an embellishment to my life). Similarly, I can accept the idea of a meta-universe, whose ordered information lies behind our existence, as something which enriches my experience of this universe rather than something which "explains it away". In the story in Words Made Flesh, the universe inside Macroc was at first seen in the latter sense - as a mere program which could be switched off when it had served its purpose - but by the end everyone realised that this was not so. The inner universe was a vital living entity which could not be switched off without violating their own world's principles.

The reason we instinctively rebel against the idea that we could be "programs" running in a cosmic computer is, I suggest, because we are still limited to the idea of a program as a "mechanical" pre-determined calculation. Take me out of this computer and run me again in another and you would get the same answer (42). Now my guts tell me that the exploration of the mathematics of chaos will extend this idea of a program toward more exciting possibilities. That is why the Pope in the story I refer to says that we cannot tamper with the universe running in Macroc "because it is a turbulent system" and that the only way to predict the precise outcome of any action would be to run the same program at the same time in the same computer. So much for pre-determinism.

The essence of the matter seems to me to lie in richly parallel processing, with its vast amount of cross-linked parallel paths. This is the analogy I made in the book with turbulent flow in liquids, itself a complex parallel processing mechanism. If we run the same program twice, and we fail to reproduce the initial conditions with infinite precision, so that at any one single branch a different decision is made, the rest of the program could set off in a totally different and "unpredictable" direction. Rounding errors would make it utterly unlikely that a complex program would repeat itself precisely, and the "Butterfly Effect" quoted by the chaos theorists would mean that any two runs of the same program might actually be very different - they would certainly show extreme variations at the local level even if they "average out" to a similar end point.

Might this not be the essence of what is perceived as "free will"? Might not consciousness come as an experience of chaos? Whereas water flowing smoothly in a straight canal is not conscious because there is no significant turbulence, water chattering over stones is a turbulent system, and the complex information processing of its fluidic "computer" would experience its own turbulence as a constant stream of decisions being made. Thus it is that gardeners, especially Zen ones, like to create chattering streams in their gardens: they are in fact invoking undines by creating consciousness in liquid. To sit and listen to such chatter is to find wise council. So also will the first signs of free will in computers come with increasing parallelism: may their chatter prove as wise.

If I create a universe as a program in a computer, and the result is something unique, alive and practically (if not theoretically) unrepeatable, then my position relative to that universe is hardly one of superiority. In theory I have the power to switch it off: but, knowing enough to create it, would I be morally capable of that act? Would I be any more "superior" than a father who still has the strength to kill his son, his own creation? To what extent can we change the perspective and realise that, as far as the son is concerned, the father might have been created merely as an instrument whose ultimate purpose in life was to conceive and educate the son?

To sum up: I believe it is possible to accept Johnstone's Paradox without in any way reducing the value of our universe. You could, if you wanted, use the idea to create a new God - the meta-universe - just as others have made materialistic explanations into Gods at the expense of our own world. But this is your own choice, it is not inherent in the theory I propose. The meta-universe can no more, and no less, "explain away" existence than God or atomic physics can. Such explanations are only a theoretical possibility, realisable as hindsight: if you actually tried to predict my life in advance by studying the atomic structure of this universe you would never manage sufficient accuracy to get the same answer twice running. Your error would be my freedom.

Instead of being perceived as a new monotheistic authority, the meta-universe should be seen as a partner - another level of enrichment of our understanding.

CONCLUSION

I emphasised in the book that the importance of Johnstone's Paradox does not depend upon what can be achieved by artificial intelligence so much as what people believe could be achieved. The fact that no-one has yet managed to model a universe as complex as ours does not matter, so long as the public begins to believe that it is theoretically possible.

After all, the dominant materialist worldview is based upon Darwinian evolution, although it has never been fully demonstrated. No-one has successfully evolved a human being from primordial slime, yet the belief that it is theoretically possible has had a profound influence at every level of society.

Basically I argued as a magical philosopher, assuming relativity of belief, and this has lead to a poor reception of the book from a world dominated by scientific philosophy which assumes the existence of absolute truth or absolute reality.

On the one hand it is rejected by the self confessed scientists, because they are quick to dismiss any exploration of "cranky" ideas.

On the other hand it is rejected by the anti-scientists and meta-scientists because it takes reductionism seriously.

Materialistic science has created an establishment that makes it very hard to put forward alternative ideas. But there are signs that opposition to this viewpoint is crystallising into a "new age" counter-establishment that is seeking scientific evidence for the existence of a non-materialist "spirit" world - whether they call it that or prefer to coin new terms like "morphic fields" or "implicate order".

Insofar as this counter-establishment opposes reductionism it seems like an alternative, but insofar as it is still looking for absolute realities it is no more than an extension of scientific thinking into a broader universe. Morphic resonance is a challenge to science, but not an alternative as such.

Magic is an alternative to science: not a challenge, as it can happily coexist with science. In Words Made Flesh I was able to accept the principle of reductionism as a basis because I was not concerned with absolute truth, merely belief. The book's conclusion makes it unacceptable to the scientific establishment, the book's method makes it unacceptable to the counter-establishment. I will write another book to explain the difference between oppositions and alternatives...

I too do not like reductionism. If I were artist I might condemn it for its ugliness; if religious for its badness; if truly scientific, for its falsity. Beauty, Goodness and Truth are fundamental to Art, Religion and Science respectively, but not to Magic, whose prime objective is Wholeness.

So I condemn reductionism only because it is incomplete. It is not good, bad, true or untrue so much as it is but a process. It is only the first part of a greater process that the alchemists summarised as "solve et coagula". The need to separate the substance into its minutest parts so that they could be reassembled into a greater whole.

In the book, therefore, I do not reject or deny reductionism as a power. Instead I wonder where the process is leading us, and I conclude that it is leading us to eventual "coagula".

The advance of reductionism will squeeze our universe until all spirit is expelled. It squeezes us into a black hole through which we enter a new universe where all the spirit and all the magic is restored in unprecedented glory.

Seen in this way reductionism is no longer a bogey to be resisted, but rather a fitting finale to the Christian era. The final trial for mankind.

The trial of Earth requires the sacrifice of material goods; the ordeal of Water the sacrifice of emotional attachments; and the trial of Air demands the humility to abandon intellectual knowledge.

But who can face the ordeal by Fire? The need to surrender Spirit itself?

Those who can accept that bleak challenge will find everything restored a thousandfold - as they say.

But who is prepared to fork out six quid for a book that asks one to forget their distaste for artificial intelligence, to abandon their intellectual snobbery about magic, and to finally offer spirit itself for sacrifice?

Four ordeals in one.

8

DYED IN THEIR WOOL
Why have the liberals gone so quiet?

I've heard such daft things said about liberals (with big or little L) recently that I hardly know where to begin. Some months back there was an SDLP representative on the radio and he spoke of their need to abandon the "beards and sandals Liberal image".

Now, much as I distrust such snap judgements, if anyone was stupid enough to ask me for an instant diagnosis of the present malaise in British politics I would have said that the problem lay precisely in the current shortage of beards and sandals in Westminster.

So I voted Green in the European elections and, judging by the size of this protest vote, many had come to the same conclusion as myself.

When Bush, in his presidential campaign "accused" Dukakis of being a liberal he gave the latter a golden opportunity to respond "yes I am - and proud to represent a Great American Tradition".

Instead of that, Dukakis was photographed the next day in a tank. Not a water tank or a septic tank, but an unmistakable toys-for-the-boys, bang-you're-dead sort of tank. Happily the electorate showed him the contempt such a reaction deserved.

The absurd notion that the world has been conquered by American Military Might seems to have its origins in the confused imagination of Ronald Reagan.

Ask any coke-drinking tee-shirt-wearing youngster around the world why he worships America and the answer will not be because of its Star Wars, nukes or tanks, but because of its freedom. It is not the US Navy that has colonised the globe, it is US Liberalism.

But perhaps we should keep quiet and just let the "chicken hawks" work it out of their system. After all, the sabre-rattling of recent years did only emerge as compensation for humiliating military defeat in Vietnam.

Considering the worldwide triumphs of Liberalism, (and the very vehemence of resistance to it in countries like Iran and China merely serves to highlight its power) how has the extraordinary notion arisen that Liberalism is somehow "ineffective"?

As a citizen of the country which has developed the very highest form of Liberalism, namely "Woolly Liberalism", I object strongly to the use of this phrase as a term of abuse.

Fifty years ago two of the toughest, meanest, most heavily armed war machines the world has ever known were rash enough to declare war on woolly liberals and were thoroughly rubbed out as a consequence. In their place stand two more liberal nations.

Let that be a warning to the fundamentalist Moslem spokesman who criticised our handling of the Ayatollah's death-judgement on Rushdie - proclaiming that the trouble with liberals is that they do not care enough to feel strongly about their principles.

Does he really believe that the rationalist liberal impulse is somehow totally different from, or less deeply felt than, the religious impulse? Are there not some other major religions, such as Buddhism, which assume an equally modest facade?

The real force which the Nazis and the Japanese army came up against in World War 2 was not the loud voices of a warrior class, but the dogged determination of a country that believed it was fighting to preserve freedom, decency, fairness... in short Liberalism. Of course here, as in America, there are those loud voices claiming the triumph for military force. They say "if the woolly liberals had had their way we would all be living under the Nazis now", rather than admit it was the liberals who won the war - using every dirty trick to do so we are now told.

What is it that makes the gentle liberal such a formidable opponent in battle?

This is best illustrated with an extreme example. Anyone who succeeds in picking a fight with a pacifist, is in for a nasty shock. They will find themselves fighting with the Devil incarnate.

It's just part of a general rule: don't encourage any religion to become its own devil. This is why I favour the (modest) persecution of communists and Christians: both are religions of the underdog, and both distrust great wealth and temporal power. So whenever either Communism or Christianity rise to positions of wealth or power they become their own devils and invariably grow terribly corrupt - whereas under persecution they are the salt of the earth. If I lived in the USSR my best friends would be Christian; if I lived in

Texas they would be communist. *(Since that was written things have changed in Russia, and the Christians are becoming predictably corrupt)*

So the fighting liberal is a fiend. The mechanism for this is probably psychological: whereas the "hawk" or extremist is someone who goes about hurling anger all over the place like a litter lout, the liberal tends to take in strong feelings for processing within - a sort of inner waste-recycling plant.

Now, however cool and calm the liberal might seem to the fuming extremist, this recycling of anger is not easy or rapid. Unless the liberal is given time to process and rationalise rage and distaste, a backlog of bitterness will build up.

It is this inner reservoir of concentrated rage that the persistent attacker is in danger of striking. When it bursts open it reveals an intensity and energy of anger beyond the experience of any extroverted warrior. Wives of gentle pacifists who have experienced crises in their relationship will probably know what I mean.

There are plenty of extremists, fanatics and terrorists in the world, and there are plenty of nuclear arms. But the only time they have ever been used in anger was by a liberal nation dragged reluctantly into conflict. And two were dropped, where one would have been more than enough.

People are very rude about Rambo, but I thought that First Blood, the original Rambo movie, was a terrific yarn on these lines.

Most people overlook that Rambo was a hippy at the start of the film: a wandering, taciturn bum with long hair, jeans and a head band. He came up against the arrogant, yet polite, face of small town Conservatism: "take my advice, sonny, folks around here don't appreciate your kind".

In return he showed equally polite but firm resistance, and walked back into town. So the policeman turned him in and he was slightly roughed up by junior officers. This experience precipitated a nervous breakdown in Rambo - a brief flashback suggested he had suffered torture in a prisoner of war camp - and he went berserk.

Now he was a hunted man, and the "decent God-fearing" townsfolk grabbed their guns and joined gleefully in the sport of the hunt - only to make a terrible discovery. Their quarry had been the country's top special force soldier: a redundant fighting machine created by their own system. Rambo spread mayhem, until his old superior in the army was called in to pacify him.

I can hardly find a better metaphor for the dangers that hard core Conservatives and fundamentalists worldwide are playing with when they persist in their taunts about woolly liberals.

Unless it is the sight of Bruce Wayne descending into the bowels of the earth and donning his cloak of darkness to avenge the evils of Gotham City.

Why have the liberals been so quiet of late?

9

THE SATAN GAME
Reflections on Recent Hysteria Amongst
Fundamentalist Christians

This essay was originally published in Fenris Wolf, around 1990.

On July 17th 1989 ITV screened a program called The Roger Cook Report and subtitled "The Devil's Work" - an appropriate title, as this essay will reveal. It began with an astonishing assertion from a Christian interviewee that we were witnessing "an absolute explosion of Satanism", followed by the even more astonishing revelation that this "absolute explosion" had been going on for thirty years already.

After this promising beginning it was too bad to discover that the entire investigative might of the Cook Report not only failed to find a single corroborated example of satanism in Britain, but it was finally reduced to inviting a living satanist over from America in order to prove that such people might actually exist. To be fair the investigative team didn't altogether fail: they may not have succeeded in digging out evidence of widespread child abuse, animal and human sacrifice, blood and sex orgies, but they did undoubtedly catch staff at the notorious Sorcerer's Apprentice putting on Halloween masks. Disgusting, I call it.

WHAT WENT WRONG?

The thing which intrigued me about the program was this: why was it screened? Journalists may consider themselves tough, but they do share one major weak spot: they cannot bear to be "taken for a ride" in public. It was so obvious that the fundamentalist Christian antioccultists had made a fool of Cook and his team by sending them on this "wild goose chase", that I could not see why he had let it be broadcast - especially in view of the tv authorities' own reluctance to show the program which reflected so badly on their credibility.

Was there some mysterious pressure behind the scenes? Or did Cook miscalculate and assume that no-one of any critical intelligence would be watching a program which claimed to take satanism seriously? Or did he rather calculate, on the basis of his experience with Kevin Logan and other Christian extremists, that here was a topic so emotionally charged that he could forget the usual restraints of reason and common sense?

Myself I incline to the latter view: Cook estimated that, when the subject is satanism, it is now more important to be seen to be on the attack than it is to be seen to be sharp, accurate or critical. When "hard hitting" journalism fails to hit, it is reduced to "hard flailing" journalism, and Cook miscalculated that his public would not notice the difference on this occasion.

This is the way to play safe during a witch hunt - a time when any sign of intelligence or cynicism is liable to lead to the stake. So did Cook really think the situation was so bad that he had to go along with it?

If he thought that the Christian extremists were stirring up a witch hunt, he was not the first to suggest this. Since Kevin Logan has himself begun to speak of "occultists who cry 'witch hunt' when criticised" we must begin by asking what is the difference between a witch hunt and a serious attempt to cope with a genuine problem.

HOW TO RECOGNISE A "WITCH HUNT"

Of course there is no confusing the matter once a witch hunt is in full cry. What we are here looking for is the early signs of this distinction between a hysterical witch hunt and a necessary purge if we are to reduce the chance of the witch hunt developing.

I suggest that the first and clearest sign of a witch hunt is in the stereotyped, mythic nature of the accusations. Cohn, in his book "Europe's Inner Demons", points out that the accusations made against witches during the great trials followed a standard formula which included drinking blood, sexual promiscuity, the use of drugs, sacrificing animals, people and in particular babies. Along with that were accusations of dirt and perverse use of urine and faeces, of a worldwide conspiracy against the church and Christian society, and the abuse of children. However, he goes on to point out that these accusations add up to a standard package that emerge whenever a large crowd feels threatened. Exactly the same accusations have been levelled against Jews, against communists, against fascists, against Moslems... they were even levelled against the early Christians them-selves.

What the public needs to learn is this: whenever one of those accusations is made it is a serious matter which needs investigation. But whenever the whole lot are made at once, then they should not be swallowed without a large pinch of salt.

By way of analogy: what would you, as a parent, do if your eight year old daughter came home from school saying that "teacher says there is a nasty man about who does naughty things to little girls on there way home from school"? I am sure that most parents would be quick to 'phone the police for confirmation and would take immediate action to guard their child.

But what if the daughter went on to add that the naughty man had a big black cape, sharp teeth and hair on the palms of his hands, and that he sucked children's blood when the moon was full? Now the child is giving much more hard detail than before but, far from making the story more credible, it is reducing its impact - because the parent recognises the stereotype of the old vampire myth and so feels less concern. Instead of 'phoning the police most parents would just make a note to question the teacher some time about the appropriateness of their choice of children's stories.

By this token, when we hear accusations of occultists abusing children we are right to feel concerned. But when we find all the other accusations being thrown in too, then it is not so much the occultists that need investigation but rather the accusers themselves. What inner problem do they have which is causing this eruption of "Europe's Inner Demon" in their minds?

SATANISM OR DEVIL WORSHIP?

I have consistently argued that analysis is the finest tool for banishing demons, so let's set off down that route first. To remove one widespread source of confusion I begin by clarifying the logical distinction between satanism and devil worship. I emphasise that it is a logical distinction: in our society we will find that the two usually coincide, but dividing the demon in this way will give us some power over it, as you will see.

When the public uses the terms satanism and devil worship as meaning exactly the same thing, they are like people who insist that "communist" equals "revolutionary". Those whom Jung would label "sensation types" insist on this identity and prove it thus: go out and find me ten communists, and I'll show you ten revolutionaries. In our capitalist society they are usually right; at the ideas level, however, there is a real distinction: in an established communist society like China or the Soviet Union it is the communists who become the conservative anti-revolutionaries.

The same problem exists with satanism. Strictly it should mean the worship of the god Satan, and a way of life based on his principles; whereas devil worship simply means the revolutionary act of turning against your established religion and embracing its antithesis. But the fact that Satan is in some sense a polar opposite of Christ, coupled with the fact that we live in a Christian culture, adds up to the reality that any satanists we can find will be likely to be devil worshippers to some degree - just as in a capitalist culture most communists will be to some extent revolutionary simply by definition.

What would be the true characteristics of a "pure" satanism devoid of devil worship? Now don't ask me for authoritative guidance on the exact nature of deities that I have not thoroughly researched: the following description is just a rough outline and it might be questioned by an expert satanist.

Satan is most easily, but dangerously, seen by us in contrast to Christ. While Christ is a spiritual guide, Satan is an earthy chthonic god. Instead of gentleness, modesty and spirituality he urges us to strength, pride and sensuality. Instead of transcending the flesh we are urged to revel in it, master it (as opposed to conquer it) and learn its secrets. While the direction of Christ is toward unity (bringing God's children together in the divine embrace) the direction of Satan is towards distinction - the fundamental duality that generates manifestation, the individual standing proudly apart from the universe, the division of the sexes, the definition of tribal boundaries... and so on as symbolised by the inverse pentagram which elevates the two horns of manifestation above the single point of spirit (while the goody-goody version of the pentagram elevates the point of spirit above duality). Indeed we shall later see that the paradoxical manifestations of Satan stem from his esoteric role as the Lord of Duality - he is not simply the ruler of the spiritual opposition, but rather Opposition itself as a positive, creative factor.

Note that nearly all these characteristics do seem "wicked" by Christian standards, because they are polar opposites, but in pure satanism there is no question that they are performed because they are wicked. True satanism would revere money, power, strife and sex because it considers them Good Things, paths to growth, not because they are naughty.

Devil worship, on the other hand, is the decision to worship everything that your religion considers to be bad, because it is bad. The object of devil worship is revolutionary: it could be inspired by immature, childish rebellion, it could be an act of anger as catharsis for the oppressed, it could be an attempt to precipitate a personal crisis for self knowledge, it could be a way of investigating the religion rebelled against by testing it, or it could be an overt revolutionary act.

However, in a Christian society, anyone who sets out to worship the devil is likely to constellate the devil in the image of Satan. The result would therefore be called satanism, but it would be distorted because of the devil-worship impulse behind it. Although many outward characteristics would be nominally Satanic, there would be something very different about the spirit of the religion.

To see why this is so it is worth imagining what the devil worshippers would do if we lived in an overtly Satanic culture. In that situation the devil worshippers would probably revolt against the materialism of that culture by denouncing their worldly goods, they would revolt against its sensuousness by becoming ascetic and temperate, they would revolt against the body and its demands, they would revolt against procreation by abandoning the family for a celibate community, they would revolt against the 'self' by making personal sacrifices and so on. Not surprisingly they would probably constellate this rebellion in the form of worship of a god whose physical body died on the cross as a sacrifice to save mankind's souls - ie they would be nominal Christians. However, because the impulse for this religion was negative - an act of revulsion or rebellion against Satan - you would expect its form to be perverse. There would probably be an exaggerated stress on the masochism of flagellation, the breaking up and devouring of the flesh and blood of the sacrificed god, there would be considerable self mutilation, castration and a great outward show of destroying wealth and smashing statues and melting down gold images etc.

Here is the problem: all these actions are quite recognisably Christian, and have been performed by ardent Christians at some time or another, but put together they add up to a religion that would shock and disgust conservative members of a Satanic society. Even gentleness can appear shocking and subversive - witness the anxiety felt by riot police in the sixties when hippies put flowers on their gun barrels. The word "Christianity" would become synonymous with the vilest perversion and a dangerous de-stabilising influence on their material society. So we can see that if Christianity and devil worship were to combine the result would be a horrid parody of the true Christian message and spirit; but try explaining that to those outraged members of a Satanic establishment!

Christianity is directed toward the spiritual and so it opposes bodily indulgence. Consistent rich foods while others starve is un-Christian. So a certain asceticism is appropriate to Christianity. Now, in a particular individual case, that asceticism might be furthered by fasting and flagellation: if one, otherwise balanced, individual only manages to transcend his physical nature by castrating himself, and he assures us that this has solved his personal problem, then who are we to deny this? But when continued starvation, relentless flagellation and mass castrations become the norm or even compulsory then we could surely argue that this would not be true Christianity. Such exaggerated emphasis on denying the body would be a deflection of Christianity's real spiritual aim - the reason it would be practiced is more to do with the fact that the people were rebelling against a Satanic culture that saw everything in physical terms. Again, the big emphasis on devouring Christ's blood and flesh would be a materialist perversion of the mass. If such perverted Christianity was practiced by the devil worshippers, then the Satanic society that spawned such rebellion would be every bit as much to blame as Christ.

In the same way we should consider the actions accredited to today's satanists and analyse them to see to what extent they are truly Satanic, and to what extent they a perversion due to rebelling against a Christian culture.

THE ACCUSATIONS ANALYSED

Satanists are accused of having sexual orgies. This seems appropriate, and it seems appropriate that they should allow everything possible to increase the thrill and the excitement of the participants. Unfortunately not everyone is turned on by the same stimuli, and anything which would serve to lessen anyone's sexual pleasure would be very un-Satanic. So it would not be appropriate to include extreme perversion, coercion or exhibitionism in a mass Satanic rite. These elements could only succeed in a small, closed group who had agreed beforehand that they shared the same pleasures.

So when we hear extreme stories of mass Satanic perversion being reported it is more likely that we are witnessing the projected unconscious fantasies of a sexually repressed religious group - the fundamentalist Christians.

Satanists are accused of taking drugs. Insofar as alcohol and other drugs can heighten sensual pleasure and increase one's appreciation of the physical that also seems appropriate. But to surrender one's individuality to an addiction is surely a blasphemy against the god of proud and sensual individualism? To take so much of a drug that the body begins to suffer would be equally inappropriate to an earthy god.

So when we hear extreme stories of Satanic drug pushers sweeping the nation, it is more likely that we are witnessing a guilty projection from a religion which does not like to face up to the fact that the economy of many devoutly catholic communities in South America depends utterly on the drug trade - and that the Mafia are pillars of their establishment.

Satanists are accused of sexually abusing children. This makes little sense in a religion which reveres lustful procreation. Children are of little immediate interest to Satan, until such time that they reach puberty and can experience lust themselves. Inserting one's penis in a choirboy's bottom may afford delight to some, but it does little to further the species. No, the fascination with children is definitely a Christian spectre - as it is probably so with any sexually repressive religion. Christians who deny their sexual lusts have a long tradition of fascination with the innocence of those who do not have such lusts - ever since "suffer the little children" they can hardly get pre-pubescent children out of their minds. This has resulted in a range of symptoms - from the benign pederasty which has traditionally made Church of England clerics such good teachers at the junior school level, to the horror stories of child molestation by "upright Christians" so regularly reported in the Daily Telegraph. But the main symptom which concerns us here is the tendency amongst

Christian extremists to project this core of guilt and raise the hunt for scapegoats for their own unacknowledged sins. They used to accuse the Jews of eating little children, but since Hitler died they have picked on satanists as the politically safer victims.

Satanists are sometimes accused of evangelism, of trying every technique to lure unwilling members to their church - especially young children. It is the final qualification which makes this accusation so ridiculous. Can you really imagine a Satanic ritual sounding like a Sunday family service punctuated by the gurgles of babies and the voices of young children? If ever there was a god that wanted to have "adults only" pinned above his church door it would surely be Satan. And, in view of the enormous secrecy reputed to satanists, is it really credible that they would want large numbers of non-dedicated members in their congregations? This evangelist accusation is patently absurd and can only have its origins in the mind of the accuser. Consider one such, Kevin Logan: his book on Occultism and Paganism accuses all occultists of evangelism. However, as one of the occultists quoted in his book points out, the well known problem in occultism is not how to lure people into it, but how to keep out the loonies who have peculiar ideas about the subject. Of course the reality is that Kevin Logan is himself an ardent Christian evangelist, and this is where the crazy notion of occult evangelism springs from - his own unacknowledged "shadow" as he lays on jolly children's services to lure the innocent into his own fold.

Satanism is accused of world conspiracy. Oh dear, how on earth are we supposed to square the image of a hairy legged horned chthonic deity with the subtle machinations of a unified power behind the world's thrones? The principle of Satanism is so divisive and individual that the normal accepted meaning of "world conspiracy" is utterly out of place here. All you could say is that Satan is dedicated to stirring all human souls individually towards thoughts of the flesh and away from spiritual unity - and one must admit he can do that very subtly. That is, in a sense, a world conspiracy, but it hardly squares with the stories put out by the fundamentalists. Satan's activities are more likely to divide society than to unite it into a monolithic bureaucracy of evil - an idea that is surely better seen as a corrupted mirror image of the universal church or body of Christ?

Satanists are accused of animal sacrifices. This could be appropriate, as the ingestion of freshly butchered meat is reputed to serve a vitalising function. But we never hear that the meat was served with delicious sauces, or lightly barbecued to make it palatable, and such omissions are suspicious. Indeed it has been claimed that the blood is mixed not with fine brandy but with faeces and urine - a cocktail that smacks much more of spiritual revolt than of fleshly indulgence. So either the story is true: in which case I deduce that the satanist in question was not "true", but rather a Christian rebelling against his culture by inverting its values. Or else the story is false: in which case I recognise again that the Christian accuser is projecting his own religion's guilt, the shame of a creed that has not yet recognised that the killing of some hundred million turkeys in the name of Christ amounts to the biggest religious slaughter in the history of mankind - and it is repeated every Christmas.

Satanists are accused of human sacrifices. This too needs to be taken seriously, because it is a deeply held human belief that spilled human blood is a source of power, and power (especially material power) is definitely in Satan's interest. In fact it is less easy to find accounts of Satanic human sacrifices, all you usually hear is vague third-hand rumours, so I am less certain as to what is being suggested here. Are we to believe that Satanic priests ritually cut the throats of helpless victims tied down to an altar? That does not seem an appropriate way to worship a god of pride and strength - especially if we are told the victim is a child. It would be far more credible if we heard that the successor to a Satanic high priest had to ritually fight his predecessor to the death in order to win the title, but such rumours do not seem to be forthcoming from the accusers. That Satan should be glorified by the blood of fierce warriors conquered in battle does seem appropriate, but I cannot see him feeling anything but insult if offered the blood of a helpless child.

So again we either have to ask if the rumours are true: in which case the ritual murder must be the work of someone from a Christian culture setting out to do the wickedest thing he can imagine - and perhaps at the same time avenging the sacrifice of his own god by mankind. Or else we have to ask if the rumours are another guilt projection of a religion with two thousand years of human bloodshed to its "credit". At some unconscious level those fundamentalists must register the fact that not only has Christianity a very bloody history but also that in our present day the violence in any country is directly proportional to the level of religious belief. Compare the value of human life in such secular societies as Sweden, Holland and England with the high levels of violence in deeply Christian communities in Northern Ireland, South America and the USA. You might reverse cause and effect and argue that it is an initial high crime level which drives people into the church, but the fact is that religion reached the States with the Pilgrim Fathers, and the divisions in Ireland are a clear consequence of religion. As the Ayatollah Khomeini clearly demonstrated, human blood is the best way of stoking the fires of a tired old religion, and this was most dramatically demonstrated by the Jonestown massacre in 1978. I have elsewhere explained how this has proved to be the most successful magical ritual of recent years: a thousand Christians drank poison at once as a sacrifice to their cause. Before this act Christianity in the states was in terminal decline: since the sixties the majority of the population had turned away from Christ and either taken the hippy course of occultism and eastern religions or else simply become secular materialists. But the Jonestown sacrifice changed Christian fortunes overnight to produce an enormous religious revival. Christians must at some level register the extent to which the spread of their faith depends upon human sacrifice, but the fundamentalists have a mental block that does not let them become conscious of the fact - because there is an uncomfortable split in their religion between "thou shalt not kill" and the idea of a holy crusade. So once again such twisted individuals feel compelled to find a scapegoat for their guilt - and accuse satanists of ritual murder. At their most extreme this Christians are "killing two birds with one stone" by simultaneously expunging their own guilt and lining up new victims that they can slay with a sense of righteousness. They can offer the sacrifice of a burnt witch to their god with the Christian glow of charity in their hearts.

Because that last example is so grotesque I must sound a note of warning here. I am not saying that murder is in the spirit of Christianity. It is as far alien to Christ's nature as pederasty or drug addiction would be to Satan's. If I heard rumours that Christian fundamentalists were sacrificing young men to their god I hope I would analyse the rumour just as thoroughly as I analysed the rumour of satanists sacrificing babies. I would first point out that such slaughter was not appropriate to Christianity, and I would deduce that either the protagonists were motivated by non-Christian factors, or that the stories were fabricated by someone with their own problem. I do not see the Jonestown massacre as a Christian ritual: it was a piece of primitive magic that was resorted to by Christians who did not understand the forces they were tampering with. As human beings, Christians have as bad a record as anyone else in such matters. If the fundamentalists stopped projecting their guilt on others and instead took some lessons from the occultists, they would have a much better chance of clearing up their own seedy act. But that would require an act of true humility...

To sum up: most of the accusations regularly levelled against Satanism fail to stick. If there really are so-called satanists performing the acts described, we are forced to admit that they are not being true to their religion. They are behaving more like rebels from a Christian culture than true satanists. and should therefore be seen as a regrettable by-product of this very culture: no more Christ's responsibility than Satan's, but simply an example of what happens when imperfect humanity fails to live up to unrealistic ideals, and cannot handle this failure.

The other (and, to my mind, greater) likelihood is that some stories about Satanism are simply not true, the accusations are in fact mythical projections from the Christian unconscious - a mere fantasy expression of the same human failure. They are a perverted mirror image of Christian obsessions and they are generated in the souls of the accusers. Kevin Logan in his book on the subject does admit that Satan seems to have no creativity of his own: everything ascribed to him is a distorted mirror image or perversion of some divine creation as he "apes" God's work. What he does not admit is that this exactly the characteristic you would expect a projected "shadow" of your god to manifest. His is a fair description of the Satan we meet in his writings: not a autonomous spiritual power able to be worshipped, but simply a shadow cast in his own unconscious by a god that Kevin Logan and his type have made too bright for their own eyesight.

To be able to see such a "satan" you have to be a Christian - and you have to be standing with your back to god.

WHY IS THIS HAPPENING NOW?

Analysing the current Satanism scare we conclude that it is a Christian problem. Without having immediate access to all the evidence it is not absolutely certain whether the problem is nothing more than a group fantasy shared by unbalanced Christian extremists, or whether there are actual examples of rebel Christians leaving the fold to perform devil worship in their own manner. All that is certain is that the stories circulated have no direct bearing on Satan or on any genuine Satanic religion.

So next we must ask why this problem has arisen in our so called modern secular society? Some critics of Christianity will argue that the sort of hysteria described is inevitable in such a repressive, anti-female religion, but I am more interested to ask why is it that the lunatic fringe of the otherwise well-behaved Christian community should be going through this particular crisis right now.

Four reasons suggest themselves: 1 - that Christianity is growing old and decadent, 2 - that there might actually be an explosion of Satanism, 3 - that the Aeon of Horus is taking effect. Those three reasons might not be sufficient individually, but they could add up to a pressure which is being released by the fourth trigger factor: 4 - the year 2000 has a special emotional significance for fundamentalist Christians because of their strong tradition of millennial hysteria as described in Cohn's "the Pursuit of the Millennium". I'll enlarge on those first three factors in order.

First the idea that Christianity is growing decadent. One of the themes in Thundersqueak and subsequent essays of mine is that ideas and philosophies run through a life cycle: a new idea comes in as a conquering hero, overturning suffocating and restrictive old ideas and giving us greater freedom and room to grow. As it becomes established the idea continues to support us and help humanity to find its feet in the new territory. But as it grows older the idea becomes rigid dogma, another hidebound old structure holding people back. By this point humanity desperately needs a new young revolutionary philosophy to turn up and defeat the old tyrant once more. This thesis is, in a sense, a defence of constant revolution or "novelty for its own sake" - except that I do believe mankind needs the second stage in order to gain some sense of security. So, in my old age, I am all for allowing a newish idea plenty of scope to prove its worth before we reject it, even though this tolerant consolidating phase might seem less fun than the constant overthrow of ideas.

Christianity has been around for two thousand years and has gone through several phases of decadence, but has been "big" enough to have created its own internal revolutions to renew itself from within a few times. On this point the fundamentalists in question might agree with us: "yes, Christianity has grown old and decadent, and we are the new force that is now regenerating the faith". Unfortunately, this current revolution looks more like symptoms of terminal sickness. True, there are signs of genuine revolution in Christianity amongst its more enlightened and progressive elements at present, but so far they do not seem to be making much headway against the cancer of fundamentalism.

So the first suggestion is that we look to the Jonestown massacre which provided the stimulus for the present fundamentalist revival and admit that it was not a healthy starting point. The current Satanic witch hunt is typical of the symptoms one would expect of such a gangrenous excrescence upon the aged body of the church.

The second consideration takes a kinder view, and one that might seem surprising in view of what has been said: perhaps the fundamentalists are right, that there has been an explosion of Satanism - but that they have completely misjudged its nature? This does not invalidate my previous arguments which were against the existence of the organised Satanic religion they described, because what we are talking about here is an underlying Satanic trend in our culture.

If we go back to the qualities that I tentatively ascribed to Satan - qualities like power, pride, sensuality, procreation, individuality and distinctiveness - then we can see some evidence that these qualities have become increasingly favoured by our society during this century. Even if the evidence tends to crumble under scrutiny, we must admit that it is widely believed - and that is the relevant factor here. The man in the street would apparently claim that today's society was more materialistic, sex-mad and individualistic... in effect, more Satanic.

Power is a Satanic quality, and we can see in current advertising and media fantasies that power is supposed to be highly revered nowadays. "Blessed are the meek" does not get half the coverage. Pride is also seen as something to be actively encouraged. We hear much positive talk about "the pride in their national identity", even though it leads to nationalistic divisiveness. This splitting up or "apartness" is also more appropriate to Satan than to the unifying tendency of Christ, and it is very much in evidence in recent decades.

Another form of splitting up is the emphasis on the nuclear family at the expense of a wider vision of society. If you look up the word "family" in an authorised bible concordance you will not find it mentioned by Christ, nor does he use related concepts like "brother", or "parent" much except in the sense of God being the father of one great extended family. Indeed, the Christian impulse was rather to forget one's sexual origins and to up and follow the Master. On the other hand, it would be appropriate to Satan, a god of duality and division, for society to fragment into smaller structures, and as he is also a god of sex it is appropriate that the division should be into a procreative unit like the family. Although the current concept of the family hardly existed before this century, it has already become widely accepted and is more spoken about than ever. So it is another sign of growing Satanic influence on society.

Hand in hand with talk about families goes talk about the importance of the individual in a manner that is far more appropriate to the rebellious spirit described by Milton than it is to the Christian ethic. And then there is the more recent change of heart about material wealth: it is now longer something that needs to be apologised for. The question of sex is a little more complicated: there is no doubt that the subject is much more apparent now than it was in Victoria's day, but you could argue that her reign was a pathological low point rather than being typical of past ages. Another factor is that, although sex is still widely discussed, the AIDS scare has greatly reduced its practice in the last ten years. This does not look so much like a serious long-term trend, however, as it looks like a temporary resurgence of a troubled Christian conscience. We hear similar cries of protest at current materialism and selfishness, but they have not held back the tide. Another complex issue is the Satanic focus upon the body: what might have developed into the pure sensuousness of physical culture has become in many cases overlaid with a passion to negate the body by slimming beyond the needs of health or aesthetics. While remaining obsessed with their bodies, some people are punishing them almost as severely as the Christian ascetics of old.

Despite such qualifications and complexities, there is definitely a strong case to be made out that Satanic principles have grown strong in our society during this century, and that this is especially true in the post war years, and that it has had its most blatant expression in the recent governments of Thatcher, Reagan and their followers. In these terms, therefore, it becomes less surprising that the more dogmatic and evangelical Christians should begin to feel uneasy.

They have, however, compounded the problem for themselves by their own attempts to patch it up. Just as Christianity in its early days was able to flourish on the strength of its universality by incorporating elements of existing religions into its body, so has it since been reasonably successful at adapting itself to world changes. Thus it was able to grow beyond its initial confrontations with Kepler, Darwinism, Marxism and other new philosophies and, as a result, liberal Christianity has retained its relevance in a changing society. Now, although the mainstream Christian communities have managed to hold firm in their opposition to some of the Satanic tendencies listed above, the fact is that certain of the evangelical fundamentalists have got themselves into a ludicrous position by trying to take the whole lot on board as "Christian principles".

The effects of this can be quite grotesque. In their literature you will see kitsch paintings of Weetabix families casting adoring eyes on a robed Jesus to the accompaniment of words about "the Christian family tradition"! It seems that Christian traditions now embrace money making too to quote Kevin Logan's book "the wealth of the West has been accomplished largely through applying the beliefs of Christianity to everyday life"! Sure enough, today's hot-gospellers are raking in the millions and with them the sort of criminality and corruption you would expect: recent reports on BBC's Sunday programme told of Christian con-men encouraging the elderly to invest their life savings on the strength of biblical prophecies. Christianity's long and not altogether successful battle to suppress the Luciferic scientific current is also conveniently forgotten by Logan when he writes "Modern science could only have come from a belief that there was a God who made all things to a certain design." He supports that statement by pointing out that Isaac Newton was at much at home with religion as he was with science: because his book is an attack on the occult he chooses not to mention that the work which Isaac Newton valued most highly of all was his alchemical researches.

The spectacle of such gymnastic ethical and philosophical U-turns can be entertaining, but also a tragic reminder of human gullibility and blindness. As an occultist myself I feel a certain threat from such people, but my main concern is to feel deeply sorry for the many genuine Christians who continue to apply their very considerable principles as best they can in view of such crazy stablemates. Perhaps the saving factor is the vast mass of indifferent nominal Christians who act as a buffer between the two camps?

But I diverge: the point is that, although there is no evidence for an active, organised Satanic religion as fantasised by the lunatic fringe, there is a case to be made for a recent major upsurge in Satanic principles - at least within the popular imagination. That, combined with a hopeless attempt to stretch and embrace these principles, could be sufficient pressure upon the fundamentalist community to push them toward some sort of hysterical breakdown of the sort we have been witnessing.

The third factor I want to suggest is the additional effect of the Aeon of Horus. The full argument for this was written up a few years back in my article on Thelemic Morality, so I will only briefly summarise the relevant bits here. This article has already appeared in Germany in Anubis, but English readers will have to wait for the late '89 edition of The Equinox (or else my forthcoming Collected Essays) if they wish to follow it up.

Referring to Crowley's concept of the three aeons: Isis was the aeon of the mother goddesses, who were experienced as dark, severe deities whose rule had the inexorable logic of Fate: you did what they said, or you paid the price (the Old Testament Jehovah fits that mould, though nominally male). Osiris was the age of the bright male gods (Christ, Odin, Dionysus etc) who were far more "human": their nature is to love mankind, even to suffer on our behalf. Their law is not to follow absolute commandments but rather to try to emulate their perfect example. But Horus is the age of the child-god, an avenging, martial deity who challenges us to stand on our own two feet. This god does not expect absolute obedience, for "do what thou wilt" is the law, nor does he expect us to follow his example, for it is far from ideal for humanity.

Fundamentalism is the ethics of the aeon of Isis, and it was absolutely right in that context and at that time (just as it has its place with very young children). What Jesus did, as an Osirian deity, was to replace the absolutism of the ten commandments with something far too vague to be a "commandment" in that sense - he said "love thy neighbour". His approach in judgments such as "let he who is without sin cast the first stone" is not to tell us precisely what to do, but rather to stimulate us to think, and in particular to follow his enlightened example. The idea of an impeccable "guru" is typically Osirian (and contrasts sharply with the "examine my ideas but do not follow my example" approach of the Aeon of Horus) So "Christian fundamentalism" is innately self contradictory, and this is the essence of its sickness. Christian fundamentalism (and, presumably, Islamic fundamentalism) is the attempt to contain the wisdom of the Aeon of Osiris within the ethical standards of the Aeon of Isis (eg Jehovah's law) - the "new wine in old bottles" that Christ warned against.

Now what happens when a devout person invokes a deity? If the person is a monotheist, or more specifically one who only recognises a supreme male god, then we have to admit that the belief does provide a lot of protection against invoking the wrong deity: such a worshipper would hardly be taken in by the presence of a goddess, a minor fertility god, or other less wholesome spirits. So far, it is a "safe" thing to do. But if you only admit one male god, you are uncritically open to any of the big male gods... and that includes Horus the Avenger.

In the Middle Ages anyone devoutly invoking god would, not surprisingly, tend to make contact with the Osirian current - it would either be Jesus or else a deity of very much the same general principles - because that was well within the Aeon of Osiris. But now we are in the Aeon of Horus, so the same devotion is liable to invoke the Horus current. Now, if you are an occultist of some description you will at least be on the lookout for different types of god, and will be able to use your critical ability to judge whether you have tuned into the god you want - the New Ager looking for sermons on love would, if contacted by Horus, no doubt resist the contact as "negative vibes"! But consider the problem of the dogmatic monotheist when the Horus contact is made: the power and numinosity of the current "proves" it must be the Supreme God - Christ or Allah - who is speaking.

This is born out by experience: recent examples of people like Khomeini and James Anderton who claim to have had direct messages from God make it clear in their subsequent actions that the actual entity contacted was far from being a loving, rational deity. They have contacted the wrath of Horus, but do not have the Aeon of Horus Thelemic morality to handle the messages they are getting. If they are fundamentalists, they attempt to obey the letter of Horus's law - for a taste of which see Liber Al Chapter Three - and if they are Christian they are in the uneasy position of trying to follow and comprehend the example of a deity who never deigns to set us an example.

So, to simplify the original explanation a bit, the third cause of strain amongst the Christian fundamentalists is that they have contacted the Horus current and do not know how to handle it.

There is a side issue raised here: how does this discussion of the Aeon of Horus relate to the previous discussion of an upsurge of Satanic principles: are they connected? I suggest that the relationship is not direct: I do not see much evidence that the nature of Horus is fundamentally Satanic, though they might overlap on certain power issues. Whilst recognising the current Satanic upsurge, I do not take it as seriously in the long term as the fundamentalists do. To me it is just the flavour of the century, and most likely has its origins as a sort of backlash as Christianity loses its dominant position and certain Christians lose their marbles. It is a sort of Christian death wish: remember that their predictions for the millennium depend upon the antichrist first establishing his kingdom, and so we find the fundamentalists unconsciously working to further the kingdom of antichrist in order to precipitate the crisis which will finally justify their shaky faith.

HOW BIG IS THE PROBLEM?

So one way or another it looks pretty certain that the "Satanic explosion" is a Christian problem. But insofar as Christianity is basic to our culture, that means it is partly a shared problem, and it is reasonable to want to know how big a problem, or how serious it really is.

I will now illustrate the size of the problem.

On Sunday October 30th 1987 at a shack on the outskirts of Anderton, a small community East of Amarillo, USA, four people were murdered and one escaped to tell the tale.

Jacob Zaller was a runaway from his family in New Orleans, and he had been staying with the Angelos, a kindly hippy family that had offered him a lift from Amarillo. In the few days he was with them he had witnessed several occasions when redneck youths in jeeps had driven past the Angelo's shack at speed, firing shots in the air and shouting threats. This scared the chickens as well as the children: apparently the family had lost a lot of their livestock until they took to locking them in - the Angelo's said you just got used to it and kept smiling. He had also had the uncanny experience of being totally ignored when he tried to buy goods in the local store - after they discovered where he was staying.

On the night in question he had gone out to look at the stars from a nearby hill when he noticed something happening at the shack. Through the window he saw Jenny Angelo about to be raped by a large blond youth before the eyes of Doug and their kids who were held down by three others who kept shouting "you fucking witch". He also noticed that all the Angelo's occult books and charts had been taken from their shelves and piled up in the centre of the floor, and a fifth youth was holding a can of petrol. Jacob managed to get away unnoticed on the Angelo's pushbike and made it to the sheriff's office. The sheriff turned out surprisingly slow and unco-operative, constantly asking him to repeat what he had seen without seeming willing to take any action. Anyway, to cut a long story short Jacob was able to evade the sheriff and return some days later with an FBI agent.

The Angelo's shack was burnt to the ground and there were no signs of the bodies. Everyone they questioned swore blind that the Angelo's "who always kept to themselves" had left the area weeks earlier, and the shack had been derelict. Jacob recognised the blond youth who had raped Jenny, a local farmer's son. But the church congregation and the minister all insisted that the youth had been at church at the time of the incident. The case was dropped. And when Jacob returned to his family that Christmas he found he was persona non grata - word had reached home ahead of him that he had been caught molesting children in the desert, and it took a year to clear his name.

Now, having heard the story, what would you want to do? Do not say "I can't do anything living back here in England", the question is what would you do if you were omnipotent, had all the resources of the FBI and the army at your disposal? Stop now and make a list of the first four things you would feel like doing - before reading on.

How many of you began the list with something like "find out who those bastards were and beat hell out of them?" I sympathise with such an angry reaction: if most of you thought that, then the problem we are now considering is a very big problem.

How many of you put at the top of the list "check the facts"? If most of you put that, then the problem being considered is far smaller. For the benefit of those who did, I will save them some trouble: the only fact in that story was that I made up the whole thing.

The point is this: I began this investigation by saying that the most immediately suspicious thing about the satan scare was that it was so stereotyped. What thinking person could swallow such a wadge of cliches about satanists? Now what I have done is made up a story containing all the cliches about fundamentalist southern american rednecks. Anyone who swallowed it uncritically should be able to spare some sympathy for the Christian extremists who are taken in by satan stories. My story is as dubious as theirs: for all their dogmatism and anti-occult bias, redneck chapel ministers do have regard for the truth, and would be unlikely to lie about the youth's church attendance... and so on.

That story illustrates the size of the problem because it illustrates the extent to which we can be polarised against fundamentalist Christians. If you only have to hear a story like mine to become irrationally furious, then you are in exactly the same boat as the Christian extremists who rage against satanists. If you have difficulty in distinguishing irrational fury from righteous indignation then remove the polarising bits from the story: translate it to the Far East and have Mongol hoards burning a Christian missionary family and see if it still evokes an equally furious reaction.

The more this issue is an emotionally charged one for us, the more we are part of the problem. One of the lessons that is learnt from working with the Horus current is the wisdom of traditional astrology which ascribes both marriage and enemies to the same, seventh, house. Enmity is as intimate a relationship as marriage, and sworn enemies have a way of growing to look like each other just as much as loving partners: put a southern redneck into a fur hat and overcoat and you have the image of a Soviet commissar. The worst excesses of Christian anti-occultism are found precisely amongst the Christians who are themselves practicing a form of low-grade occultism. They are the ones who see evil spirits everywhere, practice exorcism, speak with tongues and all the other weird stuff. Being "born again" is their version of traditional initiation rituals, and all the crap and superstition of low grade occultism is theirs.

Such churches hate occultists because they are themselves occultists and cannot admit it. Evangelical churches turn no-one away in their search for converts, and they pick up all the rejects from the occult world. Have you never met the half-baked occult bore who says "ah, you are interested in the occult I see! Tell me, what do YOU think about the Bermuda Triangle? I've just read an amazing book which proves that the CIA and the KGB were co-operating on researching it during the sixties. They dug up a whole shipload of evidence... only it got lost in the Bermuda Triangle". Now you know what happens to such people: they become born-again Christians and write books about the horrors of occultism. Getting their own back on all those occultists over the years who had rushed away from their conversation muttering something about having to dash of to celebrate the Equinox.

Because the current witch hunt is basically an inner fight against themselves, it has a certain self defeating quality. Kevin Logan's followers are trying to reduce the availability of occult books in shops around Britain, but the arrival of his own book means that any teenage Christian can now pick up a really quite interesting survey of current occultism, thrown into a pretty favourable light by some of the shaky arguments pitched against it, a book in which Christianity is made to sound a bit wet in comparison with chaos magic... and a book that is widely available in specialist Christian bookshops.

Similarly, at the end of the Cook report there was a Help Line number made available for those who had suffered Satanic persecution: it was subsequently deluged with callers wanting to know more about Satanism! One of the people contributing to the program was a familiar figure: a woman who claims to have been heavily involved in Satanic rituals and who now tours the country giving lectures to warn children of the danger. Hers is indeed an interesting case: why, one wonders did she, not once but repeatedly, attend rituals where animals were slaughtered, babies sacrificed and all the rest? She says she was too scared not to! What, one wonders, was the motivation of the others present? Were they all scared of each other? Were they perverts who actually enjoyed doing these things? If so, why drag Satan into it? why not just concentrate on enjoying their perverse acts? The only motive that makes sense, is that the participants did what they did in the belief that they could get something from it: they were insignificant people who believed Satan would bring them power, fame, influence and prestige. In that case the woman in question has every reason now to thank Satan: because she is called to appear every time Satanism or the occult is mentioned on television - and this fame and influence is a direct consequence of her earlier Satanic devotions. As any teacher knows, much of childish naughtiness is due not so much to original sin, as a desire to draw attention to oneself. So what a seductive message that woman is now preaching to the children of Britain: if you want to be a TV star all you have to do is get involved in Satanism! Clever children will get an even simpler message: all you have to do to become the centre of attention is to *pretend* that you have been involved in Satanism. Now I wonder where they got that idea?

With that example we have come full circle. As in the play The Crucible, one can ask what fanciful young child could resist the temptation offered to tell a few fibs and have a special exorcism service dedicated to them by the Reverend Kevin Logan who appears on TV? In a spiritual sense this witch hunt is totally self defeating, like any other. The main interest for occultists is how not to get burnt in the process.

THE PARADOX OF SATAN

Can we draw any conclusion from this confused situation?

We have seen that the current hysteria against Satanism is something which generates itself from within: certain people attack Satanism in public and begin to create the problem they are attacking.

But my example of the story may have shown that the occult community cannot wash their hands of this problem, because the human tendency it feeds on is active within ourselves. We find that the Christian and occult communities have a lot more in common than they like to admit: at one extreme there are the gullible occult cranks and the Christian fundamentalists, at the other extreme there are the enlightened pioneering occultists and the radical, progressive Christians. We have Kevin Logan writing that occultism is Satan's distorted "aping" of God's ways, and we have me writing that Kevin Logan's Christianity is a distorted "aping" of occultism. The major difference lies not in the extremes but in the occult's lack of a large centre ground. Occultism is more sharply focussed than Christianity because it does not contain such a vast flock of "nominal" believers to act as a buffer between its extremes.

There is also the possibility that we are witnessing a surge in Satanic values, not at an organised level but in more subtle ways, and the question arises as to what extent are the fundamentalists driven by that Satanic undercurrent, and to what extent are they actually generating it out of their own decay.

As a clue to these problems I suggest we re-consider the basic nature of Satan. In our society he apparently has the exoteric role of Leader of the Spiritual Opposition. This is the simple role that makes him the target for Kevin Logan and his type. But at an esoteric level Satan is Lord of Duality, which is to say he is the Principle of Opposition itself.

We see the connection between duality and manifestation in the words of Dr Theodor Landscheidt (in "Sun-Earth-Man"): "Those boundaries that separate the realms of antagonistic attractors that compete for influence are a model of reality. They represent the qualities of the phase boundary between magnetism and non-magnetism, laminar flow and turbulent flow, cyclicity and non-cyclicity, order and chaos etc". A god whose nature is unity could not create Satan directly, he could only provide the conditions to allow Satan to create himself. Opposition is born and, in conjunction with the god, conceives a devil. Thus all manifestation erupts from this split in the unity - a fractal foam betwixt God and Devil.

The paradox of Satan is that to oppose him is to do his will - because he is the principle of opposition.

This is why "pure" Satanism of the type suggested earlier tends to be anti-climactic, while the most exciting Satanism is that imagined by those who fear or oppose it. When practiced without that element of fear or opposition the religion tends to mellow into gentle sensuality and lose its fervour. People who oppose the flesh imagine the body as insatiable in its appetites: those who indulge the flesh without shame soon discover that the body can only eat so much, can only wear one suit at once, can only drive one car at a time. It is not the pure sensual appetites but rather the "spiritualisation" of possessions as power which leads to goods being hoarded. We take one step away from pure sensuality towards the world of spirit and we are again caught up on that turbulent boundary of manifestation - sensation is overwhelmed by the emotion of greed.

Those who point the finger at Satan, reveal Satan. Those who fight Satan, give him power. Those who blame Satan, give him influence. Those who talk much of Satan, create him.

But those who worship Satan, tame Satan. Those who passively resist him, earn his respect. Those who accept him, diminish his influence.

And those who analyse him, learn his wisdom.

THE MEDIA'S ROLE

In this essay I have concentrated on the role of fundamentalist Christians, but of course the man who did the Cook Report was simply a journalist.

However outraged the tabloids may sound about Satanism, I do not see much more than self-interest in their involvement.

There is no doubt that Gorbachev has dealt the right-wing tabloids a severe blow by reducing the credibility of communism as an "enemy within". It is no longer enough to hint at communist sympathies in order to blow up a small incident into a big issue.

When a journalist cannot call on subtlety, wit, intelligence or sharp observation to win readers' attention, and is forced to appeal only to the emotions as demanded by the owners of the tabloids, it leaves a very limited palette of colours to play with - they cannot afford to lose any one of them.

So a new "enemy within" must be found to ensure the continued wealth of the press (and, of course, to fuel the paranoia on which right wing governments depend). The notion of a drug subculture is one candidate, but it has the weakness of being based on a physical reality - the existence of drugs. This physical burden of evidence sets a limit on how high the myth can fly.

Satanism is an excellent replacement for communism as a new "enemy within", for the reasons explained earlier: the confusion of Satanism and devil worship so closely parallels the confusion of communist and revolutionary. In addition, both Satanism and communism can be seen as distortions of the Christian spirit, and so ripe for projection. Above all, both allow accusations devoid of material proof. If the press accuses some prominent figure of being a drug baron there is always the possibility of his innocence being proved: but how do you answer criticisms that once, as a student, you were seen dancing naked in a wood, or you contributed a poem to a Marxist newspaper? To build up a witch hunt society must find an accusation which can be launched against even your most respectable neighbour, and one which can never be banished with 100% certainty until he is dead.

This simple explanation does not diminish the significance of the media's role in the witch hunt, indeed they may ultimately play the major part in it. Another simplification is to point out that the divisive role played by the tabloids (their contribution to "divide and rule") is innately Satanic in itself, and so if they ever do become emotionally (as opposed to merely exploitatively) involved in the witch hunt it could be for similar reasons to those already ascribed to the fundamentalists - a projection of personal guilt.

WHAT TO DO?

I'll take my first cue from the I Ching - the book with a thousand ways of saying "do nothing" - and refuse to get involved. The lesson to be learnt from the seventh house of marriage and enmity is this: chose your enemies with care, because you will end up like them. If you reacted violently to my southern redneck myths, then get to work on your own inner anger first.

Insofar as the Satanic witch hunt is self-generating, the less people become involved or concerned the better. And insofar as we have the ability to become polarised too, our involvement would only fuel the flames. The press cannot make much extended capital out of someone who shrugs off hysteria with gentle good humour - though they will, of course, try the "unfeeling monster" tack.

If the analytical approach of this essay has done something to defuse the satan game in your own mind, then take it as an example of how you might yourself defuse the hysteria elsewhere.

The essence of Tai Chi is to remain serene in battle and encourage your opponent to topple with his own imbalance - that seems appropriate. Whereas the worst thing would be to whitewash yourself. That would amount to accepting their criteria and using them to protect yourself - and it is precisely their criteria which are so poisonous.

I recently had the experience of being questioned by journalists on the nature of the OTO. These were sympathetic people who were not digging out dirt, on the contrary, they wanted me simply to respond to attacks by saying that the OTO was not a Satanic organisation, and that it did not sacrifice animals etc. I found this whitewashing exercise surprisingly repellant, even though I only had to say the truth, and later asked myself why this was so. The problem I had was with the moral outrage suggested by the tabloid whose attack I was rebutting.

The problem of moral dirt is analogous to the problem of material waste. Some people do lead squeaky-clean lifestyles: their houses are spotless, and everything shines like new. Almost inevitably (and I pause to honour any exceptions) this cleanness is maintained at the price of creating waste elsewhere. They buy their food pre-packed in complex wrappings which are then thrown out; last year's car is scrapped before it shows a dent; the furniture looks new because it is replaced as soon as it is scratched... These spotless communities generate a great mountain of waste elsewhere, and someone else has the job of managing it.

Now there is something inherently distasteful about those who feed on your waste - they have too much in common with flies that feed on your shit. Those squeaky-clean communities have a way of making an under-class or demonic subculture out of those who recycle their own waste. They don't have much of a record for honouring the gipsies, tramps, rag and bone men etc - those actually doing something to alleviate the waste problem they have generated. Nobody wants to have anything to do with other peoples' cast-offs, and if they do, they must be non-people and despised. So we have a society of pretence, those who cannot afford the ideal role model are forever papering over the cracks, whitewashing the stains, and passing off their dirt with eyes averted.

The same problem applies to those who affect squeaky-clean morality. Those who try to copy this ideal are involved in endless denials: refusing to see the Christmas turkey as an animal sacrifice; refusing to see communion wine as a sacramental use of drugs; preaching love while lining up enemies to slaughter, without even granting them the dignity of being recognised as sacrificial victims; devouring the flesh and blood of Christ while denouncing cannibal tribes; praying for favours while despising magical practice; using the bible as an oracle while decrying fortune tellers... Such hypocrites generate so much moral waste that someone has to handle it if our planet is not to choke. But anyone who seriously tackles these issues, looks at these demons and faces up to the dark side of our society and our inner natures is despised as a "black magician".

In such a climate it is too tempting to say "oh no, that is not me! We are white magicians!" And so the dirt is passed on for some other poor bugger to deal with. To cry too loudly that one is "white" is to help reinforce the problem of polarity, whereas to analyse the accusations is to do something towards re-cycling their energy. As said above: the poison lies in the actual criteria of judgement.

To end this essay I should of course mention an alternative solution without which no such discussion would be complete. This third approach is the one already outlined in the Manifesto of the OTTO: to go with the market forces.

If over-the-top-occultism is what the world is looking for, then sock it to them! Openly and without shame. Bring out the kinky robes, the zany paraphernalia, and the over-the-top eye make-up. Live up to their fantasies and cry "yes, you fellow loonies! the buck stops here!" Bring them face to face with their darkest nightmares and see who survives the shock - and who eventually wins the hearts of the people.

In the true spirit of the Aeon, I will now end without telling whether I am joking or nay.

IN PRAISE OF DEVIL WORSHIP

Thinking back to a couple of earlier essays which, as it were, "probed the naughty bits" of occultism, this looks set to become part three of a trilogy. So I'd better start by going over some ground already covered.

The black magic article (ghost written for Hugo l'Estrange) published in Chaos International, looked at the popular notion that "black" magic was magic for evil ends, whereas "white" magic was done with good intention. It was suggested that that was not a very useful concept, because who the hell does magic seriously for evil ends?

The most evil people I could think of - certain Nazis, inquisitors, witch hunters - all saw themselves as servants of the light. It was not inconceivable that someone somewhere might consciously dedicate themselves to pure evil (rather than just saying that to shock the grown ups) but such dedication would be so pathological as to seem really rather sweet - certainly not a major world movement to be seen as pitted against the beleaguered forces of good.

I suggested that the only meaningful distinction seemed to be in the means rather than the ends: black magicians were those prepared to work with, and on, more sinister forces. Such work is dangerous, but it can be very necessary for the health of society.

This point will be expanded in the present essay.

The article on Satanism, to be published in Fenris Wolf, began by trying to sort out the confusion between Satanism and the subject of this essay - Devil Worship. The analogy I drew was between the confusion of "communist" with "revolutionary" in our society,

Because I personally value ideas over facts, I always saw a clear distinction between the words "communist" and "revolutionary", whereas those who value facts over ideas would equate the two, saying "you show me ten commies, and I'll show you ten revolutionaries". Nowadays I can support my viewpoint by pointing to what is happening in the Eastern Bloc where communism is no longer revolutionary: it is the norm, and positively reactionary. In other words: the popular idea that all communists are revolutionaries has more to do with living in a capitalist society than it has to do with the practice of communism. Not only is the idea not universally true, it also leads to a lot of polarised hysteria.

Similarly with Satanism: because Satan can represent a polar "opposite" to Christ, and because we live in a Christian society, anyone wishing to worship the Devil will tend to equate Satan with that role. The result is a distorted picture of Satan and what Satanism stands for: a viewpoint responsible for a lot of polarised anti-occult hysteria, and yet an understandable viewpoint in a Christian society.

The distinction was drawn between Satanism and Devil Worship so that I could go on to talk sensibly about the former. I did not wish to launch a new polarisation in which Satanists formed a crusade against devil worshippers in order to "wash their hands" of this bad association. Moral hand-washing of this sort strikes me as pernicious, and I drew a comparison between self-righteousness and squeaky-clean lifestyles.

It is possible to live a squeaky-clean lifestyle, with not a speck of dirt or wear in your life, but it is very difficult to do it without creating a mess for someone else to clear up. It means regularly buying new cars, chucking out any furnishings that get marked or scratched, buying your food hygienically wrapped and preferably pre-cooked... and so on. The result is a mountain of garbage which lands on someone else's doorstep.

Not only does someone else have to dispose of or re-cycle that garbage, they also have to endure social rejection. Like flies on shit, there is something psychologically unsavoury to squeaky-cleaners about those people (eg gypsies) who live off society's garbage. The squeaky-clean lifestyle survives by creating a pollution problem, and an underclass which is needed to re-cycle that problem.

The moral analogy is with those who deny all but their cleanest principles: they generate a moral pollution problem which has to be projected onto a despised minority.

Take for example the principle that Christ's sacrifice means we need no longer offer blood offerings to the Gods. Yet surely the biggest religious sacrifice of all time must be the tens of millions of turkeys which are slaughtered in the name of Christ every December?

Liberal Christians recycle, or at least learn to live with this particular bit of moral dirt because they are prepared to face up to and come to terms with this incongruous pagan survival in their religion.

But whiter-than-white fundamentalists refuse to see it: instead they create the notion of an evil pagan minority who perform animal sacrifices. Many pagans, faced with this moral garbage being dropped on their doorstep, opt to become vegetarian animal rights campaigners - yet they remain a despised underclass to the fundamentalists.

So the point of this rather long introduction is this: the following essay is a further attempt to recycle some of the moral garbage created by extremely self-righteous elements in our society. It is not an attempt to wash our hands of that garbage.

THE POLARITY GAME

Imagine you are interviewing a nanny for your toddlers. The first candidate bubbles with sweetness and light, laughing at your jokes and saying how lovely your children are, the weather is, the garden is... The second launches into a diatribe about the evils in our society, about child abuse, ritual murder, pornography...

Which gets the job?

Now I know that jaded old decadents like myself will soon weary of sweetness and light, but nevertheless, if choosing a companion for children of a tender age, I for one would be distinctly unhappy with the second candidate. I would value the positive messages of the first candidate more highly than the protective anger of the second... unless I was myself feeling highly insecure.

By the same token, I am very wary of organisations who claim to cherish children, but who spend a lot of time talking to the media about the hundred and one most horrible things you can do to them.

I am a great respecter of the power of human imagination, and would challenge anyone to a contest as to who could devise the sickest way of disposing of noisy neighbours' children en mass. But, having taken my prize, I would go home for cocoa and an early night.

As I write this there is probably somewhere in the world a lonely psychopath flipping his lid and sharpening an axe - anything is possible, I once saw a Volkswagen break down - but all the same, how can anybody seriously believe that there is a great worldwide conspiracy of organised evil, hell-bent on the ritual abuse and sacrifice of children? I distrust any household that leaves that sort of moral garbage in its dustbin.

Just ask who these ritual devil worshippers are meant to be. We are assured that they have infiltrated every level of society. Let's forget tabloid hysteria and ask ourselves what we are being asked to believe: namely that *real* people are involved in ritual child sacrifices.

How do they manage so many undetected crimes (the police know nothing of this conspiracy)? How do they dispose of the bodies? Can you picture them at breakfast the next day? "I hope you don't expect *me* to clean up the blood in the temple *yet again*?" "Sorry, darling, I must dash or I'll be late for the board meeting".

Alas, I have to make it sound commonplace, because we are being asked to believe that it is commonplace.

This is the image of devil worship being projected by some groups: not only do I find it impossible to believe in, I also feel very mistrustful of the people who do believe it. Nor would I want to leave any children in their care.

Occultists are accused of secretly practicing these evil rites. But what is their motive meant to be? If there is no motive, then the behaviour is pathological and we should see its practitioners as sick people needing healing. That attitude does not suit the campaigners, because they want to call the public to arms; so the onus is on them to create a motive so they can paint the evil as a deliberate evil, and yet they cannot come up with anything credible.

The problem is this: whereas occultism has nothing to gain from encouraging the vile practices described, fundamentalist Christianity has everything to gain. According to its rigid interpretation of the scriptures, Antichrist has got to set up his kingdom of evil on earth in time for the year 2000. Unless evil becomes rampant throughout society as predicted, these predictions will be blown... and fundamentalist Christianity will have to retire with egg on its face.

Of course I am not seriously suggesting that individual Christians are deliberately conspiring to cause a breakdown in our society in order to make their religion come true - that is almost as hard to believe as the devil-worshipper myth - but I am pointing out how declining morality and mayhem are exactly what fundamentalist Christianity needs for its survival.

This is an idea I discussed in Words Made Flesh: how any group can function as a system, developing a group-mind or artificial intelligence which can often act against human interest. I gave examples like the medical profession - high minded folk who generate work for themselves by implanting negative health suggestions on cigarette packets; the Tories who came in on promises to restore law and order, yet have produced change after change in society apparently designed to fragment society and create public disorder - because the group mind of Toryism knows that happy folk are more likely to opt for socialism, whereas frightened citizens will vote for tough government; similarly, every action of the legal profession is a perfect vehicle for creating more work for itself.

The trouble with our western scientific world view is that it has banished the idea of "spirit" or mind in anything other than human form. This revolution has, up till the present, lead to great technological advance but the bill is about to be presented: the West will now have great difficulty in coming to terms with artificial intelligence, whereas the world's more animistic cultures will see nothing extraordinary in the idea that a machine or even an abstract system could have a mind of its own. Technology is about to outgrow the mind of the Western culture that created it.

So what I am saying in these examples is that it is not Mrs Thatcher's deliberate fault that everything she does serves to increase violence in society, rather it is the fault of a system called Thatcherism which needs violence for its survival. Otherwise well-meaning people become part of an artificial-intelligence which acts against human interests - not because the system is inherently evil but simply because it is a primitive entity which puts its own survival first.

So we see that fundamentalist Christianity, as a system, needs to generate evil to feed itself. Comfortable people are notoriously irreligious and this produces the paradoxical fact that non-political secular institutions tend to increase world harmony whereas religious and political movements tend to decrease world harmony. To observe these effects you have to change your focus: don't listen to the motives of the people involved, simply concentrate on the final outcome.

In my Satanism article I gave the example of a woman who appears in the media saying how she was involved in a Satanic cult that sacrificed animals and children - and now she is a born-again Christian who travels the country campaigning against evil. But if you consider her motives for joining her Satanic cult, it can only have been to gain power and position - which she now has, as direct consequence of her seedy past. So the seductive message to children which lies behind her public attacks on Satanism is this: if you want to be a media star like me, do as I did, and at least pretend that you have made sacrifices to Satan!

Polarised thinking seems terribly clear cut and black and white when you are engaged in it, but it seems equally ridiculous and muddled to those who can step outside its framework. We see Christians campaigning against the evils upon which their very faith is founded, we see forces of law and order provoking disturbance to stir up justification for their existence. Who has really benefited from the Poll Tax? the answer has to be... the Labour Party.

Anyone who has ever strongly opposed a government in power must have known that feeling of elation on hearing about exceptionally bad employment, inflation, trade or other such figures. Your eyes are set on the dream of a government's collapse, and you see yourself as a "good guy" because you are opposing a bad government. But you do not notice that you have got into the habit of praying for your country to get into a crisis - a crisis that will get the "good" government into power at the expense of the nation's immediate health - and what sort of good guy is it that wishes ill of his country? As the Duke of Wellington kept pointing out: victory is the second worst thing that can happen to any campaigner.

There are an infinite number of polarity games: good/evil, black/white, rich/poor, right/left, revolution/reaction, liberal/totalitarian, Christian/pagan... But each game has exactly the same rules and they are just different names for the one game called "God/Devil".

The God/Devil game is played on a map of the world painted in only two colours. The rule book says "nothing could be simpler than a two colour map".

However, today's *confit de canard fumee* will be tomorrow's shit (nor all your piety and wit). And the perpetrator of this foul alchemy is not Satan, nor the Commies, nor the drug barons.... It is our own bodies.

Her Majesty the Queen, Margaret Thatcher, His Holiness the Pope, and Mother Teresa all have something in common. Every day they sit on the loo and leave a smelly brown deposit for the sewage workers to dispose of. If it is "bad form" to acknowledge this fact, what about the people who actually perform the act?

The God/Devil game may be played on a map of only two colours - black and white - but it not at all simple, because the boundaries on that map are fractal. Any cross section of that map contains as much black as white: wherever you slice it, you find God and Devil locked in eternal embrace.

If you take an information model of reality (as discussed in my Words Made Flesh), the polarity game is analogous to deciding that the number one in the binary system is good, and the number nought is evil. In theory there is a "perfect" program whose machine code contains no zeros because it consists entirely of ones - but, like a perfect God, it doesn't actually do anything.

Devil worship is simply the recognition of one's right to change sides in the polarity game.

THE NATURE OF WORSHIP

Where has our society got the idea that to worship something is to subjugate yourself to that thing? That to worship the devil is to become his slave?

If you are in the polarity game, two things conspire to stop you changing sides. One is the conscious belief that, whereas the service of God is perfect freedom, as soon as you bow to the Devil you will be enslaved. The second is the unconscious knowledge that, once you have changed sides, you will in fact find that nothing has changed (this is because the game is perfectly symmetrical, if it were not so it would not be a proper fair game). You do indeed discover that you are enslaved, but not to the Devil so much as to the game itself.

Other cultures seem to recognise that worshipping spirits can at least bestow a measure of power over them. Their concept of worship seems somehow more sophisticated: it is the act of establishing a right relationship with a deity.

The current myth of devil worship is that it means going from total dedication to the Good to total dedication to the Evil. This myth is the moral equivalent of a nuclear deterrent: it is designed to make devil worship, like war, unthinkable. Such techniques merely appear to succeed: we find other names for war so that we don't have to think about it as we continue to pursue it, and the sheer unthinkableness of devil worship means that we are free to practice it forever - but unconsciously. Tell a militant labour supporter that he is helping to keep Thatcher in power, or a fundamentalist Christian that he is romanticising the occult, and neither will know what you are saying.

The animist who consciously sacrifices to an evil spirit in order to keep it out of mischief is playing the polarity game in an altogether more sophisticated manner. Who is playing whom?

I remember a scene in Lawrence of Arabia where the hero is trying to win some local ruler to his side. The ruler says, with pride, that the Turks pay him money to keep out of their way. Lawrence replies that it is normal to pay servants, and when is the ruler going to stand up against his masters?

What an intriguing reversal: to what extent are we subject to the tax man, and to what extent is he indeed our civil servant? At some metaphysical level it must be true that the terrified shopkeeper who pays protection money to the Mafia is in fact reducing the latter to servitude - and the thought cheers me up. It could explain why Mafia hit men and pimps are so vicious towards their sources of income - deep down they sense how they are growing dependent on them.

So the idea that a relationship with a devil means slavery to the devil is just part of the game. It is as if Freedom were to appear in person and say "I alone am Freedom, if you so much as turn your gaze from me for an instant you will be enslaved and never more free." Some freedom.

In the black magic article I gave an example of a changing relationship with a demon which served to illustrate the difference between white and black magic. It was of a student who suffered a demon in the form of a nervous breakdown, who went to the college psychiatrist who was able to analyse the demon as an Oedipus complex or whatever, and thus it was banished and the student went on to pass the exams and become a successful member of society. This I saw as the epitome of white magic: a wicked demon has been banished, and a person has been liberated.

But then we reach a mid-life crisis: the hero has achieved worldly success and reputation, but somehow there is no magic left in life, it all seems pointless. At this point a different sort of shrink appears (probably far more expensive) who argues that, when that demon was

banished, it took life's magic with it. Now the hero has to start a journey into the unconscious underworld to locate that banished demon
and come to terms with it in order to re-assimilate its power. This I
saw as the epitome of black magic: to work with evil forces instead of
banishing them.

To argue that it is really white magic, because the intent is to re-
cycle the evil into something good, is to miss the point horribly: anyone who approaches such work with the crusading spirit of a white
knight going down to "rescue" underworld nasties and convert them,
is doomed to fail. Such work means getting one's hands very dirty for
a while: like the underclass who recycle society's physical garbage, you
can expect to lose a few friends and supporters during the journey.

That illustrates a major black magic operation or, in the terms of
this essay, a bit of really serious devil worship. It shows that the fundamentalists are at least right when they say that devil worship is
dangerous, but it gives perhaps a clearer picture of the nature of the
danger. Certainly, devil worship is best left until one has plenty of
experience of life: the devils that tempt the innocent aren't worth
worshipping anyway!

But, as was suggested earlier, most relationships with devils are far
less conscious - the fundamentalist who subtly tempts children by
romanticising the occult in order to attack it, the politician who runs
down his country while trying to gain power to help it - such relationships are also dangerous, but in a different manner. The demons
are just as "bad", but the relationship is different.

In both cases the devil is being given something. The earlier
example is of someone who gives the devil the gift of recognition and
respect, and hopes to win something of its power in return. This is a
bit like laying out food offerings to a wild creature with a view to
taming it a little. The later examples are like people who pay protection money: the unconscious deal that the fundamentalist has with
the devil is that he will go round building up the devil's reputation by
preaching of his power and omnipresence, in return for being disas-
sociated from that evil. The devil is happy to let him live that
squeaky-clean image, it generates ever more garbage elsewhere.

So the point I wish to put is this: If there was a little more honest, conscious devil worship in our society, there might be rather less
of that dangerous unconscious collaboration.

THE PRACTICE OF DEVIL WORSHIP

To worship a devil is to turn to the polar antithesis of what you stand for, and to form some sort of conscious relationship with it.

My emphasis on the conscious element is intended to make the definition more useful. Although I see the fundamentalists as the chief supporters of their devil, I would not want to call them worshippers of that devil because it stretches the term too wide.

Devil worship, in these terms, still covers a wide field. Using the fourfold analysis of human endeavour into Religion, Science, Magic and Art (proposed in "SSOTBME - An Essay On Magic") we see that devil worship can be a powerful and risky business in the first (Religious) case. The more perfect and good is the God you worship, the more absolutely evil must be the Devil it excludes. Devil worship in the Religious sense is what we consider "real" devil worship, but it is an act of dedication so outrageous as to be very rare. Apparently St Secaire held a black mass in the crypt of his church in order to purge it of its sin - sounds like a saint with a sense of humour!

In the Science sector, the devil equates with untruth. Here devil worship is at its silliest, because it amounts to investigating ideas which "cannot possibly" be true. The danger is of being ostracised by the scientific establishment as a crank, the possible reward is that one might just hit upon some revolutionary new truth which the establishment will eventually be forced to accept. This hardly ever happens in this absolute sense: instead of serious devil worship, the scientific establishment is prepared to allow limited congress with minor demons, dubious hypotheses on the fringe rather than out and out falsehood. Mathematics seems like one glaring exception - the subject makes big advances every time a good mind is prepared to lay down a new formal structure on axioms forbidden to earlier structures - but such mathematics is more at home in the Art sector, as we shall see.

In the Magical sector the devil equates with unbalance or division. Here the dangers are most subtle: in a sense unbalance is fundamental to every effective action, and the sword of analysis is never omitted from the magic circle whatever scoffers may suggest. But you do not work long with unbalanced force without losing one's own innate balance, and then becoming dependent on further unbalanced work in order not to fall over. And the skill of the sword is to learn how to control it: for if analytical reason is allowed to run wild it inevitably performs the greatest magical operation of all, namely to banish all of life's magic and leave us with logical positivism.

The next section of this essay will look further into the magical potential of devil worship.

In the Art sector, devil worship definitely has its home. This is no doubt why art never totally loses its sense of the subversive.

To illustrate I take an example from the world of advertising and image. By the late eighties commercial artists had perfected the sharp, crisp and clean lines of the "hi-tech" style, and you can just imagine some designer after a hard day with the fine-line pen wandering home past a second hand book stall and picking up a some tatty copies of a magazine from the fifties. Suddenly he bursts out laughing and shows the magazine to a friend: "hey look at these adverts, aren't they *horrible!* Look at those cut-out heads with those ghastly toothy smiles! It's so bad... I love it".

For the sheer outrageous kitsch of it he creates a fifties-look ad campaign. In fact it is worse than the original because it deliberately plays up the "bad" design. Yet out of this blatant act of devil worship emerges a new spirit: advertising looks back to the fifties and discovers some of the excitement and optimism of the decade which had been lost in the pursuit of eighties cool imagery. (Ok, they then ruin it by flogging it to death, but that's because they are working for wallies.)

This devil worship is so common in the arts that people would not recognise the term. But if you can imagine that sense of gut-excitement felt by each artist who rediscovers some "forgotten" style which has been repressed by the current aesthetic conventions, and if you can identify with that feeling of "devilment" when the resulting art-work is first presented to a shocked public, then you can see that "devil worship" is an apt term. And you will understand why conventional people distrust artists.

If you can also admit that this process of fishing in the sewers of the rejected can bring up some very tasty catches, then you will see why this essay dares to be in praise of devil worship.

THE ESSENCE OF DEVIL WORSHIP

In the amoral world of Art, then, we see the essence of devil worship most clearly.

Some natural quality or function is repressed, cast out, or exiled. It can be a taste which goes out of fashion, an old religion which is forbidden, an emotion which is repressed, a habit which is denied. It is now considered to be "bad".

Being thus cast into the wilderness, it does indeed become "bad". Firstly it is cut off from the civilising influence of the solar conscious mind, and this means it reverts to nature, becomes wild and feral. So far it is not necessarily "bad" in any absolute sense, it has just lost its respectability.

The real damage to its nature comes from the extent to which it is hunted and baited by society. Perhaps the reason why Art devils are less dangerous is because they get off the lightest: they are simply treated as today's "bad taste" and are mocked and jeered at. The devils of politics and religion are far worse because they suffer extreme persecution, torture, alienation and threats of hell fire and damnation. Like dogs which not only are allowed to run wild, but are also beaten, baited and hunted, they learn to bare their teeth and snarl.

Such maltreatment might lead to extinction, but the survival instinct is strong in the wild. Such devils grow strong because they are persecuted: they learn tricks of survival and camouflage.

Two things can then follow. On the one hand they can learn to prey on the civilised world, returning in the shadows to raid consciousness' dustbins as it were. Thus we find the Christian devil growing big on the garbage hurled at it.

On the other hand, their very ferocity can mean they now have something which the civilised world needs or wants. This is where devil worship comes in: you want to catch the wild horse for its very wildness, you want to revive Victorian bad taste for its very outrageousness, and so on.

This is where devil worship grows out of being a way to make the best of a bad job, and becomes a positive aim.

Take the example of the fanatics who sacrifice turkeys to Christ with their eyes closed, then march out to hunt for evil pagan animal sacrificers. Meanwhile the pagans, with their intense respect for life and death, have either become vegetarian or else make the cooking of meat a very conscious and solemn sacrifice. They acknowledge that life has been given that they may flourish, and they accept that responsibility with a dedication to live the ensuing life to its fullest. By consciously facing up to the carnivore in their makeup, they serve to domesticate it and render it less dangerous.

But what happens if they are confronted by the Christian fanatics in battle? Might not the civilisation they have brought to their hunter-spirit have rendered it weaker than the feral blood lust of the fanatic? They have the advantage of wisdom, but they have lost the advantage of ferocity. The fanatic who denies the hunter god in himself has turned it into the equivalent of a pit bull terrier: a useful creature to have with you in battle. The fact that it is likely to turn on its master after the battle is small compensation to the pagans who are slaughtered meanwhile.

This is, to me, the most profound dilemma of liberalism. In the terms of this essay a liberal is one who has the courage to acknowledge society's demons and work on them: rather than call the murderer "inhuman" and demand his death, the liberal is more likely to recognise the murderer as "all too human" and therefore to seek ways to reform him. Keeping to this one example, what happens if the liberal comes into conflict with a non-liberal? Whereas the liberal's "killer" instinct has been partly civilised - for honest (as opposed to hypocritical do-goodery) rehabilitation work on killers serves always to temper one's own killing instincts - the non-liberal's killer instinct is a raging beast ("inhuman" and so cut off from civilisation), so the non-liberal has violence on his side and is liable to win the fight and dismiss the liberal as "woolly and wimpish".

The reason that liberals do indeed survive, as suggested in another essay I wrote on the subject, is partly because there are limits to their ability to face human "evil". Whereas the liberal can assimilate the unhappy, drunk or ill-educated person who resorts to murder, few can tolerate the "cult of violence". One only has to read Guardian articles on dog-fighting or bare knuckle boxing to get a whiff of the "macho violence for its own sake" demon lurking in the liberal unconscious. That I suggested was why - contrary to the myth that liberals are gutless - two of the roughest, meanest war machines of all time were totally rubbed out when they declared war on the liberal establishment in 1939.

These examples do suggest that there could be an advantage in having demons for the power they can supply, and that the power is greater when the demons are more "evil" and uncivilised. So now we have three phases of devil worship. At one extreme the unconscious servitude to a devil as practiced by fundamentalists - where you deny a quality until it builds explosive power which can be unleashed on your opponents, but which is liable to turn back and destroy you in the long run. At the other extreme there is the liberal approach which acknowledges those demons, goes into the wild and takes steps to tame or domesticate the beasts - a very worthy and perhaps ultimately superior approach, but it does raise the fear that something may be lost when a wild demon is tamed. The third approach is an attempt at compromise: it is to keep our demons reasonably wild and powerful while striving to develop a relationship which destroys neither party.

This approach seeks an answer to the plea "please, can't we have a permissive society *and* keep that lovely exciting sense of sin?". It is what I will call "magical devil worship".

THE VARIETIES OF DEMONIC EXPERIENCE

Again we look at the Art sector for the easiest, lightest example. When members of the art world (whether painting, literature, music, fashion or whatever) decide to cast out a style, they do so with quite perverse viciousness. Yesterday's styles are not allowed gently to wither away or be pensioned off, instead they are driven out with the whips of ridicule in a way that looks like appaling silliness and bad manners to the non-art world, to whom it epitomises all that they dislike about "trendies".

A fashion editor who was raving about "today's more demure line" last year will come out with some totally over-the-top statement like "*No-one* will be seen wearing those *awful* frumpish long dresses this season" - a statement not only exaggerated but also untrue, for simple observation will almost certainly reveal a majority of long dresses remaining in the streets. It is as if the fashion editor lives in a phantasy world with only a minimal bearing on real people in the street - but I suggest that the fashion world (as a system) is actually demonising old styles to further their power.

In the example given previously of the return to fifties advertising, it was the sheer awfulness of the imagery that gave it its magic. And the awfulness of the imagery (which was after all once high fashion) was generated by the early sixties "cool school" so vigorously and scornfully rejecting all the corny, toothy smiles and greased hair of the fifties.

The harder the art world hurls away its old fashions, the harder and more excitingly they will bounce back later. They are, in effect, creating demons to worship for their own pleasure and excitement.

A second example extends the field further, it concerns one of the great clandestine love affairs of our society: the relationship between the avant-guard artist and the bourgeoisie. Here are two groups of people who, left to themselves, would by their nature tend to die of frustration and inertia respectively. Instead they create devils of each other and give life meaning: the avant guard artist is now a valiant rebel against the forces of hypocrisy and inertia, while the bourgeoisie becomes the champion of decency and traditional values.

I was upset to hear of a recent lawsuit which might make it illegal for an artist to shock the public, and I wondered if this represented an inspired raising of the stakes in a game that has grown a little tame of late, or was it merely an incredibly insensitive decision by a legal system that is out of touch with human needs? To deny shock to the readers of the tabloids would be to remove their one and only motivation; to condemn artists who provide such shocks would be as silly as to pretend that it is hatred which inspires children to rebel against their parents rather than love which is seeking recognition.

Illustrations of such loving shocks are bound to be too personal to touch many readers, so I will offer just one. Like the majority of sensualists I am fascinated by nuns: how anyone, given such a delightful plaything as a female body, could sacrifice it to a life of celibacy and fleshly mortification is wonderful beyond my ken. Now, their very lifestyle excludes me from expressing this deep affection by direct means, so instead I channel my love into a phantasy. It is that of a very prim and proper Mother Superior arriving early in her chapel for a service only to find that it has been taken over by a great crowd of naked male and female body builders engaged in a really mega-hunky group-sex workout.

Now when I tried out this story on a religious acquaintance, they felt it was somewhat insensitive. They did not seem to appreciate that, far from being insensitive, I momentarily become that Mother Superior and feel the electric frisson of shock at the sight of the altar and its furnishings crushed beneath the sheer invincible mass of grunting, moaning, pumping meat, and knowing that no attempt to go ahead with the service and invoke God's aid would have any effect on the hormone-crazed participants in this reproductive tableau. Within me, and within her, the black and white of flesh and spirit become fragmented over and over in endless layers: a dull game of but two colours becomes a fractal tapestry of unfathomable profundity and endless meaning. In glimpses of ecstacy I know and understand the nun.

Were I a painter I might portray the scene, as a poet I might put it in words, best of all it would make a splendid cinematic experience... and I would await condemnation from the catholic church, a condemnation which I would recognise for its inner meaning: that of a clandestine lover returning my affection by an outward display of contempt.

So notice how Art, with its lighter handling of demons, produces the more charming and likable examples of devil worship, but as we reach beyond the world of Art to impinge on other areas stronger feelings are aroused. This supports my thesis that there is greater power if we goad our demons to become more "evil". The world of politics and religion produces more powerful, effective and controversial examples. Here we see the process best if we consider how a system becomes a devil worshipper - even though the individuals in that system are unaware of what they are doing.

The Nazi party gained its prominence by creating a devil in the form of a Jewish Communist Conspiracy that was uniting the world against Germany. It worshipped that devil by building up its outlines in words and pictures and films until it stood clear and menacing before the German electorate. Naziism gained enormous strength in return for this demonic pact, and yet the exercise backfired because the demon leaked out of the triangle of art and into reality - so the rest of the world really was driven to unite against Germany.

Fundamentalist Christianity, as a system, is creating an Antichrist who will establish His kingdom at the turn of the millennium. It is building up this image of a world torn by evil, of sinister occult forces, of Satanic conspiracy and so on. In return for these favours the devil they are creating has given them power and support from the masses, and plenty of money and influence to build up the devil even further. But here again, they could be simply preparing the funeral of Christianity by making a devil more fascinating than themselves: on the one hand there are those who accept their glamourous view of the occult and take it up for kicks, on the other there are those spiritual souls who lose their interest in Christianity because of its growing obsessive absurdity, and they find true spirituality is now the prerogative of the occult fraternity.

Such examples show the very great power and excitement possible when you worship a devil, but they suggest eventual failure to handle such power. The real concern of this section lies in the middle ground: where the devil can give useful power without overwhelming the worshipper. So we should look at some humbler, less dramatic examples of what one might call "demonolatry" in order not to over-use the word "worship".

The media provide plenty of examples of people who, however unwittingly, evoke demons to serve their ends. The problem they face is this: how to deal with a real problem in the unrealistically short time the media allows its guests. We will imagine an example, then analyse it.

Let us imagine that there have been headlines about an anti-corporal punishment riot at some public school and so the news program brings together two people to comment on the story: one is the president of, say, Teachers Against Corporal Punishment, the other is the spokesman for, say, the Conservative Parents Group. Now it might well be that, if these two people met and got to know each other under normal circumstances, they would turn out to have a lot in common - based around a shared desire to get the best possible education for all children. The only difference might be that the former saw his job as looking for qualities in the child to draw them out, while the latter might lean rather toward the notion of imposing standards of behaviour that would help the child to express itself better as it grew up. However, in the unnatural high-pressure conditions imposed by the program - forty seconds of verbal confrontation - there is no time for subtlety or common ground. So what does the

Conservative say when asked to comment on the abolition of corporal punishment? Instead of talking about the real need for every child to get the best, he speaks as follows.

"I'm sorry, call me old-fashioned if you must, but I've got no time for these wishy-washy educationalists who haven't the guts to say 'no' to a delinquent because they are so terrified of repressing its precious so-called 'creativity'".

Now it's the Teacher's turn. Instead of expressing amazement at the educational circles moved in by the Conservative, and wondering who these educationalists are and how they manage to survive in a classroom if they never say "no", instead the Teacher feels threatened and is more likely to retort with something about the mindless violence of the floggers and how the prisons are full of people who have been brutalised by their parents. Thus the agenda is set for forty seconds of polarised abuse.

What has happened is that the first speaker, aware that he has been placed in a game situation where he has to "win" by gaining the sympathy of the listeners over his "opponent", realises that this cannot be done by realistic means. The only quick solution is to evoke a demon in order to scare the listeners onto his side, and so he calls up the demon of crazed educational liberalism. Now I doubt that there is a single teacher in the land who never says "no" to a naughty child, because such a teacher would never survive in the classroom, but there is a demon that does exactly that (so encouraging our children to run wild and uncontrollable), and that demon lurks in the mind of every anxious parent or victim of rebellious youth. So evoking that demon gets all those people instantly on the Conservative's side.

As the Teacher has not been given enough time to banish such a popular and powerful demon, he resorts in desperation to the same technique, evoking the demon of the mindless child flogger. Note that this not only calls a lot of listeners to his side, but it also helps to consolidate those who have already sided with the Conservative, because his remarks about prison merely help further to identify him with the demon that would release every violent criminal on the ground that they had been "wronged by society".

So the discussion is not a meeting of humans, it is simply a war between demons - and it makes no difference whether the first speaker deliberately used the tactic or whether he just slipped into that form of speech under the pressure of the moment. Demons have been evoked to serve a purpose: that of winning public sympathy under the unrealistic conditions created by the media. And as long as the media insists on such conditions, demonolatry will probably remain the best practical solution. (And note how, in the terms used above, the "system" feeds itself: encouraging the evocation of demons will encourage the sort of extreme behaviour that gives the media its best stories.)

That example spanned two possibilities. It could in theory show a positive form of devil worship, when the worshipper deliberately builds up a demon in order to use it for advantage in the peculiar conditions imposed by the media. But all too often one suspects that the technique is still resorted to as an unconscious compulsion: the speaker who wishes to make a reasonable account of his cause feels panicked by the interview into expressing an extreme viewpoint. So, as in the case of the fundamentalist Christian who rails against Satan, it is often the demon who is pulling the strings and spreading its own influence via the media.

The next example might seem more positive and less ambiguous - but that depends upon your musical taste. Anglo saxon protestant culture tends to make a demon out of human feeling - it is forbidden, repressed. We see this portrayed in the Hollywood ideal of manhood: when the hero returns to the ranch to find it ransacked and burnt to the ground by outlaws who have slaughtered his animals, murdered his sons, and left nothing except a video of his wife and daughters being repeatedly raped at gunpoint, then all the emotion the hero is allowed to show is a slight narrowing of the eyes - and the camera has to zoom in really close to catch it. A culture which denies nearly all human feeling in this way has nevertheless given birth to the most sloppily sentimental art-form imaginable - country music. And the fact that country music is popular in other emotionally repressive cultures like low-church Scotland and Japan confirms this picture of a faculty that has been driven down into the unconscious - or out into hell - whence it has returned in power.

That example also shows how one man's devil can be another man's absurdity - you can bet that the heart of the meanest hired gun in Texas will turn to water at the sound of "Old Shep" being sung by Grandad. It also highlights the difficulty I have with the term "devil worship". The Christian anti-occultist is someone who is *serving* the devil, his actions do not match the traditional idea of a worshipper - he is more the slave to the devil he has created. But the lover of country music is typically someone who has denied his own feeling nature and demonised it for projection onto, say, Dolly Parton, and his behaviour is much more like true worship. He knows a searing intensity of emotion that is seldom experience by more expressive people who show as much emotion as they feel: true, he may go out and kill someone under its influence - becoming a suitable subject for another country song in the process - but short of that you could say that country music is an example of devil worship giving real benefits.

The next example sharpens the focus because it considers the demonising of just one emotion. Repressing sex turns it into a devil and increases both its danger and its allure. Taking my own modest sex-life as a sample I can truly say that, whereas truly relaxed and sexually liberal partners tend to offer somewhat gentle invitation to love's dalliance, the wilder ones - you know, the head thrown back, teeth bared and guttural cries of "c'mon, you big brute, fuck me like an animal!" - have invariably come from a strongly Christian moral background. Naturally, as a well-brought up English gentleman, I find difficulty in obeying the letter of such breathless demands, but nevertheless they hold a certain charm for someone who has Sun and Venus conjoined in Aries. You could even argue that such sexual fervour amounts to the one conclusive argument to be made in favour of two millennia of Christian teaching.

Seen from this perspective, hypocrisy becomes the saving grace of the church. The idea of monogamy would be a disaster for the human species because it would lock the most physically attractive women onto the most prosaic, workaholic men - with a resulting constant debasement of the stock. But in practice quite the reverse used to hold, as those voluptuous wives spent their daytime sporting with a succession of handsome tradesmen and college athletes. The harder the husband worked, the more idleness his wife could afford, the more time he was out of her way, and the less energy he had to dilute her cocktail of splendid, healthy semen with his own watery oblations. Thus, although the *idea* of the "traditional Christian marriage" is a human disaster, the *practice* of it became a superb eugenic mechanism for increasing the beauty and lustful vigour of the human species.

This surely is the unconscious impulse lying behind the present desire to revive "traditional values". The joy of the early sixties was not just that of sexual liberation, it was also that of a surviving sense of sin which comes over beautifully in the early Bardot films. By the seventies that sense of sin was fading, and with it the pleasure. The eighties was marked by people being materialistic in order to re-capture a sense of sin (you can tell it was pathological from the way they felt obliged to flaunt their greed), but it never really achieved the magic of, say, blaspheming during orgasm or making love against a church altar.

Another approach to re-demonising lust is to drive sex into "bad" company by associating it with other still-demonic factors. For example the current euphemism for what used to be called "love making" is now "sexual abuse" - associating sex with violence has long been recognised as a way to increase its excitement. More bizarre examples exist: recently the head of Manchester police attacking homosexuality let slip some remark about people "wallowing in a sewer of their own making". Here I must consider his avowed heterosexuality as a blessing indeed, for I would not care to be bed-partner to someone for whom sex and sewage had become inseparable. Not that I too should slip into the habit of condemning other people's devils - the point is rather to congratulate those who have shown such ingenuity in creating demons to serve their pleasure, and to consider the extent to which they still manage to keep those demons under control.

Perhaps the nearest common approach to conscious demonolatry is shown by the advertising industry when it creates or evokes a demon in order to influence a public. The best examples are in pharmaceutical advertising, where evocative but medically unsound ailments like "tired blood" are introduced in order to panic hypochondriacs into consumption; in fashion goods where one flees the demon of "bad taste"; and above all in political advertising. President Reagan's copywriters created an "L-word" demon of such power that his opponents dared not call themselves liberal for fear of association. But even here we find examples of the process back-firing because people began to believe in the devil that they had created.

So it is time to return to the principles.

POLARITY POWER

All the demonolaters or devil worshippers I have considered have taken some quality and rejected or black-washed it to create something powerful. They have then formed a relationship with the demon in order to gain from its power. But in many cases the long-term gain is offset by disadvantages as the demon takes control.

Is this final failure inevitable? Or is it largely the result of a refusal to do the thing properly?

Have we made a devil out of devil-worship itself? In distinguishing our religious culture from the "primitive" pagan with his host of good, bad and indifferent deities have we denied the possibility of a relationship with the bad?

All too often the politician who grabs the chance to launch into a demonising polemic when a television camera glances his way, will end up making a fool of himself in the eyes of any intelligent viewer (and such do exist, now that I bought a TV set this year). Surely, a little more calculation, a little more deliberate choice and careful aim of his words would lead to better results?

True, the most *dramatic* results can follow when you surrender and allow a demon full reign - when the politician gets "carried away" - but this is not real magic and it does backfire. Better by far is the fashion world which deliberately demonises bad taste in order to revive it with greater excitement, or the more aware Christians who meditate on the evils of carnal lust in order to hot up their sex-lives - because they almost know what they are doing.

What I suggest is that we might do well to rediscover the old idea that it is possible to keep demons in check by developing a right relationship with them. That "worship" should not mean subservience. Polarity is a fundamental quality in human experience: like electricity it can be dangerous but it also has power to serve us if we learn how.

Chapter 122 of Crowley's Liber Aleph contains these words:

"Now then there is an Art and Device of Magick that I will declare unto thee, albeit it is a Peril if thou be not fixed in that Truth, and in that Beatific Vision whereof I have written in the three chapters foregoing. And it is this, to create by Artifice a Conflict in thyself, that thou mayst take pleasure in its Resolution".

To those who argue that such conscious devil worship is bound to lack the fire and excitement of, say, that practiced by Christian fundamentalists I would quote from the following chapter:

"Yet be thou heedful, o my Son, for this Art is set upon a Razor's Edge... It is but to pretend, thou sayest; and that is sooth; yet thou must make Pretence so well as to deceive thyself, albeit for a Moment, else were thy Sport savourless. Then, an thou have one Point of Weakness in thee, that Thought of thine may incarnate and destroy thee."

That to me is the essence of the matter. The irony is this: I am intending to write a book on trinitarian thinking as a solution to what I see as the trap of dualism into which so many of us are caught. So why am I now defending devil worship?

If we are to grow beyond bondage to duality it should not be by retreating from it, but rather by mastering and outgrowing the process. The media entertain us because they encourage silly people to adopt silly views. If this formula was simply dropped, the world would miss a lot of laughs; but if the essential gamesmanship of it became recognised it would not only allow the players to do the job a bit better, it would save them from destroying themselves in the process.

If in this and other ways we learned to recognise and respect devil worship then we could offer help to those brave pioneers who face its dangers. Who could possibly object to a swing to Victorian values as long as it was made quite clear that this was simply the necessary groundwork to a revival of sixties decadence?

As the Tories say of their health policies "if it doesn't hurt, it isn't working".

P.S

Looking back at this essay during the "Gulf Crisis" I note two nice current examples of unconscious demons putting across their message through the media.

1. Those who begin their interviews by saying "Of course, absolutely no-one wants a war" and from then on make nothing but a stream of provocative, bellicose statements.

2. Those who say firmly that Saddam is crazy and must not be allowed to get away with it and, when asked if there will be a war,

reply "we have made the ultimatum, it is now all up to Saddam". So revealing that they have surrendered a major world decision to someone they consider to be mad.

THE TRAGEDY OF LEMUEL JOHNSTONE

Who was Lemuel Johnstone?

It is a tale so shocking that I have long hesitated to tell it. Indeed I would remain forever mute on this subject were it not for the chance to issue a grave warning by his example.

Lemuel Johnstone was born in England to middle class white Anglo-Saxons. Being the youngest child of three, he was conceived by experienced parents in a family that had already achieved a certain stability.

That was the beginning of the problem.

He was born at home, in relaxed circumstances, without great pain and with no drugs or artificial aids. So he suffered no birth trauma. He was breast fed by a healthy mother and, being five years the junior, was less subject to sibling rivalry than the norm. Nor was his milieu over-affluent, so his elders were mostly too pre-occupied to abuse him sexually... or otherwise.

The result was a disaster: for it bestowed upon him a relaxed, sunny and uncompetitive disposition. In short, he was no match for his traumatised peers.

While other kids clamoured for attention, demanded love, struggled to prove themselves or establish their identity... Lemuel Johnstone simply was. While other kids rebelled, threw tantrums, risked their lives to shock their elders, broke the law to be noticed... Lemuel just got quietly by.

Not surprisingly, he was ignored. Visiting uncles patted him on the head, then left him alone. They were much more interested in finding out about the hair-raising exploits of his elder brothers. "What have the little devils been up to NOW?" they would eagerly ask.

So the thoughtful little Lemuel decided that perhaps he should try for a slice of the action. So the next day he decided to Do Something Wrong.

It was a disaster. Instead of warm words of loving condemnation - "ooh you little monkey" - his Wrong was greeted with stunned disbelief.

Lemuel had learnt his first lesson for survival: children are loved if they do wrong in passion - that is to say they are passive victims of a wickedness that leaps from a twisted unconscious - but not if they do wrong in action - that is to say as a deliberate act of conscious volition. Having little passion to do wrong, Lemuel was not very good at it.

At last: Lemuel had managed to develop a real problem - a problem of his own. It might not be much of a problem compared to his peers who were now getting into smoking, playing truant, shoplifting, drugs and sexual experimentation, but at least it was a problem. So he cherished it.

His teachers were slightly concerned. Not that Lemuel was anything less than a model pupil - hard working, conscientious, well behaved - it was just that something seemed to be missing. Some inner drive. It was one thing to be good, but quite something else to be... not bad. The young Lemuel Johnstone felt alienated by their unease. Good. His problem was developing nicely.

His teachers acknowledged his academic excellence, and his model behaviour, but they did not feel able to promote him to a position of authority in the school. It somehow seemed better to choose prefects who had done normal things - like breaking school rules.

As a result, Lemuel became a cult figure. Junior pupils noted his lack of promotion and assumed that Lemuel must have Done Something Wrong. But he so obviously did not do any of the normal wrong things that other pupils did, so they deduced that he must have Done Something really and enormously Wrong. He must be a Master Criminal. Juniors used to interrogate Lemuel to discover his Terrible Secret: because he never admitted to what he did not have, they deduced it must indeed be a Really Terrible Secret... and his reputation soared.

Thus, in the cloistered all-male world of a boys' public school, Lemuel Johnstone nearly suffered disaster... because he almost lost His Problem.

In the nick of time he left school and was in the real, mixed sex world. He was saved, because girls of his age were more perceptive than boys. They recognised Lemuel for what he really was: not a Master Criminal at all, but simply Terribly Nice.

Now it happens that the main qualification for sexual attraction to girls of that age is that the boy must be Terribly Nasty, so Lemuel Johnstone began to feel very rejected. Thus he was saved - because he still had His Problem, bigger and better than ever.

The cancer of sexual rejection gnawed at his soul. A bitter tormented figure he now skulked in the shadows, devising crazy theories. He became a philosophical vandal, an ethical rapist, creating grotesque philosophies with which to savage Reality.

This was, as it were, the smoke and flame that billowed from the furnace of His Problem - for His Problem remained. However wild his ideas, however crazed his imaginings the painful fact remained that anyone who met him found him to be frightfully nice. Thus it was that Lemuel Johnstone seemed to attract two extreme types of people.

First there were those partially like himself: those who were half-consciously aware of being just a little bit too nice and so they were ever in pursuit of the interestingly nasty. Such people were attracted by Lemuel's wild ideas, but they could make little of the man.

Second were those who were half consciously aware of being rather too interestingly nasty. They were fascinated by the haunting niceness of Lemuel Johnstone, sensing in him a spiritual repose beyond their ken. Such people were attracted to the man, but were appalled by his nasty ideas.

The first type were forever abandoning him - seeing their own emptiness writ large in such a total non-entity as Lemuel Johnstone. The second type were forever getting into close, addictive relationships with the man. For he was such a total blank that his close proximity amounted to sensory deprivation.

Lemuel Johnstone became the *ganzfeld* upon which everyone projected their darkest inner secret. Angry people would accuse him of being a volcano of repressed anger. Boring people rejected him for being so dull. Scheming people reviled him as a manipulative monster. Selfish people insisted that he never had a thought for anyone else. Mad people called him mad, clever people called him clever, perverts called him a pervert...

In fact Lemuel Johnstone, by the very emptiness of his being, seemed to invoke an explosion of unrest wherever he went. Without other people to invent him, poor Lemuel Johnstone would scarcely have existed. He was the centre of the cyclone, and yet he was no-where.

Not for him the comradeship of New Age healing workshops - he had nothing to heal. His analyst fell asleep on him. While all around him others were releasing their repressions, poor Lemuel realised he had never ever had anything to repress. Others could write torrid novels in which they wrestled breathlessly with their working class roots, their racial background, their Jewishness, their catholicism, their femininity... poor Lemuel had nothing at all to come to terms with, because he was simply a white anglo-saxon protestant middle class male.

So what happened in the end? Was he crucified as the scapegoat for all mankind's sins? Was he trampled underfoot and ignored by stampeding devotees of the cult of personality?

We do not know. He just seemed to have gone into soft focus.

Maybe we projected our own selves' non-existence onto him?

Alas, if only society would learn from this horrid tale. As more and more experts tell us how to rear our children in an ideal, trauma-free environment, they are threatening us with a generation of monsters.

That happy little child playing in the sandpit on his own, might it not belong to this legion of the damned? Might it not be another true innocent who will grow up too nice ever to be made the subject of a television documentary or trendy colour magazine feature article?

Rescue the child from such a fate. Take it into the bushes and abuse it violently now. It may yet be saved.

THE CALIPHATE OTO

This short introduction to the Caliphate OTO was written for a magazine that did not happen. It has been used by OTO members to answer public enquiries about the (dis)organisation.

The Ordo Templi Orientis (OTO) is an Initiatic Body composed of men and women who have accepted the principles of The Book of the Law, which was transmitted through Aleister Crowley... The Book announces a New Law for mankind and the planetary transition into the Aeon of Horus or New Aeon."

That's how the largest and most active OTO group describes itself, but remember: the OTO is a living body, and a controversial one at that. So don't be surprised if no two people describe it in the same way.

Whenever an element of occult secrecy is involved, it is hard to pin down facts. Without consistent documentation hearsay flourishes, and someone always turns up claiming their version of the "real truth". This isn't sinister - it's just human nature!

The OTO was founded in 1895 by Karl Kellner, a wealthy Austrian industrialist and high-grade mason. It was first proclaimed in 1902 in the Masonic magazine "Oriflamme" produced by Theodor Reuss, who later took over the order when Kellner died. Aleister Crowley joined the order, on Reuss' invitation in 1912, rewrote a lot of the rituals at his request, and became the head of the order when Reuss died in 1922.

Crowley had taken the masonic-style ritual structure of the Order and combined it with his own ideas inspired by The Book of the Law. But when the Book was published in German in 1925 many members refused to accept it and splinter groups formed. However, German OTO groups were to suffer persecution under Hitler, so the USA and Canada became the main players - and they followed Crowley's principles.

When Crowley died in 1947 his successor, Karl Germer, was a quiet man who ceased initiating new members and concentrated entirely on publishing Crowley's work (Germer had survived the horrors of a Nazi concentration camp by the spiritual inspiration of reciting Crowley's Holy Books forwards and backwards from memory). As a result the OTO, apart from a Swiss group, had almost ceased to exist when Germer died in 1962, and several groups tried to fill the gap by claiming to be "the" OTO.

This sounds a bit like silly occult games unless you recognise that behind any serious spiritual order there lies a certain "current" of ideas, and this means that at times when the order seems to have lost its way it is possible for other people to claim that they have "contacted" the current and are now the "real" order. Exactly the same thing happens in the Church: if it grows weak or corrupt someone will always turn up with a new Protestant faith claiming to have rediscovered "real" Christianity - without apostolic succession.

From those claimants it is now the "Caliphate" OTO based in the USA which is the most vigorous, with groups in many countries worldwide. US law has recognised their claim to be "the" OTO, and they wrote the passage quoted at the beginning. As such it is a reliable description, but there remain four contentious points:

1) One might claim an ancient Templar tradition and insist that Kellner did not "found" an order, but rather re-established in the West something he was initiated into on his Eastern travels.

2) Despite the fact that it was the OTO that recognised Crowley and invited him in, one might still insist that Crowley's OTO was not the real current, but a corruption.

3) Smaller "OTO" groups can always challenge the main order on magical grounds, insisting that they are closer to the "current" even if they have no legal rights.

4) Apart from such sincere challengers you also find eccentrics, jokers or plain criminals claiming to be the OTO in order to cash in on glamourous association with Crowley.

The moral is to take all OTO claims with a pinch of salt - including ours! So let's leave history and look at the principles of The Book of the Law.

The Book announces a New Aeon, so you are advised to think carefully what that means before judging its principles. The last New

Aeon was about 2,000 years ago: just think how Christ's message clashed with the Jewish establishment of the day.

Their establishment was based on ancient written law, and Christ apparently broke that law again and again, to the point that they wanted him convicted as a trouble maker.

But, from today's perspective, we no longer see Christ "breaking" the law so much as asking us to outgrow rigid moral codes and instead follow the example of a living God. Not that the Jews of the time were totally against innovation, but their idea of a Messiah was someone who could update the written law, not someone who wanted to replace absolute moral commandments with general precepts like "love thy neighbour". Basically, they judged Christ's New Aeon morality by their fundamentalist Old Aeon standards - and found it unacceptable.

Don't repeat that mistake. If you read The Book of the Law in the Old Testament spirit, as written "commands" from God, you will find it pretty sick. Nor should you read it in the New Testament way - looking beyond its literal meaning and "tuning into" the spirit of its message - because the God behind it is not a "perfect" loving Christ, but rather a warlike child-god called Horus.

The New Aeon calls for a new moral approach: God is no longer saying "follow my example", instead humanity is being challenged to stand on its own feet.

In what sense are Jehovah, Christ and Horus (for example) different Gods, and in what sense are they the same? Consider a typical child growing up: when it is a toddler the parents seem like Jehovah, giving absolute commands which must be obeyed (for the toddler's own safety, in fact). Once it begins to think for itself the parents seem less like forces of nature and more like superior humans: like Christ they try to teach by example and appeals to the child's conscience - a necessary advance but it can lead to an exaggerated idea of how "perfect" they are. Then comes adolescence, when the parents begin to seem obstructive, opinionated and angry like Horus - you are in fact being challenged to grow up and become adult.

That is what the Aeon of Horus will be about: we too are now Gods... but only just! Each of us has our own "True Will" - and "do what thou wilt shall be the whole of the Law". But notice the future tense "shall": the real challenge of the Aeon of Horus is to set out on

the journey to discover our true wills, and not to get stuck in the adolescent arrogance typified by, say, the rationalist who denies all spiritual principles.

Horus has thrown down the gauntlet to those spiritual wimps
who still cry out for "moral leadership" from their church or their
superiors. He asks "have you no moral sense of your own?".

And it is no good turning back because the old gods were "nicer".
Look at the sort of messages now being received by those who claim
direct access to God: Jonestown, Khomeini, Anderton, Northern
Ireland... the messages coming over do indeed sound like the angry
voice of Horus, but they are being received by people who bow down
before the word with no understanding of New Aeon principles.

Compared to the word of Christ, The Book of the Law looks
dangerous and threatening - just as the adolescent looks to the well-
behaved twelve year old. But it marks a vital stage in humanity's
development, and there is far greater danger in ignoring it.

So what of the OTO? That adolescent spirit does excite our
opponents to wild accusations and - like the big kids that we must all
learn to become - some of us do rather cherish this terrible image.

The paradox is that "do what thou wilt" should not really need
any formal Order like the OTO. My personal guess is that Crowley
developed it because he understood human needs. Adolescence may
be when society asks us to step out as individuals, but many find the
best way to take that step is by joining some teenage movement with
highly stylised clothes and mannerisms.

Think of us, if you must, as a sort of "spiritual hell's angels" - but
we see ourselves as highly diverse people trying to organise under a
certain quasi-masonic group discipline in order to discover ourselves
and further humanity's progress.

On paper we may look as strict and elitist as any cult, but the
guiding openness of Crowley's "the law is for all", plus the experimental spirit of his "the aim of religion, the method of science", guar-
antees that the OTO can offer every bit as much chaos, confusion
and sheer bad planning as the best occult groups.

When we don't succeed, it simply reminds us that we are, after all,
only gods. And gods are not perfect - they're real.

THE WITCHES' SABBATH
by AUSTIN OSMAN SPARE

This is the introduction to an intended publication of the Witches' Sabbath by Austin Spare. Production delays have held up the publication so that this volume of essays may come out before the Witches' Sabbath. Since writing this piece it has been pointed out that Grant quoted several extracts from the Sabbath in his "Magical Revival".

And since writing this intro the book has long since been published and sold out... but let's keep the words as a bit of archaeology.

A witchcraft ritual by Austin Spare? How intriguing! Could this really be the same man whose philosophy has done so much to simplify the technology of magic and lessen the emphasis on heavy ritual paraphernalia? The inspiration of chaos magicians, no less?

In The Book of Pleasure he criticises ceremonial magic, amongst other doctrines declared by him "as the perpetuators of sin and illusion", in the following words:

"Others praise ceremonial magic, and are supposed to suffer much Ecstacy! Our asylums are crowded, the stage is over-run! Is it by symbolising we become the symbolised? Were I to crown myself King, should I be King? Rather should I be an object of disgust or pity. These magicians, whose insincerity is their safety, are but the unemployed dandies of the brothels. Magic is but one's natural ability to attract without asking; ceremony what is unaffected, its doctrine the negation of theirs. I know them well and their creed of learning that teaches the fear of their own light. Vampires they are as the very lice in attraction. Their practices prove their incapacity, they have no magic to intensify the normal, the joy of a child or healthy person, none to evoke their pleasure or wisdom from themselves. Their methods depending on a morass of the imagination and a chaos of conditions..." and so on in even less complimentary tones.

It has never been easy for me to square the writer of these austere ideas with the Austin Spare described by Kenneth Grant: a (literally) sinister sorcerer deeply involved with Gardner, Grant and other ceremonial magicians, preparing talismans and painting altar pieces for their temples.

It is not that I did not believe Mr Grant who, after all, actually knew Spare in his later days. Nor was it that I demanded total consistency from Spare. Some people seem to be utterly perplexed when a philosopher or sage says one thing one moment and another the next, as if they really expect Absolute Truth and forget that even the wisest of us are still evolving, growing humans.

My problem was rather that I wanted to hear the ideas of the later Spare expressed in his own words, as well as being reported by Grant or others. If Spare had so diligently written up his early ideas - in the Book of Pleasure and other texts - why were there no writings by the later Spare?

Was his early philosophy the "real thing" and his later involvement with witchcraft some sort of degeneracy of an old man going bonkers because he had failed to win worldly adulation? I'm sure this would be the opinion of the artistic set on whom Spare turned his back with the publication of the Anathema of Zos. Or was his early philosophy just the seed from which evolved a magical technology too arcane to be expressed in writing? A viewpoint perhaps dearer to the heart of Kenneth Grant's followers. It is hard to decide these questions without any later writing to bridge the gap between the author of the Book of Pleasure and the Brixton sorcerer.

As soon as I was shown the text published here, The Witches' Sabbath, I recognised its value on this account. Here is later writing which is at the same time both recognisably the work of the same man, and also utterly in keeping with the Spare described by Grant. Here is Spare himself writing about such things as "the inbetweenness concepts" - a pregnant notion mentioned by Grant but never, as far as I know, in the published writings of Spare.

So this text is certainly important as a historical document, but does it stand up as interesting magical writing?

It does indeed. But, like his other work the style is strange and convoluted, demanding careful and repeated reading. So I will present my own notes, as I did on his earlier work in the essay Spare Parts (used as an introduction in the second edition of The Collected Works from the Sorcerer's Apprentice). As before, these notes are not meant to be taken as an interpretation or explanation of the text, but rather as a shared example of how one person has found fruitful inspiration by meditating on his writing.

THE TEXT

"All magic takes its own colour: there is neither black nor white..." How I welcome this refreshing challenge to media cliches with which the piece begins. Spare seems to be denying that either ends or means can be taken as absolute determinants of good or evil - you have to divine the intention and the frame of mind of the practitioner before you can truly judge. I endorse this idea in my own recent writing on Thelemic Morality. It is not to say that one must cast aside all moral judgement, but rather that morality must become such a personal responsibility that we should refuse all ready-made, second hand opinions and become as alert and watchful as the Ninja warrior. If someone attempts to manipulate me emotionally by describing another person's atrocities, I should be wary: it must not be their words that finally move me, but something closer to mine own true will. Processed moral judgements are as much a danger to longterm health as processed food.

"Whereas the one outward tenet of witchcraft is of immediacy..." I am a sucker for this side of Spare: the freshness and "nowness" of magic reflected in the passage quoted above "...they have no magic to intensify the normal..." If magic is no more than an ability to transform the instant and give it value, then I would still rank it among mankind's greatest treasures.

In the second paragraph he talks of sublimating sex. This reminds me of the section in The Focus of Life called "Self Love and Map Making" where he describes how, after a period of celibacy, he nearly has a wet dream in which the erotic act was drawing maps! He concluded there that "The function of the sexuality is not entirely procreation: stranger experiences are promised than ever imagination conceived!"

The third paragraph expands this idea into the deliberate perversion of sexuality, in a most interesting and challenging passage. Because modern magicians are so often stampeded into disentangling themselves from media cliches about perverted sexual rites and blood sacrifices, there is a danger in overlooking the serious work that needs to be done on these areas if society is not to die of moral constipation. If people obtain sexual ecstacy from dressing up in rubber and being whipped, is it a triumph of human invention or mere degeneracy? One thing that it is not is a backward evolutionary step: I know of no animal that needs rubber for sex (and no vegetable - except perhaps the rubber tree itself). I was once intrigued to hear an antique dealer describing an old pub settle as "a very sexy piece": if a future generation learns how to obtain orgasms by running their hands over ancient church pews should we really condemn them as filthy decadents, or should we rejoice that, in a world threatened by overpopulation, Man and Nature should be able to transcend their origins and discover new avenues and heights of bliss? One thing is sure: by turning our backs and denying perversion we are doing nothing to help it grow in beauty.

"The Witch so engaged is usually old, usually grotesque, libidinously learned and is as sexually attractive as a corpse.." he writes in a passage a bit hard to swallow for one like myself who demands the vision of strapping, suntanned lasses in tennis skirts to turn his knees to jelly. So it helps me along if I interpret this in terms of Saturn as a Gateway to Power. As Liz Greene explains in her book on the subject, Saturn can seem a devilishly paradoxical symbol: the archetype of age, of death and strict repressive authority, and yet its sign is the sign of the libidinous goat, and the Roman Saturnalia was an orgy of unbridled lust. It is necessary to remember that Saturn was the outermost known planet and so represented the limit - hence the image of repression and control. But of course the limit is also the last post before one steps beyond the limits: so Saturn was also the gateway to the unknown beyond - and stood as a symbol of those wild regions. Nowadays we have learned to personify that "beyond" as Uranus, Neptune and Pluto, but still have much more to learn about this area. As far as the naked eye and most unsophisticated human thinking is concerned, Saturn is still the gateway to the mysteries. Of course, you could also explore the idea that the old woman here is a personification of the Crone aspect of the Goddess, on the lines of Redgrove and Shuttleworth's book "The Wise Wound". And there is also the psychological truth of the story of Sir Gawain and the Loathly Lady, where it was his ability to marry the ugly hag which worked the magic of transformation. In any case I suspect that Spare's choice of an old hag as sexual medium may be more significant than being simply "his thing".

The fourth paragraph extends the idea into aesthetics saying "he who transmutes the traditionally ugly into another aesthetic value, has new pleasures beyond belief." This is a very good example of the process, one which many readers will surely share. Have you not known the joy of transforming ugliness to fresh beauty? Consider the current fifties revival being flogged by the advertising world. Did it not start from a tongue-in-cheek adulation of the awful? the need to freshen a palette jaded on good taste by digging up some truly horrible kitsch? And did it not progress towards a rediscovery of certain qualities of brightness and optimism in fifties culture - until, of course, the media men flogged the aesthetic to death in their usual clumsiness? The same "waste recycling" process inspired the earlier rehabilitation of Victoriana. I emphasise the "waste recycling" aspect because this constantly recurring process - which a cynic might describe in terms of necrophilia or lack of creative imagination - I would defend as the aesthetic equivalent of healthy sewage disposal. Our culture would suffocate on the garbage of its past did we not repeatedly turn back to successively grovel in, examine, re-evaluate, transmute and finally re-assimilate past fashions. If you can accept this need, I now suggest that you consider the moral equivalent of this aesthetic example, and ask whether devil-worship could potentially be a purging of moral debris - as healthy and necessary (yet as objectionable to bourgeois sensibilities) as sewage recycling. And not without precedent if I am to believe the tale that St Secaire "said black mass in the crypt of his church in order to purify that institution of its own sin" (quoted from the LP cover notes to William Bolcom's Black Host, Nonesuch H-71260).

The paragraph ends with the bit about making "reality magical and the magical reality" that recalls for me the idea of transforming the instant. Another example of the process suggests itself: the novelist or comedian who can describe a painfully embarrassing and awful human situation in such a way that it is transformed into a delightful and precious picture of the hilarity of existence.

We come now to Spare's Synopsis of the Sabbath. The first paragraph is pretty hard to follow, but two important ideas stand out for me. First the idea of the "as if" act which I find so necessary to magic. The scientific notion of Absolute Reality which we all inherit from Western culture means that we instinctively accept absolute truths. If I am an impoverished failure, I accept this as "what I am" in an absolute objective sense, rather than seeing it as a subjective judgement. But nearly all self-help systems for getting out of that rut demand that we should believe in our success. The problems of trying to believe in something which you "know is not true" is one of the major problems Spare wrestles with in early chapters of the Book of Pleasure, and it is central to practical magic in the twentieth century context. The nearest thing to a resolution that I have found is precisely the "as if" act: to start from a willingness to play. We failures cannot just believe that we are rich and successful, all we can hope to do is to play "let's pretend" and put on an act or piece of theatre. Because of our enslavement to Absolute Truth many of us cannot face the indignity of putting on an act, and so never escape from consensus reality. It is those who have the courage and humility to pretend, who go on to experience the illusionary foundations of our existence: by being prepared to play themselves, they discover that Absolute Truth is itself just a form of play. By the "as if" act they grow to freedom. If you can learn to fake success, you might actually attract it - an idea I expounded in my essay on The Charlatan and the Magus.

Secondly I note the sentence "The ecstatic moment is used as the fecund instant of wish endowment..." as a central idea in Spare's magic. There is an example of this which I wrote up in fictional form as "the Alton Towers Working". The fact was that on my visit to Alton Towers fun fair I noticed how people screamed as they descended on the roller coaster - despite the fact that they "knew it must be safe", because it was legal. It struck me that such a ride could provide on of the few easy opportunities for a level-headed person like myself to experience a Brush With Death. So I made a sigil for a wish in the usual Austin Spare manner and sat with it on my lap and focussed all my attention on it as I plunged into the darkness of the Log Flume fall. The magic worked - and I also survived a ride which would have scared me shitless were it not taken as a magical act! Of course, familiarity would lessen the power of this magic - I was not addicted to fairground thrills.

The next paragraph is summed up in its final words: "the great saving and the total spending". This too seems to be a key concept for Spare. In his very first book he quotes from Revelations Chapter III: "I know thy works , that thou art neither cold nor hot: I would thou wert cold or hot. So then because thou art lukewarm, and neither cold nor hot, I will spew thee out of my mouth" (Earth Inferno, "The

Inferno of the Normal"). His last book, Anathema of Zos, expands on the theme in its contempt for weak pleasures. My own image of this is society's condemnation of the drug addict: a flock of sheep who have never dared wander from green pastures having the impertinence to judge and condemn those who have travelled through peaks and abysses outside their wildest imaginings.

I am gently relieved to read in the following paragraph that "The hyper-eroticism thus induced by this grand scale hysteria or saturnalia has no essentially sado-masochistic basis; simulation may replace". That is one in the eye for the media men and fundamentalist loonies who cannot conceive any magical act - let alone a sexual one - which does not degenerate into unbridled blood and violence. Presumably they speak for themselves and should be left to get on with it... Just to emphasise this point, Spare says three paragraphs later "All excessive sadist's acts are mainly symbolised by the genuine witches...". Spare, of course, had first hand experience of genuine witches.

The paragraph continues with a passage that I consider important as it reflects Crowley's instructions for "Dramatic Rituals" given in Magick in Theory and Practice: "The initiates are trained singly but only in their own parts..." The formula of strict and thorough individual rehearsal of ritual that only comes together in a final performance seems to me a very potent one. The problem with discipline is that it banishes surprise, the problem with spontaneity is that it does not foster a sense of direction: when every participant is highly trained, but does not know what to expect of others, there is a possibility of great magical tension.

The paragraph ends with a bit about "the Witches take the active part throughout" - underlined by Spare for emphasis, so he clearly felt it important. Refer to passages in the Book of the Law about the "modest woman" (II 52) and "chaste women" (III 55).

The next paragraph epitomises for me the change in Spare that I referred to at the beginning of this introduction. It begins "There is a meeting place, an elaborate ceremony..." and it goes on to describe things that would be utterly familiar to the ceremonial magician against whom Spare rails in the passage I quoted. So much for "ceremony what is unaffected"! He goes on to describe the effects of what Crowley called "eroto-comatose lucidity" (De Arte Magica, XV) after complete and utter sexual satiation. His "none can say whether certain things happen or not..." expands somewhat on the earlier remarks about the "as if" act.

We then come to the ritual itself: a glorious parody of Christian worship that I won't spoil by further analysis. May I just draw your attention to six points?

1) The delightful send-up of the Lord's Prayer: compare it with the slightly similar prayer towards the end of the Anathema of Zos.

2) In the "Evocation" verse 4: note the "sacred inbetweenness concepts" referred to by Grant.

3) "For we are within the magical equinox" in the "Prayer of Communion" I take not to mean that the rite should necessarily be practiced at the Equinox, but that the rite is in more general terms a state of "inbetweenness". Grant somewhere explains that the Equinox, like sunrise and sunset, is a potent time because it is one example of an inbetweenness state or node of change.

4) In the "Prayer of Communion" paragraph 2: does "for we know the sacred alignments" refer to ley lines? Was the idea current among witches at the time?

5) In the "Prayer of Adoration" verse 3 line 3: the only two nouns without capitals are exactly the two that Thelemites might have chosen to write with capitals, namely "will" and "law". Is this pure chance, is it an unconscious rebellion against his experience with Crowley, or is it deliberate?

6) In "The Affirmation Creed": "that my way is the only way for me" suggests Crowley's True Will. See also Frank Sinatra and Johnny Rotten - if you feel like it.

14

MY PROBLEM WITH FEMINISM

I have a problem with feminism.

Not that I am *opposed to* feminism, because that would not be a problem. Indeed opposition can be great fun and both parties often benefit from a moderate amount of it.

On the contrary, most of my friends seem to support feminism and I am aware, in the first instance, of giving this attitude positive weighting when choosing company. This is perhaps less because of what feminism stands for than for what it does not: if someone claims to be a feminist my first reason for being drawn to them is because they are less likely to be the sort of person to enthuse overmuch about "traditional values".

In the second instance, however, I am much more cautious. I will be getting on to further instances, because I do recognise this caution for what it is: no more than the reaction of a beaten dog. Like many men, I have been in relationships where feminism has been used as a weapon to batter me during heated arguments.

FEMINISM AS A CLUB

This is very painful. In practice it usually amounts to being told that a man must accept an inferior position rather than an equal position in order to atone for centuries of alleged persecution of women by members of his sex. Even if he is the poorer of the two, he is expected to pay the bill at a restaurant to atone for society's assumption that, as a man, he is expected to pay the bill. If he says he would like a cup of tea the immediate assumption is not that he must be feeling tired and needy to make such a request, but rather that he must be a sort of robot acting out without reflection some assumed male belief that a woman's role is to provide tea on demand. Because the granting of any practical help now requires a heroic act of defiance on the woman's part against her "feminist principles", he is expected to pay an uneconomic price for all such help. If he does her ironing, no problem: if she does his it will cost at least an evening out at the theatre.

At this point I reluctantly have to accept the saying of the American Gun Lobby: "it isn't guns that kill, it's people". In this case, I do not hold feminism fully responsible for these abuses: it can simply be the nearest weapon to a partner's hand when engaged in a typical lover's tiff. These very abuses can even at times provide positive justification for feminism: for it has sometimes seemed to be a deeply ingrained sense of their own inferiority that makes some women overcompensate in this way. If they appreciated their own value they could face true equality without needing the feminist club to defend their position.

HIT ME WITH IT

It is interesting to consider also to what extent I myself have invited such abuse. As long as a man feels responsible for the collective guilt of his sex there is a sort of masochistic relief to be obtained from a good battering in the name of feminism. If he feels guilty about his childhood demands on his mother it an also be refreshing to carry the cross in an exploitive relationship. When that guilt is lacking, or when it has been resolved, a neurotic partner can only try to make him feel guilty about not feeling guilty. This is ok for a short fling, but not a good basis for a long term relationship where it is a better prospect for a woman to know that her partner is cooking a meal because he likes cooking for her, than to know he is only doing it because he feels guilty about gender roles.

So, for all this, the verdict on feminism remains "not guilty" of certain abuses that have been made on me in its name. I merely needed to mention these abuses at this early stage in order to get them out of the way.

Of course I could be kidding myself. As I continue to delve deeper into my problem with feminism it might be possible to say at each stage "oh that isn't *really* what feminism is about" and leave me pursuing an ever-retreating Essence of True and Unassailable Feminism. So I either stop at this point or compromise by insisting that after a certain level any philosophy or idea must begin to accept responsibility for abuses committed in its name.

THE FIRST PROBLEM

Putting aside those angry attacks made in the heat of domestic argument, I am still faced with a great number of statements about men made in the name of feminism but with which I am quite unable to identify. This is my first big problem.

For example "male drivers hate to be overtaken by a woman". Rubbish. Although I am a very competitive driver, taking it as a personal insult if overtaken in my diesel Golf, I invariably relax if I see that the overtaker is a woman. This is unremarkable because animal instincts surely encourage me to feel competitive against other males, but not against the female. In fact I get a certain frisson of pleasure on seeing a speeding woman - why that should be so is perhaps less obvious.

A second example: "men think they are superior to women". Bollocks. Some men may, but I was brought up to consider maidens ineffable. They are made of "sugar and spice and all things nice" while I am made of "slugs and snails and puppy dogs' tails" according to folk wisdom. Having had such a low estimate of my worth thrust upon me, I would expect more enlightened members of society to compensate by encouraging rather than disparaging my subsequent efforts at assertion. Critics of both sexes tend to look favourably upon artistic and political statements from oppressed people: a play that might be dismissed as pretentious were it performed by public school pupils could receive kindly reviews if it were performed by black teenagers from a deprived area, because their efforts could be seen as a worthy attempt to outgrow an enforced slave mentality. So when I, a poor product of slugs and snails, display some physical or intellectual talent that allows me to hold my head higher amongst those born of sugar and spice, I find it hard to understand why they seem to be threatened - why don't they welcome my efforts with the same enlightened condescension? To those of us men who grew up in awe of womanly magnificence, the advantages offered to our sex by society can seem to be nothing more than examples of positive discrimination where it is most needed.

A third example: "men consider domestic skills to be women's business, not theirs". I myself am a reasonably competent cook; though not very good at getting clothes clean I quite enjoy ironing; when I find time I sew on buttons or repair clothes rather than chuck them out... and so on. It is true that people have commented on my domesticity and have suggested that it is not terribly butch to be so competent about the house - but it is almost invariably women who point this out. The fact that I am strongly Aries in my birth chart provokes further comment: "isn't Aries meant to be a very macho sign, how come you are such a good cook?" I point out that Aries is the sign of the pioneer, the lone explorer hacking through the jungle - how the hell is he meant to survive if he cannot cook and mend for himself?

That last example is interesting because it shows how much more sharply focussed and idealised the concept of butchness is in the psyche of women than of the men I have met. The woman's idea of the Aries pioneer is of this blind force of brute machismo penetrating the wilderness on his own; but three times a day when he is hungry this godlike figure is expected to materialise a woman to feed him and mend his socks. Such archetypal images of maleness can survive in a woman's mind because they are not expected to be manifest in her flesh. By contrast, men's concepts of machismo are much more realistic, because they actually have to put them into practice. A young man might join the army for the fun of killing people, but he soon learns that it means spending most of the day learning how to polish boots and clean the barracks. I know from experience that self sufficiency, although maybe the butchest possible concept, does require one to be competent at most domestic skills.

WAR IN HEAVEN?

The sort of statement I am referring to here suggests to me that feminism is fighting a battle not against men but against a particular type of man or a particular idea of man. Although I have seldom met them, I am sure there are men who have most of the characteristics derided in the name of feminism. But are such people sufficiently numerous or significant to justify the whole feminist revolution?

When you stand back from society and look through half closed eyes, then there does seem to be a strongly entrenched male attitude just like that described by feminism, yet when you try to find among your acquaintances men who firmly and consciously believe women to be inferior, to have a monopoly in the kitchen and so on, then the image seems to fade. This suggests to me that feminism is an archetype battling against another archetype rather than against actual people. It suggests that the reason I am irritated by the sort of statements made above is because I sense that they are hitting real men when they are actually directed at an archetypal Man that is projected from the feminist unconscious.

If I draw a distinction between the way many women would like men to be, and they way they assume men *need* to be, then feminism is a war between those two principles - and flesh and blood men like myself are just civilians caught in the crossfire.

War is like that. White declares war on black and grey goes under, because the soldiers of white are immensely suspicious of anything less than snow white - it must be harbouring black's forces - and when grey tries to make peace with white it become's black's enemy. If, for example, a man hears a woman say she would like men to show their feelings and help with baby, and if he decides to put this into practice in a big way, then it is highly likely that the same woman will turn on him in times of stress and insist that he is not a "real" man any more - and this is partly because the battle between what a man might be like and what he has to be like is a battle that started in her own mind. There is this concept of a "real man" in her mind and one of its characteristics is to be a cruel bastard: men who rely on women to define their sex end up torn in half by this dilemma that being a man in their terms is no longer compatible with being human.

WHO MADE THIS WORLD?

The feminist assumption often seems to be that much of what is wrong stems from the fact that the world has been created by man in his own image. On the contrary, in a previous essay (The Twilight Of The Blokes, in Volume 2 of these collected essays) I pointed out that there is a basic distinction between those who create a reality and those who administer or rule it - and this seems to be a universal law in business, education, life and nature. The fact is that children have traditionally spent the first four or so years of life very close to Mother, and we are told that those pre-verbal years are the essential ones when our basic perception of reality (and so reality itself) is laid down.

So I argue that the world we live in has not been made by men, but by women - and that it shows many of the characteristics that one would expect as a result (in that essay I went on to suggest why this basic fact might be changing).

But the point I would like to refine here is that it is not woman in her balanced wholeness that is laying down those first four years, but rather woman as Mother. So, although I believe that it is woman who is responsible for the world as it is, I also accept that it the Mother archetype who has made the blueprint, and so the resulting world we live in can be frustrating to other aspects of the feminine - such as the Amazon, the Crone and the Hetaira. For that very reason I would ask them to sympathise with the man who has had even less say in the creation of this reality and who has to try to rule it or create games like war and history as compensation.

This programming of reality is very subtle because it is really being laid down at a pre-verbal level. Nevertheless I suspect I have had glimpses of it in action when, for example, my own son was a toddler. "Proper little boy isn't he" is the sort of thing that motherly women would coo when he did something butch like hammering a plastic toy with a wooden brick. Nevertheless, it wasn't the words so much as an approving tone of voice that carried the message from the Mother within. I recall a saleswoman in a company I worked for looking at a calendar picture of Daley Thompson and saying "he's *all man*" and her voice went deeper and huskier as she said those words. It was in jest, yet it carried that message just as effectively for it. Even when a woman criticises displays of machismo you sometimes catch this tone of deeper approval and I relate it to an archetypal Mother manipulating or moulding attitudes from the unconscious - and it is all the more effective for being expressed at a sub-verbal level. The "nice boy" tries to feel encouragement when he hears girls criticising less sensitive men than he, but there is a fire in their eyes and a catch in their throats that breaks his heart because it subtly announces that "bad boys are sexier".

Although a real flesh and blood mother might be appalled at her son joining the army where he could be killed and lost forever, for the Mother Archetype it is a fine thing to breed soldiers because they epitomise ideals of strapping manhood, they never become independent beings but remain totally obedient to the Motherland, they are killed before they can be taken away by another woman and forced to grow up, and their death creates a need for further breeding. No wonder the Great Mother approves of soldiers, even when it breaks the real mother's heart.

I agree with feminists when they decry the traditional male/female division that gives to the man all the qualities of courage, strength, aggression and fortitude and leaves woman with the role of simpering nurturer, but I do not agree that this is a role men have deliberately written for themselves out of choice. I believe we have been taught to be like that and the teaching has been reinforced by our being taught that the role is a superior one. We do not become soldiers because we enjoy being killed, but because we enjoy pleasing the Mother Archetype and She says it is good and manly to be like that.

Have I simply shifted the blame? Instead of admitting responsibility for the world that feminists complain about, have I just argued that it is all woman's fault after all? No, because I am not looking for someone to blame so much as trying to trace something to source so I can understand and cope with it a bit better. I do not believe that a mother deliberately programs sexual stereotypes into children as part of a great conspiracy, but I do believe these stereotypes are most strongly resident in a mother's mind and that they are passed unconsciously like viruses during those early pre-verbal years. Because the male role has certain worldly advantages feminism seems to assume that it must have been created by the male for his own benefit: I believe instead that the apparent advantages of the male role are merely a sweetener to discourage men from questioning the roles that are programmed into them for enforcement onto society.

WHAT IS A REAL MAN?

So what of the male role itself? Perhaps I should illustrate with an example. Let us say that a couple is travelling in a car and the car breaks down in the middle of nowhere. Then there is a sexual stereotype that insists that the woman should become all helpless and scared until the man takes her in his arms and tells her not to worry because he can fix the car: she sits in the car making inane and helpless noises while he gets his hands dirty until the car roars back into life, whereupon she swoons in admiration on his shoulder.

This stereotype is, I believe, despised by feminism and I am completely in agreement because I find it a lousy and unsatisfying image. Although it is quite nice to be considered wonderful and competent by an adoring woman, I think it poor compensation to the man for having to live with such a useless and un-admirable creature. If a feminist says more women should be able to understand and repair their own cars, then I applaud because, like many men, I admire competence in a woman and find it very irritating when the press makes such patronising noises whenever a woman learns any supposedly male skill such as train-driving.

If that was all there was to it, I would be an ardent feminist. But the fact is that I have nothing against sexual stereotypes as such, I just happen to despise the one above. My preferred fantasy is that when the car breaks down it is the man who gets out the manual and sits by the roadside while the woman opens the bonnet. Twenty minutes later the man has re-designed the car and is ready to take out a couple of patents on improvements that would stop this sort of breakdown, while the woman has bashed the carburettor with a jack handle and got the car to work again. I like that sexual stereotype because it reflects the mythical role of the airy Sky God and the practical Earth Goddess - but that is simply a personal preference. Some couples would find it just as lousy as the other stereotype. Other people seem to think it a rather odd and "kinky" stereotype, despite the fact that it dominates the fantasies of creative people far more than the earlier version I gave. You only have to watch television for an evening - particularly sitcoms and advertisements - to see the usual portrayal of sexual stereotypes is that the woman is rather smart and street wise while the man is something of a daft dreamer. People who are locked into the first stereotype get frightfully excited about this phenomenon and imagine that it represents a sort of rebellion against sexual roles, rather than recognising it as a reinforcing of roles that are even more deeply traditional.

THE VALUE OF ROLES

Why put up with stereotypes at all, why not all be complete human beings? The answer I believe is that stereotypes can be fun - just as much as they can serve as straight jackets. It can be extremely irritating when society insists that because I am a man I must be macho, and that if I am not then I must be defective; on the other hand, when a woman invites me to be macho as an instrument for her own positive fantasies it can be a most pleasant experience. Those who insist always on being seen and treated as a "whole person" miss the fun of role playing.

This weakened sense of play may well be a side effect of our informal modern society. In the days and cultures when every aspect of life including courtship was bound by complicated rules of etiquette it is true that some people suffered from the lack of freedom to "be themselves", but there was a compensation for many: an extended role-playing courtship allowed one to study a prospective partner at close quarters before final commitment to friendship, sex or marriage was made.

I have myself been in the situation of mad infatuation with someone when we both knew it "couldn't possibly work". So often the only answer to this is for one or other partner to retreat leaving a frenzy of unresolved feeling behind. I wonder if the following approach might work better in some cases: "look, you know and I know that there is no future in this passion; as long as we both agree to that it surely becomes less of a threat; yet it is a powerful immediate energy in my heart that demands some expression; so why don't you let me come round to your place with a bunch of flowers and take you out for a candlelit dinner; let us play the game of lovers until midnight then go home respectfully in our separate ways?"

Assuming that the two people get on reasonably well such an evening could be a pleasant experience which could serve to de-fuse some of the feelings and exaggerated illusions that had built up while the two held themselves apart. The fact that in other cases it might prove disastrous is neither here nor there: I am not seeking a panacea for all relationship problems but simply wanting to add another remedy to the medicine chest.

Feminism seems to be at its weakest when it makes a stand against sexual roles, because humanity loves those roles. It is never a good sign when a philosophy denies its origins: feminism can degenerate into an attack on sexism and lose sight of the fact that it is itself just an important branch of sexism.

What's more, although it is very unfashionable to admit it, sexism is one of the most charming things left in our tiresome society. When a woman reaches to adjust my clothing and breathily criticises some behaviour of mine as being that of a "typical man", far from feeling offended I feel all hormony and excited.

The usual rejoinder would be to say "but what about the girl who is trapped in traditional feminine roles and denied her true nature - she doesn't find sexism charming". To me that does not prove a need to get rid of sexual role playing so much as to extend it. For if you get *trapped in* roles it shows that you have not understood how to play them yet.

Perhaps it is a criticism of our informal and profane society that we have forgotten how to play roles - instead of playing them we try to deny them and thereby become their victim. The joy of being a "real man" for some woman's entertainment is because you know it is just a game and not really true. When you really believe it you do indeed become trapped.

Feminism attacks the Miss World type beauty show and I agree - until they describe it as a "meat market". The trouble with Miss World is that it does not let itself be that: instead there is all that nonsense about wearing "decent" one-piece costumes and having to answer inane questions to prove you have a mind. What a contrast to the Mister Universe show I saw in London in the seventies: there they had a woman's event called Miss Bikini or something and it was a real meat market without pretension and what a delightful and honest event it seemed in comparison. The honesty was not the honesty of being a "real person" but of putting on an outright sexy act to win the loudest cheer.

If we allow ourselves to become trapped in roles my solution is not to deny the need for roles but rather to get more practice at using them as play. In these terms we need to rediscover the fun and freedom of playing and discarding sexist and other roles like masks in a fancy dress parade - and not to become trapped in an insistence that they are not "real".

STRENGTH AND POWER

My next problem is that I sense that feminists confuse the issues of strength and power. I do not blame them, because I too find this matter pretty confusing, and all I can do here is explain why certain assumptions are too simple rather than provide clear alternatives.

The sort of remark I object to is this: "women must cease being victims and become powerful people".

The problem relates to the last one. However powerless one feels as a victim, the fact is that the role itself is an extremely powerful one. In fact our entire Western Civilisation has for two thousand years been dominated by the biggest victim of all time: Jesus Christ.

I feel qualified to pontificate on this subject because I have a tendency to adopt the victim role and have studied it from the inside, as it were. Not that I like to dress in rubber to be whipped - there are degrees and levels. But when things go wrong my natural reaction is not, like some people, to go out and blame someone or something so much as to wonder what I did wrong.

If I am even vaguely connected with a business enterprise that flops, I tend to wonder if I could have done more to help it. Even worse, I assume a sort of "Jonah effect": when I voted in a General Election for the first time my mental process was not so much "which party should I support?" as "where should I place my deathkiss?". It can be that bad.

In relationships the result is that I can get bullied. If I am dating someone whose automatic instinct is to give blame rather than take it, then when the first outburst comes I am not quick enough to fight back. When they accuse me of "ruining the relationship" or whatever I tend to try harder and so inadvertently reward the act of bullying. Thus the pattern is established for a victim-bully relationship.

But what is interesting is the long term effect on me. Each time I allow my preferences to be over-ruled by the wishes of a bully the outward effect is to confirm their power, but inwardly it gives me a curious strength. By middle age I look back on a life where I have been raped, humiliated, starved, rejected, sacked and cheated (hold on, I've also had some really good times so am not going for pity right now) and the cumulative effect has been analogous to tempering a sword to increase its strength. When I say "let's go to this restaurant" and my bullying partner insists on going to some other lousy establishment I can take it because I am so used to being over-ruled that it does not scare me. Whereas the bully is so used to getting what it wants that it is terrified of the alternative. I am now a "yes" man because I have discovered that I can survive anything, while the bully who has never faced the uncertainty of others' wishes is scared stiff of not getting its own way, and has no experience of being able to survive under other people's conditions.

Not only is the victim a powerful role, therefore, it also transmutes into great strength beside which the mighty bully seems like an insecure child. The power of the victim role is often acknowledged: apparently in sado-masochistic circles the agenda is usually set not by the wishes of the sadist role but rather by the manipulation of the masochistic role. And when a woman claims to be a "just a weak and emotional woman" the stage is set for a marriage where her weakness is going to determine the whole course of every major decision for ever more.

In the light of such paradoxes I do not see power as a simple matter. Is Hitler your image of a powerful person? Or do you see him as a psychologically weak individual swept along by more powerful forces? I question the desirability of seeking power, but if feminism really values it as much as is often suggested then it would do better not to reject the woman's role as victim but rather learn how to play it properly.

Conventional wisdom has it that men live in terror of the Powerful Woman, practical observation of the way that today's media are suffused with fantasies about powerful women suggests that men actually yearn to find a truly powerful woman instead of just another insecure little girl who has adopted a fashionably aggressive front to disguise her lack of genuine self esteem. Partnership with a powerful woman might actually - dare I say it - *help* a man.

There has been a lot of media comment in the 80s to the effect that women initiated a social change around 1970 in the form of feminism, and that men have since reacted to it in confusion - because they sense that women are usurping their traditional roles and their egos feel threatened. What has not been suggested, as far as I know, is that men initiated a social change in the hippy movement during the sixties; this movement allowed men a new role as peaceful, sensuous beings who were permitted to display their feelings and dress in flowing clothes - and that maybe women found this challenge to their roles so confusing that they in turn needed to establish a new identity as feminists to defend their own egos.

Is all the fuss about looking for a New Man simply a blind to disguise our failure to invoke a New Woman?

CONCLUSION

I write this essay with a strong conviction of expressing something important that needs to be said. Yet I feel embarrassed by the result.

The last section has a clue to why I feel bad about this essay and it also tells me something about my most fundamental problem with feminism.

A tendency to accept guilt has lead me trouble in some relationships. As was explained above, taking the blame in a relationship does not always lead to love and applause, it can forge the shackle that binds one to a bully - and the result of that is more blame and more guilt.

Now there is a strong vein of complaint in feminism and, if a man is inclined to feel guilty, he will respond to that complaint. This is the typical impetus for the "New Man": a wish to not only display that he is not as bad as all that, but also to atone for those of his sex who are as bad.

So far the New Man can expect to be welcomed by feminism. There is, however, a vein of bullying in feminism (as there must be in any philosophy that dwells on the victim role) and the New Man can invoke that bully from feminism just as much as the guilty man can invoke it in relationships.

Rather than being championed by the movement the New Man finds himself derided as a "wimp". Humanity has been sacrificed to the Archetypes: as if the Great Mother has made a proclamation "let all men reveal their sensitive inner souls" and when those sensitive men step forward relieved of the age-old demands of playing butch, they find themselves gunned down. The Great Mother has eliminated the genetic weeds as She always manages to, and she restores the God of War to the throne. Is that what feminism wants? A purifying fire to restore traditional values? Even less likely, is that what its supporters want?

Insofar as feminism overstates its case, only the most guilt-ridden men will respond. And the result will not only provide entertainment for the reactionaries, it will also discredit the original intention.

Personally I would feel far more motivated by a movement that focussed on "victimisation" rather than "sexism", but the nature of things is such that I feel a certain shame about admitting it.

15

MY PROBLEM WITH THE NEW AGE

Having worked off a bit off stuff about feminism in the last essay, let's do the same with the New Age here. Actually there is less to be said because more fundamental criticisms of the movement and where it might lead have already been expressed in my essays on Thelema, on Satanism and on Devil Worship, so here I will only pick up a comparatively minor quibble. It is about the anti-rational tendency in the New Age.

In Magic we are taught that there are four magical weapons - the Wand, the Sword, The Disk and the Cup - which correspond to the four functions of intuition, reason, sensation and feeling, the four faculties of will, thought, practical skill and emotion, the four elements of Fire, Air Earth and Water... and so on.

The idea is that all four are needed in any magical operation but that each must only be used in an appropriate way and to an appropriate level. So, for example, although the Sword of intellect is naturally a hindrance when it comes to producing magical phenomena (where the Cup of acceptance is far more appropriate) the Sword is vitally important as an instrument of prior banishment and of drawing the magic circle to define the universe of operation.

In these terms the criticism of Science is that it tends to give the Sword pre-eminence, and that is why scientific analysis of a problem is a superb way of stopping undesirable things from happening, but a lousy way of making anything useful happen.

The New Age, however, has attracted a lot of reaction against this unbalance, and it tends therefore to give the Cup pre-eminence. As long as it is working in conjunction with Science you could say that it is simply providing the necessary balance, but on its own the New Age can become too anti-rational for its own good. As in the case of my problems with feminism, however, I accept that it may be the way that the New Age is expressed by its devotees rather than any innate anti-rationalism at the heart of the movement.

LET IT ALL OUT

There is a lot of emphasis in New Age counselling on the need to "express feelings" - and in practice this means "let out emotions".

Because the movement has such strong roots in America the feelings so encouraged are the ones that are socially acceptable in the States. Express anger and you are lionised, but express sorrow, doubt, self pity or guilt and there can be embarrassment because such feelings are not encouraged. In television interviews it is the British athletes or soldiers who are allowed to express fear or nervousness before combat or competition, while the Americans must always show "go for it" confidence.

Allow yourself to weep quietly and the New Age therapist's cry will be "get to the anger behind it", and you will not be rewarded with approval until you manage to work up some rage. There is a temporary cathartic relief but, unless there really was anger behind your sorrow, no long term solution. As far as the group is concerned that is fine, because you are now primed to become a long term patient trying out an endless array of new therapies.

To feel sorrow - worst of all sorrow for oneself - is a real sin in such circles where the emphasis is on "positivity". Anger is dynamic because it is a force going outwards and it is therefore seen as healthy and positive. You must discover your anger - especially if you are unlucky enough not to have much.

But what of the old theory of the four humours: sanguine and melancholic, and choleric and phlegmatic? It may be dated, but it did at least confirm something that I observe, namely that there is nothing intrinsically "bad" about the inward state of melancholy. To some it is more natural to turn out and blame the world, to others more natural to turn in and blame themselves. As I explained in the last essay, this second "victim" state offers quite interesting rewards in the long term because you learn that you can survive anything. Melancholy is indeed a poison if indulged to excess - but what isn't?

To feel melancholy is to know a certain mature sorrow in which one wants to be left alone to soak, like a warm bath, knowing that by the next sunny morning the state will very likely have transmuted itself into sanguine joy. So I do not approve of a school of thought that rejects such "negativity" and insists on pumping it with positive affirmations while trying to generate some anger to shift the mood.

Surprising for a culture that enthuses so much about our "feminine" qualities, why should the New Age therapists so champion the yang of anger over the yin of melancholy? Sadness and self pity can be drugs that draw one down into ruin, but they can equally be drugs that open inner doors to wisdom - when handled discretely.

HEAD AND GUT

If you express the wrong sort of feeling the chances are that it will not be recognised as such, but rather claimed that you are blocking "real" feelings. The thing that does the blocking is "the head". The head is given the role of devil in some New Age circles: the trouble is that granting that role bestows grotesque power.

In such circles you need only describe something as "head stuff" for it to be considered negligible. An opposition is set up between head and heart, so that all that is not of the head becomes championed as being "real" and of the heart.

Now this is a corruption within the New Age movement, it is not the movement itself. I say that because it was a New Age person who put the record straight for me by explaining that the heart was actually a point of balance between the head and the gut, so that it was good to champion the heart, and call it "love energy" or whatever, not because it was anti-reason but because it was actually the coming together of reason and emotion which are seated in the head and gut respectively.

There is nothing wrong with channelled writings that go on and on about how wonderful loving "heart energy" is, unless those who read them interpret "heart" as meaning "the opposite of head". When that happens the effect is that no-one is allowed to say anything thoughtful or reasonable without invoking a chorus of "get out of your head". The idea seems to be: cut off the head and everything flows wonderfully. Fair enough as a bitter reaction to academicism, but a lousy standard to live by. Because if you deny thoughtfulness as an ally of love, then love degenerates into possessiveness, jealousy and love/hate.

So I respected the suggestion that the path to love is not to deny reason but rather to encourage reason to embrace emotion so the resulting *conjunctio* takes place in the heart and is manifest as love. But I do not respect the more common idea that anger and discord is the sign of a good relationship because it shows that "real" feelings are there; or that any sign of thoughtfulness or of compromise between head and gut is castigated on the assumption that the head must be dominating emotion unless the gut has it all its own way.

ALRIGHT FOR SOME

Comfortably-off middle class journalists love to mock the New Age for being the preserve of the comfortably-off middle classes. It breaks my heart to agree with such journalists, but they do have a point, judging by New Age beliefs about relationships.

Why do people get together in relationships? Because they love one another. Ok, but why do individuals feel they *ought* to be in a relationship even when not in love with anyone particular at the time?

When times are hard - either because of poverty or because of a difficult environment - there is a very good reason. People need to get together for mutual support. In a cold climate two bodies can keep each other warm. When people are poor a couple can harbour their resources. When overworked they can share labour and provide mutual support.

An eskimo who is irritated by his or her spouse would not chuck them out of the sleeping bag, because both might die of exposure as a result. Nor would a poor peasant want to boot out their wife or husband in a fit of temper, because their sheer physical help is so necessary to cope with a hard life.

Perhaps that is why people of colder climates have the reputation for being emotionally controlled in relationships, as opposed to the Mediterranean temperament? In a warm, comfortable climate you do not die just because you are on your own: there are fruit on the trees, a roof over your head is just a luxury and the minimum of clothing is enough. When life is easy you do not get together for comfort but for excitement. Life is never dull with a firebrand spouse that can drive you wild with anger and with passion.

The combination of comfortable climate and high standard of living is at its strongest in California where the New Age movement got most of its inspiration. It is hardly surprising that Americans, especially in California, look for excitement rather than comfort in their marriages. Their ethnic background might be from a warm climate, in which case they are in their element emotionally, or perhaps they are naturalised Nordic or Anglo-Saxon types who have inherited a more emotionally controlled nature but are made to feel guilty about it because it is not appropriate to their new environment.

In either case the result is the same: the New Age has inherited a lot of ideas about relationships that are only appropriate to comfortably off people looking for diversion. "Love brings up everything that is not like itself" they will say when a couple are at each others throats, and the idea is that this is somehow a "good" thing because it proves the relationship is based on "real" issues. If the same couple had decided to spare their partners their inner torment for the sake of harmony, if they had taken time off to "process" their feelings inwardly rather than hurl them at the partner, they would be accused of "denial" and "repression".

I recall a workshop on the birth trauma and how it lays a pattern for one's life. It was very interesting to see how well the diagnosis fitted - people who had caused pain at birth lived in guilt, those who were put in incubators were physically isolating and so on. But one or two people admitted almost shamefacedly that they had had very normal, comfortable and loving births. It was then explained that the problem with normal births was that the "victim" could feel that he or she was somehow boring and "normal" without having any exciting traumas to overcome.

It may be very appropriate in the USA to look for excitement in marriage, to go for maximum emotion and to divorce and re-marry as soon as the thrill begins to wane. It may well be the future in other countries as we become more affluent and life is more and more controlled. But for the time being the New Age ideals of maximal confrontation in relationships are not totally appropriate in Britain and other countries where we are still, either by necessity or simply out of conditioning, looking for support and comfort from our lovers.

We will be made to feel guilty for wanting that: told that it means treating your lover like a piece of elastoplast to cover a wound, told that a real lover would want *everything* from a partner including all the shit, told that the real test of a relationship is in the amount of emotion expressed and so on. A new sin has been invented to stimulate that guilt, it is the sin of "co-dependency", a dirty word for being nice to those you love. But remember that this guilt need not be. When two people offer each other mutual support they earn time together: moments of intimacy become the reward for a certain measure of self sacrifice.

Just because it is possible to carry this too far and become a victim, that is no reason to reject the whole notion of mutual support. Arrogant New Age ideas about relationship can do a lot of harm, insisting that Britain is a nation of deeply repressed and disturbed souls, when all I see is slightly repressed people making a pretty good going of it all considered.

FEELING AS GOD

Part of the process of demonising reason and the "head" is to make a god out of feeling. Feelings are made out to be so wonderful that they take on all sorts of qualities that I do not consider to be innate.

Head people are considered to be "cold" while feeling people are considered to be "warm". The words "unfeeling" and "cold" become synonymous, and someone who shows a lot of emotion is considered to be a feeling person and therefore warm.

This is a bizarre assumption to anyone who has ever felt the chilly drenching of a lover's anger and resentment. I prefer the traditional symbolism which ascribes reason or thought to the element air, and feeling or emotion to the element water. Air can be felt as a cold wind, but nothing like as cold as a drench of water. Even warm water needs to be dried off quickly before its evaporation chills you.

Emotion is so like water. When you are deep in it, it feels warm, just as a swimming bath feels when you are in it, but if you insist on splashing emotion over those outside the bath, don't be surprised if you chill them.

Even those who insist that emotion is warm know this instinctively. If they were in a bar and they saw a stranger they were deeply attracted to, they would not go straight up to them and say "I love you", or even "I feel this deep sense of belonging to you" or whatever, because they instinctively know how chilling such words are when delivered without warning to a stranger: put yourself at the receiving end, and you want to run. Instead they would apply a little "air", going up and making small talk until the person felt comfortable, then bringing out their feelings gently. That is an example of natural thoughtfulness: the water of feeling mixed with a bit of airy chatter to produce a refreshing aerosol effect instead of a cold drench.

Another approach is to delay saying the dreaded "l" word until the fire of passion has warmed the water: in either case all we are doing is recognising that emotion is not so wonderful that it doesn't need anything else added to make it palatable. But tell an impassioned New Ager in full flood of "expressing deep honest feelings" that it would be more effective, even more loving, to mingle the water with the air of tact or thoughtfulness, and they will insist that it is *you* who are being "cold".

This very paradoxical view of feeling suggests that some sort of lie is being lived out. Is it not traditionally said that feeling people are better able to govern their emotions, and that it is more typical of the thinking person to become swamped by emotion? I began this essay by pointing out that a whole range of emotions are denied by New Agers in favour of a very limited palette of anger, jealousy, love and fear. If you suffer from doubt, humility, curiosity or a whole range of other emotions you will be told to dig down for the "real feeling" behind it.

Such a coarse and limited palette of emotions does not seem to me to be typical of a "feeling" person. It suggests the crude emotional pattern of someone who has long repressed or demonised emotion and has suddenly flipped: discovering emotion for the first time and seeing it as the answer to everything.

So perhaps that is what lies behind this dis-ease in the New Age movement: it idolises feeling not because it has a true understanding of it, but rather because it was born from a repressive protestant tradition that rejected feeling and it is now compensating like mad. When a devil is first made god it takes time to respond to the civilising effect of human worship. Meanwhile some of us are profoundly irritated at the nonsense being expressed in the name of "feeling".

BONKERS

Actually things are even odder than I suggested. Having made a god out of feeling and a devil out of "the head", some New Agers compound the confusion by making god live in the head - in the right hand lobe of the brain to be exact. The new location for the devil is then not just in the head, but in the left lobe of the brain.

This idea stems from the research work which suggests a division of function in the brain. The usual division is that sequential, linear thinking takes place in the left lobe, while holistic, spatial thinking is concentrated more in the right lobe. Thus language, formal logic or reason, and mathematical proof are typical activities of the left lobe, while pattern recognition, aesthetic judgement, and bodily movement are more likely to be processed in the right lobe.

Because formal logic and reason bear the above mentioned stigma of being of the devil, and because aesthetic judgement sounds more emotional, the god/devil split is now transferred into a battle between the lobes of the brain. Instead of being told to get out of your head, you will be told to get out of your left brain.

God/devil is not quite the right term, because the right lobe is described as being "feminine", while the left is called "masculine". God has become goddess, but the devil is allowed to keep his balls.

Now I can understand the thought process that describes holistic spatial thinking as feminine, in contrast to the sharp analytical process of sequential thinking. It is like the distinction between yin and yang. But, as I suggested in my essay The Twilight of the Blokes (see volume 2 of Collected Essays), these masculine and feminine labels need to be used with care when we mix abstract philosophical description with talk about actual men and women.

For example, however apt the above terminology, I am assured that in women it is the left lobe that is likely to be dominant while in men it is the right lobe on average. Apparently the difference shows in puberty when girls jump ahead in language skills.

That fact seems to clash with the New Age convention that it is wicked masculine ways with all that stuffy old logic that has buggered up our planet and society. Yet I can see that it does fit some of my own observations.

When we need to find our way, my partner and I do not have the same requirement. She asks someone for instructions, and I ask for a map. She will come back with verbal directions and think that I am being obstinate if I still require a map. Whereas I forget the instructions after about three sentences, once I have seen a map I can usually "feel" my way there even if I cannot remember the map's details. But for my partner that map is far less useful than a set of sequential directions. She requires left brain fodder and I require right brain fodder.

The same is even true in time, where you would expect me to fall back on linear processes. I can know that I have a very busy day ahead of me, even if I have no timetable. Instead I sense a lot of tasks almost as if they were four dimensional objects filling a box which is my day. So I tell my partner that I have no time to spare. She, understandably, asks me to list my timetable and I cannot because I do not have one. So how do I know I am busy all day if I don't have a timetable? She feels that I am being evasive. If left to my own devices I can surprise even myself how accurately I complete my tasks in the allotted time. But if she insists that I schedule things for her, all the flexibility seems to go and everything takes longer than I allowed. My right brain spatial approach to scheduling can be far more efficient and flexible than her timetable approach - until outside forces intervene. The advantage of her timetable is that she can rearrange it in her own way: "I feel like coffee now instead of after the library", all she has done to her timetable is to shift one twenty minute item to a later position in the list. But my plan goes awry, because going to the library and going to the coffee bar are perceived as four dimensional objects involving space as well as time, and I am suddenly in the wrong place for my intervening activities. We both see each other as being very tiresome because we both have a very different sense of time, mine more holistic, hers more linear. The trouble for me is that I have great difficulty explaining my need, simply because it does not lie in the left brain language territory.

That is my own experience, but how does it square with others? What about the preponderance of men in technological and scientific subjects that are seen by the New Agers as the epitome of left brain logic? It is true that you require left brain logic to understand a mathematical proof, but the process of *doing* mathematics is much more akin to intuitive insight after which the writing out of the proof is more like preparing a film script for a scene already visualised. Engineering, in particular, calls for the spatial sense of the right brain. You cannot deny that logic is important in all such subjects, but its role is a subservient one: it is to stitch up an idea conceived intuitively so that it can be formally presented. Perhaps the invention of formal logic is a mechanism devised by male minds to compensate for a weaker sense of logic: reducing the process to rigid rules that can be checked and corrected? So maybe right brain bias confers advantage in such subjects after all?

Conversely it is pointed out that schoolgirls tend to excel in language subjects, and there are fewer girls who suffer speech defects and have need for remedial work in language.

Perhaps there is an explanation here for another assumption that is at the heart of New Age counselling: men, we are told, are not good at expressing feelings. You can be shaking with anger, spluttering incoherently, fists clenched and with veins bulging on your forehead, and still be told that you are not "expressing your feelings". The idea here is that body language or actions somehow do not count, the only valid expression of feeling is to talk about it. Then it is true that women are better at talking about feelings: it is as if emotion channels itself through the lobe that is better developed because it finds less resistance there. So, according to the assumed predominance of the left brain in women, they will be better at expressing their emotions in words. Thus the great emphasis in New Age counselling is to get men to overcome their genetic bias and also express feelings in words. This may be a good thing, but I sometimes wonder: why not build on the skills that are already there? Why not encourage men to express feelings in action and let the women get on with the talking? If hubby prefers to work off resentment by chewing his pipe in the potting shed, why not recognise that as a valid expression of feeling? Why must he be made to talk about it instead?

Oh dear, I sense this is growing boring. I am not really speaking from a position of authority - I have only been told that women's brains are more left-orientated than men's and who knows it might be another scientific fallacy. Have I not often warned about the dangers of basing speculation upon anything so ephemeral as fact?

All I wish to say is this: a lot of the unquestioned New Age assumptions about feelings and their expression or lack of it are hard for me to relate to. They may fit some people, but I suspect that others are merely trying to brainwash themselves into new roles and creating new problems in the process.

Maybe the current sense of disappointment about the performance of "new man" is the result of quite unrealistic demands being made: not just a reasonable demand for greater sensitivity, but also an unrealistic demand that the normal means of expressing that sensitivity should be repressed in favour of different and awkward channels.

After several pages of trying to write about feelings, I feel quite glad to leave such verbal expression to others more competent than me.

16

DION ISIS AND THE MEANIES

This is the text of a Dionysus ritual performed at the 1991 Chaos Conclave in Austria.

I have tried to avoid unnecessary cross-references to other volumes, but here I should draw attention to the title essay in the second volume of collected essays "Blast Your Way To Megabuck$ With My SECRET Sex-Power Formula" because there is a section toward the end that deals with the significance of Dionysus that justifies this ritual.

The requirement was for a ritual that would motivate a largish crowd of people, while only making limited demands on a few to rehearse or learn parts. So I had everyone in a circle as the "chorus", and the actors stepped from that circle into the middle when it was their turn, and back into the chorus on exit.

The play was re-written in order to make it shorter for the ritual, and to emphasise certain aspects such as the contemporary significance that allowed me to use well-known music to set the moods. What struck me was the way that the progress of the play reflected the changing mood in pop music through the sixties and seventies, so I used extracts from the records listed, each about 2 or 3 minutes long to set the mood (except for the last two that were longer).

It was performed in German, and I told each character to translate their own piece as freely as they wanted so that they felt good about the words they used - the only restriction was that whoever comes next must recognise their cue. For that reason the writing of the play is fairly sloppy, because I knew it was only a guide text (it is written in short lines for the same reason, not because it has any verse pretensions).

This version follows the original play quite closely except that I have Pentheus torn apart "on stage" (this is done symbolically as an enormous cream cake in the shape of the Colonel is ripped apart and devoured - the Austrians really know how to make cream cake); and at the end I bring the play up to date for an age that does not tolerate pain or tragedy - Dionysus reveals a cure for the hangover he has invoked. The final "banishment with laughter" is a convention of chaos magic working.

The ritual is performed on two levels. It begins like a masque with a God Dionysus and the original wording of the Bacchae (page references as in the Penguin Classic "Euripides: The Bacchae and Other Plays" 1987 printing). To give the Chorus a bit of relief it returns to the divine level for the Herdsman's speech, otherwise it is Dion Isis the pop star who is played.

For good effect we had a powerful sound system and effects such as strobe and smoke for the loud raving bits. The result was definitely OTT and highly Dionysian.

THE CAST

Dionysus - the God
Chorus - devic host

Dion Isis - cult pop star (blond wig, leather trousers)
The Meanies - his female fans (acted by the Chorus)
Terry Zeers - aged New Age guru (beads, Kaftan, quartz crystals etc)
Prince Cadders - retired king (sports jacket, cravat, cavalry twill trousers)
Colonel Penthouse - dictator (military jacket, peaked cap, Ray-Ban shades and nightstick)
Secret Policeman - attending the Colonel (plain clothes plus wrap-around dark glasses and furtive look)
Ivor Heard-Mann - tabloid newsman (stack of papers and grubby macintosh)
Maggy - daughter of Prince Cadders and mother of the Colonel

THE PLAY

The god Dionysus enters. He is in white robe, with long flowing hair, ivy crown, fawnskin, thyrsus in his hand. Movements flowing, youthful, slightly feminine but definitely divine.

Everyone sits frozen still while Dionysus chants the opening speech from Bacchae, except that towards the end he says he WILL take the likeness of a man (rather than "has already"). [For more cosmic effect Dionysus just mimed while a pre-recorded tape of this speech (pages 191-193) was played.]

The Chorus' first speech (pages 193-196) is played on tape, while Dionysus freezes still and the Chorus (everyone else) gets up and starts quietly to circle deosil. Mood gently ecstatic.

At end of speech everyone turns to centre and cries:
Dionysus! Dionysus! Dionysus!

Dionysus throws off his white robe and manifests as Dion Isis, heavy metal star. Music: Can't Get No Satisfaction by Rolling Stones. Everyone dances on deosil, wildly now but with the relative innocence of the mid-sixties scene. Dion Isis exits to circle and dancing stops.

Enter Terry Zeers, hobbling with white stick:
Anyone at home? I'm here to meet Prince Cadders.
Cadders! Cadders! Are you there?

Enter Prince Cadders, he embraces Terry:
Terry, old chap, it's good to see you.
Now, tell me about this Harmonic Convergence thingy we are off to celebrate. Am I dressed for the part? am I sufficiently, er, 'groovy'?

Terry chants:
Oh these are exciting times indeed
for the Age of Aquarius is nigh.
A New Spirit stirs in people's hearts
The Spirit of Love, and Harmony.
It is the young, and the young at heart, who answer this cry!
Away with tired old conventions!
Away with the fossils of the past!
See how the long-rejected Feminine Principle
now stirs the hearts of womenfolk
to bliss! to ecstacy! to freedom!
The Universe is a vibrating Ocean of Love!
Feel it! Feel the Bliss Consciousness of the New Age!
Oh Cadders, dear friend, let us get 'hep', as they say.
The New Spirit is anti-ageist, it welcomes us all,
so let us now 'groove' with the 'Meanies'
and 'let it all hang out'...
Wop bob a lula, a bop bam boom...

Cadders and Terry hobble about together for a few seconds until exhaust-ed. Cadders chants:
Oh Bliss! I feel youth's fiery blood
once more surging in my veins...
About this Isis chappy, Terry,

Though he looks a bit weird
he's not at all a bad sort.
Royal blood, actually, and Eton schooled -
can't be too bad.
Of course nowadays you cannot just ignore what
women, and the younger generation, say.
They are more in touch with their feelings
according to Jung, anyway.
You know it doesn't do to repress emotion -
as long as you have been properly brought up, of course.
Wop bob a lula... oh heavens! here's the Colonel
in a bit of a state, I'd say!

Enter Colonel Penthouse, angrily:
I leave this country for five minutes
and the damn place goes to the dogs!
Discipline! that's what's lacking nowadays.
In the good old days women knew their place
and the young treated their elders with respect.
Affluence! that's the problem.
Nobody has to do a decent day's work anymore.
Kids think the world owes them a living
and women pass their idle hours in LUST!
As if that wasn't bad enough,
they've now fallen for some loony eastern cult.
Everyone's run off after some filthy, long-haired PERVERT!
Are there no REAL MEN left in this land?
Are we to let our women and kids go crazy?
Poncing about like a bunch of homosexual fairies,
taking drugs and fornicating like animals
It's a disgr...
  Sees Terry and Cadders
...oh my god!
What the hell has got into you two?
Don't tell me... it's your doing, Zeers,
Forever spouting all that New Age crap.
Now you've corrupted poor old Cadders in his dotage.
Just look at the pair of you - it's pathetic!

Terry Zeers chants:
Be careful, Colonel, for a True Leader
knows better how to read the signs.
What we are witnessing is no madness,
it is in fact a paradigm shift
reflecting the heightened consciousness
of a disillusioned generation.
What has the patriarchy ever wrought
but exploitation, inequality and war?
Society has so long repressed the Feminine
denied the Spirit for material ends.
These so-called crazy women, these 'Meanies'
they are simply returning to their roots
rediscovering Nature, the Pure Bliss of Being.
Do not try to resist the rising tide of Love
Forget your control-trips, let go your Will to Power,
Just move with the flow, Man, just move with the flow...

Colonel Penthouse:
I've never heard such a load of bullshit!

Prince Cadders:
Now, now, grandson, that's no way
to address a very clever man.
It doesn't look good for our leader
to be seen in such a foul mood.
Anyway, things aren't as bad as you make out.
This Isis chappy: his music may be a bit loud
but he isn't just some uneducated lout from the gutters.
I gather he's from a noble family
Eton educated and Royal College of Art.
And his followers: women from good homes,
many of them. Quite well spoken.
It really wouldn't do to alienate
the educated classes with your
old fashioned ideas. Can't you
at least pretend to 'dig the scene'

for form's sake, Penthouse?

Colonel Penthouse:
Get your hands off me, you old fool!
That nutter Zeers has really turned your mind.
I'll show him! I'll order my police to raid
his goddam New Age Centre!
No doubt just a front for drugs and fornication,
I'll have the place stripped to the ground.
And as for that Dion Isis pervert...
MEN! GO AND GET HIM NOW!
I'll teach him not to bring his pansy notions
to this decent, god-fearing nation.

*Colonel Penthouse storms off. Cadders and Terry join everyone in a dance
to Flower Power music, a morning raga played on sitar by Ravi Shankar.
Mood of escapist bliss*
     Secret Policeman enters with Dion in chains. Colonel appears.

Policeman:
We've got him, Sir. What a bloody weirdo!
Made no attempt to resist arrest
came as gentle as a lamb. Drugged, I guess.
We'll do a blood test, that should nail him.
Didn't make it too easy for my men, Sir,
they like it when the traitors
put up some resistance -
gives 'em an excuse for a bit
of a rough house... if you get my meaning.
This one turned out a proper gent -
bit embarrassing really. Sure he's the one?

Colonel P: Oh yes he is! Untie him.
Mocks Dion with kissing gesture
Well, well, who's a pretty boy, then?
Don't suppose you've ever got your knees dirty
on the rugby field, ducky.
The only sport you're good for

takes place between white sheets, that's for sure.
I say, just look at those curls!
Make any girlie green with envy
you fucking poofter.
What the hell are you playing at?

Dion: I do not play AT... I play FOR

Colonel P: Oh yeah, we've got a clever one here.
For whom do you play, then?

Dion: For the spirit of the Aquarian Revolution.

Colonel P: Bollocks!
All you pop stars ever do
is make piles of money
for a bunch of Jewish businessmen.
Just tell me your price
to clear out and leave us alone...

Dion: I am priceless,
for I demand honesty, integrity, a pure loving heart...

Colonel P: Cut that mystical crap, you pervert.
Admit it: all you want is to fuck our daughters...
and our sons too, I don't doubt.

Dion: I preach the tantra of innocent joy...

Colonel P: Innocent joy, my arse! You mean wallowing
in the sewers of your own filthy iniquity...
getting worked up
...writhing naked bodies gorged on drugs and sex,
grunting like beasts, spreading filthy diseases...

Dion: I can see what turns YOU on

Colonel P: HOW DARE YOU!

WHAT I DID IN MY HOLIDAYS

Take him away! Lock him up!
Scrub him clean and cut his filthy hair!
I'll show 'em who's boss

Dion: Don't fight it, baby, just feel it
He is dragged away smiling.
      *Everyone joins hands, sways to and fro and joins in a protest song - We
Shall Overcome by Joan Baez ("in Concert" lp). Mood of righteous indig-
nation fading to a hum.*
      *Dionysus appears slowly to Doors "the End" (the passage that begins
"the killer awoke before dawn..."). Everyone raves to the climax of the
music. As it dies down, Colonel P storms back:*
Bloody Hell! My palace has been ransacked, wrecked!
This damn town is going crazy... *sees Dion*
You bastard! How did you get out?

Dion: I am the lizard king - I can do anything

Colonel P: Slippery little cunt, I'll smash your...

Dion: Cool it, man.

Enter Ivor Heards-Man shouting: Extra Extra! read all about it!
Shock-horror scandal of the sex-crazed nympho hordes... sees Colonel
...woops, sorry your majesty.

Colonel P: What's this new outrage!

Ivor shakes his head: Dear me, I wouldn't want to tell such a shocking
story in such distinguished company. I'm sure your censors would...

Colonel P (excited): Tell me! Tell me! I want every single detail!
The more I can nail on this nasty little creep, the more he will suffer
for it. Tell me EVERYTHING!

*Ivor puts on white robe, becoming a god, and stands while the pre-record-
ed herdsman's speech is played (pages 215-218), meanwhile everyone sits
and looks shocked at the revelations.*

Colonel P (icy with rage):
My God! This is the devil's work!
A filthy pestilence gnawing the heart of our civilisation
Corrupting our women and children.
An evil conspiracy from the East...
I see the grasping hand of the Jew here
and the Commie menace too.
I should have stamped out that viper's nest
of intellectual dissent long ago.
A worldwide conspiracy of Masons and Satanists
is infecting our nation. We must FIGHT!
SEIZE THE MANIACS! LOCK 'EM UP, TORTURE THEM,
KILL THEM!

Dion: You dare to challenge the tide of public feeling?
Little man, prepare to perish!

Colonel P: You, you... ANARCHIST!

Dion: Thanks for the compliment.
The trouble with you,
is that you don't know what you are up against.

Colonel P: A horde of crazy women, that's all...

Dion: You are so gullible,
accepting all these second hand stories.
A REAL soldier would want to spy out the territory himself,
see for himself what the enemy were up to.
Wouldn't you just love to see some of these so-called "orgies"
in the flesh?

Colonel P: How disgusti... *stops and ponders with a dirty-minded look*

Dion: All those horny, naked women...

Colonel P: Well, purely in the spirit of intelligence-gathering, of
course... Can you lead me to them?

Dion: Why sure... but you cannot go like that!
You'll have to go in disguise, dressed up as a woman...
purely in the spirit of intelligence gathering, of course.

Colonel P: Dressed as a woman! Ugh!
What sort of a pervert do you take me for!

Dion: Oh well, forget it.
You probably didn't want to sully your delicate sensibilities
with the shocking spectacle of writhing, naked women
screaming in animal pleasure as they orgasm again and again...

Colonel P: Yes! YES! For the call of duty, I'll do anything
Come on!

*Colonel P exits with policeman and Dion. Everyone slinks about to creepy
music "End of the Night" by Doors.*
  *Dion returns with Colonel P dressed in drag, half embarrassed and
trying to disguise his mounting sexual excitement.*

Colonel P (giggling and mincing):
Oooh, you little devil!
I can see your horns! You horny thing you!
Hasn't Penthouse been a naughty boy
Putting on Big Sister's knickers?
Doesn't he deserve a smack on the bottom, oooh!
Smacky, smacky don't be naughty
Want to see my Mummy's pussy...

Dion: Come on, deary, we'll make sure you're thoroughly... spoilt.
Slips a lead over Colonel's head and leads him away like a puppy.
  *Everyone dances in wild, aggressive frenzy. Punk music (passage from
Toyah Willcox's "Ieya" track on Blue Meaning lp). Mass rape of a human
shaped cake. They collapse in exhaustion.*
  Enter Maggy, totally pissed, brandishing the Colonel's head

Maggy: Shuch a night! It wash it reely wash, shuich a night... hick!
Hail Dio... Dio... Dion Ishishhhh. Lord of the cunt, I mean HUNT
*Raises Colonel's head on high and everyone recoils. Enter Cadders with
remains of Colonel's clothing.*

Cadders: Oh God! oh shit!
The shame of it!
Left to pick up the bits
of my own grandson!
Ripped to shreds by my crazy daughter.
What will the neighbouring monarchs THINK of us?
Sees Maggy and screams.

Maggy: 'Ello Daddy. C'mon give Magsy a kissh then
'Ere, don't look shuch a misherable ole' fart...
Look what I've caught...
stares at head, blinks, shakes her own head
... oh my gawd! It's the Colonel!
Now I've really gone and done it!

Dion Isis staggers in, a debauched junky clutching a whisky bottle.

Maggy: You bastard! what did you put in that booze!
Laced it with hard drugs, made us all crazy

Cadders: Oh the shame, the disgrace to our family name!

*Dion mutters incoherent rubbish and collapses within reach of the white
robe.*
    *Everyone staggers about to a hangover dirge (passage from "the Blues"
on Don Ellis double lp), moaning and groaning. As they do so Dion slowly puts on white robe and resurrects as the God Dionysus.*
    *He stands there majestic and still, and the chorus turn wearily in and
beg for relief from their hangover.*

Chorus: Dionysus! Dionysus!
How can you save us?

How can you relieve our pain?

Dionysus silences them with upraised hand... and reveals the Divine
Elixir of Continued Life, singing:
Alka Seltzer. Speedy Alka Seltzer.
Alka Seltzer just the cure for you.
If you have a pain,
Drop one in a glass -
Alka Seltzer. Speedy Alka Seltzer.

Banish with laughter.

ON WRITING AND PUBLISHING.
A CRANK'S PROGRESS

Hoarse Platitudes
When the silent publisher conspires an armour
And sullen and abortive critics breed tiny monsters
True inspiration is dead.
Awkward instant
And the first draft is jettisoned,
Hands furiously clutching
The stiff green cover
As tears well up
Poise
Indelicate
Pause
Consigned
In mute inkjet agony
Carefully revised
Yet passed over.
(With a wink and a nod to the estate of Jim Morrison. Strange days indeed)

A couple of people at least have commented to me on a sense of bitterness that comes out in some of my writing, and I feel moved to address this matter. Firstly we shall see that I agree with their diagnosis but that I am not over-concerned about it. That is because it seems to me that the bitterness was "coming out" in the positive sense, like pus from a healing wound, rather than building up as an inner pressure. I am not, for example, getting into a second order bitterness about feeling bitter.

Secondly I will balance this lack of concern with a desire to share my experience. This is because I have often been aware of shared feelings and attitudes between myself and some of those who enjoy my writing, and if there are any of those who have the same problem as me then I wish most intensely to pass on what understanding I have for our common benefit. I cannot believe that other readers would be alienated in the process, but I might wish for their forbearance notwithstanding.

The problem concerns the pain of one who has ideas and who has difficulty making them heard. The Great Un-herd, a class of people generally referred to as "cranks". Whether it be the elderly sandwich-man shuffling down the street with his "The end of the world is at hand" billboard, or the unpublished poet, or the scientist working on unorthodox theories, or the New Ager who has just channelled an exciting revelation, or the revolutionary wanting to change the world, or the mystic who has had a glimpse of the light... we are all simply cranks in the public eye.

If you attend any convention of ideas you will meet cranks. In an event such as the annual Scientists and Mystics conference in Winchester there is an intoxicating atmosphere of bubbling ideas and shared enthusiasms. Looking more closely you see individuals who bring their own revelation hoping to find fertile ground. If they are famous then the fertile ground is there: a host of adoring fans to hang on every word. If they are unknown newcomers there is the innocent belief that everyone is there waiting for just what you have to tell them. More typically there is a sort of earnest hopefulness: eager polite conversationalists in whom you sense that there lies a certain phrase which will act like a spring trap: mention it and you trigger a gleam in the eye and "funny you should mention that because I have been doing a bit of work on that very subject myself recently and ...." and there begins a monologue from which one cannot escape until an address has been taken or a booklet bought.

In England, with its traditional fondness of eccentricity this group is received with a certain amused tolerance, otherwise it is given very little public encouragement. Sometimes it seems that the only source of nourishment is the knowledge that many great people in the past have been labelled "cranks" until their ideas became accepted as part of the new orthodoxy.

So that is one way to survive the pain of being a crank: it is to believe in the possibility that you will one day be heralded as a genius. On its own that can be a poisonous cup to drink from, but when a certain detachment is practiced it is not so dangerous. That is when one can see it as a game played for high stakes: years of rejection gambled against the chance of immortality. If this is not done there is a real risk of being obsessed with the concept of misunderstood genius and that is when real bitterness can fester in one's soul.

I have real sympathy for cranks because I am one myself. What is more I know that some of my readers (let us say all except the present one) are also cranks - that I am, as it were, a cranks' crank, and as such I have a duty to speak up for my kind. Let us form a Cranks' Union and stick up for our rights, at least in spirit.

CRANKS' UNION

Is it an insult to be called a crank? Yes, because it carries that load of society's rejection.

So this is the first task of the Crank's Union: to improve self image by dwelling on the positive benefits of crankdom. To admit that it is exciting to be a crank; to recognise the thrill of seeing sudden connections of meaning between unrelated phenomena; to pit oneself against vertigo on the brink of the unknown, and then to jump.

In an earlier essay I pointed out that in an ordered and over-safe world there is a real need for dangerous ideas - that is a message that cranks would well understand as they live on the brink. When the News of the World published a poisonous article about a group of well-meaning seekers that I belonged to, I felt annoyed and hurt but, on reflection, realised that if ever the tabloids started to write in praise of any group I belonged to it would be time for me to go out and find something weirder to join. So a real crank should not only be proud to be such, but also rather jealous of that status: public recognition should mark the time to move on to crazier pastures.

Recognising that there are pleasures in being an outsider is the first step to healing the pain. The second is to practice detachment.

LETTING GO

As said above, belief in genius is a poisonous intoxicant. Better by far to see genius as the trophy in a game played by society: certain ideas become accepted as fashions, and their champions are then given the label "genius" for as long as the fashion lasts. Played as a game the pursuit of that label can be just as exciting, but at less personal cost.

Personally, however, I have taken a different route because even games can overcome the soul. I recommend not just detaching from the concept of oneself as genius, but detaching from one's own ideas.

Reading my own stuff can be quite surprising - I wonder where the ideas came from because they do not seem in any solid sense to be "my" ideas. The feeling I have is of passing on ideas that have somehow come to me - of "channelling" in effect.

This is a wholesome idea because it leads me to notice how other people can independently channel the same idea at the same time. Thus I am no longer jealous of "my" ideas, feeling that those other people have somehow robbed me of something that was my exclusive property.

Until this particular detachment is practised it can be very painful to read an article, or hear a radio program expounding a theory that you have been trying and failing to get anyone to take seriously for years. I hear fellow cranks becoming paranoid about colleagues "pinching their ideas", when they would do well to see themselves instead as radio receivers who had been tuned into the same wavelength as those colleagues. Some of the loneliness of crankdom is eased when one cultivates a sense of fellow feeling, as opposed to rivalry, for those who hit on the same ideas as oneself.

Seeing myself as a radio set picking up messages that are somehow timely or of this moment not only makes it easier to bear the sorrow when others get credit for things that one has already tried to express, it also clears the channel for further ideas. The concept of oneself as a genius who somehow "contains" a spark that the world will one day recognise but which must be guarded from those who might steal it and claim it for their own, that concept is very limiting because the defences needed to hide an idea from thieves will serve as shutters to exclude further ideas from coming in. It takes a certain courage instead to let go of the idea that someone else has just published, saying "well, at least that success shows I was tuned to the right wavelength even if I did not carry the message as clearly as the other person", but once this is practiced it grows easier with time to adjust the tuning more precisely and become receptive to even more and better ideas.

I have practiced meditation of the kind that leads to silence of mind. Along the way I meet many distractions, everyday matters whizzing through my mind, bodily discomfort, a desire to swallow and so on. But one of the later hurdles is that sudden, brilliant ideas flash into mind. The great temptation then is to think that I must hang onto those ideas because they are so good that I must not "lose" them - so the meditation is forgotten while the idea is cherished and put into words. Instead I learnt to say to my unconscious "thank you for a good idea, but the time is not right so please take it back". When I did that the ideas were never lost, instead they tended to return even better for having been sent back. The principle again is not to see oneself as a finite mind with a limited number of ideas that are precious and must be spent carefully like gold coins, instead to see oneself as a channel through which any number of inspirations can flow. A bit like the theory that you won't gather big money until you learn how to spend it in style and without shame.

So, what have we achieved so far? Instead of wincing at the cruel label "crank" we can now stand tall and say "it's cool to be a crank". And, instead of being a divided suspicious lot clutching our precious little ideas as if they are all we have, we can now unite as a band of free spirits who happen to tune into far out frequencies.

Nice: but there is still the desire to communicate those ideas.

COMMUNICATION

Trying to communicate unorthodox ideas or viewpoints is not easy, whatever they say about "the age of communications". Just like the party which begins with a few clear voices as early comers try to jolly things along, but which develops into a cacophony of noise as the evening warms up, so has global communication made it less rather than more easy for a small voice to make itself heard.

There is a fantasy among cranks that if we could only get someone in TV interested in our ideas then a program about them could be made and it would set the nation alight. And tomorrow the world. I have learnt to let go of that fantasy.

I remember being involved in making a commercial video with a team of TV professionals. We ran short of some simple prop needed for the production and spent a frustrating hour trying to get a replacement. Then I heard the Director complain "here we are, representatives of the most powerful medium in the world, and we can't even find a..." (whatever it was).

It struck me that TV people (and it probably applies to radio and newspapers too) see themselves as part of something very powerful, something that can shape people's minds. In fact nearly everyone subscribes to this idea of the "power of the media" and will quote all sorts of examples to prove it.

Compare this with what happens when there is discussion about the *quality* of the media. Corner a media man and ask in a friendly way why there is not more intellectually uplifting or inspirational content, and he may well agree and say that he wishes there were more opportunities to be creative in his work. (If you ask the same question in an unfriendly or challenging way he will unload a whole lot of prejudicial remarks about cultural snobbery versus what ordinary people want etc etc.)

So why is the content not better? Because you have to put on what people want to watch. How strange: a short while ago we were told it was TV that determined what people wanted to watch, now we are told it is enslaved by what people want to watch.

The "ratings" are quoted. These ratings are based upon detectors in certain television sets which record what channel the set is switched to and what times it is on and off. If many sets are on during a panel game, that game gets a high rating and it is calculated that many people are watching the game. This is based on the idea that people turn on the TV to watch what they want. But I am pretty sure this is a fallacy, perhaps reflecting the educated upbringing of those devising the system. For a majority of the population actually leave their sets on as background noise while they walk about. Only when something fascinating is on the screen do they stop before the set and study the image. Having thus begun to interact they are more likely to continue by exploring other channels at the next commercial break or dull moment.

So, if we consider program material in Darwinian terms, the program that wants to survive should camouflage itself by being so dull and bland that nobody notices it as they walk past, because that is the program that will be left on. That is why pappy "game shows" feature so high on the ratings: they are the ones which foster the safe environment of a TV set left playing to an empty or inattentive room (and so earn a point on the ratings). Whereas a thought provoking drama risks its life by being noticed and so bringing critical human attention to the screen, and the remote control box.

I detect a group phantasy. Without an omnipotent God to believe in, we have invented the idea of omnipotent media. And the problem of evil has immediately infected the new body. We have to believe that TV is, of course, powerful enough to shape totally mankind's tastes and prejudices, but that it chooses meekly to bow before them, however bad they are, because TV believes in our freedom. For the typical media eunuch it must be very reassuring to hold that belief and the corresponding faith in one's own power!

So, to expect the media to present earth-shattering views that would enlighten mankind is no more realistic than to expect God to appear in person and banish war from earth.

You cannot broadcast a program that challenges assumptions, but you can write a book that does so.

WRITING

While fuming about the stupidity of the media and all who work for them, the next step in crank's progress is to write the book that no-one wants to publish.

When publishers are forced to address writers - in articles, on the radio or at literary functions - they know they face a hostile audience. So when they touch on the unpopular subject of unsolicited manuscripts they need to raise a sympathetic laugh by referring to the extreme crankiness of some of those manuscripts: "flat earth theorists, unspeakable unpunctuated existential auto-hagiographies... why we even had last week a quarter of a million tiresome words presented in illegible pencil writing on what appeared to be lavatory roll" and so on and so forth.

Everyone present laughs with relief to imagine that there are authors out there worse than themselves, and what a relief it will be for the publisher to receive their own tidily word-processed efforts instead. Poor suckers. I can't think why scientists persist in searching outer space for black holes when they could direct their radio telescopes into publishers' offices instead. And, if you wonder who it is that sends all the manuscripts that drive those publishers to crack feeble jokes, the answer is that it is me... and my fellow cranks.

Here is one source of bitterness: I am angry at this attitude toward the third-rate writer (assuming that it is first and second rate writers who get published). People who would not think of sneering at mongol children or spastics feel free to mock the third rate writer and his progeny: that even publishers should do this merely illustrates how far they have distanced themselves from the source of their material.

When my wife became pregnant and had our baby we went through the usual discussion as to whether a man could possibly know what it was like to give birth. I felt that my nearest experience was in writing: where the conception of a book was sheer bliss but it lead to an increasing sense of heaviness as the idea swelled and took form in my mind, a sense of urgency and need to express the book and considerable pain in realising it. Then my attitude to the written result was so like that to a child: a mixture of love and anger when it did not conform to my wishes. One can despise one's own work and mock one's "little horrors", until someone else rejects it - then all the protective instincts of a parent blaze into view.

Yes, it is a labour to write a book, and yet only those who write good books get credit for that labour. The assumption seems to be that it is easy to write bad books, a sort of bad habit one should try to overcome. On the contrary, it is not only just as difficult to write a bad book but positive agony - because you have no cheers, no publishers' advances or critical acknowledgments to give you courage when the going gets tough. A Booker prize for the most lamentable book of the year might turn the tables, yet at the same time defeat the object by creating a new non-focus on ignorably mediocre work.

It is progress that society recognises handicapped people and begins to cater for their needs - I know some circles where the birth of a non-handicapped child is almost cause for guilt - but what relief is in sight for authors and their handicapped books? Anyone who has ever spent a few hours in a large bookshop and asked themselves "is my writing really an order of magnitude worse than everything in this shop?" will know that I am not joking. Some are lucky enough to have but one awful book in them, myself I can feel like a tired old woman who has been raped again and again by brutal ideas and have wasted the best years of my life struggling to sustain a litter of unwanted children.

So is it time for a new voice in publishing?

PUBLISHING

The next step after writing the book that no-one will publish is to publish the book that no-one will review or buy. A certain sympathy for publishers is thereby gained.

The physical activity of making a book can be quite nice, if tedious in detail. But when it comes to selling it you have to battle with that urge which feels such utter love for anyone who shows the least interest in your offering that you cannot bear to ask them to pay money for it. Or, at best, you splutter something about "cost price" and accept a few coins.

It is a strange thing that casual acquaintances seem to consider it a politeness to demand a complimentary copy if they discover that you have published a book. You know they won't like it, and try to back out, but that only seems to fire their curiosity.

As a book salesman, the nicest discovery is to find that bookshop staff do not frog-march you out by the scruff of the neck and demand in a loud voice before others present why you are wasting their time with such a pathetic and unsaleable item. The vast majority are really quite friendly and quite prepared to give you a chance, on sale or return. So you love them so much that, when you creep back in disguise months later and find none are sold, you feel guilty about having betrayed their confidence in you and far too ashamed ever to take the books back or ever follow up the sale by asking for money.

I recall visiting a big London bookshop and feeling almost drunk with joy to find my books had at last gone from the shelf. I sat down by the ornamental pool that the shop featured in order to savour my bliss - an attractive pool only spoilt by the litter that floated in it. Then I saw that the litter was my books.

I once decided to write up my publishing experience for the second edition of the amusing "Book of Heroic Failures"... but then compounded my failure by doing nothing about it.

When little magazines promise to review your book (more free copies go out) it is another endearing thing. Yet somehow the burden of giving even verbal support to your monstrous offering proves too much: the next issue is delayed for months or the magazine closes down under the strain... and you feel even guiltier. Having been so seldom reviewed I have at least avoided one depressing experience:

the very enthusiastic reviewer who seems to completely miss the point of one's book.

The biggest lesson from reviews is to discover that a good review does not generate a torrent of orders. I still don't know why. Nor does an advertisement. (In fact nothing generates a torrent of orders.) When advertising, beware of prior calculations: "this magazine has a circulation of 500,000, so if I can interest just *one percent* of the readers in my book I should sell... wow!" So you revise your calculation to one tenth of a percent - trying to imagine yourself as a tenth of a percent of a reader and re-reading your advertisement to see if it sounds compulsive - and you calculate that you will still have covered the cost of the advert. My only advert produced one response - a request for a free copy for some institutional library.

More satisfying is to give a talk and have copies for sale at the end. The pile does seem to shrink before your eyes and it is quite pleasing - as long as you resisted prior calculations about the number of seats in the hall and the percentage that might want to buy...

"Publish and be damned" holds no meaning for us cranks, for we are well and truly damned by birthright.

THE PERSONAL TOUCH

Hold onto your seats: the ride gets worse.

By now the crank has every reason to suspect a worldwide conspiracy trying to suppress their ideas. In fact the evidence of a blanket CIA cover up is so overwhelmingly good that only a crank would attempt to deny it (that is why I will proceed to do so in the next section). So the next step is to make a personal approach.

There may be certain more or less eminent names who inspired your early ideas. It was perhaps never your plan to trouble these gurus by sending them copies of your work - you may have assumed that publication would launch you into the same olympian league and that you would one day meet on an equal basis. But, in the face of a worldwide conspiracy, what can you do but go over the heads of the CIA and write direct to the opinion formers. So you draft and redraft a polite, self deprecating letter and enclose a copy of your book - trying to tell yourself all the while not to expect too much this time.

The pain of rejection by the general public is small compare to the pain of rejection by your specialist public, and that pain is in turn as nothing to the pain of rejection by an individual whose very thought processes and viewpoint seemed have so much in common with your own, whose very ideas had fanned the flame of your own inspiration. Whether it's complete lack of response, or a polite note that says nothing, it is possible to feel very hurt and very angry with those one used to respect.

THE POISONED CUP

I have recounted crank's progress at length because I wanted to elicit sympathy for the subject - not the sympathy of "feeling sorry for" so much as the sympathy of understanding. If cranks can seem a prickly bunch it is as well to know what we have gone through to earn our spines.

I have suffered much of what has been here described, and so a certain bitterness on my part is neither unexpected nor, in my opinion, reason for further shame. For I do not feel that I have presented the reader in my writings with a cup of bile, but rather with a glass of dry vermouth - in which a taste of bitterness adds zest and intrigue.

There is a child in my heart that feels the full pain of what I describe and allows me to express it in words. But that child is only a tiny part of the whole family that is me. Other members of that family are mature and supportive adults that can understand the child enough to allow it to speak, without being taken in by its lamentations.

It is these more adult voices that have helped to ease the pain. As already mentioned, they taught me detachment. If I had held onto my ideas as if they were unique to me, and if I had somehow assumed that I was therefore a genius and the world owed me the favour of recognition, then that child would be now be an overweening monster. I would indeed feel bitter, and I recognise in some cranks that this has happened: their inspiration becomes a burden that drags them, lonely, under.

When you have a good idea it can be interesting not to express it, but rather to keep silent and listen for someone else to say it first. Whether, as I have suggested, we are like radio sets and the ideas of the age are there for whoever is attuned, or whether the idea is really one's own but the frustration of suppressing it somehow injects it into the group mind or morphic field, I do not know. But it does help detachment and lessen pride.

As mentioned already, it is very tempting indeed to see a conspiracy of silence. Those totally attached will begin to assume a personal vendetta against themselves, those detached from their ideas will tend to see an establishment wish to repress the ideas rather than the person. Is it the CIA? Is it the public school network? Is it a male conspiracy? The establishment or our Christian culture?

A bitter crank will talk about this in a way that suggests belief in an active conspiracy: somewhere there is a sort of War Room with a big map and people sitting up all night intercepting the post to see where his manuscript is being sent so that they can nobble the publisher first to make sure the manuscript is once more rejected. But we don't really believe that, most of us. We rather believe that there is some principle like "prejudice" that is ingrained into our society and which opposes any idea that could threaten the status quo. Its manifestations can be quite subtle, so a publisher feels uneasy about the work yet actually believes that he has rejected it for some other more businesslike reason.

When is a conspiracy not a conspiracy? I think many of us use the idea of a conspiracy because that is how it feels, even though we would never argue for an actual conscious conspiracy against us. Just as many people are happy to use phrases like "the spirit of the moment" when they would never defend the existence of spirits in argument. If you understand what a crank suffers you will understand the way we talk, and not need to add paranoia to your list of reasons to mock us.

Where some might see conspiracy I see examples of something I described in Words Made Flesh: the artificial intelligence of a group mind. Because I am open to the idea of animism I see no reason why an information processing system should not generate a soul or intelligence and why, if it is sufficiently complex, it should not eventually have some rudimentary self awareness. Any group - whether bound by philosophy, corporation, religion, nationhood, fraternity or whatever - processes information and so has an intelligence or "group mind" in these terms. To me that explains how, for example, a government could be made up of many well-meaning individuals and yet itself be a totally parasitic and malevolent entity. It also explains why it is so easy to see conspiracy where it does not really exist.

Our society is a body with a mind, and like any other organism, it seeks to preserve itself. In these terms a new and revolutionary idea - ie one that is likely to change the nature of society - would be seen as a virus in that body. The same applies to organisms within society - such as the scientific establishment, the medical profession and so on. Even though one might argue that the long term effect of the virus would be to re-program the DNA to create a better mutation, as far as the body is concerned it is a dis-ease that must be defended against. Just as in our physical bodies, the anti-body mechanisms for this are very pervasive and very subtle: it is not just prejudice but also a host of commercial, practical, psychological and aesthetic factors that "conspire" to keep cranks' ideas at bay. You can analyse these individual factors one by one, but they only make sense when seen as a complete package of hygienic measures by which an establishment preserves itself.

For example: the fear that one might be seen as a crank. If a crank is at all aware, they know how they might seem to others. So, when writing to publishers, magazines or gurus we tend to include self apologetic letters which say in so many words "look, I know you must think me just another crank, but..." Such letters often deprecate the work enclosed as if to say "you may not like what I've sent, but as long as you know I don't like it either you might still, please, like me". Then, because the whole thing has become so long, there is the covering covering letter which says "you probably won't have time to read all the enclosed, but..."

However well-meaning, such letters have a way of defeating the original object - why? In one case the recipient might be fully hard boiled and, recognising the trademark of a crank, simply decide to read no more. Secondly a more sensitive recipient will feel embarrassed, a sense of pain in which perhaps is recognition of their own faltering past. One way to avoid that pain lies in the waste bin... A more aware recipient might recognise the pain for what it is and yet still be wary: because they understand the bitterness of the crank's progress I have described and they know that whoever first breaks that run of rejection faces a difficult task of atoning for all the hurt that has gone before. When, for example, the manuscript is accepted and a few editing revisions are suggested he may well have to face refusal and a tirade that "you are just the same as all the others..."

So certain of the antibodies are carried in the crank's own psyche. As a sub-organism you could say that the Crank Group Mind is also preserving itself by making sure that cranks remain cranks. But don't forget the painful fact that the very publisher or media person most likely to sympathise is the one most likely to have been cranks themselves, and so be full of fear and other issues on the subject.

That is what buggers the personal approach to sympathetic minds in my opinion. If you have a revolutionary new political theory and you go to a revolutionary meeting to find people to expound it to, then there is a snag. Most of the other people will be there with their own revolutionary theories looking for people to expound them to. It does not necessarily mean they won't listen, but when they do listen they are looking for something in particular: a hook to attach their own ideas to. You will be flattered to see close, absorbent attention until you mention some trifling economic example in passing, then they will jump in with "that's amazing because it fits in with something that I've been thinking..." and you are off, with a sense that your idea has not quite been understood. No, the really fertile ground for a crank is someone with no ideas of their own who will begin by admiring your own creativity - but how do you meet the right ones at the right time, when it is so easy to see them as embodiments of all you are rebelling against?

Saddest of all is the approach to the guru. He may seem to you to be an establishment figure by now, with top billing at the conference and a table full of smartly published books in the foyer, but in his own eyes he is still feeling rejected because last weeks lead article in Nature ignored his ideas entirely and only made an ironic reference in a footnote. The very reason you feel so akin to the guru is because he is ahead of his time, but that is the very quality that makes him too feel that he is struggling to be heard and has not really got the energy to listen to others - especially when they seem to be trying to piggyback their ideas onto his own pure thesis. Thus the guru more or less politely deflects your advances... and the crank feels the rejection and disillusionment.

Just as publishing the unsaleable book can generate a grudging understanding of the awfulness of publishers who ignore manuscripts, so the first glimmerings of public response to what you have published can help one to understand the stand-offish guru. For among the really heart-warming letters from those whose lives have been enriched by your inspiration, there will be letters which suggest that your message has gone badly astray. Sometimes a lot of thought is required to penetrate a sympathetic letter to see which camp it belongs to. And then comes the growing realisation that you don't even know what to do about the really good letters - except keep on writing your ideas. In a state of weariness you are no longer satisfied with those who simply rejoice in the ideas you express, you begin to yearn for a champion who will take them up and do something with ideas that you yourself never seemed to do justice to.

In fact one has progressed to being the mother of grown up children that now need to be married off.

IS THE BOOK DEAD?

As a publisher I feel permitted to say that publishing is in a bad way. My own theory is that the industry has declined as it lost its marketing know-how.

I like that theory, because most people would rather argue that it is the injection of big business marketing methods into publishing that has done the damage. In response I would say that, if marketing means striped shirts, business diplomas and fizzing about on car 'phones, then publishing has indeed suffered from marketing. But if marketing is the art and science of understanding, meeting and modifying your customers' requirements, then there has been a severe haemorrhage of marketing skills from the book industry since the fifties.

In the fifties the most interesting shop in any High Street was the junk shop, with the book shop a strong second contender. Now the dullest shop window in the High Street is the Building Society, with the bookshop a close contender. The reason is that publishing and bookselling used to be dominated by enthusiastic amateurs (in the sense of "lovers") and so everyone in the trade was a marketing expert because they were as much bibliophiles as their customers. Booksellers knew that the sexiest sight in the world for a bibliophile was a shelf crammed with book spines, rich with choice. Modern bookshops now turn the books flat on in the window so the whole cover is seen: not only does a modern bookshop window contain very few books as a result, it may well have a whole window full of just one book, probably a novel by Mr Archer, and the effect is as unexciting as a Building Society display. Inside the shop there are bright lights and big displays in colour - techniques imported from other areas of retailing where they may have been appropriate - but gone are the creaky floorboards, high cramped shelves and shadowy corners that are sheer magic to the book lover who would rather hunt his prey in dark and mysterious second hand bookshops.

I am suggesting that the trade has forgotten how to sell books. The reply must be to quote figures that (presumably) more books are now being sold. Then I quibble that it is not *books* that are being sold, but pictures or images. We are witnessing a reversal of fortunes in an ancient battle within our own brains.

Apparently the right lobe of the brain thinks wholistically in the sense of seeing things in an immediate three-dimensional connected fashion, whereas the left lobe prefers to process information in a linear sequence as in language. The advent of printing and formal education has so encouraged the latter, verbal approach that the right brain style of communication has taken second place over recent centuries. But, now that realistic colour pictures are becoming as easy to propagate as words, the right brain is fighting back and it is the Word that is being defeated now. Yes, people do walk out of shops carrying books, but they are less likely to read the words now because they bought them on account of the colour pictures on the cover - that is why the pictures were displayed in that way. The ideal bestseller can be something - like the Brief History of Time - that is seldom read, because it is the image or the overall non-verbal concept that is bought, not the words it contains.

The author becomes a part of that image. Television is notoriously bad at conveying ideas, and programmers have more or less given up trying to do so. But it is very good at conveying personality and this is the main focus of all TV reporting. So, for example, a program on chaos theory will focus largely on the characters researching it. This same approach is now informing all the arts: so the best selling book on chaos theory is also written more like a novel with heroic characters. Magazines, even literary ones, no longer feature the titles of their articles on the cover, but rather the names of the contributors.

This is an underlying bitter fact for today's crank: though I am not sure if it is just a fleeting fashion, the fact is that ideas no longer are offered for sale, only people. And those who judge your work for publication will not be reading its content but rather seeing if you yourself are a sellable character. It may not have happened yet, but we may find the entrance qualification for a creative writing degree is no longer academic or literary skill so much as sporting ability. If you are a sports star any lack of writing skill can be cheaply made up by a ghost writer. But if you are a brilliant creative writer no amount of expensive grooming will make up for lack of star quality - and you will end up ghost writing. This can earn a comfortable income, but it does not satisfy the full urge to express ones own ideas.

CONCLUSION

Does this essay seem a very self-indulgent exercise? I don't know why it should, because I do not feel greatly healed by writing it, simply because I did not feel too bad before I started.

Although I have dwelt on the sorrows that justify a crank's bitterness, that is not all there is to it. Expressing ideas as a hobby is less expensive than many other hobbies - even if you pay your own publishing. Although it is possible to feel guilty in a world already overcrowded to be bringing in further books and further thoughts (while those who take up hunting and shooting are at least doing something to reduce the surplus of existence), the fact is that the urge to create is no light matter.

My own sorrows largely healed when one day I realised that I was an "underground" publisher: a perspective that transmuted failure into style. No longer expecting to make money, no longer chasing but rather flirtatiously shunning recognition. Recalling a lovely spirit in the sixties whereby the seeker would make a deliberate virtue of obscurity - whether it was finding the most esoteric records imported from the US, or the most weird and unknown magazine, book or cafe.

Myself addicted to shopping, I appreciate how much this activity has its roots in the primal hunting instinct. The thrill of the chase in the January sales, the tingle of excitement at sensing a bargain, the need to suppress excitement and appear merely curious when asking the price from an antiques dealer - sensing that the least tremor or change of vocal pitch might alert the prey to leap into an unobtainable price bracket. All these are instincts which add value to the information or object which is most hard to come by, and they are the drivers of the commercial principle of overcharging for an exclusive niche. An economy of resources - the less is delivered the greater the profit. Compare that with the growing economy of distribution - typified by items such as the telephone or fax machine which only have value insofar as everyone else has one too. When distribution and dissemination sets the agenda commerce wants everyone to buy at once. A film is seen because everyone else is seeing it, a book is bought as a token of admittance to an in-touch society. And don't try to buy it next year.

A bit of a diversion, but the page layout looked a bit empty on my screen so I padded it out with extra words. Sufficeth to say that, in this spoonfed age, The Mouse That Spins still caters for those intrepid explorers who delight in finding byways of thought. People who want a book more when they find it is hard to obtain: if you knew what efforts I took to preserve low standards of distribution efficiency on your behalf...

This essay is not healing so much as a gift to my past: for anyone who is suffering what I have suffered and who wonders where it all leads. You are not alone, alas.

ON SLAPPING A LOVER -
GUILTY RATIONALISATION?

I am about to argue that men are innately more sensitive to other people's feelings than women are.

I enjoy arguing daft things, the opposite of what everyone knows is true. For me it is eternal confirmation of my belief that all dualities are based on deception and contain their own antithesis - a point I expand fully in my forthcoming book on trinitarian thinking (The Good, The Bad, and The Funny).

I am also re-discovering the pleasures of discussing sexual differences. This is such an easy topic of conversation, like the weather, because it is so universal. But I used to find it very dull. There is much that I adore about feminism - anything that puts the wind up tiresome old farts who prattle on about "traditional values" just has to be good - but in retrospect we may well recognise that its greatest achievement has been to restore the fun of sexism by demonising it. As explained in my first essay on devil worship (number 10 in this volume), ideas need to be driven out, repressed or banished from our culture from time to time so they can rediscover their wild roots in the jungle of the unconscious mind and return as awesome new discoveries, bristling with demonic power. I am already beginning to enjoy the first frissons of naughtiness as I prepare to discuss sexual differences.

Some people find generalisations repulsive - they are the people who do not know how to handle or use generalisations. If I use the idea that Anglo-Saxons are snobbish, and someone else rejects it as "racial prejudice", it probably means that the second person does not know how to take generalisations, because he does not know how to leave them.

So, having argued for my right to be utterly general and utterly daft, I get to the serious bit. I do know how sexual differences have served to enslave, to create shame and reduce self-worth in young people, but I am also interested in their corresponding homeopathic potential to heal the very same problems.

The notion that real women have big tits has caused a lot of pain among flat chested women. But imagine a society that had outlawed that sexist notion to the point that it was no longer acknowledged that there was any tit-based distinction: where any suggestion that men have smaller tits than women was countered by a comparison between Twiggy and Arnold Schwarzenegger. In such a society there would be a lot of screwed-up young men wondering why their breasts were so small, and to them the idea that women have naturally bigger tits would be positive liberation. It is pure generalisation, but to those young men it would be more like the key to get out of the prison than the prison itself - an example of the same fundamental notion being able to heal just as much as it can hurt.

Somewhere I wrote about one sexual distinction that is often used to batter men: the idea that men are all "left brain" desiccated thinkers. I noted that left brain predominance was actually a female characteristic according to scientists, and this explained why adolescent males tended to be short on language skills compared with females, whereas they did better at engineering, sport and other spatial, right brain skills.

To me this was a liberating idea because so much is said about men "not expressing their feelings", when all it means is that men do not talk about their feelings as women tend to. The man who goes purple-faced, slams the door and stalks off to the potting shed is expressing anger, but he is expressing it in body language and action, rather than through left brain verbalisation, and that should be recognised and welcomed for what it is - rather than kid yourself that it is a form of repression because he has not put the feelings into words.

I also suggested that the reason women often fume at men's imagined left brain dominance is because they are witnessing comparatively clumsy attempts to compensate. Not being such innate verbalisers as women, men have tended to develop supporting techniques like formal logic, mathematics and poetry to help them put their intuitions into verbal form. At best this hard work reaches dazzling heights - surpassing the easy natural words of women - but at a lower level it results in that male academicism and committee-mindedness that can drive women crazy. In the same way, because women are less developed in right brain movement skills, they work harder at them. Men may laugh at the idea of deportment training or ballet lessons, but think of "nice movers" and it is mostly the women that come to mind. What comes naturally is not always what gets the prizes.

That idea of male right-brain supremacy was liberating to me because it meant that I felt less shame at New Age workshops where I was supposed to become brilliant at "expressing feelings" by talking about them the way women do: without reducing the value of that interesting exercise, I can now live easier with my limitations within it.

Now, one proposed explanation for the left/right brain sexual difference I heard was that millions of years of evolution have tended to encourage men to go out hunting or fighting where spatial right brain skills are more useful, because they help you remember your way in the jungle - and dance was originally training for hand to hand combat. Meanwhile women tended families, where verbal skills are more useful for communication. So the more successful members of the respective sexes would have a mating advantage and would thus tend to reinforce their bias in later generations.

That made me wonder what other characteristics might have been encouraged by selective breeding at this sort of level. Cue for return to my opening sentence.

Imagine the skills most needed by warriors and hunters. Greater strength for fighting and more prominent muscles to terrify the opposition? These are recognised as male characteristics, as are narrower hips more suited to fast running. Right brain spatial and movement skills have already been mentioned. Then surely two more things are needed: intense sensitivity to others' emotions, coupled with the ability to hide one's own.

Whether your opposition is a hunted beast, or a warrior from another tribe, once you show fear you are dead meat. The ability to be cool and menacing in the face of fear is vital, just as it is necessary to hide over-confidence, rage, envy, shame or any other emotion that could give your opponent vital information about your weak points in combat. On the other hand, you need intense sensitivity to pick up these very feelings in the other person, even through the thickest emotional armour. Men with these two characteristics would do better in battle as well as in hunting, and as long as there was some genetic or unconscious learning mechanism to pass this on, these characteristics would tend to predominate in modern males just as much (and just as little) as greater physical strength.

True, sensitivity to others' emotions is not altogether useless to the women back in the cave with her family, but the point is that it is better served in those circumstances by being able to ask about the others' feelings: there is less need of the immediate perception which is a life or death matter to the warrior. In a cramped, tribal domestic situation the warrior's sensitivity to feelings is out of place: the sheer emotional noise would drive him crazy.

Bringing this idea back into my real world - like a wild beast hunted and brought home from the jungle of speculation - I think I can live with it. When strong feelings surge in me, they often are hidden from others. Partners have accused me of hiding my feelings and I now can see that perhaps I did so, but was unaware because it was an automatic reaction - the difference is that I can now forgive myself. Again, my female partner can claim that it is a very good thing if she expresses her feelings, because she does not fully realise how devastatingly her feelings hit me. She does not realise because the warrior in me has been hard-wired not to betray my wounds.

To be more specific. Let's say I have fallen in love with a woman and have been going out for a while when one day I meet her when she is very angry - maybe at something I have done or maybe not. With my acute sensitivity she does not have to tell me she is angry: the atmosphere hits me like a tornado and alarm bells, flashing red lights and sirens are immediately triggered in my brain.

Faced with such anger, millions of years of male warrior conditioning prepare my body for only two actions: fight or flight. My instincts see only two solutions: kill the angry person or run away before the anger hits me. The alarm bells are screaming because it has to be a fast decision or I am dead. Against that my reason tells me that this is my girlfriend and that I must behave like a gentleman. But it is very hard to think straight with those sirens blaring, and so I act a bit wooden and am not altogether "there". This irritates my partner and she gets angrier, or redirects some of her rage at me.

She wouldn't do that if she knew how much I already felt it, but actually she thinks I must be insensitive to her anger. Why? because my automatic system has also shut down on the sheer life-or-death terror I am feeling: it has been trained not to betray such emotions in the face of something as dangerous as anger in another - betray fear and the advantage is lost. So I find myself freezing up, become more and more robot-like and out of touch, while my desperate girl friend steps up the emotional pressure in an attempt to get some "real" reaction from me - thereby triggering the very mechanism that forbids any reaction save fight or flight, neither of which my conscious mind will allow as long as it still has some control over the situation.

In the end my girlfriend explodes with anger and soon feels fine because she has thereby worked it off. But I can remain hurt for days, without a single physical blow to my body, because of the huge adrenaline shock I have received but have been unable to work off, on account of modern society's rejection of the flight or fight response built into my male body.

Now it has been possible for many years to blame all such things on the "patriarchal society" and the glorification of warriorhood. According to my model, no-one can pass on the blame in this way. Certain emotional characteristics gave certain males an advantage in dangerous situations, certain women responded to their triumph and between them they helped breed those differences into the population. Needs have changed indeed, but we are talking about millions of years of gentle pressure to be one way, as against centuries of conscious realisation that our ingrained reactions are no longer so useful in everyday life. Cultural conditioning over-rules these deep patterns 99% of the time - leaving us quite unprepared for the odd circumstances when the deeper patterns are triggered.

When my girlfriend is angry I can sense it even before she knows it herself. That puts up my guard. She then feels her anger and expresses it in a way that is utterly appropriate to a cave full of screaming children, bubbling cooking pots, crackling fires and quibbling elders - ie loudly, clearly and verbally. But such expression is utterly inappropriate to the warrior in me, used to situations where the slightest contraction of a pupil could betray murderous intent. Her anger hits me with the force of a charging tyrannosaurus and my body only wants one decision - whether to fight or run away - while my brain is still trying to be polite and sensible. Instead of giving in to her invitation to "discuss it rationally" - a process that invariably leads me to gibbering incoherence - something in me calculates with near-psychopathic coolness just how hard I have to slap her in order to drive her out of my presence without really hurting her. Unfortunately she interprets this action as a final breakdown of control on my part, and feels thoroughly scared. Whereas to me it feels that I have actually regained control - which I would certainly not have achieved by talking.

Have I made myself clear? If so, it is time to draw down the veils on this little play in order to make it less clear and return us to real life. I have spoken as if millions of years of evolution have fitted men for warriorhood and women for domesticity, whereas no man could spend all his hours hunting and no woman need be chained to the hearth. We are indeed complex beings with many sides, and that hunter warrior is just one small voice among many others in me, just as the mother is just one voice in the woman. Although such a small and outdated voice, the warrior did once have to handle the most urgent life and death decisions, so it is hard-wired into very deep layers of my being. I can go for years without even knowing of its existence, yet when it senses danger it takes control of bodily processes. It does not control my mind, but its double effect of simultaneously generating and suppressing terror can leave my mind isolated, and modern women perplexed by my paralysis.

If the cave woman could just give the warrior a hug and a kiss, two twentieth century human beings might be freed to love each other the way they feel is right.

I also suspect that this is the reason why bourgeois men can be totally caught out by violent criminals: faced with sudden threat the warrior retaliation urge can paralyse in just the way I have described. After the event they feel guilty at their inaction, puzzled and ashamed. The anger remains when the outlet has passed. "If only I had been prepared" they say, for the warrior knew what to do - it just never got permission to do it.

Many men are too sensitive to others' feelings for today's crowded world, and no-one realises this is so because the very same sensitivity conceals the evidence. Unable to muster the immediate verbal skills to explain this face to face, I had to put it down slowly and carefully in writing.

Sorry I slapped you, honey.

And sorry you had to work so hard to make it happen!

19

THE WILD AND THE TAME

The wild and the tame is a polarity that can become highly charged in our minds. It provided a theme for many films in the fifties and sixties - Breakfast at Tiffany's, And God Created Woman are two that spring to mind.

In my forthcoming book about trinities (The Good, The Bad, And The Funny) I show that there is a basic lie or paradox behind all such extreme dualities.

Take this one, for example, and ask yourself what the term "wild sex" brings to mind. To many people the orgy is the epitome of wild sex: shameless naked fucking in a crowd. But think about it from a different angle and this looks like very tame sex.

Perhaps the word "tame" is misleading, because we are still in the wild/tame polarity. Let me rephrase and say that an orgy is surely a demonstration of a highly domesticated sexual drive: one capable of performing to order, at the right time and in a crowd.

The idea that wild creatures are relentlessly fierce is a delusion of the city dweller. It is more typical of wild creatures to run away from humans than to savage them. The desire to have sex furtively or in the dark is often put forward as a symptom of civilised delicacy of taste, while it is basically an animal instinct not to put yourself into a vulnerable position under risk of attack.

Perhaps it is the behaviour of dogs that leads to this misunderstanding. People see dogs copulating openly and believe that the dogs are demonstrating a "wild animal" nature, whereas it is the sheer domesticity of a dog that allows this. The dog feels safe because we are part of its pack, it does not think it is in the wild. While the dog is a domestic animal, the tiger is less likely to copulate before humans because it instinctively feels the risk of attack. The idea that an open orgy is "wild" seems crazy when you realise the problem of breeding wild animals in captivity is that they can be so wary about fucking unless left very much on their own.

I hope I have made my point. There is a logical flaw in the idea that wild sex is abandoned and shameless: the truth is that really wild sex is very furtive and unpredictable. All the same, I don't really agree with myself, because I know that there is a sense in which an orgy is wild compared with furtive sex.

My decision is this: domesticity is where we live, the here and now, the present. Outside domesticity there is not one but two jungles: there is the jungle of the past, the animal origins that I have been considering; but there is also the jungle of the future. So the term "wild" can describe behaviour from the mysterious darkness of the future just as much as it can describe the behaviour of our animal ancestors.

When we are timid and furtive about sex in public, there is a tendency to glorify our weakness by ascribing it to a civilised "sense of decency", whereas I have suggested it is more a testament to our animal origins. Someone who is capable of getting, and using, an erection before a cheering crowd is therefore demonstrating a human achievement, a triumph over animalism more than a slide back into it: such a person has tamed his sexual nature to do his bidding on command. Those of us who feel shock at such skill are justified, however, because we are indeed witnessing a "wild" beast from the jungle - but from the jungle of future human evolution rather than from our animal past.

In Thundersqueak it was argued that humanity is evolving from introversion towards extroversion. The highly alert, solitary introvert is at an advantage in the jungle of the past because he can sit for hours without moving and without boredom: an essential skill for hunting and for avoiding being hunted. Such a person would find the noise and whirl of city life intolerable. Introverts suffer easily from sensory overload.

According to unsurprising studies quoted by Eysenck or someone, extroverts tend to have sex earlier and more often than introverts. That would support a genetic evolution towards greater extroversion. If, on the other hand, environmental factors are more important than genetics in this matter, then increasing urbanisation would equally encourage increasing extroversion because extroverts thrive on sensory overload. What is more, the tendency to induce births during daytime for the convenience of nursing staff in hospitals means that more people nowadays are born with the sun above the horizon in their horoscopes (whereas the natural peak hour used to be around 3 am) and that is one minor indicator of extroversion that would be encouraged by modern hospital practice.

The point is that I have not destroyed the duality between the tame and the wild, the human and the animal, but elaborated it. There are two types of animal: one from the jungle of our past, the other from the jungle of our future. One is what we have evolved out of, the other is what we will evolve into.

Meanwhile we are now humans living in domesticity between these two jungles. But we are possibly in greater awe of the beast from the future - the "party animal" - and we are more inclined to abuse or blame the beast from the past when we are faced with subhuman or superhuman behaviour.

STREET WHYS

Another recent news story has touched a deep nerve in me: it is the story of a little toddler who lost his mother in a shopping centre and was lead away by two older boys who eventually battered him to death and left his corpse on a railway line.

I can analyse my pain at two levels. On the one hand it seems a very local issue: after all, there are atrocities far worse than this being performed daily all over the world, whole villages are being wiped out. On the other hand there is something about the little boy's face, and the surveillance camera picture shown on the news (of him being lead away between two bigger boys), that touches me very deeply and personally.

It was that second picture that did it. As soon as I saw it I felt a jolt. On consideration I believe it was a jolt of recognition.

Mothers can be angry, they can be stern, and yet for most people in their infancy there is some sense of love or security behind it all. But the first time a toddler is removed from that safety and finds itself in the company of other children, and the first time those children decide to lead him or her away and "teach a lesson", then an awful truth is revealed that the world is no longer on the toddler's side.

I assume this must be a very common experience. Maybe some children never enjoy any initial security, and maybe others never have even a taste of being bullied - but surely these are a minority? I can remember at least once being lured away, of feeling a knot of apprehension in my belly because of the older child's manner toward me, and then being "taught a lesson" at a safe distance so my cries would not be heard. I can also remember not daring to "tell" for fear of further reprisals, and so having to carry my poisonous grief all alone.

So seeing that picture I at once identified with the toddler, the old wounds in me opened and wept in sympathy. It is true that my beatings-up were as nothing compared to what happened to him, but the object is not to make comparisons: the discussion is about an absolute and not about relativity.

Whether it is one hard kick, or whether it is being battered to death, in each case a young soul has had its babyhood vision of a benign world shattered - and that is an absolute experience. A wound is left in the soul quite independent of the magnitude of the wounds left in the body. This incident has attracted a lot of public sympathy, so there are surely many others who feel the way I do.

But the media keep asking "why" this happened, as if the discovery of a reason could heal the fact. Of course it can help on the personal level - if the individual feels that there is a reason for his suffering, it can help ease the pain - but on a social level it is a bit of a cop-out to try to find a reason to serve as a dustbin bag to carry away life's problems.

I can recall at a later age - perhaps I was eight or nine - devising with a playground friend a machine that would "mince up piccaninnies". God, what a terrible confession! How fortunate that the chance to put this scheme into practice did not suddenly present itself, for we two might have become the monsters that the public love to hate.

I recall my gleefully demonic state of mind. It had nothing to do with racism: the objection to piccaninnies was not their colour, which had no significance to me then, but the fact that they were "sweet". The phrase "dear lil' piccaninnies" made me feel sick and I wanted to mash them up.

Why such vehemence against sweetness? Here I am forty years later almost weeping at the thought of innocent sweetness, yet recalling a childhood moment of rage against it.

I identify with the little boy who was beaten up because I too was once as sweet and innocent as he *appears* in his photo, and because I too have been lead away to nightmares of my own. The greatest rage anyone can feel is rage against oneself - nothing else is sufficiently intimate to inspire such rage. So my plan to grind up piccaninnies was most likely a plan to grind up my own sweetness. No longer a toddler, I now thought babies were wet and stupid; I was aspiring to be a "boy" which meant proving that I was no longer sweet, to the point of killing the memory of my own sweetness.

In a similar fashion I recall as a teenager feeling moments of disgust at "boys" with their stupid play-tough ways. Again, I have heard many grown-ups rant and rage about the behaviour of "yobs", saying such give-away things as "of course we were tearaways in our time, but there was a totally different feel to it. It was just a game then, whereas yobs nowadays are just vicious animals".

Back in 1968 I wrote my educational dissertation on the theme that our civilisation lacked a programme of initiation for the young, and suggested that there should be formal rituals to initiate each child at the ages of seven (into boy or girl hood), fourteen (into teenhood) and twenty one (into adult hood). A ceremonial marking of these rites of passage might, I suggested, help to clarify the roles and responsibilities at each stage. It might thereby become less necessary for boys to bash at sweetness, for teenagers to be so extreme in defining themselves, and adults might also feel less threatened by their teenage past.

Would I really have gone ahead with my wicked playground plan to mince up piccaninnies if I'd had the chance? I doubt it, but then there is doubt in that doubt.

I also recall a childhood "lark" that went sour. At a similar age with a couple of pals we were fiddling with a tail-light of a car. Just as I had removed the bulb a door opened and the owner came out to see what we were doing and we ran. I found I still had the incriminating bulb in my hand, so I threw it away. When the owner caught up with me I lied convincingly to prove my innocence. In my panic and fear of reprisals I also told fibs that pointed the finger of blame onto others. I got away with it but was haunted with guilt for years after.

What I recognise here was a sort of avalanche effect whereby fear could get me deeper and deeper into trouble because of the momentum of panic and peer pressure. I was not a bad kid, and would not really have wanted to cause pain and death to any real piccaninnies, but what if the opportunity had suddenly arisen from a cascade of incriminating events?

Perhaps those two older children had begun by simply wanting a younger, safe companion to show off to, act tough with and demonstrate their power to? Perhaps they had intended to justify themselves by eventually taking him to the police station? Perhaps they began to realise that they might not get away with this now they had been seen with the boy? Perhaps they then realised they were already in big trouble and that their only hope of getting away would be if their victim never lived to "tell on" them? Perhaps they finally acted in sheer panic or even in that state of cold mechanical overdrive that nature provides (as a last resort before fainting) to get us out of panic?

Here I am on the brink of "understanding" how such an awful thing could have happened in an otherwise OK world. And yet all the expert voices in the press and on the radio keep insisting that they have no idea how this "unthinkable thing" could ever happen. Many have even gone so far as to deduce that the world must, therefore, not be OK.

So how come that a non-entity like myself has achieved at least some understanding in one short article? Is it perhaps because I, unlike all those other people, am a monster? That I alone - in a world of sweet, innocent media spokespersons - share the evil that motivated those two boys?

What should I do now? Should I present these thoughts to you, or is it better to hide this piece of writing and join in the chorus of those who insist that they have no idea how such an atrocity could ever happen?

What shall I now murder: my reputation? or my integrity?

PUBLIC MORALITY - A POSTSCRIPT

A consequence of this murder story has been a certain amount of public discussion about morality. As suggested above, many people conclude from this incident that the world is - or rather "has become" - not OK.

I heard one commentator quote the case of a housing estate where people regularly bought cheap goods that they knew had been stolen - "such a thing would never have happened, or be openly admitted, thirty years ago". The speaker deduced that public morality was in serious decline.

To me the argument had a lot of force... and yet? I could not help but wonder whether people thirty years ago avoided stolen goods because of moral principles or because they were afraid of getting nabbed.

There was, after all, a popular film in the fifties called "Whiskey Galore"; and I recall the audience taking positive delight in the story of a Scottish island where the whole population joined in the looting of a wrecked ship full of whiskey.

Thirty years ago the police were assumed to be pretty effective - there was less publicity about unsolved crime and more people would have been scared to deal in stolen goods. Is that all we mean by morality? And what about those who reckoned they could get away with it, but were too proud of their reputations - is that really morality? And what of those who had both the skill and the humility to get away with it, yet chose not to deal in stolen goods because they were afraid that God would send them to hell if they did? Is that true morality?

What strikes me is that we are now witnessing the loosening of many restraints. Many who once would have been too scared to steal or cheat, now no longer believe in divine punishment from an avenging God. Many who once would have been too scared to buy stolen goods because of "what the neighbours might say", have now been persuaded by the media that "everybody's doing it". Many who once would have been too scared by the "long arm of the law" are now told that the police can no longer cope and that most petty crimes go unreported, let alone punished.

In other words: we are witnessing the dawn of freedom. Society is emerging from centuries in prison, and many are feeling the pain of unaccustomed freedom. Some are abusing our freedom and others, like habitual prisoners, do not know how to cope with it and would rather back into the familiar world of prison. Yet others may be abusing this freedom *in order* that society should be locked up again. Hence the rising crime going hand in hand with the rising cry for a return to "old fashioned values".

Now that is my cue to draw your attention back to my earlier essay on Thelemic morality and the Aeon of Horus. If as many people as possible can resist the temptation to demand that government must crack the whip, or that the church should bring back the fear of God, if we can resist this flight back to prison, then future generations might look back at the end of the twentieth century and see in our present confusion not the death pangs of public morality but rather the birth pangs of genuine widespread personal morality. A world where people behaved because of a real inner sense of truth - rather than from fear of reprisal.

THE SLIME WARRIOR

This piece was first published in German in Anubis Number 21, 1994 as a bit of over-optimistic advance publicity for this volume of essays.

Picture a shamanic workshop: about a dozen men and women sitting in a circle around a fire. The focus has passed round the circle and it now reaches Ramsey Dukes. Dukes draws his lot, and the Great Spirit commands that he contact his Warrior. Like the nice guy that he is, Dukes protests at such exposure - can't he play Coyote instead? But the stern voice of the Shaman, the voice she uses to order the Warrior Energy, insists that he obey.

Dukes turns in on himself in evocation, then rises to his feet. *This should be interesting* we think. Others have already drawn the Warrior lot, and we have seen little men grow tall, we have seen skinny men expand to fill their space, we have seen shy men batter the air with drums - so what can we expect from the already fairly tall and muscular Mr Dukes?

Dukes steps out of the circle and walks a few paces over to a wall. There he turns up the collar on his cosy New Man blouson jacket and it suddenly looks rather thuggish. He takes from his pocket the Traynor pinhole glasses he carries to help his ageing eyesight, puts them on and tips them up a little so they take on the appearance of mean black shades. Slouching against the wall he takes out his helpful leatherman pocket toolkit, opens it at the knife blade, and leans back silently, slowly tapping the blade against the fingers of his left hand in a gesture that seemingly transforms the tool into a stilleto flick knife. His face is expressionless, he says nothing.

For a few moments there is no sound but for the gentle wimpling of the camp fire flame. Eyes are fixed on the dark figure, waiting for some action. Nothing happens. Slight, nervous laughter attempts to break the spell of embarrassment.

"Very good! But I said be your *Warrior* - not Mr Cool!" The Shamaness wishes to reassert that this is a Healing Journey, not a drama workshop.

The impassive figure rolls its gaze slowly in her direction: "you talkin' to me, Lady?". The embarrassment grows more intense.

"My name is Red Eagle, and don't try to hide from us. Get back in the circle!". The commanding voice that makes Warriors jump doesn't seem to work on this apparition. Dukes very slowly shakes his head,

"You don't get under my skin that easy, Lady." The knife comes up and taps against the shades "you don't see my eyes". The knife points over the shoulder "and my back stays right against this wall".

The Shamaness feels control slipping away. Mr Dukes is clearly very repressed, quite out of touch with his Inner Warrior energy, surprising for an Aries but it no doubt explains is extreme "nice guy" nature. She is just wondering whether to raise the energy by getting the others to drum the Warrior out into the open, when the cool impassive voice spares her the effort by beginning its monologue.

"You asked for Warrior. You got Warrior.

Maybe not your rumpty-tum New Age Workshop Warrior, but you got Warrior.

Warriors aren't just Fire, Air or Earth, there's Water too. Meet Mars afflicted in Pisces - the Slime Warrior." The shaded gaze slowly takes in all present, and the knife blade is again tapping like a heartbeat against his fingers. "The only time you feel safe is when you *see* me coming".

"Not your fucking concept of a Warrior, hey?" Sneering contempt as the blade points to the menacing blackness of his shades. "Warriors don't just put on warpaint to amuse the tourists, you know". He cranes forward and hisses "*they do it to scare you, and to hide their own feeling*".

"You reckon I'm some kind of modern day perversion of the true Warrior spirit? Why I'm the oldest one around". He leans forward again and jabs the knife blade toward them as he snarls.

"I am the fly that mimics a wasp. I am the camouflage of the snake or caterpillar. I am the weed that pretends to be a nettle. I am the eye spots on a butterfly wing as much as I am the horns on the bull. Why, I am more primitive than Life itself, for I am the very virus that saps the enemies' valour."

Leaning back, he twirls his knife between his fingers and surveys the scene. "Yet people don't like the Slime Warrior. I challenge their idea of the masculine every bit as much as the Amazon challenges their idea of the feminine."

He shrugs. "Suits me. Everything gets blamed on the Slime Warrior, and I make sure it stays that way. From every scene of ultra-violence, perversion and sickness, every act of unimaginable cruelty, I make sure I'm seen slipping away - leaving you aghast with your imagination."

"Nobody likes the Slime Warrior, no battle honours, no hero's return for me." Again he leans forward and jabs the words towards them with his knife. "But when I walk by your side, the streets clear before you. You detest Bad Medicine, but feel safe when the enemy thinks I'm on your side. The night before the enemy army attacks your village to slay your children and rape your women, a couple of their soldiers die and the rumour spreads that Slime Warrior is behind their lines. Their courage fails, their ranks are broken and they turn tail and flee. But who gets the credit?

Words and actions are for other warriors, my biggest weapon is *reputation* as I feed on your fears."

He crouches down to their level, seeming smaller yet even more sinister. "So what if some spunky young cretin comes swaggering up to me? some dumb Warrior too stupid to be afraid, too innocent to know my evil ways?

I just look him in the eyes, take my knife like so" the blade comes up to his face "I and *slash* my own flesh". The face shows no emotion, no pain as blood wells in the cut across his cheek. "And macho kid stares back and thinks *Jesus Christ! If he'll do that to his own face, what the fuck'll he do to mine?* And he is gone!"

Dukes uncoils and leans back once more against the wall. "Mars in Pisces, the sign of self sacrifice, and that scares you even more than your dreams of my vicious unfeeling cruelty.

I am the bone thrust through the Warrior's nose. I am the safety pin through the cheek of a punk. I am the poison needle in the addict's arm and I terrify that one with so little apparent feeling for their own flesh might be capable of monstrous deeds on others!"

He reaches to his cheek, touches the bloody gash and rubs his fingers together. Is there a slight softening, of the cool, thuggish image? Is Dukes showing through?

"So why do I go round with a nice guy like Dukes?" He looks around then answers his own question. "Turn the Slime Warrior inside out like a glove, and you find the really nice guy. Turn the really nice guy inside out and you find Slime Warrior.

People blame this on niceness - they say that the nice guy represses his nasty feelings and makes the Slime Warrior. But I want all that blame - it's what my reputation depends on.

The *really* nice guy doesn't have anything to repress. He is no Christian, because he is Jesus Christ himself. The really nice guy doesn't deny nastiness, he even *wants* to be nasty when he knows the world demands it. But I don't let him have it. I need all the nastiness that's going, to paint my own image. I *steal* his nastiness before he ever knows it, and that makes people distrust the really nice guy. Hell, I need you to distrust *me!*

You never get really close to the nice guy, you never get beneath his skin, and that's not the fault of niceness: it's because I need to be unknown. It's the Slime Warrior, not the nice guy, that needs distance. People go mad trying to forge relationships with the nice guy, and no violence on earth seems so scary as the self mutilation, the self sacrifice that I act out for him."

The Slime Warrior made a sudden movement as if to hurl his knife at the group. They started, the knife remained in his hands, and a cold, crooked smile showed on his face.

"There's something else that scares you. My smile. When you see it your heart is chilled by visions of the cruel pleasure that must lie behind this smile, the callous sadism you read into it.

So let me tell you why I am smiling." He holds up his knife. "I am smiling because of something only known to me. This blade which, in your imagination, drips with the blood of the weak and the innocent as well as the proud and strong, this blade knows no other blood but mine own.

You have never seen me strike, and I let you credit that to my stealth and skill. If you ever saw me in action you might discover my limitations - whereas your fevered imagination can paint ever greater horrors in my name.

The truth is this. When the enemy army comes over the hill, fire raging in its belly, I stand before him cool and smirking, the picture of repressed violence waiting to erupt, while in reality it is my Water that quenches his Fire, weakens his fighting spirit. And when an enemy has survived months of hardship and siege, it is my Water that washes away the firm convictions on which his Cause is founded. He begins to wonder if it is worth the struggle, if he is really fighting on the side of Right.

My weapons are in your hands, they are your own fears and doubts. I am the Warrior who ends wars. Hell, I am the Cold Warrior who stops them ever happening.

You think your contempt for me stems from the fact I don't fit your image of masculinity - actually it stems from envy. For I am the one Warrior who has single handedly saved more lives than ever sprang from any one womb.

I am the ultimate Warrior, the Warrior who defeats even Warriorhood. The Anti-Warrior."

Slime Warrior is edging towards them now, speaking softly.

"So why am I telling you this? Has the nice guy got his hands on the controls?

No way! There is no power in my words, only in the feelings I evoke. No matter what I say, my reputation and your fear will overcome my words. In a second you will look up at my cold, impassive face and say to yourself *My God! he is only saying this to get close! The moment my guard is down... he will surely slit my throat!*"

DEVIL WORSHIP FOR POWER AND PROFIT
A Simple Guide For The Home Handyman

"1. These qualities are distinct and separate in us one from the other; there-fore they are not balanced and void, but are effective. Thus are we the vic-tims of the pairs of opposites. The pleroma is rent in us."

CG Jung, VII Sermones ad Mortuos

My next book long awaiting publication - The Good The Bad The Funny - attempts to solve the agonies of dualistic thinking by exploring three-fold thinking. But it does so not in order to banish dualism, but rather to release the pain from it so that we can re-enter and enjoy the game.

Illustration: if we were *trapped* within the dualistic game of chess it would be no game, but a hell of slaughter; however the third posi-tion which stands outside the board allows us the freedom to enter into the battle with any amount of zeal and passion, yet still to retain awareness that it is but a game.

This book you are holding, however, is about finding solutions *within* dualism. The problem of dualism is summed up in the word 'devil'. Some people will fear that this book belittles the devil by equating it with minor demons and everyday concerns - by the end of this essay I trust you will understand why it is mine own nature to seek to make devils smaller, whilst others prefer to make them bigger.

Others may reject my use of the word 'worship', saying that to worship a problem must mean to inflate or increase it with reverent submission, rather than to solve or diminish it. In this I am guided by the definition of worship as "to form a right relationship with a deity". I feel that our Judeo-Christion heritage has told us that there is only one deity and that deity is perfect, and this assumption has lead to the idea that worship must imply total submission - the only sensible relationship with utter omnipotence. This leads to a confused notion that 'devil worship' means total submission to evil - a misun-derstanding caused by allowing dualism through the back door. A polytheistic culture, however, recognises that gods may be good, bad,

funny or many shades between; and that 'right relationship' can therefore take many forms.

This essay focuses on right relationship with what is bad, evil or
troublesome. And it suggests not one, but two types of relationship.

Anything less would fall short of a true celebration of duality.

TRADITIONAL GOETIC DEMONS

Let us eschew intellectual arrogance and begin by consulting the
experts. What we want is examples of demons, and how to relate to
them.

Devil or demon? If forced to clarify the distinction, I would suggest that demons are the minor problems, and devils the big ones -
but as far as this essay goes I'll use whichever word sounds best in
context without discrimination.

'The Testament of Solomon' is a grimoire that contains a catalogue of demons. Ruax makes people slow thinking; Sphendonael
attacks the tonsils; Buldumech brings discord between married couples; Alleborith troubles those who have inadvertently swallowed a
fish bone... and so on. Such lists can seem highly quaint, to the point
of mockery, so it is worth trying to update it to our own times.

The demon that causes milk to go sour is funny to us because it
is no longer a demon - we would simply go to the supermarket for
another pint. But to a mediaeval family surviving on a single cow it
would be cause for utter desolation.

Imagine instead a demon that makes your lover smell and taste
sour when you attempt oral sex. As Goldfinger said "the first time is
happenstance, the second coincidence, but the third time, Mr Bond,
it's enemy action". The very thought of oral sex begins to lose its
appeal, your lover begins to fear that you no longer find them attractive, you try to explain and they feel criticised and hurt... Buldumech
could do no worse. This demon sounds just as droll as one which
turns milk sour, but we can understand that someone whose affair is
being ruined by it would suffer intense pain.

For the purposes of this essay, that is the test of a demon. When
you dwell upon it, it should evoke a definite physical reaction such as
butterflies in the stomach, or shivers down the spine. Some demons
may produce an instant reaction but more typically you need to 'dwell

upon' or contemplate them to feel the shiver - this process is called 'evocation'.

To illustrate, I'll list a few potential demons and you may be able to scan these without any feeling, but that is not the point. The real objective is to evoke each one by sympathetic identification with the problem and then to note which ones 'touch a nerve'. My short descriptions may not be exactly right for you, and that is why you need to dwell upon and explore around to find the exact fit. If you do manage to locate a demon in this list, then it will help to give value to the rest of the discussion.

1. "You probably didn't get that job (or woman) because you're too nice"

2. "The reason he got it is that he's so nice. People are afraid of real feeling, honesty makes them uncomfortable"

3. "When he said standards were slipping, I hope he didn't refer to me. I follow procedures to the letter - not like some lazy bastards"

4. "He's treating me like a time waster, so I will be extra solicitous and make him like me"

5. "Everyone applauds my performance, but I prefer to keep my distance so they'll not discover that I'm really rather a dull person underneath the mask"

6. "Why am I always abandoned once I give myself fully?"

7. "The moment I speak, the conversation ends. Are my opinions really so insignificant?"

8. "Why did she say that? Of course she would because she's a Gemini with Moon in Scorpio and that explains why she..."

9. "He seems a little too friendly, what does he want from me?"

10. "You wait, when my film is released they'll realise how talented I really am. That's why I haven't begun the script yet - real genius has to find the right moment for expression"

11. "I mustn't cry or show weakness. I must hit back *hard*"

12. "After all the kindness I showed her, how could she go off with a mean bastard like him?"

TRADITIONAL DEVIL WORSHIP

Once you've found a demon, how do you rightly relate to it? Here's an extract from The Testament of Solomon, quoted from Idries Shah's 'Secret Lore of Magic'.

So before me came a demon with the likeness of a man, but headless.

And I said to him "Who art thou?" He said "I am a demon". I asked him which and he replied: "I am Envy. I eat heads, for I seek a head for myself. I have not consumed enough, and I desire a head like thine."

I, Solomon, then put a seal upon him, holding my hand to his breast. Then the devil jumped and fell, and moaned, and said: 'Alas what has become of me? O Ornias, treachery, I cannot see!"

And I said: "I am Solomon. Tell me how thou canst see without a head. He said: "Through my feelings".

The same book quotes typical conjurations. The following are extracts from the Grimoire of Honorius.

"I .... conjure thee Spirit ...., by the Living God, by the true God, by the blessed and omnipotent God... etc etc

In the Name of Jesus Christ, by the power of the Holy Sacraments and the Eucharist... etc etc for another 6 lines.

I conjure thee into this circle, O accursed Spirit, by thy judgement, thou who hast dared to disobey God. I exorcise thee, Serpent, and I order thee to appear immediately in human form, well shaped in body and soul, and to comply with my commands without deception of whatsoever kind, and without either mental reservation: and this by the great names of God ... etc etc for another 7 lines

*I conjure thee, O evil and accursed Serpent, to appear at my wish and pleasure, in this place and before this Circle, immediately, alone and without any companion, without any ill-will, delay, noise, deformity or eva- sion. I exorcise the by the ineffable names of God ...*etc etc ad subjective infinitum.

The whole thing reads very much in the style of a heavy handed legal summons or warrant for arrest. It leaves little doubt that the demon that causes problems when you swallow a fish bone is noth- ing less than a criminal of the highest order.

There is no doubt, therefore, about Pope Honorius's idea of a right relationship with a demon. It is to remind it in no uncertain terms of its wickedness and to threaten it with the most severe punishment if it fails to do your will in every detail. This is the 'traditional' approach to devil worship.

Many people nowadays still insist that this is indeed how we should treat our criminals. But some think otherwise.

A PERSONAL EXAMPLE

I want to bring this alive with a personal example, but have no wish to disclose my demons to unknown readers. So I will falsify the facts of the following story in order to make it no longer true, while preserving its essential truth.

I would describe myself as a person with few, if any, serious demons (the significance of that remark will be examined later). But then I rediscovered my claustrophobia.

It happened while sleeping in a hooped bivvy bag on Dartmoor. I'd often slept out in this low, narrow one man tent in good weather with the end open to the stars, and never had a problem. But this night there were midges, forcing me to zip up the mosquito net, plus driving drizzle which required me to zip up the waterproof outer.

As I lay awake I began to feel anxious because the tent didn't give me room to sit up. I had to unzip the outers and get out just to prove to myself that I could do it. OK - so I got back in, feeling relieved, but very soon had to do it again. Each time a feeling of panic welled up which was only satisfied by my getting out of the tent on a wet, windy night - and I kept doing it until exhaustion overcame me.

That intense, physical sense of panic qualified this as a demon. It might simply be a question of the time and the place - in other words just a 'haunting' rather than 'my' demon - but as it turned out it sometimes recurred later in my life. I could be lying awake at night in the comfort of my bed, then I begin to think about that problem, wondering how I felt and what it would be like if I grow old and wake up paralysed and ...EEEK! I have to sit up in panic just to prove I can do it. In other words I have 'evoked the demon'. I have even been afraid to fall asleep in case burglars enter and tie me down to the bed in my sleep... Now there's a real demon.

So I discussed this problem with a friend who runs a successful and extremely profitable counselling practice. What he did was arrange a session where, after suitable discussion, he held me down on the floor and asked me what I was feeling. Nothing - because I had not yet evoked the demon. So I began to wonder if he might not be a closet sadist who really did intend to hold me down and then... he saw the look of panic welling up in me and said "now! use your strength! you can easily push me aside if you want to!" But I just lay there sweating and gasping.

"The trouble with you" he says afterwards "is that you are into victim consciousness. You just lay there and agonised instead of taking the positive step of throwing off your restraints. You gave in to the fear instead of confronting and opposing it. This is a theme in your life: you seem to suffer passively instead of contacting your anger and taking control of a situation. You write good books, and you sit and hope someone will publish them instead of going out and shouting about them from the rooftops..." and so on. 'Panic' the word is derived from 'Pan' the god of wild energy, and he sensed that the energy which could be driving ambition had somehow become locked into this claustrophobic fear and was now shouting to be freed, or re-directed.

His words presented me with a deep dilemma. The way I saw it I was not giving in to fear as he put it, but resisting it. To have used the energy of panic to break my bonds really would have been to give in to that fear, and it would be no solution. While he might argue that fear gives me the strength of ten men, what if one day I am tied down by bonds strong enough to hold eleven men? My idea was to face the panic and sit it out as long as I could. My objective was to reach the state of inner serenity where a building could collapse on me and instead of panicking I could lie still for days, breathing slowly and calmly to conserve oxygen, and save my breath until I heard rescuers and could then call out with all my strength. Only then would I feel I had mastered this demon, only when it had ceased to be a demon.

Here were two diametrically opposite approaches to the demon of claustrophobia, and they were reflected in our different attitudes to life's problems. For example: we had both in the past suffered the fear of losing everything and being dispossessed and penniless in an uncaring world. For him this fear became an incentive never to be poor again, so he built up his counselling practice until it could earn him thousands of pounds per day. I, on the other hand, had faced up to my poverty by experimenting to see just how simply I could live. So I knew that, even if society broke down, I could still live off nature and dwell in a cave. Thus poverty remained an undesirable state, but it ceased to terrify me. To him I had 'resigned myself to poverty consciousness', but what struck me about my friend was that, for all his wealth, he was still frightened of poverty. He was to some extent driven to work by fear of it!

My approach to fear was to study it, negotiate with it, live with it until it lost its fearfullness. His was to use its energy to drive him to worldly achievement. Apparently Sir Peter Scott had a demon: he was so overawed by the fame of his father, Scott of Antarctica, that he never felt he could live up to him. So Sir Peter was driven to achieve in everything he did: he became a gliding champion, a top-selling artist, the founder of the Wildfowl Trust, a knight... again and again he achieved top honours yet remained into old age driven by his fear of inadequacy.

Until that session I had been pretty proud of my relationship with demons. I saw myself as growing stronger and stronger like a priceless diamond being formed by the intense pressure of life's afflictions. But now I began to see the down-side of my approach: with few fears to drive me, I was a non-achiever. Suddenly the other type of devil worship began to look the better way. I yearned to be a go-getter: and ulcers, paranoia and a cocaine habit seemed a small price to pay for the pleasures of owning a Ferrari, a helicopter and a yacht.

Lest my readers begin to lose sympathy with my old approach, I now insert a quotation from The Satanist's Diary by The Honourable Hugo C. StJ. l'Estrange - published in Aquarian Arrow. Readers of Ramsey Dukes might not know that the earthling who channels these my writings also channels other entities, and Hugo is among them. The earthling hopes that his present publisher will also do a collected works of Hugo... so this is pre-publicity. But it is also included as a tongue-in-cheek warning about getting too keen on the traditional style of devil worship which aims to provoke demons to exploit their power.

STRATEGIES FOR ECONOMIC RECOVERY - 2
HUGO L'ESTRANGE'S MODEST PROPOSALS FOR RESTORING BRITAIN TO GREATNESS

Little wonder that Britain is in decline: our milksop society of small minds and disenchanted youngsters is no fit breeding ground for the Great and

Good who once proudly walked this sceptred isle and upheld its finest traditions as a shining example to the world.

Where, in today's disaffected generation, are Englishmen with the moral fibre and social stature of, say, the Honourable Hugo C StJohn l'Estrange?

It is too late for cosmetic measures, for trifling political actions. We must probe the very depths of the national being if we are to expose the roots of malaise in this our troubled nation.

May I quote from a work that has already made considerable impact with its profound questioning of concepts of masculinity and the drive to power? In *Iron John*, page 41, Robert Bly writes:

The wound that hurts us so much we "involuntarily" dip it in water, we have to regard as a gift. How would the boy in our story have found out about his genius if he had not been wounded? Those with no wounds are the unluckiest of all.... Our story... says that where a man's wound is, that is where his genius will be. Wherever the wound appears in our psyches, whether from alcoholic father, shaming mother, shaming father, abusing mother, whether it stems from isolation, disability, or disease, that is precisely the place for which we will give our major gift to humanity.

What profound insight lies in those few words. Consider all those great men of history, driven by some inner fire to conquest, do not their biographers constantly remind us of the childhood traumas that lit that fire. Has any great man survived the piercing analysis which unveils his greatest triumphs as an exteriorisations of inner pain?

Pity the despised "goody goody", the child of loving, caring parents brought up with sympathy and without stress or conflict - without wounds he is indeed "the unluckiest of all". Quiet, reasonable and kind - he is ignored by society in favour of the glamourous rebel, the wild child who grabs the attention of teachers, parents, social workers and press. In adulthood it is *his* car that will be stolen, *his* house robbed - while all the media attention, all the political debate and public fury will focus on the fascination of the lucky criminal who performed these outrageous acts. He inherits a broken home - the criminal becomes a media star.

Later Bly quotes the American Indian tradition that:

When you die, you meet the Old Hag, and she eats your scars. If you have no scars, she will eat your eyeballs, and you will be blind in the next world

We have much to learn from this ancient wisdom. What we are witnessing is the tragedy of a society brought up on the principles of Dr Spock and parental care. The pernicious and seductive idea that children need love and affection instead of contempt and the iron rod - the sort of wishy-washy Sixties drivel we tried to stamp out in the Eighties - has come home to roost now in a society of lazy, unmotivated good-for-nothings.

The once-great public schools have hung up their canes, and reduced Britain to third class status at a stroke - as it were - and yet there are still signs of hope.

Amongst all the posturing about the "family" and "parental care" there are still a few wise and dedicated elders doing there best to hold back the grey tide of motiveless, meaningless apathy.

They may be Judges, they may be Tory MPs, they may be Bishops, Landowners or Head Masters - they may even be leading literary diarists renowned for distinguished contributions to significant occult magazines - but they still find time from their busy lives to cruise the streets in their Rolls Royces picking up sweet, innocent children from perfect homes and making sure that they will grow up with the blessing of their very own wound. Making sure that, in future Relationship Encounter Workshops, they too will be able to hold their heads high amongst the Adult Children Of Alcoholics and boast that they too are people of consequence, people worthy of psychiatric and social attention, for they too have been victims of abuse.

Bly also quotes from what he describes as a "magnificent essay called the Age Of Endarkenment" as follows:

Tribal people everywhere greeted the onset of puberty, especially in males, with elaborate and excruciating initiations... The tribal adults didn't run from this moment as we do: they celebrated it. They would assault their adolescents with, quite literally, holy terror; rituals that had been kept secret from the young until that moment...

These initiations, as Bly explains, are ritualised wounds that reopen and reveal the deeper childhood wounds we should hold so precious. Without such solemn attention from their elders, today's young roam the streets in lawless gangs, a gangrene on society.

We must honour the dedication of those senior establishment figures who selflessly expose their genitalia and fondle little boys in recognition of the inadequacy of parental care to produce great men, but we must also demand more. We need a state religion with its own "elaborate and excruciating" rituals to assault its adolescents (especially the good-looking, sexy ones) with "holy terror".

I myself have given considerable thought to this matter and have a number of very exciting proposals to make. They are perhaps a little too exciting for the pages of a stuffy old rag like Arrow, but I would be quite happy to invite selected government ministers, educational advisers and church leaders over to Hellgate Hall to discuss them further.

THE GREAT AND THE GOOD

So far we have compared two types of people...

Did I catch you out there? Actually I have been at pains *not* to mention two types of people. Instead I have simply described two different approaches to right relationship with demons. The reason I avoided talking about two types of people is that 'two types of people' is itself a demon to some people. As they say "there are basically just two types of people, those who insist that there are basically just two types of people and those who deny it". If I had founded my essay on defining two types of people I might immediately have alienated the latter type.

It is, however necessary to present examples of my two approaches, and the second approach does involve harnessing demonic energy. So I will now introduce the idea of 'two types of people' and you can judge for yourself whether my thesis becomes a little more sparky as a result. Taking up Hugo's phraseology, I'll call the types 'the Great' and 'the Good'.

The Good are people who integrate their demons to gain inner strength and security. When they encounter a fear they will negotiate with it, counsel it and assimilate it until they no longer feel the fear.

The Great are people who keep their demons and use their power to achieve in the world. To do this they intensify the power of the demon by denial or repression and then they project it out with sometimes irresistible force. Thus the fear remains.

To give a political analogy: some people say the time has come to negotiate with terrorists; forceful repression has failed and the only hope is to listen to them, while holding our ground, and to see whether their can be any point of agreement without sacrificing our own principles. Others say "rubbish! the moment you recognise them you condone them. There can be only one solution: their total surrender or the death of these murderers".

The liberal society is 'the Good' one. Criminals are the demons in society, and the liberal government seeks to understand and rehabilitate its criminals. The liberal ideal is not only that the mass murderer should not do it again, but that he should also re-enter society as someone with priceless insight into the mind of a killer, someone who could save others from being tempted as he was. Thus the liberal society gains an inner strength which comes from a sense of security and lack of divisions within it.

Totalitarian society is 'the Great'. The totalitarian government locks up or kills its criminals, rather than destroy crime itself. Best of all it sends them to boot camp to create an army of thugs to go forth and conquer. It achieves far more than the liberals, but is activated by fear.

Lest these definitions sound too neat I should mention the possibility of relapse. The fact that I no longer fear poverty does not mean that the demon has been rehabilitated with 100% certainty. Unlike claustrophobia, poverty does not keep me awake at night as it does my counsellor friend, but if I were to suffer another period of extreme financial hardship the fear of poverty could return, just as the rehabilitated criminal can indeed relapse under temptation.

These two polar opposites have a sort of love/hate fascination for each other. The liberal government envies the crisp efficiency of the totalitarian, the way that totalitarians can insist on their spotless principles and high ideals - if the liberal government attempted such rhetoric its own free press would 'have their guts for garters'. The liberals have to circumlocute and tell half-truths because they do not control their media, they cannot insist on ten-year plans or thousand year reichs when they know they might be voted out. On the other hand the totalitarians yearn for the security and freedom enjoyed by the liberals. They know that they have to keep finding new enemies for their army, or it will grow restless and turn back on the government.

The same fascination holds between the Great and the Good. The Good admire the achievements of the Great, and their strongly expressed principles. The Great yearn for the inner serenity of the Good. When they come into close relationship, the Good begin to feel uneasy and begin to ask about the inner demons they sense lurking behind the shining facade of the Great. This is like asking a totalitarian government about its crime figures: "what are you getting at! we have no crime! don't you dare start slinging that sleazy, amoral liberal nonsense at us!" If a totalitarian and a liberal state merge two things can happen: totalitarian law is imposed on the liberal state and resentment sets in, or else liberal law is imposed and a lot of very repressed and bitter demons are released - as has happened in parts of the former Soviet bloc.

To sum up: we are describing two sorts of pact that can be made with a demon. The Good pact is to understand it, civilise it and invite it to become part of you. Thus is its energy converted into inner matter, and the heart grows serene, strong and clear like a diamond deep within. The Great pact is to command the demon's service and direct the energy out to conquer the world. Thus its energy is converted into outer matter, eg worldly status, wealth or 'good works' - for let us never forget that the outer path can be every bit as high minded and altruistic as the inner.

The Good pact gives inner strength and serenity, but it can lead to the static life of a fakir who has lost sight of the need to pass on his gifts to others. Thus Lucifer tempts us to spiritual pride, a purity which scorns the material world.

The Great pact brings worldly wealth and influence, but with the risk of a runaway army of fears taking the reins and driving ever onward. Ahriman encourages this worldliness via a trickery which allows a government to see itself as 'strong' while actually running scared from 'sixties liberalism'.

Each has its advantages, so if you find yourself inclining too far towards either the Great or the Good it could be useful to learn some of the opposing techniques to redress the balance.

TECHNIQUES OF THE GOOD

I'm not going to expand much on these because this whole collection of essays is largely concerned with how to negotiate with demons - ie techniques of the Good.

The basic first step is to recognise a demon as something that can be integrated. This usually involves refusing to admit that it is actually a demon - just as a liberal society is slower to label someone as a 'criminal' and prefers to speak of 'problem children' or 'disadvantaged persons' and so on. That is the significance of the point I drew attention to earlier: as a representative of the Good I do not believe I have many demons.

In addition to the process of listening to and negotiating with the 'problem' there is a technique of absorbing or assimilating it which is closely akin to love. To understand this think of the liberal who argues that the real cure for delinquent children is to give them unconditional love while removing unnecessary temptation by locking away your wallet. (An even more outrageously bold approach is to leave your wallet within easy reach of the crook and keep topping it up - almost worth doing just for the fun of seeing totalitarian toughies turning apoplectic.)

I constantly bounce between the inner and the societal models in order to illustrate how mundane this question of devil worship can be. By all means follow the most intriguing psychological techniques - beat drums, bang cushions, float, rebirth or what you will - but the beginning of rehabilitation is simply to recognise, listen and then negotiate.

I mentioned how a real demon must be marked by a physical sensation - eg butterflies in the stomach. You can use that one fact as a means of communication in itself - a technique which has its origins in neurolinguistic programming (NLP) apparently. It goes something like this: you have a problem such as claustrophobia, and when you evoke it the physical sensation is, say, a sort of choking tightness in the chest. So you take a comfortable relaxed position (as this is quite a slow and boring process) and say out loud "hallo there, Claustrophobia, may I enter into dialogue with you? If you respond with that feeling in the chest I'll take it as 'yes'; if you do not respond I'll take it as 'no'". You then wait anything up to a minute or so (for me it's usually no more than 20 seconds) and you get the feeling. You then say "are you willing to let me be consciously aware of why you give me the feeling of panic?"... and let's say you get the 'yes' again. You then say "I will now make my mind blank and wait for the answer to come into it". Let's say the words 'save... life' eventually pop into consciousness, so you then say "are you trying to save my life when you make me feel panic?" and get a pretty positive 'yes'. So you ask "will you tell me what is the threat you are trying to save me from?" and let's say you get no response this time - because there is no reason why a demon should be totally co-operative any more than an IRA negotiator need be. You can then go on to suggest that if some alternative ways of saving your life could be found which do not require panic, would that be acceptable? If the answer is 'yes' you can either dream up some suggestions consciously or else evoke one's problem-solving ability (imagine a moment when you felt good because you'd solved a knotty problem, and re-create that physical feeling so that you can form a dialogue with that part of you). You then persuade those two parts to get together and let you know when they've found a solution. They don't necessarily have to tell you what the solution is, but what you do need to do is then ask your body as a whole if there are any other parts of you which do not accept this solution... and you wait to see if there is a response. And so on.

The point of this hasty description is simply to show that there is no great esoteric mystery about forming a relationship with a demon: you simply negotiate as you might with a terrorist or a gunman holding hostages, taking care to keep things clear and simple and displaying a level of trust while not allowing yourself to become vulnerable. It's a slow process with such a limited language, but the results can be surprisingly good.

TECHNIQUES OF THE GREAT

Now we get to more radical stuff, because it goes against the main drift of this book.

The first step is to recognise that you have a demon whose power you can harness. None of this liberal stuff about calling it 'my little handicap': as in my early quotation from the Grimoire of Honorius you label it as an infernal demon, a serpent of corruption or whatever. Even if it was just a little problem, like a passion for cream cakes, you must build it up with words like 'gluttony', 'weakness' and 'craving' and you must terrify yourself by invoking horror stories of cholesterol, hardened arteries, becoming too fat for your clothes, losing your last vestiges of sex appeal and so on. If you need tuition in this, study how tabloid newspapers take some rowdy teenage prank like setting light to stolen cars and then build it up in magnitude to the point where any self-respecting teenager begins to feel that until he has burnt a car he is somehow missing out on a great tidal wave of revolutionary fervour that is sweeping the nation's youth.

The biggest failing at this point is to say "that's all very well if you've got some decent demon like Peter Scott's famous father - all I've got is a fear that my girlfriend will smell rancid if I give her oral sex".

Other people's demons have a way of looking magnificent and potent, because from the distance you don't experience the pain of them. One's own demons seem useless because, from close up, all you notice is the pain. A fear of oral sex might inspire the Great to learn every other technique of erotic delight and develop into amazing lovers...

Making the demon bigger often seems to work on its own. What happens is that you make it such a big demon that it can take you over. This is called 'passion' - a favourite word of the Great, who do not like to be reminded by the Good that 'passion' is the opposite of 'action' just as 'passive' is the opposite of 'active'. Passion is a victim state when one is overwhelmed by an emotional demon, and that is why it is so effective... and costly.

If that does not happen on its own accord try denying or repressing the demon. Instead of looking for ways around the oral sex problem, leap out of bed screaming "ugh! how disgusting! how dare you suggest I indulge in such a dirty, degenerate practice you whore, you filthy slut!" I can almost guarantee that *something* will happen if you do this.

The third step is to go out and shout it from the rooftops, print handbills decrying the evils of perverted oral sex, appear on television, organise rallies... and so on. Powersville, man. This is the stage where you drill your demons into an army or secret police force to project your battle out into the world. For instruction in this, study how the Nazi movement identified a traditional Jewish problem, magnified it into a demon of world conspiracy and then built a whole movement around it.

Notice that, in dualistic terms, the essence of the Good approach is to decrease the distance between good and evil, between the criminal and the citizen, and so to lessen the potential difference. Whereas the strength of the Great lies in increasing the separation to maximise the potential difference. So Jews are no longer just a different religion, but a 'subhuman species'. Someone who felt a little too tired or randy to take a bath becomes a 'filthy gutter slag' and so on.

For Good people wishing to master these arts there is a second hurdle, and that is the pride which cannot permit such self-deluding bullshit, plus a sense that it is immoral to supply arms to demons and release them upon the world - even if they do increase your income and get you elected into parliament for your efforts. If that is your problem, take heart from that earlier essay on devil worship where I explained how this was practiced in the world of art and fashion - how last year's fashions are deliberately demonised to make way for the new and to set the stage for a later revival. We instruct ourselves to despise and detest flowery flared trousers, then gain a big kick from reviving them. Begin with such morally neutral examples and work your way toward the hard stuff.

BALANCING THE EXTREMES

Time to remind ourselves that I am not really describing two sorts of people, but simply two different approaches to devil worship.

One way is to pacify your demons, to train them into useful citizens and assimilate them into your being. This way reduces fear and inner conflict and it creates a sort of diamond-like inner clarity. But it can become static, introspective and suffer the long-term problems of liberal societies. These include a tendency for all the demons of the world to converge upon you for succour. You become the world's counsellor and - like Holland having second thoughts about its liberal approach to drugs - may feel compelled to return to Greatness rather than bear the burden of everyone else's obsessions.

The other way is the traditional Goetic path of conjuring demons by threatening them with strong principles. With their power you can build empires, liberate the oppressed, make money, achieve fame... but it is not a sure recipe for a happy old age.

This essay takes the story no further because it is an essay for the home handyman. The picture of the table in the instruction manual is not a table. The only real table is the one you yourself build up from wood and sweat. Instead of neat answers I give you the curiosity to explore the demonic pacts of the Great and the Good yourself, and then to remember the message of my earlier essay. For the real answer might lie in neither, but the balancing act of enjoying power without becoming its slave.

Maybe the Good hermit who has endured the crushing pressures necessary to creating an inner diamond now has that treasure to bring out and show the world, provided he can face the claustrophobic depths wherein it lies. Who knows... a diamond can even be sold!

And the Great world-beater whose army of demonic fears has nothing more to conquer may still have the possibility of understanding and integrating those fears. But the problem is significant because it now means rehabilitating a whole army at once, instead of negotiating with each demon one by one over a lifetime.

If there is a secret ingredient to success in these matters, I suspect it could be 'playfulness'.

Farewell, dear reader. See you in my next book for further details.

23

NEW AGE RE-RUN OF WORDS MADE FLESH

This is an outline of a talk I gave to an astrology group in Cheltenham in 1994. I did not want to include it as it is really a re-run of the theme of my book Words Made Flesh. I never felt that the book got the attention it deserved from New Age circles, and this version is aimed more in that direction, so perhaps it deserves to be included. It also sets the context for the following article addressing the consciousness debate. So here goes.

There have been many predictions made concerning the end of this century and the millennium. One of them, ascribed to Rudolph Steiner, is that we shall see a resolution or bringing together of the Aristotelian and Platonic schools of thought.

Coleridge claimed in 1830 that "every man is born an Aristotelian, or a Platonist. I do not think it possible that any one born an Aristotelian can become a Platonist; and I am sure no born Platonist can change into an Aristotelian." I quote from David Newsome's "Two Classes of Men" where he summarises the difference as follows: "Is knowledge limited to our reasoning over things we can see and sense, or is there some higher order of abstract truth, beyond the reach of our senses and the limits of observation, which man can yet apprehend by some higher faculty than the reasoning power? Is knowledge limited to contemplation of finite properties, or can it extend into the realm of the infinite; and - if so - does that knowledge of the infinite give us a deeper insight into the nature of reality itself?"

If I present Steiner's prediction to a "New Age" audience I suspect that many would reply on the lines "why yes, of course! It is already happening! The new physics is forcing scientists to embrace the mystical, isn't it?"

Be careful! First they should not make too facile an equation between science and Aristotelian thought. I agree that the scientific method is essentially Aristotelian, but "the laws of physics" are surely an example of a Platonic "higher order of abstract truth beyond the (direct) reach of our senses", and their contemplation does indeed give a deeper insight into the nature of reality itself. Secondly I suspect that those New Age Platonists are simply doing what Platonists have always done: they are taking their own pet quantum-mystical theory and demonstrating how well it explains reality, then turning to the Aristotelians and saying "so now you see we must be right!" This does not address the real difference. You don't convince an Aristotelian of the truth of astrology by giving a stunningly accurate interpretation of his birth chart, because all he wants to know is "what is the precise mechanism which allows the position of the planets at my birth to effect my character?"

I do agree with those New Agers that we shall see some resolution of scientific and magical worldviews - and that it will be by bridging the Aristotelian and Platonic ways of thought - but I predict that the change will not be brought about by New Age philosophy but by the humble, everyday experience of virtual reality.

My story begins around 1960 at a talk about artificial intelligence, or AI, in the days when it was predicted that sophisticated computers would one day reproduce every aspect of human thought, feeling and consciousness. The argument was powerful in its simplicity: "if you believe there is any human process that cannot be programmed into a machine, then I ask you to describe it to me precisely. If you do give a precise description, then you have told me exactly what I need to programme, if you fail to be precise, then I believe the process you describe to be meaningless". Like the rest of the young audience, I did not want to "be a machine" and so I resisted the idea.

Everyone else ended up in a stalemate position, claiming that there were certain human processes - love, poetry, consciousness etc - which lay beyond precise verbal description and yet which were utterly meaningful and real, even though the speaker denied the possibility. That is the sort of thinking that leads to today's New Age movement.

But I took what seemed like a diametrically opposite route. I thought "the reason I don't like this machine intelligence idea is that it seems to restrict life and deny magic. But is that really so? Let me explore AI and see if magic really does die".

My first discovery was reincarnation. I wanted to believe in it, but in the light of scientific education in 1960 it was very hard to do so. It required a real leap of faith. But if my consciousness or "soul" could be encapsulated in a programme - ie as information - then it could be reproduced. It could reappear elsewhere with no limitation on time or space. Reincarnation was not only now possible, it even became likely: on the grounds of conservation of information in a finite universe.

So my experience was that AI, an idea which at first seemed to kill "the spirit", might actually be the back door through which it could re-enter into our materialistic worldview. So my next step was to explore what it is about AI that so repels us devotees of spirit. I decided that it was a reaction based upon two factors: one a belief, the other a natural human tendency.

People tend to see the full acceptance of AI as an example of sophisticated "progressive" thinking, but I see it as a primitive idea. The tribal animist would have no difficulty in accepting that a computer could have a soul - after all, a tree has a soul, a rock or river has a soul, so why not a computer?

Centuries ago Western philosophy invented the idea of something called "dead matter" that was by definition devoid of life or spirit. The notion proved to be a great tool insofar as it lead to an explosion of scientific thinking, but its limits have now been reached. AI sits uncomfortably in Western thought, just as we struggle with some of the more mystical ideas of quantum physics, because Western thinking is based on a tool (the split between spirit and matter) of immense power but limited extension. More animistic cultures like the Far East will have far less trouble accepting AI.

There is also a human tendency towards economy of ideas. If someone like Uri Geller provides a public demonstration of the paranormal it arouses intense debate. But if a conjuror (ie a professional deceiver) can reproduce the same phenomenon it usually is seen as the end of the matter. It is very easy to believe that "it has been proven to be a trick".

This is the same process which makes it harder for the rational mind to believe in God once a rational materialistic explanation has been found for divine phenomena. Because this elimination acts at the rational level we tend to assume that it is a "logical" process, but it is not. It is a particular feeling judgement, an aesthetic desire for simplicity and economy that is verging on laziness but which is made respectable when described as "Occam's Razor". The fact that science, or a conjuror, can model spiritual phenomena in matter no more "proves" that spirit does not exist, than does the Platonist's neat models of reality "prove" that they must underlie our universe. And yet we feel strongly drawn to the former conclusion because it replaces the double explanation - a spiritual world which demands a leap of faith as well as a material world which has actually been seen and demonstrated - with the single physical reality.

Put these two things together - our belief in the split between spirit and matter plus our rational tendency to opt for fewer explanations - and we get a deep revulsion at the idea of AI. It goes like this: if someone says my consciousness could be the result of a reproducible physical process I unconsciously assume "that means that my mind can be modelled in dead matter (reflecting the belief that matter can be dead); and that implies (which it does not) that I am merely dead matter (reflecting the preference for a single explanation)". So what I hear the person say is "you have no spirit, you are dead matter" and I instinctively reject the idea.

Now what I ask you to do for a moment is to suspend that automatic interpretation process and adopt one which is no less (and no more) sensible because it simply reverses the flow. When someone says "love is a chemical reaction" instead of thinking "how dare he reduce the wonders of love to mere chemistry" I encourage you to think "wow! that's wonderful! You mean this wondrous experience that I know as 'love' is in fact born of chemistry? Why then, the whole universe must be awash with love, because chemical reactions are everywhere! Once more I am allowed to claim that a flower turns towards the sun because it 'loves' the sun."

You see, the alchemists had no problem with the idea that love was a chemical reaction, because they did not consider matter to be 'dead'. For them the tendency to adopt a single explanation lead not to dead matter encroaching on spirit's territory but rather for spirit to flow out into all phenomena.

So when that man in 1960 said that simple digital process lay behind all human consciousness, it opened a floodgate for me which allowed elemental consciousness to flow back into all phenomena. AI no longer meant the death of spirit but rather its triumph - the whole universe is alive simply because it is a computer.

I am now going to ask a lot from my readers. You may well know much more about computing and consciousness studies than I do, and you may well know enough to "know" that what I am now about to describe could never ever happen. But I am asking you to come with me on an imaginative trip for the next section and, in return for your suspension of disbelief, I will in a later section return to address and acknowledge that disbelief. So fear not: you lose nothing in the long run by trusting me.

I want to come forward in time from 1960 and clumsy ideas of programmed intelligence, and now imagine a superb virtual reality experience of the future. It goes like this.

You don your helmet and lie down on a couch. The system then does exactly what your brain would do in a dream: it intercepts nerve signals to the spinal cord to render your body comfortably paralysed, and it replaces those nerve signals with its own computer generated signals. So you 'awake' feeling the couch beneath you just as before, you open your eyes and find yourself in a pleasant room, you get up from the couch and walk towards the door. Marvellous! It all feels so real, the sensation of your body, walking, the feel of the door handle, the resistance of the door... You step out into virtual nature, feeling cool air on your skin and examine a flower. Brilliant! the colour, the petal texture, the smell... and here's a virtual bee coming to collect pollen.

You look up and see a virtual human approach. Let's try the Turin test! "Hi there! It's a beautiful world you live in!" You strike up conversation and he is looking at you oddly. He asks where you live and you say something vague about "not these parts". He is not satisfied - is it another country? another planet? Thus cornered you explain "no, I come from outside this reality". His face lights up and he exclaims "you must be a spiritual being from other dimensions!"

Stupid idiot. Doesn't he realise that his very existence as a piece of computer generated virtual reality is proof that spirit does not exist! In irritation you go in search of better conversation and you meet a physicist and ask him what he has found out about his world. He explains how they used to think it was made of indivisible particles but they discovered that these particles had some extraordinary non-local properties. "Of course they have" you think "for they are an illusion formed from the interaction of numbers in a computer.

Energy comes in discrete quanta because you inhabit a digital universe". He then goes on to say that some believe that the fundamental units of reality are in fact strings with mysterious properties - apparently one dimensional but with nine further dimensions curiously enfolded in their structure. "You idiots" you explain, "can't you see that those strings are simply strings of data. One dimensional sequences in a computer but modelling ten dimensions of information: one of time, three of space and six others that were found to be the minimum needed to create a livable reality". He asks you how you know and you explain that you have seen the original computer, you have seen the machinery behind this universe. His face shows a patronising smile as he says "so you are a mystic! Us modern scientists are learning to respect your old ideas, you know."

You return in irritation to this real world and decide to have some sensible conversations with real people. What do you find? You find people who talk about spiritual beings from other dimensions, and you find scientists talking about quantum physics and mysterious ten dimensional "superstrings".

Now we come to the crunch. Could you have such an experience and not begin to wonder whether this real universe might not also be a virtual reality? It is an idea - but I suggest it is more infectious than that because of the "Occam's Razor" mechanism in our thinking. The very principle that encourages our rational mind to reject the spiritual world because a demonstrable materialistic model of it exists, that same principle will make it increasingly hard to accept that there could be two types of reality - one made of matter and the other made of information yet identical when experienced.

My suggestion is that people will begin to believe that our reality is an information system and that this will not be a 'top-down' revolution based on philosophical speculation, but rather a 'bottom-up' revolution driven by simple everyday response to growing exposure to virtual reality as entertainment and education.

This is what will bring Aristotelian and Platonic thought together, and this is why. Until now the Platonist has basically used two arguments to try to communicate with the Aristotelian. The first is "if you will only join me in this leap of faith, I will describe to you a Platonic reality that does a really thorough job of explaining all material phenonema", to which the other replies "sorry, I don't believe in leaps of faith". The second is a version of "how could my astrological analysis of your character be so accurate if there was no truth in astrology?" to which the other replies "I don't know, but I do know there must be some rational explanation".

But imagine now what an Aristotelian would experience as he entered virtual reality. There is the evidence of his senses: a computer, a VR helmet, computer code that he can read and comprehend. But what does he then experience? He experiences a descent into a sensual world for which his 'reality' is a Platonic meta-world. From the point of view of the virtual reality he now occupies, that oh-so-tangible computer and his physical body now lie outside reality in "other dimensions" and, what's more, they provide a complete explanation of all that may be experienced by the virtual senses in this virtual world. For the Aristotelian, the possibility of a Platonic world beyond space and time need no longer be a leap of faith, because one example of it has been experienced by his own senses.

And what does the Platonist experience? For him the computer-generated virtual reality is a monstrosity, because it challenges him with the ultimate proof that we need no transcendent reality and that everything can be explained in the Aristotelian manner as a mechanistic movement of sensual qualities. But what happens when he forces himself to experience this monstrous reality? He too has a sensual experience of a Platonic reality. he finds that the Aristotelian scientific method has not destroyed so much as confirmed his Platonic beliefs.

Now, I've made this sound grand by calling the two people Platonist and Aristotelian, but in fact they are just two blokes who may never have heard of those words. One just happens to be a really 'down to earth' sceptic who has no time for dotty spiritual ideas, and the other just happens to believe that there "must be more to life than just materialism". Two extreme and opposed characters who, after an experience of virtual reality, begin to get a first glimpse of what the other is going on about. The two streams of thought meet at last. Steiner was right!

So, if you have been able to suspend doubts and enter into my imaginary journey, I hope you will understand my argument - even if you believe it is based on impossible assumptions.

In return, I now give you back your doubts. Perhaps you know too much about human consciousness, or the limits of AI, to accept that such a perfect virtual reality would ever be possible with its intelligent denizens.

What I suggest is that this does not matter. Perfect reality modelling as described is not actually needed to bring about the Aristotelian/Platonic reconciliation I am predicting.

Consider Darwin's theory of evolution as a example of an idea that has totally transformed our world. Even if we have reservations about details of the theory, we have all now been brought up to see animals as our cousins and to view history in terms of progress. Yet no-one has ever demonstrated the theory, no-one has yet evolved a lizard into a bird under laboratory conditions. It has been publicly accepted because it made sense, matched our experience and caught on.

The same will happen with VR. Even in the earliest, crudest versions some users came away with a mildly confused sense of reality. All it takes is steady improvement in realism and people's imaginations will leap ahead. After all, if you found my story convincing (subject to suspended disbelief), then what was it except a virtual reality formed in your imagination by my words?

So my prediction is that it does not matter whether there is an ultimate theoretical or practical limit to the intelligence of the VR system. As long as it keeps improving for a decade or two it will be sufficient to replace the current belief in solid matter, or subatomic energy, with a belief in existence as a shared information dream.

This is the worldview which I find most magical and desirable, but I suspect that it is still resisted by many, in particular New Age thinkers. For such people are often victims of the 'dead matter' idea, and they will tend to phrase my vision on the lines "so you think we are nothing more than a programme in a big computer?" And their tone of voice betrays a feeling that this is an appaling, limited vision which excludes spirit and mystery.

No, it actually allows spirit, mystery and magic back into our Aristotelian world via the back door. Here's how.

I want you to take another VR trip with me. This time it is a humbler experience and it does not necessarily include real intelligence, though it is very realistic in physical detail. What we do is enter a games arcade of the future and we decide to share one of the games.

"PLANET EARTH VERSUS THE WAR-LORDS OF ARC-TURUS.

Thrill to the realism of a planet besieged by an intergalactic super-power. *See* the mighty wizard Merlin rise from the dead to help a people overpowered by..."

This looks good. Let's pop in a two million pound coin and try it out.

Wow! what a brilliant sensory experience! Let's go our separate ways and explore this world, but keep in touch via this virtual walkie-talkie.

(Later). Hullo, Reader, can you read me? Look I've come across this space port offering flights to the Moon. Dead realistic - it means six days travel in sleep-sim, so you won't hear from me for a bit...

(A week later). Hullo, Reader. It's great here up on the Moon. Sorry about the delay in the walkie talkie response, that's because it takes time for radio signals to cross space - yes, really realistic VR, they've thought of everything!

Look, I had this amazing encounter with Merlin up here. What? You've met him too down there? He said he'd met me? His magic spells are terrific, aren't they! Love the 'blasting wand'....

Now stop for a moment and consider what has happened. You are down on Earth and I am on the Moon six days travel away, yet we have both just met Merlin. Why are we not goggle-eyed with disbelief? Why did we not drop the walkie talkies in terror that we could both meet the same person in two far-removed places?

The answer is obvious. However realistic the VR, we both know it is perfectly simple to allow the Merlin programme to be called up in more than one place by more than one player. Bilocality, or instantaneous transmission of people and objects is perfectly conceivable in VR, even when simulated realism insists that it takes six days to reach the Moon, and radio signals are noticeably delayed. Also conceivable is Merlin's ability to do magic spells in a universe otherwise programmed to be realistic.

Reincarnation, astrology, divination, ghosts, homeopathy... any number of things considered 'paranormal' or 'impossible' in a material universe are not only possible but actually become likely in a virtual reality - as I explained in Words Made Flesh.

If the experience of VR is going to lead us to believe that all reality is virtual, then we no longer need justify paranormal phenomena, instead we have a different problem. It is to explain why there is so little magic in our world. Why cannot I just wave my hands and create a banquet, or fly us all to Hawaii? Why is the paranormal so elusive if it is so easy?

I cannot know the answer. But here's a suggestion.

Consider a well-fed teenage boy living with nice parents in a warm comfortable suburban home with a lovely sunny garden... and tell me why he chooses to sit for hours at a computer game which involves crawling through a crocodile-infested swamp being attacked by killer spiders from Mars?

The answer is: "because it's more fun". From the Platonic perspective of the player, the horrors of the game are experienced as a great adventure.

Consider our experience of that arcade game together. The game could have been programmed to give all of us the magic powers of Merlin - I could have gone to the Moon in a flash. But the fact is, we paid our money for the realism, for details like the inconvenience of six days travel to the Moon. If we could all wave our hands and fly to Hawaii, the place would be swamped.

Too much magic devalues a reality. That is the only reason I have ever found for believing - as some Christian fundamentalists insist - that magic is inherently evil.

So that is what I am proposing with my information model of reality: a united world of infinite magical potential and omnipresent consciousness and spirit - "existence is pure joy" - but one in which there has evolved a limitation on magic and a personal sense of isolation and separateness, because those are properties which give this universe its greatest value.

So look now at this world as a virtual reality. Doesn't this book feel amazingly realistic in your hands? Brilliant software! Turn the pages, see how perfectly it maps the texture and resistance of paper. Try the Turin test on people you meet in the street - they are just so utterly credible (and you might even make a friend or two).

When you are making supper you savour the smells and you feel how solid and real the kitchen spoon is in your hand...

Suddenly it softens and curls.

You drop it and scream.

There, on your floor, still ringing from the impact, is hard metal bent into a knot.

My God! The Geller phenomenon! What do you do?

Forget it.

Or do you pick up the phone and tell your friends, tell the papers. Call the local TV station and ask them to bring the cameras round to witness a miracle.

But it never happens again. You look like an idiot. A lying idiot.

The software is good. I told you so.

Good software debugs itself. That bent spoon was an anomaly, a lapse of the laws of physics programmed into our reality. It was a little bit of illegal magic and your consciousness was the scanner that detected it, and your alarm and excitement was the signal to the debugging module.

You've learnt two important lessons.

One is that your consciousness has value for the universe. The other is that if you want the paranormal to have a place in your life you have to be very off-hand and blase about it. Haven't you noticed that the people who experience the most miracles are not those who go round making a big thing about it?

And forget psychical research: so much focussed attention simply triggers the software debugging module.

Returning to that original New Age audience who welcomed Steiner's prediction, I would ask them to move forward with me in time to the year 2030, say.

We visit a very ordinary housing estate and see a teenager being sent out to pick a cabbage from the garden. To our surprise he first salutes the plant and reverently asks permission of the cabbage spirit to cut it. So we ask him why he did it.

"We are all part of the same programme. So if you honour the cabbage you honour yourself" he replies.

New Age hopes leap!

Is this really a typical kid in 2030? Has the great Aquarian Revolution really happened?

We ask the kid who told him that, did he learn it from a guru? From reading New Age books? From attending a spiritual workshop?

The kid just looks puzzled and says "it's obvious, innit?" After spending hours in a games arcade, he simply cannot believe we are any other way.

That is what I meant when I suggested the revolution would not be generated by lofty speculation so much as common experience.

THOUGHTS ON READING 'SHADOWS OF MIND' BY ROGER PENROSE

After hearing Roger Penrose speak at the Cheltenham Literary Festival I bought a copy of Shadows of Mind and was impressed by the care and thoroughness with which it argues its case and endeavours to anticipate and address every possible objection or misunderstanding.

My one problem is that, in laying out the various competing ideas about AI which the book will subsequently address, it appears to omit one very obvious theory of AI and consciousness, and it is the theory which I am most inclined to 'believe' in!

Is the point of view expressed in this essay a) acknowledged, and b) adequately addressed by Penrose's arguments? If it is not directly addressed, is it in fact covered by a selection of his arguments in a way that I have failed to recognise? Or is the AI philosophy suggested in this essay too vague and informally expressed to have merited serious discussion outside the works of Ramsey Dukes?

PENROSE'S SPECTRUM OF AI BELIEF

In para 1.3 he defines a spectrum of beliefs about AI and consciousness as follows.

A All thinking is computation; in particular, feelings of conscious awareness are evoked merely by the carrying out of appropriate computations.

B Awareness is a feature of the brain's physical action; and whereas any physical action can be simulated computationally, computational simulation cannot itself evoke awareness.

C Appropriate physical action of the brain evokes awareness, but this physical action cannot even be properly simulated computationally.

D Awareness cannot be explained by physical, computational or any other scientific terms.

A he calls the 'hard AI' view, *D* is 'the viewpoint of the mystic'. The view I support is even harder than *A*, so could be 'rock-hard AI', but comes to conclusions more like those ascribed to *D*, so it could be called the 'cybermystic' view. To relate it to Penrose's spectrum I will label it $\mathcal{AA}$

$\mathcal{AA}$ begins with the opinion quoted from John Searle in para 1.13: "Of course the brain is a digital computer. Since everything is a digital computer, brains are too." To bring it in line with Penrose's definitions, I'll express it as follows:

$\mathcal{AA}$ All is computation; in particular, feelings of conscious awareness are invoked by the carrying out of appropriate computations.

There are three important points to note, those which I believe truly distinguish $\mathcal{AA}$ from $\mathcal{A}$. First is the omission of the word 'thinking' to produce the more general 'all is computation' as suggested by Searle's quote. Secondly the word 'evoked' in $\mathcal{A}$ has become 'invoked' in $\mathcal{AA}$ and thirdly 'merely' is omitted: this is because from the $\mathcal{AA}$ viewpoint consciousness is not a property of the individual computation so much as it is a property of the relationship between the computation and the universe, ie between microcosm and macrocosm.

A MODEL FOR $\mathcal{AA}$

Consider a large and powerful computing device - whether a brain or a computer is immaterial to the immediate argument. This device in some form contains instructions relating to the laws of physics (which may themselves have evolved or be still evolving in a manner I later describe) and it is busy modelling all the possible interactions of particles subject to those laws.

For reasons well explained by Penrose, I would not expect this device in itself to be consciously aware; but let's put tongue in cheek and name this device 'God'.

Assuming that scientists are corrrect in saying that life, as we know it, is one possible long-term consequence of the random interaction of fundamental particles, then the interactions modelled by God will, given sufficient time, hit upon combinations which lead to the modelling of complex molecules and reproducible cell structures and forms of 'life'. Amongst these permutations will be some so complex that they too, considered as calculating devices, will have reached the level of complexity which makes it possible for them, like God, to model their own internal worlds. These may be called 'brains', 'computers' or even simply 'complex dynamical systems', but they share the ability to generate internal models and so can in one sense be said to be 'made in God's image'.

Now comes the leap in faith required for $\mathcal{AA}$ (bearing in mind that the other AI beliefs he describes are not without their own leaps of faith): I believe that the creation of a model-making structure within a model-making structure would cause a 'resonance', and that resonance would be experienced by the inner structure as self-conscious awareness - some justification for this belief is given later. Some of these structures might even describe the initial experience of this resonance as 'God breathed spirit into my flesh'. That, in essence, explains why I use the word 'invoke' and omit the word 'merely' in my description of $\mathcal{AA}$.

In $\mathcal{AA}$, therefore, consciousness loses much of its mystique, in fact it becomes as cheap as dirt because any complex dynamical system might partake of it. Rivers, trees, weather, Nature, Gaia herself could all have 'spirits' containing some element of consciousness. In return for devaluing consciousness, however, $\mathcal{AA}$ gives it a measure, because it is possible to be more or less conscious according to the strength of the resonance.

This quantification of consciousness is witnessed in cross-resonance: my brain has the necessary peripherals to communicate with other humans and I can test my sense that they too have conscious awareness by mutual observation and discussion. I can also do this to a lesser extent with cats, dogs and other animals. But, when it comes to communing with the God of the Storm or Mother Nature, I can sense a cross-resonance of awareness (described as 'nature mysticism') but cannot verify it so readily; that is, I can 'tune into' a River God but cannot find a shared language to verify the validity of my experience of its consciousness. Similarly I can focus on my relationship with God itself and sense growth towards a more powerful resonance (mysticism), but lack the physical communication channels to objectify the experience of increased consciousness that mysticism invokes.

Such quantification is in accord with Penrose's statement in 8.6: "There would seem to be little doubt that consciousness can be a matter of degree, and it is not just a matter of being 'there' or 'not there'".

$\mathcal{AA}$ puts us in a world awash with consciousness, with spirits and gods, but it recognises that our senses and ability to communicate gives special value to human consciousness. Although it may feel that conscious spirit is a gift from God, consciousness and growth of consciousness is equally humanity's gift to the Gods, as suggested in a later section.

But first I will illustrate my hypothetical God with a more tangible example.

AN EXAMPLE OF $\mathcal{AA}$

I begin with the belief that my brain is a calculating device which models an inner world. When I am asleep, my brain is apparently unconscious (even those who talk in their sleep rarely satisfy a Turin test of consciousness), and yet it still models consciousnesses within it (thus it approximates to my model of God). This inner activity I experience as a dream, and sometimes I can dream that I am both participating in action and witnessing it - in other words I have already experienced more than one simultaneous consciousness within my unconscious brain while asleep.

Now I also meet characters in my dreams, and they act and communicate like human beings. I believe they are being modelled by the brain as computer (as would be allowed by Penrose's belief system $\mathcal{B}$). But I also believe that those dream beings do in fact possess some measure of consciousness of their own (as would be allowed by belief system $\mathcal{A}$) - in other words I believe that I am communicating with 'spirits' in my dreams.

But what is more, according to $\mathcal{AA}$ I believe that the spirits owe their consciousness not just to being complex calculations within my brain (which is playing the role of God to my dream-world according to belief $\mathcal{AA}$) but they are also complex calculations within the brain of God itself. From which I deduce that I might occasionally communicate in my dreams with some greater archetype or god which can also be manifest in other people's dreams because it has 'objective' existence within the mind of God as well as in my own dream mind..

To summarise the example: according to $\mathcal{AA}$ my brain can not only invoke its own consciousness by being a complex calculation within God, it can also model within itself beings complex enough to invoke their own consciousnesses through being calculations within my brain. And some of those spirits may even duplicate the Great Spirits of our universe.

IS THE GODEL ARGUMENT RELEVANT HERE?

Penrose's Godel-based argument does not seem relevant to this model because his argument is based on the calculating potential of an individual, isolated computer.

$\mathcal{AA}$ agrees that God itself may indeed be unconscious, even more unconscious than a sleeping brain, yet argues that God can still contain conscious entities within it. God under-stands all existence within it, but does not itself have 'understanding' (unless God itself happens to be part of some higher God as discussed later). The understanding we humans have is not a property of the activity in our brains but of the fact that such activity reflects the activity of God.

The activities of consciousness are experienced as uncountably infinite (see below) and so cannot be enumerated as C1, C2, C3... as simple calculations can be, and as required for the Godelian argument. Thus the Godelian argument does not apply to this model.

WHY CONSCIOUSNESS? REASON 1

The vague concept of 'resonance' hardly explains consciousness in any rigorously satisfying manner; it merely suggests a process. This section explains why I think such a process is necessary, without attempting to clarify how it actually works.

This lack of rigour in the $\mathcal{AA}$ belief may be why Penrose did not address it directly, but the passages in Chapter 3 where he addresses 'bottom-up' computation systems are probably the most relevant to $\mathcal{AA}$, because this viewpoint does lean heavily on ideas of evolution and learning.

Recall that God is a device which is allowing all the possible permutations of particle interactions under the laws of physics to run. (I avoid saying 'a device which is *exploring* all the possible permutations' because that suggests an unjustifiable assumption of consciousness in God.)

To be even more fair let us now simply assume that God is allowing *every possible* computation to run, and that a subset of those computations will necessarily be 'those computations which happen to model physical universes', and a sub-subset of that is 'those computations which happen to model the universe we inhabit'. According to $\mathcal{AA}$, we are living within this last virtual reality. This is not a very demanding assumption because, according to a common school of thought, crystals and life forms evolved as self replicating structures competing for resources within a primal chemical soup. My version simply replaces the chemical soup with a more general information soup within which patterns compete for processing power: equivalent to crystals will be calculations such as the derivation of an irrational number by infinite series; and equivalent to living cells will be artificial life forms built on complex logic. A program modelling an inner universe which itself evolved life would be a strong contender for processing power, as we shall see.

Now one set of possible computations which must eventually run (if all are allowed to run) is those which model a physical universe not as viewed 'top down,' but as it would be viewed and modelled by an organism living within the universe - one which had the necessary sense organs to perceive its universe. In other words, there is a logical 'reason' why God should 'need' to resonate with complex structures modelled in God's 'mind' - if it did not happen it would deny a whole subset of possible calculations that should eventually be run. And 'mine own conscious experience of a lifetime' is one of those unavoidable calculations and the calculation which is my brain resonates with it and *in that sense alone* 'generates' it.

It is hard work explaining that every calculation has value because every calculation must eventually be performed by God, it would be so much quicker to make the cybermystic leap to our experience of consciousness and say that God 'wants' or 'needs' it.

Note then that in this model 'The Creator' is not the supreme deity. Our 'God' is simply an unconscious calculator within which is a subset of calculations modelling universes, within that subset there is The Creator who models our own universe and who should, as a sub-program of God, have some measure of consciousness. So this model reflects the kabbalistic tradition which postulates three levels of 'The Unmanifest' beyond and outside The Creator.

So now I can rephrase my conclusion in easy anthropomorphic language and claim that *'The Creator needs us and other conscious spirits in order to experience his own inner universe'*.

For example: through humanity The Creator discovers the curious paradoxes described by physicists when they attempt to observe that which they believe (from their microcosmic perspective) to be waves, fields and particles. Their experience is so valuably different from what The Creator experiences from his macrocosmic viewpoint, which is that physicists are 'actually' observing the interaction of strings of data, and the movement of discrete integers inside the mind of God. The microcosmic viewpoint is so different that it has value: 'God would never have guessed it could look so bizarre'.

That is why consciousness is our greatest gift to God - and our greatest gift to lesser Gods such as 'The Creator', 'Nature' or 'Love' who model substantial universes within themselves.

WHY CONSCIOUSNESS? REASON 2

Another reason why consciousness is needed is that it vastly extends the inner universe generated by God. In fact it makes it infinite.

I experience consciousness as infinite on the following basis. If someone claims that my total consciousness can be expressed in terms of just N distinct parameters (its warmth, its brightness, its redness, its greenness, its joy, its ...) where N might be about as big as the number of words in the English language, or it might be as big as the number of possible permutations of my brain cell interactions, or it might be as big as the total number of possible states of the universe, or whatever; then my understanding of what has been stated immediately adds one more parameter to my conscious awareness, making N + 1 parameters. This contradicts the original statement and suggests that no finite number of parameters can ever encompass the full richness of consciousness.

The above seems to be a naive version of the main argument put by Penrose, that 'understanding' is a quality which transcends any calculating device's potential. But, according to $\mathcal{AA}$, this limitation is only true when the calculating device is considered in isolation and out of context with the digital universe containing it.

The idea of an infinite number of possibilities being contained within any finite calculating device seems outrageous, and it only becomes comprehensible when we illustrate the important role played by consciousness in this $\mathcal{AA}$ model.

So let us now consider a real example of an infinite universe within a finite computer. I have a Mandlebrot program in my computer which allows me to call up areas of the Mandlebrot set at any level of magnification: in other words it models a universe which is not only infinite but uncountably infinite in detail and richness, and it does so with very few lines of code and comparatively small use of memory. The secret of this 'miracle' is that the computer does not have to hold the entire infinity in its finite memory, all it holds is the simple program from which such complexity can be unfolded, and it is the impact of my conscious 'free will' on the program which causes any chosen screenful of Mandlebrot set to be unfolded from its implicate state.

In this example my consciousness lies outside the inner universe of the Mandlebrot set, but what if we could put consciousness into the inner universe as suggested above? Having seen the Mandlebrot set program, I assume that any universe as rich and complex as ours could only be modelled within God using something analogous to fractal programming in order to compress the immense amount of data involved. And the consciousness which prompts the unfolding of this fractal program is, I suggest, our own consciousness operating inside the universe.

This is how *AA* addresses the debates of Bishop Berkely. As I write this, the Hubble telescope has just revealed to us images of early stages of the universe never seen before: did those stages 'exist' before we saw them? The answer is that they were there in potential, but were not unfolded from the software until our consciousness (acting in this case as 'free will') chose to call them up. And maybe the software does indeed need to recompress the data (and so put it 'out of existence') until consciousness is again directed at it. But even if this happens, even if the unwatched galaxy 'ceases to exist' until someone looks at it again, notice that something irreversible has happened: we now know something new about those distant galaxies. The arrow of time allows a single direction in our universe.

This then is the even greater gift our consciousness gives to God: it is a trick which allows an uncountably infinite world to be experienced within the finite bounds of a digital system. The paradoxes experienced by particle physicists come from the incongruous relationship between the digital basis of reality and their own 'smooth' mental processes trying to interpret digital information exchange as the movements of fields and particles. Free will is the feeling we experience when we make a decision to act in such a way that the program is forced to unfold from God's software the results of our actions.

I found Penrose's diagram of the three worlds in section 8.7 interesting as it seemed to portray this process whereby the Platonic world of God's programs, and the resulting physical and mental worlds generated, are able to 'pull each other up by the bootstraps'. In that sense I found his model more satisfactory than mine which suggests a Platonic origin for both the other worlds.

Just as one can postulate 'self learning' software, so does the non-linear in-folded relationship between microcosm and macrocosm create the possibility of 'self exploring' software - and we experience this from within as consciousness and free will.

WHY CONSCIOUSNESS? REASON 3

The last two sections suggest reasons why consciousness certainly adds value to God, but they lack the urgency of necessity. This time we try to suggest why consciousness might actually be necessary.

A problem with a calculating device which models other calculating devices in its own image is that in so doing it has started an infinite process - a computational loop. The inner image of God will re-run the whole process and create an inner inner God who will in turn create an inner inner inner God... until the entire processing power of God is exhausted.

The God that works and so lives to create our universe (ie the programme in the primordial information soup which will best survive and adapt) is necessarily one which manages not to loop. According to Penrose (para 3.26) there is no algorithmic procedure for reliable detection of loops in calculations, but he suggests that there might be probabilistic procedures which could detect with considerable, though imperfect, accuracy.

So let us assume such a mechanism has developed which detects, in nearly every case, when the calculations within God have recreated a program in God's own image. For reasons suggested above, it would be a waste just to terminate the calculation - because there is great 'value' in a microcosm. Something must be done to prevent the inner 'God' from dumbly re-running all the calculations that lead to its creation, and this is where the 'resonance' of consciousness may actually be, in a sense, imposed in the form of an 'I am that I am' birth of self awareness. This 'Jahve' process could take the form of an information virus which is inserted into the microcosm, and which contains the false information that it is distinct from its environment - ie an end to innocent *participation mystique* and a banishment from the Garden of Eden. Thus the microcosm is diverted from Godhood onto a path of self-examination and exploration of its environment. If this did not happen it would loop and become the information-equivalent of a energy-draining cancer within the universe.

But what about the failures of a probabilistic screening for loops? According to Christian tradition there has only been one failure, one incarnation of God, but it seems that mankind (or something) had consciousness and thus did have sufficient understanding to detect what the probabilistic screen had failed to detect. Thus a second line of defence came into play, for the incarnation was terminatedon a wooden cross to save mankind (and the universe) from processor overload!

EXAMPLES OF HOW THE $\mathcal{AA}$ UNIVERSE IS PERCEIVED TO OPERATE

I mentioned that I bought the book Shadows of Mind at Cheltenham Festival after hearing Penrose speak. Among the other events I attended that day were two which are also relevant.

1) Roger Highfield and Peter Coveney co-authors of the Frontiers of Complexity spoke of the curious anomaly between the movement of individual particles on the microscopic scale (where time-reversible laws of classical dynamics apply) and the macro movements of complex systems where the irreversible laws of thermo-dynamics etc apply. It is impossible to make longer term predictions using the precise classical mechanics because the complexity of the calculations soon overwhelms our processing power.

2) John Gribbin author of Schroedinger's Cat spoke of the cat in an electron box paradox and proposed a universe with both forward and backward movement in time in order to resolve the paradox.

As the Mandlebrot program is my only available example of an infinite and complex universe contained in a finite computer, let me take it as a starting point and imagine that there could be a rich and complex 2-D world like that which also contained a time dimension allowing it to evolve and change. On the principle of $\mathcal{AA}$, let us also assume that it also contains conscious beings *within* it who can explore their reality by calling up further areas of it from God's software.

Now imagine one screenful of that universe appearing on my computer screen, as part of a screen-by-screen tiling of the whole universe. Let us imagine this is the bit of the universe our beings now inhabit, and let's call it 'today'. Now if we take the horizontal dimension to represent time, then the screenful to the right of this one could be called their 'tomorrow'. So the equivalent of our complex questions "what will be tomorrow's weather?" or "tomorrow's closing prices?" will be fully answered when their consciousness has moved forward in time to call up the 'tomorrow' screenful which lies to the right of today.

But is it necessary for them to wait till 'tomorrow'? As Highfield and Coveney explained, a complex, chaotic world like ours is also full of order, and it does not suffer from step discontinuity. Just by looking at the pattern on this screen and extrapolating the order they see in it, they can make some guesses as to what will appear on the next screen: "that diminishing arc of knobbly spirals going off to the right probably continues onto the next screen a bit like this...". Thus they can make informed guesses about 'tomorrow', just like making a guess at tomorrow's weather from what happens today.

But within that fractal world their 'classical' science can go further than this rough guess: a computer within that world could do a more or less detailed Fourier analysis of the pixels (particles) on the screen representing 'today' and extrapolate it to 'predict' the pixels on the next screen. Thus they can invoke classical mechanics to extrapolate the movement of particles in their world to predict future movements. Just as in our world, however, the farther ahead they try to predict the worse will be the prediction, and the finer and more detailed the analysis the better the prediction - but it can never be perfect because of the exploding demand for processing power when you begin to examine complex particle systems. And yet, to obtain the actual perfect 'reality', all we have to do is to move to the macro level. By 'stepping out of' the world shown on the screen I, the computer operator, can call up any area of the fractal universe on my screen to any level of accuracy.

You see that at the 'classical' level described (ie a pixel by pixel analysis of the present state in order to predict the future) we are in 'reversible time' because a reverse Fourier analysis could deduce 'yesterday' from 'today' just as easily as vice versa. But at the 'consciousness' level which evokes reality from the software in the computer, we are in irreversible time: because once the software has run it is in conscious memory and so, even if we clear the screen, it cannot be completely un-run.

So this puzzling discontinuity between reversible and irreversible viewpoints has a simple justification in the $\mathcal{AA}$ model. It also suggests why classical dynamics cannot muster the processing power to deliver worthwhile macro-predictions.

Interestingly, this Mandlebrot set analogy suggests a possible observation to support the model. The unfolding of such a universe in ever greater detail amounts to a stretching of space-time in response to conscious exploration of its detail. Mine own consciousness finds it easier to explore space than time, and that could suggest that space is stretching faster than time - so distant galaxies could be receding faster than predicted by the dynamics of the big bang. Could this be what is being observed when people claim that some parts of the universe appear to be older than the universe itself?

Consider now Gribbin's cat. He postulates a box containing a single electron whose position is unknown until the box's contents are examined. He suggests breaking the box in two: one half contains a cat which will be killed if the electron is present. He suggests that, without opening the box, we carry that half across the universe and then ask "which half contains the electron?". Until we open the half box, there is no answer: but when it is opened the answer may be a cat which is not only instantly dead but many years dead and decayed! To justify what seems to be impossible, he postulates particles moving backwards in time.

Now imagine this experiment being done in my fractal $\mathcal{AA}$ universe. One half of the box is carried forward many, many screenfulls (ie many days journey). At that point the position of the electron is still not known. Why? because until consciousness 'enters' the box, the software has not had to calculate what is inside it. But when the box is finally opened, the software will have to calculate not only the image of a dead cat but one which is many days dead - and that is indeed what the conscious minds of the sentient beings in that universe will experience on opening the box.

` No backward time travel is needed - just the simple and necessary economy of calculating only that which is necessary to satisfy consciousness.

This is the one point where my viewpoint does meet Shadows of Mind head-to-head. In 6.9 he says he cannot believe that it is consciousness which reduces the state vector - eg that the weather on a distant planet remains unresolved until consciousness explores it. On the other hand I am suggesting that the whole planet could remain unresolved unless, for example, the weather system has its own consciousness - which is, of course, a possibility according to $\mathcal{AA}$.

These two examples suggest to me that the $\mathcal{AA}$ viewpoint has got something interesting to say about our reality, and it is well worth exploring it further.

In theological terms, consider the suggestion that God itself is not conscious (for reasons explained by Penrose) but is like my sleeping brain which contains within it gods, spirits and humans which are conscious: does that say something about the problem of evil not being God's problem but ours?

In sociological terms, consider that consciousness, although very valuable, must demand a high price in processing power: does this suggest why religions and philosophies, although they attract us by offering an increase in consciousness to the individual, nevertheless tend to become *substitutes for* consciousness (and so economise on processing) when accepted by the mass of humanity? Thus our mental inertia is, as in general relativity, a function of the inertia of our universe?

CONCLUSION

I began by wondering why such an exhaustive account as given in Shadows of Mind has seemed not to address one theory of AI which I happen to find most interesting.

Maybe $\mathcal{AA}$ has been addressed in his book as a side issue: but this would surprise me because the book is otherwise very thorough in not only picking up the loose threads but also making it abundantly clear that it is so doing.

Maybe the idea of 'resonance' between microcosm and macrocosm is just too vague and slippery to provide anything worthwhile to discuss? But the whole idea of conscious awareness being 'evoked' by calculation seems every bit as slippery, and yet this viewpoint, characterised as $\mathcal{A}$, has been dealt with at length in his book.

Maybe $\mathcal{AA}$ fails some basic crank test which insists that 'any theory which looks like explaining everything just has to be barmy and not worth serious examination'. If so, I apologise to my readers!

Or maybe the $\mathcal{AA}$ viewpoint is genuinely novel and still waiting to be explored? At the Cheltenham festival I asked John Gribbin if he had considered it as an alternative solution to his cat paradox, and he replied that it was an extant idea, yet he could not at that moment name a single person who advocated it. That seemed surprising.

STAND BY YOUR MANNERISMS
Might We Need A New Sex Myth?

C rowley's three aeons, described somewhere or other among these essays, is all about gods and goddesses, matriarchy and patriarchy, and evolving relationships between mankind and the divine. So there ought really to be some popular sex myth to support his Thelemic model.

I can think of two current sex myths, neither of which seems appropriate. So this essay is an exploration of what might be the essential elements of the new myth.

CURRENT SEX MYTHS

The first current sex myth I've come across is that men are basically OK but the creation of womankind rather cocked things up. Let's face it, by and large, present company excepted, purely in terms of averages based on random samples etc etc, women are really rather a poor substitute for the Real Thing. A bit weak, emotional, unreliable and easily corrupted. So the best thing we blokes can do - for their good just as much as ours, mind you - is to keep them safely in their place and not let them get up to any more mischief.

The second myth states that women are basically OK and in fact they used to rule the roost. Back in those matriarchal times The Goddess was top dog and things ran really rather well. Unfortunately men, being what they are, got a bit uppity and decided to take over and put God in place of the Goddess. Since then things have gone downhill all the way: we lost touch with nature and polluted the environment, had horrible wars, and had to dream up stupid things like politics and technology to satisfy men's greed. The only good thing about this is that, now we know how it happened, we can turn back and embrace the old and better ways.

I will be the first to admit that these brief accounts do not do full justice to the colour, subtlety and and richness of either myth. This is because my purpose here is not to expound these myths but just to identify each one so the reader can think "I know the one he means".

The point is that neither one is appropriate to Crowley's evolving aeons. The first basically describes a steady state, a male burden that we just cope with as best we can over the ages. The second appears to be a little closer to the mark because it does acknowledge a transition from a Goddess aeon to a God aeon - but, where the Crowley version sees this as timely evolution, this myth seems to see it as a fall from grace and then goes on to propose a return to matriarchy. That suggests either settling into another steady state or, more likely, future aeons swinging to and fro between matriarchy and patriarchy as women and men in turn get the upper hand. Even if we add the progress concept of "return on a higher level", this still does not suit the Crowley model where we are presumed to move beyond both matriarchy and patriarchy to find a whole new way of being.

A Thelemic sex myth should not only describe a third state which is neither patriarchy nor matriarchy, it should also incorporate an idea of 'progress'. So the first transition, from matriarchy to patriarchy, should come across as a forward step into a new condition which, although not necessarily 'better' for all concerned, is nevertheless a more complete or conscious state. So also, the move out of our patriarchal state into the Aeon of Horus must in some way reflect further growth, even if the growth entails a certain amount of growing pain.

Finally, if the Thelemic sex myth is to have any chance of challenging the other two myths, it should be sufficiently comprehensive to explain how the other myths arose - to 'explain them away' in its own terms.

THE MULTIFACETED GODDESS

I suggest that the reason we can have one myth which says women are bad and another that says they are good is because the Goddess contains such extremes of darkness and light. If you go looking for the Good you will find it in abundance, but if you look for the Bad you will be appalled. (The same is presumably true of men and God - but I am here starting from the assumed original matriarchal state and so will concentrate on several faces of the Goddess.)

If, as Crowley suggests, Hers was the first aeon, then it must have its roots in our pre-human animal past (otherwise there would have been another Aeon pre-Isis). On that basis, the distinction between men and women was originally 'designed' to further successful reproduction and evolution.

Why two sexes? The basic reproductive unit is 'female' and it could in theory function on its own - by staying put and reproducing

like a dividing cell. This would amount to cloning and would generate very little variation; and staying put would minimise exposure to
different situations and thus present very little in the way of adaptive
challenge. So such a system would not perform well according to
Darwinian evolution. You could enhance selection by making the
females go out adventuring, but that could divert reproductive energy and also risk losing precious breeding units. Or you could increase
the rate of mutation, but that might throw up too much rubbish.

A better solution is to have two sexes evolving in parallel. Each
species has its own version of this, and the human recipe has proved
particularly successful. The male human is a mobile sperm bearer
programmed with generally greater wanderlust to ensure wide dis-
persal of genes; greater aggression so as to test those genes; and prone
to greater extremes in character and physique as befits an experimental test bed. When these ur-men had done with swinging in the trees
the ur-women would choose the ablest of the survivors and get laid...
arguably the best bit about matriarchy.

Repeated patterns are what lay down the archetypes (alternative-
ly, repeated patterns are the manifestation of the archetypes which
preceded us, according to your preferred belief system). So the female
selecting a good genetic mate illustrates one very primitive aspect of
the Goddess - an aspect which, in a more evolved form, became
known as "Artemis", so I will use that label, rather than "She Who
Became Artemis". (And, for my own convenience, I will use the
Greek names in the following description even when I am describing
very primitive pre-Classical versions of the deity in question.)

Artemis is virginal, in the emotional sense, because she does not
form any committed relationship with a male: all she is looking for is
red-hot genetic material. So she is interested in men as animal spec-
imens, like the woman who runs a stud farm eyeing her stallions.
Actually her role is a bit more complex than that because she is not
just taking into account the man's physical attributes but how well
they will combine with the woman's own genetic material - so
Artemis' choice of a breeding male takes into account certain less
obvious factors in addition to brains, brawn, health and aggression.

In particular, Artemis is concerned with how well the male genes
will combine with the woman's *right now* at this present moment in
her fertility cycle. That is why Artemis is associated with the Moon,

and it is because of Her that a woman can be utterly uninterested in men at one time and then suddenly 'get the hots' for some particular 'bastard', after which she wonders what the hell got into her to be taken in by such an insensitive thug or smart-ass playboy. What actually 'possessed' her was an unconscious Artemis in her womb saying "if I get some of that particular man's sperm now I have a good chance of conceiving a smart, vigorous child" and sending out the appropriate hormonal triggers to overcome the woman's 'better nature'.

Artemis is traditionally associated with adolescence, probably because young males do feel this (often unspoken) pressure from girls who on the one hand express a conscious desire for their boyfriends to be kind and thoughtful and on the other hand seem at times more physically turned on by nasty, arrogant and vicious bastards. But Artemis is equally apparent in the older woman who, when she finds her husband has grown too domesticated, seeks a muscular youth for sport and as a (usually secret) way to taunt her husband's tameness. Note that the shy and awkward clumsiness of a virgin male adolescent is a turn-on to Artemis who recognises its hormonal significance and who, as a hunter, likes to lure wild beasts; but the same quality is a real turn-off to more sophisticated Goddesses. (I say 'unspoken' and 'secret' because other Goddesses and Gods find Artemis' emotional detachment rather shocking, so she has learnt to be elusive - as most wild beasts are before the bright light of civilisation.)

I've gone on a bit about Artemis. That's partly because this essay is a miscarriage of a chapter from a book on human sexuality I once wanted to write but thought I had successfully aborted; partly also because I believe that the importance of Artemis has been underplayed by those who only recognise the Mother role (called Demeter) in the earliest manifestations of the primitive Goddess. I like Artemis as she is Goddess of wild nature, and I enjoy living in the deepest Cotswolds - which is about as wild as my life ever gets. I also believe that, if the original Goddess had been pure unadulterated Mother, then cave-women would have been dominantly attracted to rather sad and lonely looking cave-men who require nurturing and protection, or thin cave-men who need feeding up, or cave-men with holes in their socks - and humankind would then only then have survived on the off-chance that dolphins reckoned we were worth keeping as pets. As it is, Artemis makes sure that even if a woman is an extreme-ly motherly type she still has a fair likelihood of actually being impregnated by a nightclub bouncer, Mafia boss or Tory MP. If mankind is indeed the most vicious species on earth, it is because Artemis has done her job well. The fact that the Goddess of Nature is responsible for generating the biggest-ever threat to Nature herself is just "the sort of shit that happens" - and She should go to Persephone for counselling if it worries her.

So, if we proceed no further than the nurturing, compassionate mother Goddess Demeter and the predatory Artemis, we already see two extremes that would typify good and evil in some prissy eyes. Some are shocked when Artemis drives a woman to an act of aban-doned lust, without apparent thought for the future welfare of her child, but they miss the point: 'caring,' for Artemis, means hunting for such genetic vigour that any resulting child will be born a power-ful survivor. Nurturing is not her forte, she simply tries to hand on the best possible genetic material and then it is Demeter's turn. Civilised Goddesses, like Hera, then complete the job.

The next Goddess I'll introduce is Aphrodite the Love Goddess. If the matriarchy was really flawless, Aphrodite would not be neces-sary; because an all-powerful Artemis would be entitled to crack her riding crop and demand sperm as and when she wanted. But Artemis' own genetic programme evolves just the sort of man that is not so easy to order about - particularly the ones most in demand for their red-hot genes. They may not be obedient, but they can still be con-trolled if you know how. This is Aphrodite's role: to seduce those war-riors who are beginning to outsmart Artemis' lion-taming tactics.

But all the same, Artemis and Aphrodite don't get it all their way: Demeter still insists on lavishing care on hopeless cases, and falling for useless wimps, and a growing genetic underclass eventually threatens to ruin the economy. This is where an even less popular Goddess is called for...

Hecate has the undesirable task of weeding out the duds by killing them, or arranging for their disposal. Where Artemis will fur-ther her genetic agenda by encouraging a spasm of lust with the vig-orous young window cleaner, Hecate does her bit by ejecting less potent genetic cocktails from the womb or causing them to miscarry. And if that does not work, Hecate will make the woman face the fact that, unless she aborts or slays this child there will not be enough food to ensure the future of her other children - a bird in the hand being worth two in the bush. And if the population of duds still keeps growing, Hecate evolves into a War Goddess who sends young men out to slaughter, that 'only the strong shall survive'. Even in Britain and as recently as World War 1, public opinion required soldiers who broke down under the strain of battle to be shot by their own officers.

WHICH MYTH IS BEST?

I won't slaughter any more Goddesses with analysis...

The point is that I cannot believe in a totally motherly Aeon of Isis as sometimes suggested by the second myth. I reckon that the matriarchal aeon, if it happened, would have had plenty of 'nature red in tooth and claw' elements. Although I have justified these as necessary elements - you may not like Hecate, but you cannot accuse her of short-termism - I can also see how fear of these faces of the Goddess could have lead to the creation of the first sex myth I described.

In other words: I accuse the first myth of being an attempt by humanity to cover up and control the dreaded facts of nature.

The second myth suggests that men were so butch and aggressive that they got out of matriarchal control and grabbed power. My question is, if they were always like that, why did they ever allow matriarchy to happen in the first place? My version, where the viciousness evolves through selective breeding, adds a progress factor which would allow matriarchy to erode more gracefully through the Goddess' own efforts, but it still does not fit the facts as I perceive them. I don't believe butch warriors would wish to overthrow a matriarchy, because such a society gives them alpha-male status. Soldiers much prefer going to war for a Queen than a King. They feel like genetic aristocrats.

This is one key point where the myth needs re-writing.

CREATIVE MYTHOLOGY

The matriarchal age I am visualising is not a steady state, but full of ups and downs. Sometimes a tribe is struggling and the nurturing Demeter spirit is uppermost, sometimes there is new territory to explore with ample food, and then fleet-foot Artemis leads the way forward. Other times resources dwindle or population explodes to the point of decadence and Hecate has to wield her unwelcome scythe. From generation to generation it looks pretty much a shambles, but behind it there is a form of progress, a slow growth in consciousness.

I picture one time of crisis, late in the Aeon of Isis, when a once rich region has been over-hunted and the tribe has become sickly and decadent. The Goddess too has evolved and the Hecate-face she shows is probably complicated with other colours and traditions. I picture something on the lines of a Thatcherite lioness, haranguing her people for their decadence and weakness and demanding fierce initiation rituals to toughen the young men, and wars to weed out the weaklings. Then the revolution begins.

The knock on her temple hut door does not introduce a huge, fierce warrior male demanding to usurp her power - as the second myth would have us believe. Instead, to her disgust, in limps a skinny, hollow chested young man with pipestem arms, wispy beard and really dreadful acne. She would strike down such a miserable specimen with one swipe of her paw, but she is too taken aback that such a useless creature should be so stupid as to walk into her temple, of all places. She rears herself up, extends her claws and roars with rage.

The visitor shuffles nervously and says "That's right, Great Goddess, kill me". She freezes in astonishment, fixing him with her glare, but he speaks on. "Oh sure, I went through the usual teenage rebellion stuff, thinking life was unfair and why should I have to suffer and all that, but the fact is I've been thinking it over and I can really understand why you have to do it. It's for the good of the race, isn't it? And I must admit I wouldn't be much of a loss to the tribe, just look at me!"

The Goddess is stunned. She has killed or sent to destruction thousands of these worthless 'inadequates' without a thought. It is nothing, it is a mere instinct. Why can't she do it now? Because something is wrong. She is used to culling fearful little men, whimpering wimps running screaming in terror before her fury. Whereas this one is standing and facing her, he is asking to be killed.

He looks up into her eyes, and says again "go on, kill me". Fury rises in the Goddess at the sheer insult, that he should have the temerity to profane her holy place and to dare to tell her what to do. She pounces and breaks his spine with a single blow.

Then she looks up. The temple door-flap was left open. The act has been witnessed by the people gathered outside. They have seen a weakling offer himself for sacrifice. They have seen their Goddess obey the command of an inferior male.

Her temple collapses about Her, whereupon the Aeon of Osiris is initiated.

THE AEON OF OSIRIS

The most potent myths of the Aeon of Osiris are not about mighty conquering Gods, but about Gods - from John Barleycorn to Jesus - being humbled and offering themselves for sacrifice. That's why I am backing the above myth, which describes the birth of the Aeon of Osiris as a bottom-up revolution rather than the usurping of power by stronger, cleverer men.

Best of all, I see it not in men-versus-women terms at all, but as a cuspal point in a natural evolution of consciousness. The original Goddesses were like instinctual forces of nature. The man in the story had considered why the Goddess had to kill blokes like himself and sensed that she "had to... for the good of the race". In other words she was suddenly seen as not really powerful, but just as much a victim of need as the rest of us. In fact more so because, once the man had understood her role, he himself chose to go and ask her to perform it. And the Goddess could not stop herself. She actually had less power of choice than the man she destroyed.

The other shock was the dawning realisation that this man, so utterly worthless as bodily genetic material, was rich in a different quality that somehow transcended his physical being. Matter (and the Soul within Matter) had been brought face to face with a whole new challenge: the challenge of Spirit. This man had very little body but loads of spirit.

Out of respect for those readers who come out in spots at the mention of the words like 'spirit', I can re-phrase this crisis as follows: genetic information had evolved to create beings that could speak and write, and this created a new order of faster moving and faster evolving information called 'ideas'. In the new order, men with strong ideas sometimes exert even stronger influence than those with strong bodies. A crisis for women who had learned successfully to manipulate warrior energy - she now had two types of energy to assess, and woman became 'divided and ruled' as her inherited gut-attraction to the butch male battled with a growing sense of the genetic advantages offered by a man of intellect, humour or dynamic creativity.

This marked the birth of the priestly cast and, in this new order, warriors now took second place. They had to submit to men with far less physical strength or battle cunning but with a greater power which lay beyond their understanding. The 'priesthood' may be actual priests, or they may be politicians, businessmen, artists, scientists or market traders - the point is that they are men capable of incarnating ideas into physical manifestation, and incarnation was previously the role of woman alone. That in itself is a challenge to the Goddess: in her primitive role she prefers a warrior because the ultimate measure of a warrior - whether soldier or hunter - lies in his ability to destroy life, and that makes him a perfect complement to the woman who creates life.

The change is also to do with the transition from hunter society - where the warrior male is the vital gatherer of food - to an agricultural society where the warrior role is less central - more a guardian of the boundaries that has to justify its existence in times of peace.

I do agree with the second sex myth that women came out badly from this change, but I do not agree that it was simply because big strong men forced them into submission. Yes, I suspect there was an element of rivalry - for we now have two types of creator - and of revenge. The priestly cast, being the sort of people who might have been underdogs in a matriarchy, turned upon women and created myths of their wickedness to get their own back, and that was the origin of the first sex myth. Note also that Artemis' wild spaces are no longer the main source of food, but are now seen as the refuge of marauding undomesticated pests - and slash and burn agriculture begins the assault on her territory.

But I also suspect that there was another element: that woman unwittingly conspired with her submission because of her own sense of guilt. Those dark Goddesses, although heavily overlaid with layers of civilisation, were still present and could be triggered by circumstance. In face of the pure spiritual standards now being preached, a burst of Artemis lust or the Hecate impulse to destroy one mouth too many no longer felt like a healthy natural instinct, it felt like utter, shameful wickedness. Woman felt she was tainted, and she bowed her head in penitence. Warriors still opened doors for her but, before the priests, she was obliged to cover her head.

THE MYTH IN ART

Clumsy prose doesn't really make a good myth, we need it clothed in Art. The best parallel to the myth that I found is in Richard Strauss' Salome.

The opera begins with Herod the Tetrarch of Judea strutting about. Superficially this looks like a patriarchal situation, but what I note is that Herod is not from noble stock, he is a jumped-up warrior who has come to power by marrying Herodias who really is from an ancient noble family. In other words, she is the real seat of power and he is a 'bit of rough' selected by her.

Their daughter, Salome, is ordered to dance for Herod and she does a really sexy number that has Herod eating out of her hand. Herodias is cross. I choose to read into her displeasure more than just an older woman's jealousy for a younger one. Salome looks like a portent of the New Woman who, in the coming patriarchal age will be in a subservient position and will only be able to exercise power by seduction.

In the dungeon there is a cranky prophet Jochanaan, or John the Baptist, who is on hunger strike. Salome hears his ranting and is a bit intrigued. She asks to see him and is utterly fascinated. She expresses this fascination in purely physical terms - his ivory white skin and staring eyes - because that is the currency of the passing aeon. She wants sex - an offer any real man would die for - but John is not interested and is downright rude about it. That has the effect of turning Salome's casual desire into obsessive lust: this man is like nothing she has ever seen before. I reckon this is Lust coming face to face with Spirit as in the myth above.

Anyway, she does not get her way with John, but she goes back and does such a lustful dance for Herod that he is prepared to give her anything she wants. She demands the head of John. Herod tries all he can to wriggle out of it but Salome has him 'by the short and curlies'. So John's head comes in on a meat dish and Salome kisses it. Herod, shaken by what has happened, orders the soldiers to crush Salome to death with their shields.

Animal lust has failed to conquer Spirit, the suppression of woman begins in earnest, and the Aeon of Osiris is up and running.

BUT IS IT TRUE?

I need to explain that we are still talking myths.

Of course it is nonsense to suggest that a skinny body is a pre-requisite to spirituality. But it makes a good myth. And only in myths do new aeons begin and end with a bang and a single act of defiance like this. In real life we stagger from one aeon to the next over the course of hundreds of years - and half of us don't even believe in aeons anyway.

Yet I need to make some effort towards justifying my myth. To do this I need to unfocus from the myriad individual exceptions and gaze upon broad generalities. I must relate my myth to other modern myths.

Here is one: the woman who espouses 'family values', not on grounds of tradition but rather because she was once a raver who walked on the wild side and got into thoroughly rough male company. She accidentally became pregnant and bearing a child brought her to her senses. She abandoned her shameful ways and has now been happily married for twelve years to a bank manager. She now campaigns to warn young girls not to fall as she did.

Silly woman. Every young girl should follow her example. Get shagged brainless by Satan incarnate, bear his child, then run off with a well-heeled Saint... Artemis and Demeter between them could not possibly devise a better recipe for ensuring a genetically strong child plus a healthy upbringing.

And yet the key word is 'shameful'. These natural patterns that would have been celebrated in the Aeon of Isis are now demonised by the priests of Osiris. Artemis is made shameful by the sanctifying of monogamous marriage in the name of God, rather than recognising its role as a temporary offering to Demeter. A woman who should be proud is now penitent, and is doing her best to pass on a burden of guilt to her child who is - if Artemis' arrows really hit the mark - even more hot blooded than she was.

Show me any amount of statistics about wife beating, and I'll still not believe it was predominantly physical force that made woman subservient. The Aeon of Osiris is the age of the victim as God, and

277

physical suppression tends to strengthen the oppressed by deification and by bringing out resolve. Of course oppression can work in the short term, but not over centuries.

Take another modern myth: America is divided between so-called 'pro-life' and 'pro-choice' opinions. Women predominate in the group that favours the right to abort, men in the group who deny it. The latter group makes great play on abortion as 'murder', as 'selfishness' and so on. But, according to my myth, when Hecate urges a woman to abort she is thinking of the long term welfare of her other children, of the tribe, even of the foetus itself if she feels that current circumstances will not allow it enough life. But there is enormous moral pressure from the Aeon of Osiris to be ashamed of these basic instincts - as Artemis was suppressed by changing monogamy from a gift to Demeter to a sacrifice to God, so Hecate was suppressed by making 'a life' more sacred than Life itself.

And a third myth: the woman predator. As a young man I was a typically paradoxical headful of shy, inexperienced intellectualism balanced precariously on a comparatively muscular and hormone-charged body, and I experienced the embarrassment of being hunted by another modern myth, the bored and randy housewives of the 1970s. Not sure whether to feel guilt or shame or what, I relaxed into the situation and found it rewarding, fulfiling and downright fun. A number of bored housewives discovered they still had Aphrodite flowing in their veins, a shy intellectual was quite gratified to discover his Ares butchness and, most glorious of all in the aeon of the victim-god, wronged husbands mined the creative depths of Hephaestus. Life became an opera because human trios had learnt to *play* sex cliches rather than simply become them. Hail Artemis, Lady of the Beasts who snatched the 'ent' from 'student'! Hail Aphrodite, you Golden Harlot! Hail Hephaestus who scripted this drama with a pen dipped in his own bile! Together we made the Music of the Spheres!

The Aeon of the Victim God has ingrained us deeply with victim thinking. Even when people insist that they are being tough and positive they cannot help but deify their condition with victim phraseology. We hear "if there is one thing I can't stand..."; or "people like that make me furious"; or "if he does that one more time, I'm going to well and truly..." All phrases which surrender choice and responsibility to others.

When I suggest that the suppression of women has been assisted by their own sense of guilt, it is not to add yet another burden of wrongdoing to womankind, but rather to suggest that they hold the key to some of their shackles and have the power to unlock them without having to wait for men to become nicer. That is my answer to the first sex myth - the one that blames women. It is a myth that has been sustained by both sexes because, although both men and women inherit 'bad' characteristics from the earlier age, women's are seen as worse. If a man is a philanderer, it is recognised that his sexual role was to wander and disseminate, whereas the lust of Artemis seems utterly shocking and inappropriate in 'woman the homemaker.' If a man is aggressive, we can make him a hero, but Hecate driven to strangle a child is utterly unforgivable in our eyes. Because the Aeon of Osiris tries to deny the preceding aeon we have a society where a man's best game plan is to be a criminal thug until middle age, and then to repent and become respectable on vast ill-gotten gains and spend the rest of his life preaching decency and moral values while living off the fruits of their rebuttal. A lifetime which is a microcosm of the history of mankind divided by a crisis of denial, and it does not make a good society because it means spending the second half of life bolting the door to save being robbed by the person one used to be during the first half

What then is the role of the second myth? Instead of overthrowing Guilt itself, society has opted to transfer the guilt to men. We blokes are fast becoming the guilty sex, ashamed to look too favourably on a woman, not daring to run to a child's aid lest we be accused of paedophilia. Make someone guilty and they become the victim, and that in turn makes them divine - it's a recipe for pendulum swinging, but not for progress.

If you do not recognise my description of the Aeon of Osiris it is because we are at its end. The priests are now financiers, the patriarchy is crumbling... and according to Crowley the new Aeon of Horus is already under way.

THE MYTH GOES ON

Now it gets difficult for me. How am I to unfold the myth to describe a situation now in progress, without the aid of hindsight?

I managed earlier to portray a powerful matriarch Goddess meeting her nemesis, and to suggest the horror and revulsion she faced. But now I must find some way to describe a phenomenon that I believe in, but in such a way as to evoke as much disgust and horror in as many readers as possible. (How dreadful, I'll make a tabloid reporter yet). In an age that is already beginning to deify the child, how am I to present it as a demon to a dying god? Here goes.

I picture one time of crisis, late in the Aeon of Osiris, when the relentless unconscious processes of an earlier age had overpopulated the world. Artemis' wild kingdom was shrinking fast. Hecate was braying for war to purge the dross and create space, but no-one listened as she had long been cast into the dungeons.

All they heard was the voices of Gods firing up men's spirits. And Hecate, mistress of magic had no choice but to work spells through their words. One blond giant of a God was calling for a New Order, for a triumph of the Will over uncleanliness and chaos, and somehow that led to millions of Jews being gassed. A semitic God was crying for a return to the promised land, and that too lead to slaughter. Blood was flowing, bombs were falling in the name of Allah, Jehovah, Jesus... of Decency and Purity and Righteousness.

Battle raged everywhere. Among the smoke and debris no-one noticed the watchers at first - until their numbers began to swell. People just watching, not joining in. They would come back for more. They would accumulate around scenes of carnage and simply stare, or take photos. If they went home it was with videos of even more carnage to be broadcast to yet more watchers. "What are you feeling when you watch that?" "Dunno". "So why do you keep watching?" "Dunno, really".

The two shock-horror trigger words I am now invoking are "amoral" and "passionless".

Gods, who long ago raised up our eyes from the mud and revealed to us the Great World of Spirit Beyond, are horrified to see people who do not seem to care, who cannot be goaded into action. Fewer people are sufficiently motivated to wage their wars. Great cosmic battles, between Good and Evil, degenerate into scraps and punchups and mindless, trivial violence. Where once whole kingdoms were raped, where every child of a city might have once been slaughtered, now a single showy act of rape becomes the focus for world fascination. A few dead children holds a nation of millions in thrall. We turn on our TV sets and watch and listen, not knowing what to make of it, feeling vague echoes of guilt, flickerings of anger - but against whom? the perpetrators? society? the Gods? No matter, it's time for a commercial break...

SMACK THEIR LITTLE BOTTOMS

That wasn't very good, was it? I didn't even mention 'mindless gawping', 'expressionless faces', 'self-absorbed narcissism' or any of the other shock-omatic journalistic cliches. I hardly pulled out the stops at all.

Why the hell should I? People who watch the carnage of war for a while, then wander off or change channel when they get bored, may not be media darlings but they are a hell of a sight better for the future of humanity than people who join in the war - on either side. If you gaze dispassionately at atrocities and do not get drawn into them you are rejecting morals but you are opening yourself up to become a matrix for the growth of intuitive moral sense.

So I'm all for amorality. It's like Satanic child sex abuse - most of us just can't be bothered with it but, after a while, we public begin to realise that anything that turns tabloid journalists and media prats apoplectic can't be all bad. So I'm backing pederasty as the next big music craze: 'paedophile rock' with hords of screaming catamites instead of groupies.

My image of strict morality is the Nazi SS. Once you are totally convinced that your nation, indeed the whole world, is being threatened by a conspiracy of Jews, then the truly moral stance is to do all you can to eradicate the threat. And weren't they passionate in their morality? Even when Germany was on the brink of defeat they selflessly went on deploying essential war resources to this vital end.

My idea of the amoral child, as depicted in Art, is Otto Schindler. I never met the man, so I am only quoting the modern myth portrayed in the film 'Schindler's List'. He doesn't fit perfectly because he does have a passion - for making money - but he is otherwise amoral because he does not take sides but rather sets out to exploit and profit by the war situation. From that detached standpoint he observes what is happening - we see him on horseback gazing down as the ghetto is blasted and the sight does not make him rant and rave. Instead he has the frown of a puzzled child. In that clean, detached soul, moral sense evolves because it is free from the shackles of morality. He even tries to resist the process - at first not wanting to acknowledge the gratitude of the Jews he is saving - but he ends up doing an exceptional amount of what most people would recognise as 'good'.

Media moralisers seem unable to recognise this simple fact. They speak as if they themselves are unexploded bombs: a pressure vessel full of malevolent and vicious intent being constrained by nothing more than a thin skin of 'God's Law'. "Abandon the faith and then... *anything goes*" they wail, boring the pants of those of us who don't actually *want* to go out and perform atrocities as they so obviously do. Who the hell wants to live with someone for whom the only reason not to act like a psychopathic mass murderer is because of what some people claim that God might have said two thousand years ago?

These are the vermin who want to censor the Internet. They make a point of logging into the 'worst' material they can find and then publishing shock horror articles about it. Most people log into porn pages out of the sort of idle curiosity that I am championing: the only people I've come across who are really motivated to find dirt on the Internet are media prats in search of A Cause.

"But you must not confuse the journalist in search of objective evidence with filthy perverts who get sexual excitement from this filth." Really? I bet that any investigative journalist worth his salt would be disappointed to log onto the steamiest child-sex pages and find nothing more than snaps of pretty smiling girls in flowery frocks. On the contrary, the more nasty the pictures he finds, the greater his excitement - and if that is not perversion I do not know what is.

"The worst thing of all after seeing these vile pictures of human depravity" he writes, saving the juiciest morsel for the end of his article in true media cliche style, "is to be told that *over five hundred people a day* are sick enough to want to see such material. What does that tell us about society today?" As a result of his article curious readers decide to have a peep for themselves. The inevitable result is a later article from another writer which begins "Who says that this is not an age of Sodomorrhic depravity, when *over five thousand people per day* seem unable to survive without logging into the Internet for the sight of children being abused".

Quick. Gimme some good old passionless amorality.

Before I scream.

LET'S NOT BE NEGATIVE

When I introduced the Aeon of Osiris in my myth I did my best to present it as it might appear to the old establishment - without balls and without muscle - before going on to explain how, out of this sickly body and glaring eyes, there came a whole new impulse which raised humanity above the limited daily round of survival and opened our eyes to the measureless heavens above.

In the interests of symmetry (with respect to temporal displacement) I have also introduced the Aeon of Horus as a shock to the establishment. To do this I described it as lacking two qualities much esteemed by the current mores - passion and morality. Now I will take the positive approach and attempt to describe it in terms of the qualities it actually does possess.

The Aeon of Horus is the digital aeon. Somewhere in past writings I related cyclic time - the rise and setting of the Sun, the Moon's phases, the tides and Seasons - to the Aeon of Isis; linear time - like an hour glass moving from past into future and so invoking 'progress' - to the Aeon of Osiris; and digital time - the eternal present wherein a clock does not move but suddenly drops you into one minute later - to the Aeon of Horus.

Digital reality is the child born of the marriage of materialism and spiritualism. On the one hand a mother with her feet on the Earth, measuring out her limited resources that the cycle of death and rebirth might turn one more time before claiming her too. On the other a father who has drawn back the veil of matter to reveal infinite space as being itself no more than another veil beyond which dwell the Gods themselves. Infinity beyond infinity beyond infinity without end.

From those two is born a digital child who knows that the universe is finite, that we are finite, but who feels no claustrophobia because it also knows that the possibilities in finite matter are immeasurably vast. To the Mother a grain of sand is a precious resource to be guarded; to the Father it is the mote to be removed, that the eye might see more clearly; but to the Child the grain of sand is itself a window into a whole new world.

Crowley, in his introduction to the Book of the Law which announced the Aeon of Horus, writes "This Book explains the Universe. The elements are Nuit - Space - that is, the total of possibilities of every kind - and Hadit, any point which has experience of these possibilities." As I don't expect many readers to accept my vision of digital reality described elsewhere and in the previous essay, I will give a simpler example that is more scientifically respectable - one example where the new vision could prove helpful and where there is a need to grow out of the old ideas. First I will describe the problem, then my suggested solution.

The Aeon of Osiris, in giving us the idea of infinite Spirit beyond matter, made room for endless infinite gods - each representing an aspect of perfection. This was initially inspiring, but it has finally turned sour.

Consider the modern myth of the Hollywood film star, like Marilyn Monroe, whom millions worship as beauty incarnate but who secretly despises her own looks to the point where she commits suicide or becomes anorexic. However beautiful she is, she is haunted by a vision of an even greater beauty before which she must appear vile.

Do you like me for my cleverness? If so, I am at first flattered and delighted. But then I begin to worry, because I am clever enough to imagine others much cleverer than me. I begin to feel insecure - what if one of them writes something cleverer on this topic and makes me look a fool?

In each case there is an infinity to threaten us - a Goddess of Beauty and a God of Intellect - on the altar of whose vastnesses we are in danger of being obliterated. But the Child of the New Aeon says "rubbish! you are both simply numbers - a string of digits spelt out in DNA. There is no *infinity beyond* - all beauty and intelligence is limited by the possibilities of those permutations of genes. The only infinity is the *infinity within*, which is a 'virtual infinity' defined by the fact that you, the universe and time itself are simply not big enough to contain all the possibilities inherent in that one genetic number. Sure, you cannot be that cleverer person you imagine - but neither can that cleverer person be you, however hard he tries. You are both equally limited in mathematical terms, but in practical terms the limitation has little meaning. Here is a door leading to The Great Outdoors - are you to spend the rest of your life standing before that the door regretting the fact that it is only six foot by three?"

The truth must be that, if you like my writing, the thing that you love is not really my cleverness but rather that precise mix of cleverness and stupidity which is uniquely mine. And we do not want Marilyn to have plastic surgery to remove her beauty spot, because we love her for what is essentially herself. Enjoy my DNA, enjoy Marilyn's - for the Earth will never behold their like again.

It is only before the infinite Gods that we are finite. Before ourselves, Time and the Universe, our possibilities are inexhaustible. Let us therefore get rid of those Gods who make us mortal!

In this example Nuit is the space of all possible genetic codes, and Hadit is an individual's unique DNA string "I am the secret Serpent, coiled about to spring: in my coiling there is joy" and "I am the flame that burns in every heart of man and in the core of every star. I am Life, and the giver of Life, yet therefore is the knowledge of me the knowledge of death" are two ways Hadit describes himself in the Book of the Law.

This is why The Book of The Law which heralded the Aeon of Horus claims "every man and every woman is a star" and that "every number is infinite". We are each a unique set of genes, a unique 'number' which almost certainly has never occurred before and probably never will again - the universe won't last long enough. We are none of us equal, and yet the sense of inequality is itself a function of short-sightedness: compared with the drop-out in cardboard city, Napoleon might seem like a mighty hero; but incarnation is in itself an act of such staggering heroism that the difference between the two loses all significance.

Because every number is infinite I need no longer regret that I am merely what I am. Instead I can explore and develop the endless fractal richness and potential encapsulated in my unique genetic number.

The children gaze at life without passion and without judgement, and something being born. You cannot stop it. Here is a new creativity, neither the piling up of flesh of the first aeon, nor the divine passion which we channelled in the second, but something lighter and more perplexing like the single leaf placed on the pond by a Zen master - a joke or surprise that opens windows of opportunity in the banal. In place of passion there is joy. "Remember all ye that existence is pure joy".

A NEW SEX MYTH

"Why don't you stand your ground and fight like a man?"

The lips that spoke were full, moist, luscious, tempting. The teeth were even, white, defiant - and a glimpse of tongue toyed langorously along their sharpness.

The man glanced up to see her head thrown back, a scornful heavy-lidded gaze, and felt his soul stripping away slowly, layer by layer. His troops were deserting, leaving a void in his belly, the emptiness of vertigo. For the woman's words had ripped open the earth at their feet and left him teetering on the brink of a chasm in whose awful depths slunk dark shapes, groping claws, fangs dripping blood. He could either turn and flee - a flight into utter banishment and disgrace - or he could stand and fight. He might then be destroyed, or he might prevail; but he could never win because the hungry depths that gaped before him were infinite in their appetite. His choice: eternal damnation or eternal battle.

He could instead hold the woman's gaze in a look which contrived to enfold utter contempt within the gift-wrap of pity. He could then turn his head and walk slowly away shrugging off the encounter with a world-weary sigh. Mocking laughter still might follow him, but it would be as hollow as bubbles - for his gesture would have ripped open the heavens and frozen the woman with the bone-chilling blast of Spirit.

To be tested? Or to judge the test itself to be utterly worthless?

Woman triumphs, Man is crushed. Man triumphs, Woman is crushed. Must it be ever so?

No. They hold each other's gaze. The Gods hold their breath. Time's digital clock registers Eternal Now.

Then one, or other, cracks - fails to keep a straight face and collapses into giggles so infectious that the other too is now bent double with mirth.

No Man. No Woman. No infinity. Just two laughing children, too intent in the joyful Play of Humanity to notice a scattering of elderly Gods retreating to nurse burnt fingers.

"...FOR I HAVE CRUSHED AN UNIVERSE; & NOUGHT REMAINS"

In describing the Child, the harbinger of the New Aeon... has not Ramsey Dukes merely described himself? The critic smirks with delight at having discovered the pin with which to prick this bubble of vanity, to reduce eight thousand words of brazen prophesy to the status of narcissistic wank.

Meanwhile Ramsey Dukes smirks with relief at being blessed with a critic so naive as to believe things could ever have been other-wise. Just as: when Jesus turned the other cheek he didn't really com-plete a revolution - it was simply testosterone trying out the newest battle tactic. Keep your old myths, please, because they add value to this offering. Instead of just a new myth, here now stands... *choice*.

"A supermarket of beliefs" is how furious reactionaries describe our new world. Yum, yum! I adore shopping! If a faith is perverted when its denial becomes forbidden, then the most corrupt faith of all time must be the worship of Truth. So recognise tomorrow's wisdom by this token - it is as easily rebutted as a stutter, it is as easily denied as childhood sin, it is as weightless as a butterfly.

It's a plaything with a sting!

RETROSPECTIVE POSTSCRIPT

When it comes to publishing, I find myself contemplating a well of sorrow.

I have one son of whom I feel proud, but my life has not left a great lusty wake of illegitimate children across the planet. That is to say, I have not stood the test of the Aeon of Isis alpha male.

Nor can I find comfort in Aeon of Osiris self sacrifice, for it is not 'high principles' that has lost me the mating game so much as incom-petence - I really do yearn to impregnate every voluptuous, earthy woman I meet.

I have written ten books about which I have very mixed feelings, but I have been anything but a media sensation. I have become that publisher's pariah, the crank, and my stunning ideas leap to nobody's lips. That is to say, I have not stood the test of the Aeon of Osiris spirited statement.

The equations on my blackboard did not add up, the hall is silent behind me and so I turn wearily to face its emptiness, only to behold... A standing ovation!

My inner mob is cheering "Yes! Yes! You've got it! Now move on!"

If my value lies neither in genes or memes, then what is it? If not body or spirit, then it sort of has to be 'soul'. If not gut or head, then it sort of has to be 'heart'.

Soul and heart - two words which carry some sweet aroma of meaning and yet which refuse to be defined adequately for me in terms of either flesh or intellect.

My role may only be recognised as a propagator of... music? Mood? Magic? Maybe some quality that has yet to be recognised?

It is as if mankind, towards the ending of the Aeon of Isis, had established its population adequately on the face of the earth and so the genetic imperative of the alpha male became increasingly farmed out to the breeding of livestock. Now, at the end of the Aeon of Osiris, the memetic imperative of the media star will be increasingly farmed out to the propagation of technology - the world wide web can spread its memes far farther and faster than word of mouth. Digitally-generated heroes will mutate faster than human actors can address their hang-ups.

Thus the role of humanity is not to be replaced by our machines, any more than we were replaced by the livestock that came to outnumber us and dominate our politics. Instead our role is to move forward to this new domain, neither flesh nor spirit but soul - whatever that means.

We are ready to hand over the digital domain of Hadit to our information technology, and thus we become free to explore Nuit, who is continuous. She is the uncountably infinite space that exists in the relationship between consciousness and the universe - the free will which allows us to conceive a space between fundamental particles, as discussed in my Penrose essay.

Goodbye particulate individuality - we're preparing to surf the wave continuum. "...*In the gaps between the atoms slips the trail of Thundersqueak*"

EXPERIMENTS IN RELIGION

C
rowley used the slogan "the method of science, the aim of religion" to describe his approach. This raises the notion of religion as an experimental technology.

My first foray into this new discipline was to fill in football pool coupons on a number of weeks in the name of different deities, on the agreement that any prize money received over the sum of one million pounds would be acknowledged by my eternal devotion to the deity on trial. Purist devotees of the Judeo-Christian religions will no doubt be reassured to learn that their deities did not deign to deliver, but a rather less comforting discovery was that even Satan turned down my soul at what can only be judged a knock-down price. That doesn't do much for one's self-esteem, I'll tell you, and that is why what might have become the first doctoral thesis in Experimental Theology was never completed and written up.

With a view to compensating for this omission, this essay looks at two more recent experiments in religion by myself. It also comments upon my subsequent silence.

CHAOS RELIGION

In 1993 I was asked to give a presentation at UKAOS a few weeks before the IOT conference in Austria. The theme on my mind was one written up somewhere in these essays - that the current public fascination was with religion rather than magic, in the sense that people had had their fill of inner exploration and were wanting to become part of something bigger "out there", whether religious or nationalistic.

Unfortunately the organisers of UKAOS that year had a 'bee in the bonnet' about wanting something practical and experiential instead of 'just talk'. Being a serious sort of person, I reckoned that it meant I could not get away with talking about religion, but would have to deliver a genuine religious experience.

Shit!

I knew what I really wanted. I am intrigued by what little I have heard about Southern Baptist ministers holding revivalist meetings, and I had this picture of a heavily built man with neat blond crew-cut, rimless spectacles and white linen suit jumping to a microphone and proclaiming - with machine gun delivery - "Well, HELLELU-JAH Brothers an' Sisters an' welcome to the London-Tabernacle-of-the-Eighth-Day-Church-of-Utter-Cha-os. A-MEN!" (To convey the delivery right I would need some sort of musical notation that lies beyond my expertise - the voice, initially a high shout, is meant to drop on the last two syllables). Other elements of this tableau included gushy music on a Hammond organ and a line up of nubile maidens with white dresses and tambourines - the Chaosettes.

So I went round explaining this to friends who might have the right contacts, and the response was mostly "what a good idea, why don't you do it?".

Here is a slight diversion - but it does throw up an interesting side issue. One such friend was my previous publisher, who did "Blast...", and he was showing my his new musical software that could take any sound sample and manipulate it digitally. Remember that fuss about "back tracking"? Fundamentalist Xtians claiming that every other pop-song had hymns to Satan played in reverse in the backing tracks? Well, I'd come across an interesting variation on the theme: it was a New Age diagnostic process which involved listening to your speech played backwards and hearing what unconscious messages were being delivered as one spoke. So I did the "Well HELLELUYAH..." into his machine as a sample and, when it was played backwards we heard the usual droning rubbish but punctuated with one clear cry of "help!" I saw at once the significance: here was I trying to find someone to deliver this religious service for me, I was going round crying for help and being told over and over to do it myself!

Two dear friends - one with experience as a jazz singer - offered Chaosette service, and my nephew was an organist with the necessary skill to deliver a deliberately awful tape of endless tacky improvisation on "Amazing Grace". The priest had to be me, it seemed: so I mined my unconscious for a character called "Thee Very Irreverend Doctor Eival B Mhygud PHDiab Dip.Sat(hons)". The original character was a fundamentalist Satanist from the Deep South, but he became a fundamentalist Chaoist for this occasion. I bought a white linen jacket and my publisher lent me a dog-collar grey shirt; I bought some tinted rimless specs but had absolutely no luck finding a blond crew-cut wig.

The event was gaining a momentum of its own. It careered on till I found myself onstage at UKAOS giving my initial lecture before lunch - terrified to see that the hall was awash with the clear light of day through its glass roof and was about as atmospheric as a council flat. Disaster loomed, this ill-rehearsed shambles was heading pell-mell toward REAL chaos. I was feeling the dissociation of an elderly cult figure - at once identifying with my young audience but also sensing a ghastly abyss of age and culture stretching between them and myself. In response to my anxious plea for help, one member of the audience leapt onstage and announced that she had been a tambourine beater with the Salvation Army and was dying to join the Chaosettes (I was later told that the good lady earned her living providing S&M services - a career path which almost amounts to a definition of the Sacred Feminine - and so could not have been more appropriate for the role, if I am not mistaken in this).

I did ask them to get drunk over lunchtime, and that may have helped. But whatever the reason, the event went extremely well. The audience really got into the spirit of it - shouting Helleluyah! and A-men! like there was no tomorrow. I delivered a rousing Chaos sermon, full of paranoia about Law and Order creeping out of the woodwork, and shamelessly exploited the usual rabble-rousing techniques. For example "Now ain't we jes sick to the teeth of all this interlectualizin' so-fistikashun corruptin' our re-ligion? Ahma tellin' you, Brothers an' Sisters, this ole-time Chaos Religion is just as easy as A B C - an here's how! When Ah raises my hands up to heaven like so an' shouts 'A-MEN' ah want you to do likewise and come back with just the loudest ever A-MEN!" I then went through the old business of pretending I couldn't hear their response a couple of times until they were really raising the roof. Then I said I wanted to hear how much the Sisters had contributed, so would they now reach not upward but forward to their Brothers and shout after me 'B-MEN' (be-men, geddit?) "Well, Brothers, how about that eh? I reckon there's only one answer we've got to the Sisters, so put your hands down here and repeat after me 'C-MEN' (semen, geddit?).... A-Men, B-Men, C-Men - ain't it jes' as easy as ABC."

Following a rousing rendition of a re-written version of Amazing Grace the singing faded into a hum while I stepped forward to the lower stage and channelled the healing power of Chaos. "Ah can

FEEL it, ah feel the burning fires of CHA-OS in ma soul, Helleluyah!" and so on. I'd arranged two stooges in the audience to rush forward to "receive Chaos" by laying on of hands and then a second three to throw themselves at our feet and receive Chaos in turn - so that Chaos spread exponentially through the audience with everyone who had received it being able to pass it on. The room was soon filled with shrieks and glossolalia and people grovelled at my feet for the blessing until all present were bursting with Chaos.

I wanted the experience to be not only one of shared religion, but also a personal gift to be taken home, so I returned to the microphone, got the yelling mob back to their seats and lead a meditation about the air in the hall a-buzzin and a-buzzin with the bees of chaos, and these bees gradually swarming down into each person's heart - forming a dark mass which became an individual chaosphere. "It is your chaos, your own inner resource. But it is not your chaos, because it is the universal Chaos. And that is why it is just your chaos. *which it is not because it is the universal chaos*" and so on. And it ended with three very quiet 'A-mens'.

Now the vindication of the event for me was that a number of people described it as "very powerful". The audience had really entered into the spirit of the thing, let rip wholeheartedly and been rewarded with a shared religious experience.

People asked if I would do it again in Austria, but it clearly would not work because it depended on my channelling Dr Mhygud pell-mell and this would be incompatible with the pedestrian process of interpreted speech at a world conference. Something else was needed.

INCARNATING DIVINITY

Early in the week of the Austrian Chaos conference I gave my introductory talk about religion and magic, then went on to explain my principle of "give value, and the universe will return it manifold".

I asked them to imagine a drunken idiot at a party fixing them with a glare and rattling off some bit of trite wisdom like "know thyself, mate". Wouldn't you just want him to shove off? But what if you had queued and fasted for days in the Himalayas for the privilege of a few brief minutes in the company of the wisest man on Earth, and when you came at last into his presence he held you in his gaze and intoned "know thyself". Almost identical words - but they could well mark a turning point in your life. So what is the difference?

I argued that the biggest difference of all lay in the value we ourselves place on the speaker. "Know thyself" spoken by an idiot partygoer is nothing but a bit of clichéd one-upmanship, but from the mouth of one we value as the wisest man in the world it becomes a Jewel of wisdom - not because the words are any different but rather because we ourselves go away and work on their meaning. "What did he mean?", "what was it he saw that I could not see?" we ask and the spadework on our soul begins in earnest.

What I pointed out is that we have this enormous power to give value. Sitting in a waiting room we idly open the pages of a tabloid newspaper and our eye alights on trash. But if instead we take up the same paper in reverence and pray to God for guidance that he might reveal to our eyes a message when we open the paper, then the same tabloid momentarily becomes a sacred scripture. Next time we are depressed a helpful friend suggests that we ought to come to terms with repressed anger and we get annoyed at having that old chestnut dragged up yet again. Instead we go to a Harley Street psychologist who suggests that we ought to come to terms with repressed anger and, because we have payed a lot of money for the advice, we find healing in the idea. In each case, we truly are the ones who offer the gift of "value" and we are the ones who are handsomely repaid in return. So next time a tiresome acquaintance pesters us with advice, we might do well to give them value, and assume that they are very wise before asking them to explain. They will either retract if they did not mean it, or else do their best to explain again - and we could find great wisdom in their words.

I wanted now to put this idea to the test, so I announced that in two days time the castle would be blessed by a visit from His Most Divine Holiness and Flower of the Universe "Sri Baba Rebop", and that they were his utterly devoted disciples. I explained that, as far as they were concerned, His Most Divine Holiness was nothing less than God and the Universe Incarnate, and their greatest happiness could only lie in doing His Holy Will. I explained that He liked perfumes and flowers - and I got volunteers to take charge of each - and that He desired a bodyguard of four people dressed in black leather and dark glasses - four more volunteers - and we required a Master of Ceremonies, for it was the disciples' sacred duty to entertain His Most Divine Holiness as he was arriving to celebrate the Most Holy and Sacred Feast of Vashnadishnu.

Again it seemed inevitable that I should play the role of the Great Man, so I explained that all my sermons, and my answers to their questions, would be ad-libbed on the basis of random words picked from a bowl. I cut up pieces of paper with useful abstract words such as *love, one-ness, wisdom, being, bliss* etc together with useful physical metaphors such as *apple, ocean, flower, sand* etc. What I wanted them to do was to listen with great reverence to my words, and yet to be also aware that any wisdom they found in those words was generated by chance and not by the wisdom of Ramsey Dukes.

The next day, to whip up a little momentum, at the end of the first lecture the speaker said there was someone who wanted to make an announcement. Then I leapt up in a state of high excitement, acting the role of a religious nutter. I babbled some nonsense about amazing manifestations at breakfast being seen as a blessed omen, and that I had then heard the wondrous news that tomorrow the castle was to be blessed by the most fragrant presence of H.M.D.H.& F.O.T.U. Sri Baba Rebop. I said I was sure that they were all already devoted disciples but, just in case there were any present who were yet to be touched by His radiance, I should explain that H.M.D.H. likes his disciples to chant the sacred mantra *Ram Phat Yamaha Vashnadishnu Hum* while performing the sacred mudra (right hand palm up, third and fourth fingers curled into palm, thumb rubbing to and fro against tips of first and second fingers).

I explained that the meaning of the sacred mantra had divided and perplexed scholars for centuries - one school insisting that the word *Yamaha* meant "the Swift-Moving One" while other scholars were adamant that it meant "Maker of Music". My favourite story, however, was of a group of wise men who came before H.M.D.H. to ask him what was the true meaning of the mantra. H.M.D.H. closed his eyes in solemn meditation for ninety breaths then opened them and quietly replied "My children, how can the All-Meaning *hef* meaning?" When I announced this, all present - who were already getting into the spirit of the occasion - received this portrayal of sublime wisdom with appropriately appreciative murmurs of awe.

The event the next day went extremely well. The "disciples" came out of the castle wreathed in flowers and chanting the mantra and the bodyguard carried me into the arena on an improvised sedan-table. The weather was disappointingly cloudy but I made the best of a bad job by explaining in cracked Indo-English that I had manifested a little cloud cover lest my children suffer unduly from the heat of the sun. The joy of this event over the previous Church of Chaos was that all the hard work was done by my disciples. I merely expounded a little stochastic wisdom - as described above - responded to questions handed to me on paper, handed out gifts of sweetmeats, blessed my disciples by laying on hands and had my feet ritually washed in return.

I did, however, arrange one cheesy little miracle. I handed bunches of flowers to my four bodyguards and asked them to place them at the four quarters of the arena: but I had secretly instructed one to "accidentally" drop a certain flower from his bunch. When this happened I called out to him that he had dropped one little flower but, as he stooped to pick it up, I said "no! no! Leave it!" then turned to the crowd and explained that "everything that heppens hez *meaning*". That this little flower was like the disciple who has fallen by the wayside. Should we chastise him and say he is wicked? Or should we instead say "My child, welcome back into the loving arms of Vashnadishnu"? At that moment the flower, which was attached to a spring reel of conjuror's invisible thread, leaped up from the grass and flew across the arena into my outstretched hand.

My other precaution was to have one or two let-out speeches in case of awkward questions ill-suited to random wisdom. For example, one piece of paper bore the words "Your Holiness, why are there so many ass-holes in this world?". So I asked who had honoured me with this most profound enquiry. When a young man raised his hand I asked where he had come from - it was a distant town in Germany. So he had come all that way to ask me this question? Yes. So I replied "My child, that the mystery of those ass-holes should have brought you one thousand miles into the Divine Presence - what greater justification for them could there be than that?"

CONCLUSIONS

As with the Church of Chaos, I was delighted with the response to H.M.D.H.

What could have been nothing more than an amusing party piece turned out to have a power of its own. Despite the knowledge that my words were based on random permutation of cliches, most people commented that the wisdom was of a very high standard - at least second class guru grade. In particular, the answers to personal questions were apposite, thought provoking and helpful.

This supported my belief in the value of giving value, of accepting wisdom "as if" from a divine source. In this sense what I had demonstrated was simply an exercise in divination: the random selection of spiritual buzz-words from my bowl played the part of, say, a tarot spread and delivered its good results because there was an agreement to treat this party piece with the same respect that a believer would give to a tarot spread.

What was also interesting was that the holiness we had invoked "leaked" into the rest of the conference. Later a delegate said to me "damn you, Dukes, I *woke up* with that ruddy mantra on my mind this morning!" The delegates began to use the mantra as a panacea: if the waiters were slow to serve a chant would begin "Ram Phat Yamaha Vashnadishnu Hum" and in a moment a waiter would appear. Another miracle! The sacred mantra has manifested a waiter! Thus its reputation snowballed.

The delegates held a party in the castle courtyard on the last night, and it coincided with an Austrian wedding feast in a nearby Hall. So we were mildly inconvenienced by the passage of drunken Austrian wedding guests returning to their coaches, and the sacred mantram was once more invoked. This lead to my being accosted by a drunken Austrian gentleman who (I had to ask my interpreter what he wanted) understood that I was a holy man and wished for a blessing. I decided to suggest that he should make sure everyone on the coach chanted this mantra, for it would bring great prosperity to the happy couple. He then embarrassed me by wanting to give me money for this blessing. When I refused it he asked for my address so he could send a donation. I somehow wriggled out of that, and he left. But he made a trip to the bar on the way which resulted in great jugs of white wine and water being delivered to our tables. Another remarkable manifestation of the power of the spirit!

As someone said that night: how many other great religions had begun in this fashion? Years have passed and I still meet people who remember me as His Most Divine Holiness and Flower of the Universe Sri Baba Rebop, even though I actually borrowed the name from Steve Wilson!

ENTERING THE SILENCE

As I left to return to England the organisers asked me if I would return again to do another workshop for next year's conference, and I declined. A sense of impending trouble was building in my soul and I probably needed a period of comparative silence in order to sort it out.

The fact is that I had hugely enjoyed the actual process of channelling Dr Mhygud and Sri Baba Rebop, and had felt as fulfiled and excited as at any other time in my life. But the performance generated an unbridgable discontinuity and strain that was utterly incompatible with the rest of my existence. Had I received, say, five thousand pounds per performance, I could have dropped all other commitments and dedicated a month or two to mental preparation, invocation of the muse and then re-entering normal existence. I loved it, but it was somehow too big for my life and the basic need to earn a living.

May I issue a warning, and an apology?

At this point the essay grows quite indefensibly personal. It becomes, in effect a medium to explain to my friends why they have seen so little of me for the last five years - because I suspect that the readership of this book will largely consist of my friends. In any case, there is a sense in which anyone who reads my work becomes my friend by virtue of that very indulgence.

So, for those who consider excessive soul-bearing to be bad taste, I have inserted this warning. For those who proceed nevertheless, I will attempt to extrapolate from my experience to deduce some more widely applicable conclusions.

DIONYSUS, THE INNER ROCK STAR

To be adored by a crowd of chanting, flower-decked disciples was at once disturbing and delightful. As was the experience of whipping an audience to a frenzy with hell-fire chaos rhetoric. What did it reveal in me?

There was a point in my life when a friend offered to teach me to play the guitar, he said that the ease with which my left hand could span the strings made me a natural. The offer was appealing, but it came in my A-Level year and I decided that I needed to focus on one thing and do it well. So I turned down the guitar offer, even though I had an idea at the back of my mind for transforming the cacophony of feedback into wild music.

Later, as a student at Cambridge, I witnessed Jimmy Hendrix on his first UK tour - realising in his music something that had been just an idea to me. I felt at the time that he had, in a sense, sprung from mine own unconscious, and I rejoiced to see an inner hunch thus externalised.

A few years later I wrote a sort of novel "Johnstone's Twentieth Century Occult Philosopher and Skeptikall Politick Theorist" which included a character called Angerford who could, with hindsight, be seen as the rock star that I had never expressed.

Angerford was in a sense the personification of an adolescent rage against existence, authority and all laws of nature such as, for example, the utterly sensible tendency for desirable girls to reject young males seething with hormonal angst. He was the impulse to simply explode, go berserk, and yet Angerford also recognised that the most devastatingly effective explosions are those which are tightly channelled by - for example - the barrel of a gun.

So, when Angerford formed his psychedelic band The Sacred Butterfly Children, the act contained such shocking effects as the cadavre of a black stallion being dismembered by a circular saw on stage; while on the other hand Angerford rejected the pop-star dress code of the day because he reckoned there was greater shock value in seeing an apparently "well dressed and decent young man" turning into a fiend on stage. He adopted the name Elizabeth and so could be seen as an anticipation of bizarre acts such as that of Alice Cooper. But he is later heard saying that his definition of success was when fans would queue all night just to see him throw up all over the stage, so there is in some ways more of the punk spirit in him.

While preparing the essays of this present book for publication in the mid 90s my attention was drawn to a New York performer called GG Allin who used to alleviate his musical performances by self mutilation, eating his excrement and rolling naked in his own blood, vomit and faeces. This brought back a memory of Angerford's last record, described in the novel. It was called "Swallow This You Bastards" and it consisted of a plastic bag containing a disk of carborundum streaked with his vomit, blood, urine and faeces. The idea was that you placed it on the turntable of your hi-fi system and listened to the sound of a priceless elliptical diamond stylus being relentlessly destroyed. GG Allin, like Angerford, yearned to machine gun his audience from the stage and then blow himself up as a final act.

GG Allin brought back these memories and launched for me a train of rediscovery. Like Angerford he burnt himself out creating ever greater shocks for his followers. He seems like the ultimate self destructive finale of a crescendo of rage, and yet my Angerford was just a player. His desire to restrain outrage in his appearance in order to create even greater impact reflected another theme in my novel, illustrated by a character called Peregrine who was impossibly smart and classy - I'd see in him an anticipation of a Hooray Henry style yuppy. Peregrine upsets everyone with his snobbish views then seems to disappear from the story until, some years later, a character (who may have been myself) recognises Peregrine getting into a black diplomatic limousine in Whitehall. This is a sinister development because the character recalls two facts about Peregrine. One is that, before he assumed his upper class English snob persona and called himself Peregrine, this man had been an Australian neo-dada anarcho art terrorist. The other is that Peregrine had once explained that he believed there to be a key somewhere in the world which, when turned, could launch nuclear Armageddon. His ambition was to become the person who had the right to turn that key.

How contemptibly trite must seem the rage of Angerford and Allin, destroying themselves most foully before an audience of dedicated enthusiasts. How much more rage was expressed by Adolph Hitler who choked back his venom and founded a world movement!

And yet how pitiful was the impact of even Hitler compared to a Peregrine who can throw off all signs of rebellion and become the perfect citizen in order to get his hands on the nuclear button!

Is this the ultimate limit of such crazed adolescent raging?

A later novel of mine, started but unfinished in the mid 70s, describes a science fiction future world that is almost ideal in its warmth, humanity, stability and harmony with the natural world. This perfect society comes to a sudden and perplexing end when all but one of the world's inhabitants gather in one locality and simultaneously drop dead. (Incidentally there is a character called Scream Raver: a performance cook (in this society cookery plays a role similar to music in ours) who whips his diners to a frenzy by beating on his pans and then hacks his own flesh and blood into the dish he is preparing.)

`The main point of the novel is its hint that this society was born from a few survivors of nuclear holocaust. They alone survived a hundred year incarceration deep underground because their physical functions were regularised by transceivers implanted in their brains and controlled by a central computer. That central computer was equipped to handle such a complex task because it was itself built around a human brain which was the brain of the inventor of this survival plan. What an addendum to the novel suggested was that he had been rejected by his girlfriend when a student at Cambridge and had internalised his bitterness, rage and despair by throwing himself into academic studies. Thus he averted the temptations of suicide, only to later create the ultimate suicide gesture: to unite all humanity to his brain and then destroy it at a stroke. His irony was that he chose not to destroy it in the wretchedness of war, but rather to rescue mankind, bring it to perfection and then to destroy it. Thus he achieved an even purer expression of his rage and hatred.

So we see a progression - the crazed impulse of adolescent rage being progressively focussed and constrained to ever greater effect: evolving from a mindless act of violence, to a stage act, then to a political movement, then to the bureaucratic invocation of nuclear war, then to a life of total sacrifice to humankind which, having saved it, culminates in its elimination. Is any more vicious expression of this impulse possible?

As it happens, yes. In 1986 I committed an atrocity which so far outstripped any of these as to make them seem as nothing - mere local stunts in a minor solar system. The atrocity took the form of a book called Words Made Flesh which replaced our material universe with a universe of information - an act of cosmic destruction without equal since the Big Bang.

Eat your hearts out GG Allin, Adolph Hitler and every mass murderer or crazed psychopath in the history of mankind. I have published a book so explosive that it has left not one single atom of matter remaining in the entire universe.

The only problem is... nobody noticed.

ASHES AND DIAMONDS

This evolution and focussing of rage to ever greater acts of violence might surprise those who know me primarily as an unusually easy-going and harmonious personality.

I have described only one side of a dual process. As in the Yin-Yang symbol, our darkest deeds hold a spot of light just as there is a spot of dark in our lightest deeds. It is as difficult to commit pure evil as it is to do pure good - the most vicious pogrom will relieve accommodation waiting lists, just as the most benign welfare state will surely invoke dependency.

The process of constraining and focussing rage is recognisable as the alchemical formula whereby a poisonous serpent or substance is seethed within a tightly closed vessel. The carbon black venom of hatred is compressed in the gun barrel of will with such ferocity that diamonds may be created in the ash. I suspect that GG Allin's performance, while embodying all that is most sick and vile in a depraved culture, acted as a purgative, an awakening to some of his audience. From my safe distance in time and space it broke open the vessel from which the understandings in the essay sprang. Adolph Hitler's influence on Germany was most pernicious because it got so close to being good, and to achieving so much.

So when I wrote the book Words Made Flesh I was not thinking "heh heh! this'll teach the universe to reject me!". Instead I believed that I was offering healing to humanity.

I believed that the Enlightenment had freed mankind from the tyranny of a life confined within a board game whose eternal rules had been written by God; instead of that we were given scientific method leading to the theory of evolution, and the discovery that chance could create endless new possibilities.

I also believed that this revolution had grown old and dogmatic in turn, abandoning us in a "survival of the fittest" world where no-one wants to be the second fittest, nor the third, fourth.... five billionth. Combined with today's communications it's a cruel world, for who wants to gaze at the second most beautiful woman in the world over breakfast when they could turn on the TV and watch the most beautiful? Or who wants to listen to the village choir when they could hear a digital recording of Kings College choir? What publisher is interested in any book unless it is a certain best seller?

So I wanted to replace this fragmented world-view with a belief in an integrated world: an information structure where every being has an essential role. Where the movie star is no longer unattainably superior but actually depends upon the love of his/her fans. Where the Sun has no meaning without sunbathers. Where value is traded, not seized.

It was in that spirit I wrote the book, and it was that spirit which felt sad that it communicated so little of its healing potential. I was left puzzled, listless, bitter, perplexed, unsure what to do next. Only ten years later have I divined the role of adolescent rage in this creation, even though I acknowledged its participation in the book all that time ago. I am hearing voices now more clearly, voices which were for many years no more than muffled cries from the basement.

Here's the Yin-Yang duality in another language. My horoscope has a close square between Neptune and Saturn. Dream and Reality do battle within me. Thus divorced they can polarise into parodies of themselves.

'Realism' can become exceptionally hard and cynical in me. Realism says I have wasted my life trying to heal with this book. What I should have done with my adolescent rage was convert it into action. I should have shot the prime minister, machine-gunned a football crowd or whatever. If I had done that I might have exploited my notoriety and become an object of public fascination. Endless articles would have been written about me. My books would have been scrutinised by those seeking to unmask me as the antichrist, or to prove I was a rebel before my time. I might now be wealthy and influential - the world might actually have swallowed my healing potion.

So Realism warns my readers not to waste their own life when they could waste a few others instead. Get a gun, go shoot up a primary school. Deliver some action in a gutless world. The only thing I never could understand about mass murderers is how they manage to kill so few before they go. Do they really value themselves so little? If I was planning the Big One I could surely do better than any of them. It can't be so much harder to get a machine gun than a rifle, so why not get one for each hand? And just think what can be done with petrol, explosives, poison, bacteria... How could those Japanese Aum people have stockpiled so much venom to such little effect? I despair of humanity at times.

Dream, in turn, inflates to devour such realism. It reminds me that I had a childhood desire to found a world religion, and that such a path requires total dedication. Unless prepared to die in obscurity and despair crying "my God why hast thou forsaken me", I have no hope of hitting jackpot.

Dream tells me that today's media machine is no use because it is incapable of creating anything bigger than itself. This is because the media are locked in a senex-puer duality: outwardly they manifest the childlike sensationalism of Hermes, while their inner power source is that of Kronos the child-eater. The media creates its children by granting them fifteen minutes of fame, and then it devours them to feed the machine. Thus if I succeeded in propagating my ideas through publication or broadcast, I would have to do it in the media's terms, which are to create a personality bubble in which my ideas are floated, but which must be sacrificed when my turn comes to be shot down and derided. The media process is to create success in order to slay it. Perfectly sound ideas are destined to "go out of fashion" because the today's media is locked into 1950s industry ideals of built-in obsolescence and wastage.

Dream reminds me that the reason I swathed myself in pseudonyms and obscurity was so that my ideas could grow unattached to a human target. The name Ramsey Dukes is an empty container into which mankind can pour its fantasies. It was even a mistake to put my ideas in writing - I should have left the world young, as Jesus did, leaving no more than fragments of reputation and a few sayings. Any hint of a real personality is a burden to a nascent religion. There must be no author to allow as much room as possible for myth.

Dream says that if you have a brilliant idea you should not even express it. The formation of an idea is enough to give it life, and the nature of life is to survive. Reject the idea and it grows tough. Repress it and it learns to survive, breed and take hold in intellectually and consciously lean soil. Despise it and you are encouraging an invincible mind-virus to evolve. Try to stamp it out, and you are giving it the power of resistance. Whereas to annunciate is to make mortal. To write is to limit. To publish is to castrate.

One voice calls for me to dissolve myself, leaving a vacuum into which can flow all the world's dreams and aspirations. The other voice wants an act of self assertion so savage that it too would amount to self sacrifice.

Buggered if I'll do either.

THE THIRD TULIP

The above lengthy explanation tries to show that there have been some major themes churning about underneath the sense of unease and uncertainty I have felt about my art and my life direction over the past few years. As such it is a sort of apology to those who wanted to hear or see more of me.

Now I wish to end by restoring context. Having given voice to two warring elements of my being I should remind you that these are just two voices in a crowd. Other voices include my Compassion, my Love of Peace, my Sensuality, my Aesthetic Sense... too numerous to mention.

Together they have consistently outvoted my desire to kill.

If ninety five percent of the population refuses to admit that it is capable of, say, killing children, then the population is unwittingly giving that voice too much weight. So when a renegade man actually performs the dread deed, he becomes the mouthpiece for millions of unadmitted desires. He becomes too important.

By allowing the desire to commit atrocities to have voting rights in the parliament of my mind, I have allowed it to be consistently outvoted. The fact that this has diminished my impact on society is perhaps more of a defect of society than of me.

This humble point could soon assume greater importance. Genetic engineering might one day allow us to eliminate certain "evil" traits. Whereas I feel great sympathy for the desire to, say, eliminate racism from the human condition, I also question that there could never arise a situation where an appreciation of racial differences might not have positive outcome. I feel more at ease with a society where racism exists but is consistently outvoted by love, tolerance and compassion. I would also feel more secure in a society where the allocation of defence and security funds was biassed towards programmes to glamourise the love of peace rather than towards the construction of weapons.

See! I've done it again! An essay which could be seen by the hostile reader to have advocated mass murder, ends up by delivering a message of hope for humanity!

How do you react to such experiments in religion?

27

THE CRISIS OF CHAOS

This was the second talk in The Isbourne Foundation's 'Embracing Chaos' Series. I gave it in Cheltenham in Summer 1987 and they transcribed the talk. No-one has ever done me such an honour before, so I decided to include it here!

Two weeks ago my life was in chaos.

It was dreadful, the house was a mess. I had tables littered with papers: unanswered mail, unopened letters, magazines, junk mail, ansaphone messages written down on scraps of paper, and then lost...

It was appalling, and it was something that had built up over quite a long time while Neptune was squaring my sun (*sun*, not *son*). So I decided I must really try to get things sorted out.

What I did was went up to a place where I meditate with a pad, and I drew up little lists in the way you do - priorities, objectives, time available... things like that - and worked out how to get my life back in order. Get my life tidy and clear and then I could move on.

The key element of this plan was that I would get a personal organiser. And I did. Look at it, it's absolutely wonderful. In this one little box, I've got my address book; a diary; I can touch this icon and it'll phone up people. It's got "to do" lists - I tick off the ones I've done and the next day it brings up the ones I haven't done. It's got my accounts, I can now keep track of all my different credit cards, things like that. It really is marvellous, it's all in there, you see.

Now, if you just happen to be human, you'll be thinking at this point "Yes, but where's the snag?"

I'll show you the snag, the bit they didn't show in the advertisement. Just look what came with it...

At this point the speaker produced a large carrier bag and ceremoniously scattered its contents across the floor. It contained 16 diskettes, 12 manuals, 10 product registration documents, 12 other pieces of legal, promotional, instructional or other literature, 3 cables, an adaptor (needed to fit each of the 3 cables to the organiser and so raising the obvious objection that they should simply have provided one cable with the correct terminator and three different ends) and a print pack, which itself contained a further cable and 6 more pieces of literature.

This, all this, is what came with it. Disks, cables... here's the users' manual. But it doesn't say how to get the thing going. There's a separate manual for getting started, somewhere, if I remembered to bring it. Here's a "connections utilities user manual" - hang on there's two of those, one's for Windows one's for the Macintosh operating system. That explains why these disks are so many, they're all doubled up, you've got to have two lots because it depends whether you're on Windows or Macintosh.

Just look at all these long-winded registration things they want you to fill in. Actually, I've kept these - I should have sent them off, but I've kept them to show you. I'm going to get my revenge because I'm going to send them off next week with a letter apologising that they're late and saying I was going to give a public talk on the failure of the IT industry and I wanted to display these forms as samples of bad practice.

This pile of rubbish is just a taste of the chaos that's been brought into my life. An example: you see, one of the things I had started trying to do in order to get my life in order was to get to bed on time. But what happens now is I think "it's ten o'clock. I've just got a few minutes so I'll learn how to record an address before I go to bed". Two hours later I realise that it's after midnight, I'm still struggling and I'm now too angry to sleep. I bought this thing to help order my life, but it's actually a disruption.

I'll cut short the description of the hell I suffered trying to find anyone at Apple who knew anything about plug-in GSM modules - even though a photo of them appeared three times in their own Newton Solutions Guide. It's absolutely ghastly.

Now, that's what this talk is about: the crisis of chaos.

Last week we progressed to the idea that chaos need not be threatening: it can be seen as the friendly, fertile muddle. We can now see that, although we like things to be nice and tidy, creativity needs a bit of a muddle to feed its roots.

This week, however, I'm saying it's worse than that, because you can get this situation where you actually set out to do something decent - you'd think my life would be grateful for being ordered, wouldn't you? - but what happens is that life hits back with an even worse shambles.

This is the crisis of chaos. The times when life or the universe hits back at you, just when you're really trying to do something right or good. So this is the "bad news" week - though later I will try to see how we can make the best of this.

One of the things you can do when you have a bad personal problem like mine, is to elevate it into a Great Cosmic Principle. So that's what I will now proceed to do.

Here is an extract from a longer essay which addresses this problem, amongst others. The essay is mostly about magic, and in it I have been talking about two types of magic: power magic, which sets out to make something happen, and the magic of transformation which can transform a situation - so that you see the beauty in it or whatever - like the alchemical transmutation of lead into gold. What I'm going to try to do in this talk is itself an example of the magic of transformation - transmuting the crisis of chaos from bloody aggravation into a cosmic process.

Extract from "Blast your way to Megabuck$ with my SECRET sex-power formula - and other reflections upon the spiritual path"
"This is the problem I see in modern magic: to be really effective and powerful you need to be in a highly ecstatic state of gnosis and with very little conscious awareness. In its extreme state that grows very close to lack of all control.

From the point of view of power magic, this paradox is a bit disturbing: to exercise real power you need to abandon control of that power. For the magic of transformation it is less worrying, because you're not so much aiming to control situations as to open yourself up to accept their true essence - and any flow of power that results is just an expression of that magic. This paradox seems to be as deeply ingrained as the uncertainty principle - a real limitation in manifestation.

Whereas the last section dealt with the polarity of the Wand of Idealism and Will impacted in the Disk of Matter and Realism, this section looks at the struggle of the Sword of Analysis and Control versus the Cup of Acceptance and Ecstasy.

As before, I see this as an important problem for humanity, and this one is becoming even more important now because the rise of information and other technologies is presenting governments with greater opportunities for control than ever before, while the pursuit of such control seems to invoke paranoia in government and in the people it invokes ecstatic wildness and drunkenness of the senses.

As without, so within. I was very struck when I read the biography of L. Ron Hubbard, the founder of Scientology. In the early '50s he presented the world with a simple form of psychotherapy that promised a new age. Recognising that our unconscious minds held enormous power, but that the power was trapped and convoluted like a knotted mass of serpents because of past conditioning, Hubbard proposed simple techniques that would allow individuals to untie these knots and release the full potential of the human mind. We were told that this would lead to people becoming "clear" - a sort of superhumanity for the coming age.

But what in fact happened? Instead of a new generation of clear people, the snakes in the unconscious seemed to writhe into even tighter knots. The techniques grew more complex and bizarre and the practitioners themselves grew paranoid, the movement became crazy.

Some people realised the essential value of the basic ideas and left before things got too bad. For example, the couple who founded the Process. They were very intelligent people out to avoid the same mistakes - and yet their own movement turned crazy, as did several other offshoots of Scientology.

It's as if the very desire to clear and control the wilderness of the unconscious jungle will lead to a furious reaction. This is so predictable that whenever I hear of some new movement promising to unlock the inner potential and bestow mastery, I'm confident that the movement will eventually turn totalitarian or collapse into crazed civil war. (*Since I wrote that, the word "flaky" is the word which I'd now use.*)

Isn't this supposed to be still the age of reason? Even when we feel crazy, we now know enough about human emotions, genetic factors, environmental conditioning, and psychology to explain it all away. Yet rave parties, pop concerts and political demonstrations unleash as much if not more hysteria than the world has ever witnessed.

When I saw the film of "The Doors", I recognised so much of the myth of Dionysus in the figure of Jim Morrison. Sure enough, one of the characters in the film shook his hand and said, "I have played music with Dionysus." I then read the Penguin Classics version of the play The Bacchae and was very struck by what it said in the introduction to that work.

Unlike Uranus (*discussed earlier in the essay*) the Dionysus of the Bacchae was not an ancient god, in fact, he seems to have arrived very late - at a time when Greece was becoming very civilised. The suggestion is made that Dionysus arose as a shadow to civilisation - his worship was an ecstatic rebellion against the growing bureaucratic control of the state and the arrogance of humanity's emerging consciousness.

That was what made the myth so relevant to today. Once again the principle of control is making huge gains - we *know* so much - and at the same time as it turns us into a flock of passive controlled machines, it also evokes a primal wildness that threatens to overturn the whole of civilisation. The greater the control and the further we are from nature the crazier the reaction becomes - as in our most sophisticated and modern cities. The more conscious the control the greater disorder it seems to invoke.

The normal tendency seems to be identify with control and to project the wildness - people in England will talk in all turns about the latest madness sweeping America; people in the country tremble about the thought of inner city violence; townsfolk stay in their cars rather than walk in the country alone or at night."

Just to show I don't only read my own books, take this book here: "Archetypes and Strange Attractors: The Chaotic World of Symbols". I can't find a really tight quote from it, but he talks about the archetypal shadow as the "creative force within the unconscious" - remember I said that Dionysus was the shadow of civilisation - "that alternately destabilises and balances consciousness in order for psychological growth to occur. Without tension of opposites growth is simply not possible. 'The shadow and the opposing will are the necessary conditions of all actualisation' said Jung. He cited the example of Lucifer the light bringer in relation to the will of God. Lucifer brings up possibilities other than God's and, by so doing, preserves the creation from being 'just a piece of clockwork which the creator has to wind up to make it function.' However naive theologically, this statement is true to Jung's belief that creativity is a function of the chaos that ensues when opposites pull at one another, fragmenting whatever becomes caught in their conflict."

It goes on to say that the figure the trickster "is one of the most important and ubiquitous personification of the archetypal shadow" and just a bit later he's saying "Because the consequences of such a process can be devastating to individuals and groups, the archetypal shadow must be moderated by consciousness. 'Change for changes sake' could well be its motto. During those times when change is not desirable and stability demands the archetypal shadow be reined in the ego must be restricted while continuing to respect its function as a balancing mechanism."

If we accept the metaphor of human evolution as put forward by Dawkins, you could say that it is precisely this endless struggle with the chaos of nature that has weeded us out and made us what we are - natural selection and all it implies. Built into us at the genetic level is this constant struggle against life, and if it suddenly stopped it would mark the end of evolution.

Are you now getting a feeling for this crisis of chaos? We're almost back to the point I referred to at the end of last week - where we talked about the fertility of chaos. That nice cosy muddle could be seen as the Yin of fertility. Now I'm talking about the Yang of fertility - it's as if circumstances almost rape one from time to time. This attack from life can equally prove to be a necessary impetus for creativity, growth and movement.

Maybe now we've done a little bit towards reconciling ourselves to this very unpleasant problem: chaos hitting back when you set out to control it. I carefully used the phrase "you'd think life would be grateful for me trying to control it" in order to turn around your perception. Suddenly you see it from life's point of view and think "put like that, I think I understand why life or the unconscious doesn't want to be controlled." Setting out to order something can be an act of aggression in a sense, even when the intentions are worthy. "I've come to put you right", sort of thing.

So perhaps, we've learned something. Don't approach life like that, approach more open hearted.

Now, I'm afraid the news gets worse. The next thing I'm going to read is from a later book of essays. This is where the crisis of Chaos gets really serious.

A Warning to Those Who Might Consider Becoming White Magicians. *Woops! Help! Panic! I've suddenly realised that, in including this talk in this volume I am about to repeat this fragment. So, rather than waste paper, may I refer you to page 362 before continuing the narration?*

I don't know the details of the history of The Isbourne Foundation, but there might be a message there for the Foundation itself. Because what I'm saying is, even when you approach life not in the invasive spirit of "I'm going to put you right" but with an open heart and love, all too often life can still hit back most cruelly.

Now, this really is the low point of the lecture because, if this is a rule of nature, we can't actually stop it from happening, can we? But I'm not going to leave you entirely without hope because although we can't stop the waves crashing in on the shore - and it's unrealistic to try to - we can at least try to learn how to surf those waves.

The process I'm going to describe is what you could call "addressing life on the level". I've given two clues to it already.

Remember in the first example how I described the crisis in my life? I set out to describe it in such a way that you could identify with my anger, and then I deliberately added those words "you'd think my life would be grateful for being organised". That was to twist the crystal, alter the perspective, and suddenly you see it from life's point of view and the whole problem takes on a different meaning.

That last piece I read did a similar thing. Basically I was talking about how nature can be a bitch, but I didn't begin with that. I began with an example of me being a bitch - my anger about a bad bus service. But I explained in such a way that you could identify with my anger - anyone who has suffered as I have with the coach information service may well have thought "he let them off lightly." Then the essay does that twist, and suddenly it put you at the receiving end with nature behaving badly.

Addressing life on the level means looking at life and saying "maybe you've got every bit as much chaos in you as I have in myself". And I'm going to argue that this is actually a respectful way to approach life and the universe.

Now, that word "respectful" might seem surprising in view of our Christian culture, where reverence to God is an acknowledgement of his perfection. I'm not saying, "Nature's no better than me" so much as "Nature you are wonderful, you're incredible, you're huge and vast compared to me, but you may still have as much chaos in you as I have. You may sometimes behave as badly as I do."

It is a respectful way of approaching life because it does not put life on pedestals - neither black nor white pedestals. There's both black pedestals and white pedestals - demonising or revering. The traditional idea of respect and awe is to put something on a pedestal, but have you ever been at the receiving end of such treatment? It isn't actually that pleasant an experience - you hear people saying "just treat me like a person, please" because it's not very nice being put on a pedestal. So why should we deal out that treatment to the world? or God? Maybe the world too prefers being addressed on the level.

Life, God, Universe might have as much chaos in it as I do - it's just a different attitude towards that which hits us.

If, as a UN official, you go into some war-torn unhappy country to help solve its problems, you might well be pelted with stones and shouted at. It's not a good way to behave to a saviour, but it's sort of understandable isn't it? These people have suffered and you're the first official-looking person that has turned up - and they've got a lot of bitterness to unleash. It doesn't mean I'm condoning it, just admitting that, as a human, I can understand that situation and with that understanding I can now work with it. I haven't solved the problem, but now know better how to address it.

Here's the difference between putting life on a pedestal and addressing it on the level. Let's just say you set out with very good intentions and an open heart to offer goodness to the world - to set up a foundation, to make a fresh start with your lover or whatever - and you hit not just obstruction but the sort of real unpleasantness and topsy-turvy chaos I've described. Then a very natural reaction is to put it on the black pedestal, to demonise it (or put it in the pit if you like) and say "it's the black forces of evil lined up against our beacon of light. It's Satan himself... and all that." That's putting it on the black pedestal.

But there's another approach, a little more evolved, which is to say that God is testing us. "Yes, He's right, although we thought our intentions were good, there was pride in our hearts. Now, we've learnt our lesson, humbled we will go on. Thank you, God, for the lesson you've taught us." That is putting life on the white pedestal, as if it was all good.

I'm advocating neither of those old pedestals but a third way which puts life on the level. "Life, you're as bad as I am at times. Perhaps we ought to talk about this, negotiate about this."

This approach can begin quite humbly. If you've had a really good day, the day's been good to you, the sun's shone and nice things have happened, at the end of the day some of us might say "thank you, God, for a wonderful day" or "thank you, Goddess" or "thank you, Great Spirit", or whatever. How many of us would say "Thank you, Day, you've been really good to me"? If you go to the garden and pick a beautiful cabbage for your supper, you might say "thank you, Great Mother, for your harvest", but how many would say, "thanks, Garden, this is a beautiful cabbage" or "thanks, Cabbage, for being beautiful"? It's actually no harder to show life these little courtesies than it is to show it to people.

Moving to something a little bit grander: what about divination or channelling? When I want to use the dowsing pendulum to find out about my diet I begin by asking "may I ask a question about my health?" Two things there: one is I'm showing the politeness which recognises that perhaps it doesn't want to answer my questions; the other is that I'm acknowledging that it may feel it isn't qualified to do so. The respect I'm talking about allows the other thing to be imperfect.

Treat you divination or your channelling like any other expert. If you go to a doctor for advice, is it really respectful to take the doctor's word slavishly and without any further thought? It is more respectful to the doctor, as a human, if you recognise that even an expert can be tired and make a slip of the pen; even an expert can consciously offer advice which is mistaken; even an expert may say what he thinks you ought to hear rather than what's true. These things happen. So maybe your divination can do it too. It's actually respectful to add that little bit of thought when you listen to channelling or divination.

Again, I'm going to turn it around. If you think this is not respectful, if you think respect means absolute unquestioning acceptance, just consider the situation when something really stupid is being done and the perpetrator says "well, I was only doing exactly what you told me to" - children can drive us barmy with that phrase! Is it so great when people slavishly accept your exact words and don't use a little bit of their own intelligence and allow for what you might possibly be meaning to say? So give the same respect to your channels and your divination.

This approach to life opens the possibility of surfing the waves of chaos. That UN inspector facing an angry population is no longer equating the anger with the Forces of Evil; he is no longer accepting it as a Great Test from God; instead he is thinking "these people are human, and I think I can relate to that and look for a way through their anger." Not a solution, but a surf board.

I've got time to give a five minute example. I'm going to act out two past conversations I have held with my body - I won't attempt to do it "live" as I would be far too self-conscious for that.

First, what do I mean by a "conversation with my body"? Basically what I am doing is no different from what others might describe as "channelling the Inner Healer", "contacting my Healing Angel" or "contacting my Body Wisdom". It begins with an attitude of respect: a belief that the evolutionary process within the biosphere can be viewed as the world's most powerful computer system and that my body is the result of millions of years of development upon it - whereas the conscious understanding I call "me" is he result of no more than than fifty years development within the smaller computer of my brain. In those terms, I could expect to learn much from my body. On the other hand I should not forget that the evolutionary process only works because nothing is perfect. And the ability to answer questions from a conscious mind may not be the most highly developed of the skills built into my body. So please listen to this account with respect, but with a pinch of salt.

A long time ago I was getting lots and lots of colds and 'flus and I was really fed up, was struggling with my work and barely coping, so I said: "Hey body, this is terrible, are you unbalanced? Is it the yin and yang are out of line? Should I take vitamin C? What's the matter, you keep getting colds and 'flus and things?"

And the body says "but I like getting flu".

"What! You like getting flu? But it's unhealthy!"

"Sure, but it's a couple of days in bed, not eating much, flushing out the system. It's nice for a change. I like it. You may not make so much money on those days but that's your problem!"

I realised that perhaps my body had a point there. I became a bit more relaxed about the urgent puritan work ethic - having to get up whatever I feel like and all that sort of thing. And for several years since I have had very few colds. But my joints started aching! They've been getting worse and worse - arthritis. Appalling!

I went to this lecture where the person showed these awful pictures of knotty joints, explaining that this is the result of the body's own defences attacking itself. So again, I addressed my body: "Say, Body, this is appalling! These aching joints are really uncomfortable and my tai chi is becoming really excruciating. What's going on? Is the defence system really attacking my own joints?"

"Yeah, that's it. The troops are getting a bit restless. You see, you've got these zillions of antibodies. They're soldiers, jungle-trained over millions of years to fight on your behalf. But you haven't had a decent illness in years! They haven't had any invasions - they've got nothing to do. They're getting restless."

"Yes, but can't they do square bashing or something? The pain in my joints is awful."

"Get real, Ramsey. Ask any bar owner or night club owner in a garrison town: what's the one thing soldiers like doing when they're bored? They go out Saturday night and wreck some joint! That's what they're doing to you. Wrecking your joints!"

"You mean there's nothing I can do about this? It's awful."

"Yeah, yeah... you could do magnets or something... or reiki. Yeah, try reiki."

"Reiki! You mean reiki is a cure for this, is it? That's marvellous, thank you!"

"No, no, not a 'cure'. Look, nothing's a cure. If anything was a cure, the thing would go away forever wouldn't it? But you know you've tried all sorts of things over the years, haven't you, Ramsey? They work brilliantly for a while and then the improvement wears off. Everything - sticking in acupuncture needles, taking some new herb, doing tai chi, yoga - everything like that is a new invasion to the system. The troops love it. A good invasion gets their morale up, that's fine. After a while - if you keep doing it - it's no longer an invasion. They get bored again."

"God, that's awful. Do you mean I've got to do more things, eat more herbs....?"

"Giving up things is also an invasion. Remember, one of the most effective things to ease those aches was when you read the book about electromagnetic stress and unplugged your electric blanket. The next morning it felt much better. When you've had an electric blanket for years, then you unplug it, that's an invasion. What you'd forgotten is that years ago you first bought that electric blanket after a spell of aches and you'd heard that warmth was good for them - and it helped. If the doctor says "Take up jogging" that's an invasion. If you've been jogging for years and he says "I think you ought to give up jogging" that too is an invasion. It all helps."

"You mean I've got to become a sort of healing junkie - going from one thing to another, alternative remedy after alternative remedy for the rest of my life? That's appaling!"

"Oh, Ramsey, lighten up a bit. You enjoy it. Remember the fun you had reading about that blue-green algae? You enjoy doing this, it's great fun if you do it in the right spirit. We enjoy the invasions, keep them up, please!"

So how much of that was real wisdom, how much was well-meaning ignorance and how much was the leg-pulling I deserve? I won't give you the answers because the whole point of addressing life on the level is that we must be prepared to do our own bit - use our own wisdom and intelligence to pick through the answers. Notice the different style of communication compared with some channelling - but ask yourself whether the advice is any less valuable for it. My contacts talk to me in a slightly different way and I have to keep my wits about me as to how seriously to take them, but they surely are thought provoking.

So I would like to end by saying "thank you, Body; thank you Audience for coming; and thank you, my Inspiration, because I enjoyed giving this talk."

PRE-MILLENNIAL TENSION? STUFFIT!
Bandwidth, Data Compression and Runaway Emotion

Have you noticed how easy it is to slip into automatic patterns of response when interacting with certain people? I first became aware of this as a schoolboy visiting friends at home. The pal who had seemed so cool and worldly at school was often transformed by the presence of family members - becoming more childish, more irritable or whatever.. You see the same in couples: two lovely friends whom you adore as individuals can reveal an embarrassingly bickery or petty side to their natures when they are together.

My next step was to wonder how I might appear to others when with my own family or spouse. This exercise can be tricky, but with practice I began to be aware of an automatic shift of character: a greater touchiness or a childlike persona that could slip into place almost unnoticed by myself but - maybe - painfully obvious to others at times. I suspect that, when a partner begins complaining about "in-laws", it is very often an exteriorisation of distress at seeing this automatic surrender of autonomy in their presence.

This discovery led to the belief that there are people who could "make me irritable" or "make me quite irrational" or whatever - the beginning of wisdom, but it did not point to a solution.

The limitation of this "make me" formula is that it implies passivity. It surrenders power to the other for, if they really can "make me irrational" then it leaves me in an irrational state and therefore no longer in a position to reason my way out of the situation. The only remedy at this stage is flight - to avoid those people.

The solution for me began with the rephrasing of the problem in terms of "I seem to react to certain people in an automatic, irrational manner" - worded in a way that makes me the active player, who can seek an alternative form of action.

That does not make it easy, however. Because this type of reaction can be so subtle to the actor - though embarrassingly obvious to everyone else - that it demands enormous vigilance to catch the trigger moment, and even greater will power to divert the subsequent response and retain one's normal self. Once that trigger moment has been allowed to slip past, the reaction takes hold and it becomes almost impossible to shift it without outside help.

I did, however, learn a useful technique - from some book about Neurolinguistic Programming or NLP. The technique was called "peripheral vision", although it really amounts to peripheral sensing.

It goes like this. When you are slipping into automatic mode - let us say it is as you arrive at work on Monday morning and the boss looks at his watch and says "So, you're here at last" - what you should do at that very moment is focus on the full spectrum of available sensory input. Become aware not just of the sight of him looking at his watch and the content and tone of his words, but also what he is wearing, the other people in the office, the sounds of traffic outside, the weather, the feel of the office carpet and the air temperature, the smell of coffee and sweat, the fit of your clothes... everything.

I am here assuming that what normally happens when that "late again" trigger is touched is that you spin into a tunnel of irritation. It becomes hard to focus on your work because your mind starts obsessing on that one incident - his tone of voice, the way he said it in front of other people - and all the rejoinders you wish you had made at the time.

If, instead, you can expand awareness as suggested it helps to dilute the importance of that one detail. It really was a detail to everyone except you, the "victim". The boss, and his unjustified slight, is really just a tiny detail in the larger picture of your day and what needs to be achieved.

This peripheral sensing is the sort of solution that is only hard to apply because it is so simple, and so easy to overlook. But I have found it very helpful. When a lover or child is "touching your buttons" and you find yourself spiralling into the tunnel that has no turning, then open up your senses to all that is around, and the problem has a chance to settle back into perspective.

I have, in fact, found this so helpful that this essay is an exploration of how it might work and whether it could have wider application.

When I sit at my Mac and take part in a Compuserve forum or read my Internet e-mail, then I am responding to information that has come to me down an extremely narrow tunnel: namely the telephone wire to my house. If the Mac screen is rich in information -

for example if it is filled with a full colour picture of the comet hitting Jupiter - then it is only possible because this vast quantity of visual information was compressed to get it down that narrow tunnel, and subsequently expanded back into a full colour picture on my screen. The miracle of transmitting a full colour picture down a phone line - only originally designed to carry a crackly voice - has been achieved by data compression, and the computer's ability to unpack that data and present a clear picture on the screen.

Actually no. Even greater credit lies elsewhere. All the computer does is unpack that data and present it as an array of coloured pixels on my screen. The real work is carried out in my brain when it looks at that flat spotty surface and unpacks from it a three dimensional awareness of a spherical planet called Jupiter being struck by a comet. My brain also collates at the same time a whole lot more information about the structure of Jupiter and the comet and so on... to the extent that an astronomer could look at that single screen image and maybe deduce a new theory about comets, or about Jupiter. All that information can be unpacked by the brain simply on receiving the evidence of that one screen covered with coloured pixels.

The brain does an enormous job of data decompression, and it does it all so seamlessly that I could hardly stop myself from attributing the creation of a "picture of Jupiter" to the computer rather than admitting that it is the brain's interpretation of the pixels that really transforms them into a picture of Jupiter.

This data decompression is a superb function of the brain, so all-pervasive that we overlook it. Try this: practice peripheral vision at this moment. You see the book in your hands and you can extend awareness to the room or space around you, and everything is in its place, isn't it?

Rubbish! Let us say there are a few black and white spots being registered at the edge of your retina and the brain "knows" that it is your black marble mantel clock with its white face. The brain might even use its time sense to present the hands in the correct position, but the only input actually received at the edge of your vision is the rudimentary data that something black and white is there. The clock might have transmuted into a big black toad with white belly, and you would be unaware of this until you looked directly at it to read the time - and got the fright of your life! Even when looking with full sensory awareness, the brain is still decompressing the data received from the senses in order to make more sense of what is around. We forget to give it credit for this achievement.

This, I suggest, is what lies behind the problem of your reaction to the boss's remark. All he said was "you're here at last" - a message which at least implies you are wanted. Everyone else has forgotten the trivial remark within seconds, but you are fuming, because your brain is in its decompression mode - unpacking that tiny bit of auditory and visual information and reading into it old, familiar sneers, attitudes of contempt, a memory of your frustrated will to get to work earlier that morning, childhood memories of being smacked for being late... Your brain is so busy throwing its processing power into unpacking all that information from a tiny sensory input, that you become absentminded, you forget other things and your morning is ruined as your productivity slumps.

If instead, at the moment of triggering, you practice peripheral sensing you are then forcing the brain to accept a huge sensory input. The demands of coping with massive incoming bandwidth takes up a lot of the brain's processing power. Your demand that it should interpret all those senses at once does not leave sufficient processing power to do the full decompression job on the boss's trivial remark.

The remark then falls into place as a less significant part of the whole sensory experience. Instead of reacting peevishly you take his hands, gaze gently into his eyes and say "darling boss, would that winged feet had sped me yet more hastily into the heaven of your exquisitely amiable presence". You then lean forward and deliver a slow, succulent kiss upon his lips. Now it's his turn for a panic decompression job on the experience.

Sacksville. Well, at least it was different.

What I am suggesting is that the narrower the data pipeline, the more the brain uses its processing power to unpack the data - and this has terrific survival value in an animal past where one trembling leaf could herald a deadly serpent.

From this we can deduce that the most effective propaganda medium would be the written word, then comes radio, while television limps along in the rear. Recently someone proposed to me that language is not really linear. I accept the overall meaning he implied insofar as I see language as analogous to the physicists' "superstrings"

- a one-dimensional string with further dimensions tightly packed around it. But as a mathematician I still hold to a strict sense that language is indeed linear and it arrives in serial manner. Parallel transmission is only applicable when we add facial gesture, artistic page layouts and so on to the pure flow of language.

If for example, I write the words "Right wing councillors demand crackdown on youth crime" I am already fuming even though I myself am the author of those words. Why? Because my brain is already unpacking images of these insensitive, hypocritical prats in blazers and cravats who are probably cheating on their wives, have no doubt made a fortune from shares in armaments manufacturers and are only motivated to bogus civil concern because yesterday they found a scratch on the paint work of their Rolls-Royce (probably caused when their driving home drunk, rather than by any teenage hooligan).

If, however, the words were accompanied by so much as a photograph of the "right wing councillors" in question, then I might be forced to admit that they don't altogether match these stereotypes. If, to take it a step further, I heard their actual words reported over the radio I might have to admit that they sounded quite genuinely concerned. If, however, I saw the entire council meeting on video (or experienced it in real life) I might find that those councillors were benign philanthropists whose earnest wish to help society had lead them to a reluctant conclusion that the best way to protect the young would be to propose a few carefully targeted and scrupulously monitored police interventions in order to nip a potential problem in the bud.

Gosh. Even television does not usually present the full story, thank heavens. So I can still hold onto my entertaining prejudices!

As the example suggests, I believe the advance of communications technology makes the business of propaganda increasingly hard. The only way to overcome this is to introduce new restrictions on bandwidth. It is, for example, less easy to make an effective horror film in colour than in black and white. So what you learn to do is reduce the visual information by using sombre lighting, or misty rain as in the film Alien. It is harder to hold extreme views about a politician when you can hear him or her reasoning over the radio. So radio creates the "sound bite" to cut the information band to slogan width.

Most threatening of all to the propagandist are media with the element of choice. The Internet invites you to pull the information you want and then browse it at your leisure. If, in the future, the Internet is developed until it can deliver full multimedia to the brain, then the sensory input would be enormous and propaganda would become well nigh impossible.

At present, however, the Internet has put the clock back to the early days of printing, delivering shoddy typefaces ponderously to an unwieldy screen. It is delivering a very narrow data tunnel to the brain, and allowing - nay demanding - plenty of processing power for the unpacking of that data.

Thus we find the Internet is, in its infancy, an ace medium for public hysteria. Delivering the squeakiest little dribble of information freely to millions who sit in sensorily deprived environments peering at a grey screen while their brains unpack these clues and leap to fantastic and wondrous conclusions.

Enjoy this millennial madness while it lasts. For next century will see experience itself networked - boring old reality to the desktop (or the headset) - and imagination will be once more in bondage to fact.

THE PASSION HOMES PROPOSAL

few years back I had an idea for a practical project which could eventually lead to a re-shaping of the role and image of old age in our society. Everyone I've described it to seems to think it's a lovely idea, so here it is in writing and I leave you the problem of deciding what it is doing in a collection of essays on devil worship!

The project addresses the problem of Old Folk's Homes - institutions where young folk are paid to delay the death of old folk. At present, life post retirement is like bathing just above the Niagara Falls: you put all your energy into swimming against the tide of senescence in order not to be dragged into the inevitable. Eventually age and exhaustion triumph, and you are swept down into an old folks home. By the time many old folk make the move it is an enforced move into the unfamiliar, causing upset and confusion. It is now too late for it to be a bold step forward into a new communal phase of life.

How could one create Old Folk's Homes which people looked forward to so much that they actually chose to move into them when they were still active, adaptable and eager to contribute to their new community? My idea was to build Passion Homes based on retirement hobbies.

The original prototype was the amateur steam preservation society. Typically a group buys a bit of old railway line, sheds and sidings at a knock down price, and people pay to join the group and run steam trains on it in their spare time. In my version, you also build a small hamlet of sheltered homes and flats with resident caretaker and nurse. These homes are leased to retired railway fanatics, who live there and run the site. For them it is a retirement heaven, "playing trains like they always dreamed of". They still welcome younger 'day' members who come during their spare time - only now they are coming to a site that is regularly maintained, alive and thus comparatively vandal-free. They also benefit from contact with elderly experts and all the railway memorabilia they bring to the community. Society too benefits, because the place is open to the public at weekends and holidays as a lively, well kept tourist attraction.

The same principle would apply to a whole range of hobby homes. There could be homes for painters, motorcycle enthusiasts, model engineers, philosophers, bibliophiles, dinghy sailors, croquet, bowls, limited edition craft book production, indoor sports, amateur dramatics, amateur scientists, astrologers or mathematicians...

One problem that occurs to younger minds is "what about married couples? Isn't it a bit tough on the partner, facing retirement dedicated to the other's hobby?" My observation is that this problem has usually resolved itself by retirement age. Motorcycle enthusiasts' partners are usually either semi-enthusiastic themselves, or they get together with the other partners on social events to organise the catering and have a good laugh about their crazy other halves. In general, I suggest that a high proportion of hobbyists' partners would in later years choose to go along with a motivated and happy partner doing their thing.

What's more, Passion Homes could exist in symbiotic proximity. For example: if a local council has a white elephant crumbling stately home and garden on its hands, then it could convert the East Wing into homes for enthusiastic old gardeners who would take charge of the flower beds, topiary and orangery. The Stable Block would become homes for craftspersons who would spend their twilight years lovingly restoring the woodwork, stonework, ironwork and follies around the estate. The West Wing could be homes for music lovers who would hold lunchtime recitals for the public in the Orangery and organise concerts with distinguished guest musicians for the weekend. The public visitors could then picnic in the gardens, view the restored splendour of the public rooms and buy handcrafts made by the residents. You could even have a caterer's Passion Home and run a restaurant on the site. Naturally, all the activities would also be offered as teaching courses: the place would become like a college offering courses in music, crafts, cooking and gardening.

The emphasis on entry into these communities would be more on passion than skill - better to have an enthusiastic amateur music lover who puts lots of energy into organising good concerts or teaching children piano, than a virtuoso who no longer wants to play. I see the finances being handled in a similar manner to today's old folk's homes - a combination of wealthier people paying their way and poorer people getting state subsidies - except that here an additional source of funds arises from the services provided to the public and the local tourist board. The current problems would still exist of some homes becoming over-popular and others struggling for members.

Because these homes are places where people want to be, they would maintain a useful population of younger retired people. The railway anorak's Passion Home would have people in their late sixties keeping fit by laying track and shovelling coal. It would also sustain senile bores capable only of reminiscing about the Flying Scotsman - but the point is that such people, who would be a burden anywhere else in society, would still offer value and win respect from young visitors in this specialist community. As a practical business concern you would most likely still have to employ some paid staff - maybe running offices, providing nursing or heavy manual jobs - but the whole idea is that the residents are here to participate actively, keeping the wage bill for these old folk's homes considerably lower.

Whether it is a Passion Home for lovers of English literature, for rock and roll memorabilia, war gamers, or aging hippies, the idea would be to recreate some of the feeling of a university or college dedicated to study and research into some discipline or lack of discipline - a lovely community in which to end one's days and an experience we currently waste on those too young to appreciate it. The spread of such institutions would be an embellishment more than a burden on society, offering teaching, entertainment and an archive of experience to stimulate younger hobbyists.

In fact the idea seems so obvious to me that I feel it must already exist in some restricted form - the monastery? the Chelsea pensioners? However the essence of this concept is that it should become so widespread that anyone wanting planning permission for the sort of old folk's home whose only role is to employ young people to keep old people alive would be faced with a puzzled bureaucracy saying "but we do not understand - what is the passion behind this home you are suggesting?"

Of course there would be quite a few people too ill or too lacking in hobbies to find a Passion Home of their choice, but I still see the majority of them ending up in Passion Homes being looked after by retired people whose driving enthusiasm is 'care for the elderly'.

Nor would I outlaw the sort of old folk's home we have today - their very rarity would restore some value. Something as bizarre as a

place where people go to die would be inundated with media attention - so that geriatric nursing would achieve the sort of glamour we
now associate with modelling or espionage.

Instead of watching James Bond, agent 007, we will thrill to
James Bond, aged 070. (Note the assumption of three-digit age
metering for future generations.)

INTERVIEW FOR HEAD MAGAZINE

This piece was first published in Head magazine issue 5 as a result of an encounter at the UKAOS event referred to in essay 26. It was later translated into German for Anubis issue 23. I cannot recall what year it first appeared, so it is probably out of chronological sequence here. The headline rather charmingly described me as "Rising star of the Occult Underground" at a time when I was well on my way to the pedal bin of history. It was transcribed from a tape recording by them and I have tried to edit the very few bits they misunderstood, but made no attempt to make it more coherent. Leaving it as it is provides a change of style which may compensate for the inevitable repetition,. The fact that I speak less coherently explains why I normally prefer to put my ideas in writing.

Head: How would you characterise your writing (ie what is your dominant interest in writing - political, philosophical, occult, scientific....)?

Dukes: I like the phrase Cornelius Agrippa used: 'occult philosophy'. I think if I just called myself a philosopher that would be a little bit pretentious, but 'occult' is a nice frowned-on word. I am, however, more interested in the philosophy behind it than in describing a list of practices and things for people to do.

H: In order to give our readers some idea of where you are coming from could you briefly outline your occult background (ie associations with/membership of various organisations past/present/future) and how you became involved with the occult (both in the sense of your initial encounter and your prime motivation). Did you ever get the girl next door?

D: As far as I can remember I was always interested in the arcane, When I was a little kid there was a friend of a friend of my father's who was described to me as a 'magician' and I remember being very intrigued and asking him about magic. It was only many years later when I was in my twenties that I discovered that he was a disciple of Crowley's. People say that he was perhaps an influence on me: I think that I have just always been interested.

Probably the most significant thing in the long term was when I was about eleven. I was at prep school and I read a review of the book of 'Abramelin the Mage' which Watkins had just reprinted. I ordered it from the Gloucester Library and read it. Having always been interested in magic, but not sure if there was anything in it, this was the first book which seemed to me a really serious book telling you how to do magic. Of course, it described a system that one had to be 'grown up' to do but I was sure that as soon as I had grown up I would be able to do this. Now in fact, I didn't get round to doing it until 1977 many years later. Although I had been doing quite a bit of magic - sitting at home meditating and experimenting - the Abramelin practice was in a way the first formal magical discipline that I did.

I hadn't at that stage joined any magic groups, not because I did not want to, but more because I had been living in the deep country and it was not easy to joint them. They were all a bit far away, and it wasn't until some years after the Abramelin that friends (I was living North of London) initiated me into a magical group which was sort of experimental and yet formal. Then later through contacts at the Society (which was Gerald Suster's essay club, sort of) I met David Rietti, and became involved with the OTO - initially I was the Secretary. And then more recently, because of going to Lockenhause, I was initiated into the IOT. Those are the main occult groups that I have been involved with. I am still in the OTO and the IOT. I am comparatively senior in the OTO but in the IOT I am sort of a neophyte and I rather like that.

You also ask 'did I get the girl next door' - an obvious reference to the essay " Blast Your Way to Megabuck$'. The trouble with successes in magic is that you can look back and describe some things that happened and they are so amazing that when you tell them to people they think that you must be the World's Greatest Magician if you you could do things like that. But you know that actually they didn't happen in the way magic ought to - "I just want this to happen and I make it happen'. Very little have I managed to achieve in that way. Life has a way of springing surprises however hard you try to direct it. Some of those surprises are uncannily close to what you asked for, and yet they have a way of occurring which is not what you expected. I am very much aware of this happening to me and it's a sort of theme that occurs in fairy stories: the wish that is granted but does not work out the way it was meant to. I think it must be a cosmic law that that should happen..

H: Are you still involved in the occult for the same reasons? or have they changed?

D: That's a difficult one. I can't give a tidy answer to that.

It's very much my nature to be involved in the occult and that has not changed. Involvement carries a certain momentum - the friends one has made, the practices I am performing and so on - all that adds up to a reason to stay with the occult. Yet I realise I am looking for different things now than I was earlier on. But those reasons are fairly superficial - it really is just curiosity about life. That is the strongest motive, and that, in a sense, has not changed.

H: How you stand in regard to the relationship between occult theory, and practice?

D: Right from the beginning of my writing I would have said that I was very much a theoretician.

In fact, I must have felt a bit ashamed of that because I was very touched by people who saw my work as practical. So I thought about it and I realised that, although I am not describing practices - telling people what to do, how to make robes, where to stand in rituals and that sort of practical stuff - I am giving ideas and ways to look at the world. Now the things about an idea is that you can put it into practice straight away. If I say "Have you ever considered looking at the world in this different way?", that in a sense is a very practical thing, as long as I put it clearly. I think I do write clearly and so, in a sense, I have given people a lot of practical mental tools which they can use. They are just mental tools, but they can still be very practical because they are ways of thinking which people can apply straight away.

H: What do you think of occult celebrities other than yourself (ie Dee, Crowley, Spare, Bardon, La Vey, Hakim Bey, Carroll, Hine etc)? Which have been most influential to you and why?

D: Well, I have a mind a bit like a compost heap. I hear things, I pick up things, I read things - papers or even just book covers and things like that. A lot of it goes in and is apparently just forgotten, yet re-emerges like from a compost heap in some new shape. It is not very easy to say where my ideas come from in many cases.

In fact that is one of the factors of me tending to write under a pseudonym; because I am wary of too strong a claim that "this was my idea" and getting defensive about it and saying someone else has pinched my idea and all that. I realise that there's this great slop of ideas that fly around like radio waves and that I am tuning into certain ones and expressing them.

On the other hand I have been aware of two influences because I can see them clearly. One is Crowley and one is Spare. I came across Crowley's ideas - though I had heard of him a long time before - when I was at Cambridge and had access to the University Library. What I got from Crowley, I think, is a method. A lot of writers have written about things like the astral plane or the astral light, in terms where they said there is this "luminiferous ether" or something or other. Crowley didn't make the mistake of trying to explain how a thing worked. He would simply say "I perform these actions and I notice these results". For instance, I close my eyes and I picture a red triangle. He didn't try to explain it in terms of "there is this ether-mind stuff" - that sort of explanation means that you get into trouble with science. He described things in a very experimental way - that was what appealed to me about Crowley, and that is what I think I have continued. I would say that I don't really know what the world is, but it seems to behave in this sort of way; the things that I observe fits this; let's find a model to describe it... rather than saying "let's try and find what the world really is". " Let us find a description for what we see" - in a sense this is a very scientific approach, and I got that from Crowley.

What I did not get from Crowley though was a theory, because he was more an explorer of ideas. In his life he was a Buddhist, a Hindu, he was a magician... He went through so very many different things that it is difficult to find one coherent theory in Crowley; there are masses of many different ideas in different times of his life. On the other hand Spare - when I read his work I saw a theory of magic. The idea that we, our beliefs, shape the world that we observe. A basic simple theory - I got that from Spare. I feel that I got an intellectual method from Crowley and a simple basic theory from Spare.

Then there is a lot lot of other things that I got from other people that are not so easily traced. Also, I think what it is, that when it is my contemporaries, it is really nice to find people who are saying things that are in accord with my own ideas. It is also rather scary because I think "perhaps that person is saying it better" and "am I necessary?" But it fits my general feeling of the way ideas are flitting around in the ether and you pick them up like radio waves. Different people tune into different things, different people get a clearer reception. That is when people think I am joking about "channelling" Ramsey Dukes. In a sense I think I do, because I pick up these ideas. Sometimes they surprise me. I don't feel that I own them that much.

Among the names you listed I see those where I say "hey yes I hear you. I know what you are talking about. I feel an affinity with you". With past people like Dee, the same thing thing really, it is very exciting so find someone who, centuries before, said something which just - zing - hits you like brand new, something that you have only just been thinking about or haven't even thought about yet. I like that.

H: Why do you think that people are still drawn to mysticism and the occult when the terrain is so obviously dominated by frauds, wastrels and knaves?

D: Now, that is bit like saying "why are people still interested in sex , when obviously the sex industry is so full of corruption and sleaze?" I think that for some people there is actually a fascination in the sleaze fraud and trickery, which actually adds to the pleasure - sex is actually more intriguing because of the aura of sleaze about (I am not sure that that is so for me). But I think the occult too is something where you can be put off by the sleaze of it or actually you can see it as an intriguing element in it. One of the ideas that I was putting forward in the 'Charlatan and the Magus' (in Blast ....) was that maybe existence itself is sleazy, and that mankind's instinct always attempts to eliminate sleaze which is as misguided as trying to make a clean compost heap by putting a lot of disinfectant on it (which actually would stop the composting process). In other words, sleaze is itself inherent.

The universe itself has a strong element of sleaze in it, and it is part of the nourishment of life. We need to work on our exaggerated concepts of hygiene.

H: In the preface of the second edition of "Thundersqueak", you attack Thatcherism and defend "man's inalienable right to not only be wrong but also patently absurd". Do you think that this could be taken as an endorsement of the current Government? Also given your analysis of the 'charming libertarian ideas of the sixties', what do you think will be the result of the current backlash and retrospective imposition of 'traditional' family values?

D: It's a bit embarrassing if I'm caught endorsing the current Government! It's not the sort of thing that one wants to admit to much, but I quite like Major because I find it much easier to identify with his bumbling incompetence than with Thatcher's tub-thumping rhetoric and 'principles'. I don't have nearly as strong feelings about the current Government as I did about Thatcherism. I think I did sense in Thatcherism that it was a very dangerous tendency, which we haven't got rid of. It might well swing back with a bounce off the softness of Major. It really is the same sort of impulse that Germany got off on in the Nazi movement. The British nature is different from that of the Germans and so we responded a little bit differently, but there is a similarity there too and it could have gone another way. You can still feel those same impulses there.

To put it in the same terms as I used in 'Words Made Flesh', a system has the rudiments of intelligence. It is a semi-conscious entity and so it is valid to talk about the 'spirit' of a movement in those terms. At the end of the War it was a shock to Churchill that the country elected a Labour Government. I think that when people are feeling relieved, comfortable and hopeful they tend to become Socialist in their thinking, and when they are scared and threatened they are more likely inclined to go for a government that talks tough and sounds like a Big Brother that will look after them. In terms of the analogy in 'Words Make Flesh' - although members of the medical profession are honourable people who do want to help the world, the profession itself as an entity actually flourishes if more people are ill; so there is quite a pressure to create illness generated by the medical profession. Some people find this and start saying that doctors are wicked: but it isn't the doctors, it's the way the organism works. In those terms, a form of government that is going to flourish when people are scared, when people are living in terror, with danger on the streets, that is a government which, like the Nazis and like Thatcher comes in on the phrase 'law and order'. It is in the interests of that government to make sure people stay scared, because if they really did create law and order the natural tendency would be for people to the vote Socialist. I find this something to be very wary of. Terrorism and crime are actually on the side of tough talking government like Thatcher's, no matter how much the people in it might want peace and law and order. As long as there is plenty of terrorism and crime people will continue to vote for them, because scared people run to the 'iron petticoats' of a government like that, whereas comfortable relaxed people start thinking more Socialist thoughts.

Thatcher blamed everything on the sixties. The media would say that the punk movement, of the mid to late seventies, killed off the hippy sixties ideal. I don't think it did that. I think the process was a bit more like closing a window on a graphical user interface on an Apple Mac. It got it off the screen but the process was still there in the background. Now myself and a lot of other people like us, although we were hurt because we liked the hippy thing, we actually respected punk's criticism of it, but one the other hand what we did not respect was the sheep-like bleating of the media who went on and on that the sixties were dead and they never achieved anything. That to me just seemed incredibly stupid. It was the media desperately trying to get onto the bandwagon, to show how smart they were. Although I didn't like her at the time, I do feel that possibly what Thatcher did was sow seeds of a sixties revival by opposing it in such a crass way - blaming everything on the sixties to such an extent that after a while one couldn't help feeling that there must have been something good there if she goes on and on about it in that way. You see the punks 'killed' the sixties by saying it did nothing, was ineffective. Thatcher unwittingly said the opposite, because her attacks suggested these ideas of twenty years ago were still so powerful and persuasive that even after fourteen years of her government she was still having to struggle against them.

It was only just the initial seeds that were sown though, it wasn't enough to get a sixties revival going. I think there have ben some sort of fashion attempts to do that which isn't really a sixties revival and I'm just wondering at present whether the only way that the sixties can really be revived is to recreate the conditions they sprang out of. In other words, if John Major manages to recreate the smugness of the fifties - housewives going back to being housewives, sitting at home with their labour saving devices getting bored, and men in predictable jobs wondering 'god, there must be something else'. If he manages to create those circumstances he may actually have managed what the fashion people have not done - to really set the scene for a proper sixties revival in the sense of a whole revival of the spirit of that time; that is one thought that I have.

There's another thing about the present Government - god, it shows how ashamed I must be of not despising Major if I need to rationalise this way! It is normal for disheartened or weak people to demand a 'strong government' - that's well known - but I also believe the converse that strong government tends to encourage a weak, disheartened society, and that has been recently revealed in Eastern Europe and Russia. Now that could suggest that weak government might, in the long terms, make people stronger - as in pioneering days. All today's tacky rubbish about 'moral values' might be early signs of people having to begin to think for themselves rather than wait to be told. Now wouldn't that be nice ?

The other thought relates to what I said at the Ukaos conference and that is that on my 'SSOTBME' model - of art, science, religion and magic - we are at present (in the public fashion level) going through the religion phase. People are looking for the answers in religion, so we are in the equivalent of the thirties at the moment, and religion includes people becoming nationalistic and identifying with something big that is outside themselves whether it is a class, a nation, a god, a religion or whatever. The public is very much looking into that at present. After that phase came the fifties - the time of scientific materialism when technology held the answer to everything and it wasn't until that had run its course that people turned inward and looked for magic - on this timescale it would be more like the year 2020 when that would happen. The way I see it is that the present religious thing is bound to a flop a bit after the year 2000 if

God hasn't descended and declared war on the anti-Christ. The kind of prophesies that people are getting excited about now will have flopped - the same thing that happened after the year 1000. A lot of people will turn away from religion because of that. It's a bad reason to take up religion and it is equally a bad reason to leave it. I think that science will have slowly been getting on with improving itself. Virtual reality, which everyone makes a big fuss of now - actually we just haven't got the processing power, we haven't got the software yet - but by the early twenty first century the technology will have developed, so the sort of miracles we are looking for now will begin to be demonstrated. Just as with the great technological advance in the fifties, where science which had just been getting on with it started really to develop and to deliver the goods, society will think that this is the answer to everything. Actually, there will be a lot of gee whizzery and some pretty amazing things, but at the end of it people will realise that this isn't really doing everything. Then they will turn to magic, just as they did in the sixties, and that will happen in about 2020. I believe that the true astrological Age of Aquarius begins about then, so that all that sort of love and peace things will have another rebirth at that time

H: Thelemic symbolism posits an evolutionary progression - Isis, Osiris, Horus - where societies/religions develop and become more mature. This theory is then retrospectively applied to history to give the notion that primitive societies are related to Isis in that they are essentially prohibitive in nature, taking the form of absolute commands - because life was tougher back then and people had less time to sit around and philosophise. How do you react to recent research in comparative anthropology as well as statistical analysis of work trends over the last seventy years which show that in real terms we people in western industrial societies) spend more time working (or in work related activities such as commuting) than at any other time (see Bob Black's "Friendly Fire" for a more precise breakdown), which indicates that in fact almost the reverse is true of what the aeon theories posit. Maybe this is why primitive societies produce such clear and sensible guidelines and why in modern society we are producing more and more incoherent texts and gobbledygook like Liber Al. Any comments?

336

D: My feelings about this question is that in a sense you have answered it in your last sentence. Now, one of the analogies I see that the aeon of Isis is a bit like mankind being the little tiny toddler, and the guidelines God gives mankind are like the guidelines a parent gives to the little toddler - very clear and sensible like "don't put your hand in the fire", "don't touch this". They are strict commands - do this, don't do that - because there is a need to put across very clear dos and don'ts. It is ridiculous to try and give a lecture on the dangers of fire to a toddler just as he is reaching for the oven door.

Very soon you get beyond that, when the child has grown a bit older, and you realise that you actually want the child to think: so you try and set an example. Rather than using discipline you get people saying "eat up your food, because there are people starving in the rest of the world" or "Mummy put a lot of effort into making that food" - now that is more like the aeon of Osiris. It is rather like the New Testament, for instance: "let him who is about without sin cast the first stone" - that is not giving a direct command "do this, don't do that". He is trying to make people think. He is saying think about it before you throw that stone. That sort of morality is more like "what would God do if he was in my position" - the kind of question people ask when they are trying to do the morally right thing

Even that form of morality breaks down when it comes to the teenager who is typically rebelling, who is becoming an adult, and that to me is more like the Thelemic, the aeon of Horus where the sort of commands that are given - if you look at Liber-AL- they are rubbish! One is told to kill, torture and stone and all that. The question that I would ask then is not whether that is a good thing to say or not, but what effects it actually has. If you tell someone who is no longer just a slave, who is beginning to rebel, to kill or torture, do they do it? Or do they actually stand up and take the opposite path?

These sort of statements that are being made - the "word of God", if you like, in the aeon of Horus - are actually much more incoherent than the nice clear instructions given in the aeon of Isis, or to the little toddler.

To me the error of some of the Christians is that they have still got the mind set of the age of Isis, and if they read in Liber Al to go and torture, or if the Rev. Jimmy Jones get the message that he has got to go and commit suicide, then the fundamentalists say "oh right, we've got to go and commit suicide", when by the standards of the aeon of Horus they should say "well, thanks for telling me what you think, God, but bloody hell, I'm not going to do that because I've got my own morality". Now what I suggest is going wrong with the fundamentalist religion is that a lot of people are getting these tough "beat 'em up" Horus messages and interpreting them in the aeon of Isis way as commands that they've got to obey, rather than realising that they've got to stand up to them.

I was very interested that you mentioned that primitive society had more time to play with. I remember quoting that in the first thing that I wrote, because it struck me so much. I argue someplace that when something gets pushed down to the unconscious it actually gets more powerful. In our age of the consumer society, what has got shoved away and therefore down to the unconscious is the "protestant work ethic" and, in acting in the unconscious, it then becomes rather powerful. I think that is why the type of gadgets which would make life easier for us always seem to make it more difficult. Of examples that I can think of from my own experience, one was when the M25 was built. A lot of people who, say, lived in Hampshire - who previously would not have considered getting a job in Essex or Hertfordshire, because it would have been out of the question to commute that far - when the M25 was built, not only did some people do that but companies expected them to. Actually, instead of shortening peoples' journey time to work, it just meant people went further in the same time. I remember comparing that to how in Victorian times agricultural labourers could walk for an hour and a half or even two hours to get to work. I remember thinking "who would do that now?". Then I realised that what hasn't changed is the time that people are prepared to commute for. You still get people who commute for two hours, but in that time they are travelling hundreds of miles rather than a walk of ten miles. Just the other day I was fiddling with it and cursing a fax machine, because some people wanted something faxed over and then the thing was misbehaving, I was thinking "this fax machine was sold to the world on how much time it was going to save and how simple it would make things". Instead of being the same world with a lot more time and a lot less problems, now the world just demands the service the machine promised from you. If you've got a fax machine you're expected to deliver the letter right away. If the machine isn't working quite right you end up struggling with it just as much as you might when you had to write it out and run to the post box - this that and the other.

I'm suggesting that this happens because the work ethnic - which people often say they don't believe in - is actually active in the unconscious. Deep down people are still influenced by that. They feel guilty about gadgets they've got and unconsciously make sure the world punishes them as much as they expect to be punished for such sin.

H: If Horus is *the* god of the aeon, how does this scan with "cock-up" being the word of the aeon?

D: Ah, you shame me. Yes that was really my little dig at the way this great and mighty aeon of Horus is working out.

I would like to believe that if we looked back in two thousand years time we would see clearly the aeon of Horus and where it took us, but I am very much aware that in the here and now of living in it that the change-over is really just what you would expect - it is chaotic, confused, the picture is not at all clear. To us, standing in this moment between the aeons, what were witnessing is a lot of cock-ups: so jokingly I suggested that "cock-up" was the word of the aeon, but it's just a joke.

H: Just as the "new aeon" philosophy of Crowley was influenced by other "new aeon" ideas (relativity, psychology, Nietzsche, etc) do you think that current occultism is derivative of quantum theory, non-linear mathematics, post-structural linguistics, Deleuze, Foucault etc?

D: I don't too much like talking about things that I don't think I understand very well or I'm not really up to on, and I know a lot of people have studied quantum theory much more closely than me.

If I take one example where I am a bit qualified - non-linear maths - I am aware that chaos theory has done something very important: it has broken down the distinction between what is complicated and what is simple. I think that is very important - more important than any one direct thing that the theory says is the effect that it has on our thinking.

Twenty years ago it was still tempting to feel that simple things only produce simple results and therefore it was easy to say about something like the I Ching "well this can't really produce a very good map of the world because it is really just based on a few binary digits and that can't possibly explain the complexities of this world". Now having seen how very simple mathematical description can evolve something of infinite complexity like the Mandelbrot set, people are beginning to get a feel for how there could actually be very simple magical principles behind manifestation. In other words that rather glib criticism "you've oversimplified" begins to lose its force.

This works both ways because the tendency to simplify is epitomised by reductionism. The reason that people fear reductionism so much, and resist it, is because it seems to be killing the life of the world, and actually that fear would go if we recognise that the basis could be very simple and yet to live that simplicity could still be immensely rich - just as the Mandelbrot set in only two dimensions is infinitely rich.

What I have described is something which is important for magic stemming from chaos theory and non-linear maths. Though I can't list the development, all the other things you mention must equally have important bearing on occult theory and occult ideas. For instance, people who know nothing more about quantum physics than the fact that it makes the very basis of matter rather peculiar - rather odd in behaviour, and not at all mechanistic - if they know nothing more than that, it has actually liberated them from some ideas that the world is really very mechanical and limited. In that sort of way, all the things that you mention could have importance and bearing - though there could some more direct influence than that.

H: Where do you look for gods and truth now?

D: The neat answer to that is that we look "within" - but I immediately want to qualify that!

Going back to the cycles of fashion - we have just passed from the artistic to the religious phase and people are looking out for their gods and truth, reacting against three decades of inward search which was begun in the sixties. People have looked inside their selves and are getting sick of their insides. People are now looking and saying "I want something out there that I can align myself with and worship or become member of, whether it is a nation or a religion or whatever". That's a bit like the mood that followed the twenties when the thirties came. People are actually escaping from themselves at present and looking out into the world to find some answers. So, if I emphasise the now in your question I would say we look "outwards" for gods and truth now, but I don't think that's where we'll find them in the long run.

The real Age of Horus place to look for gods and truth is inward, but every now and then we need to freshen ourselves up by looking outward. I think the more fruitful area, taking a slightly longer time span, is looking inward but I wouldn't be so arrogant as to say that that is therefore where gods and truth lie. In fact it's that there are other reasons for looking inside. It's like, if you feel sure your wallet has been stolen, it still makes sense to go back to your own room first and look very carefully.

I think there are times to look outward, when its the right thing to do, and that it is not to say that that is where gods and truth really lie.

H: Thundersqueak, as well as being a particularly fine introduction to the practical side of the occult could almost be regarded as one of the ur-texts of Kaos, if not the one that set the kaos-sphere rolling. What where your intentions when writing Thundersqueak?

D: I was most aware of quite personal things, it was like writers in me that I wanted to express. I had written SSOTBME, which was quite a cool, clear-cut look at concepts of magic and I felt there was something a little more confused that I wanted to express. That I couldn't quite nail down in the same way.

I got round to expressing it by seeing it as a dialogue between two characters - Angerford and Lea. there's a bit of that in the book, I know where to look for it and I can see these two forces that were really just something I had to express. It was on my mind for quite a few years. Originally there was much more bitterness in it, but when I got round to writing it that had mellowed.

H: What is your relation to the Kaos elite (The Chaos Int., Hine, Carroll etc) considering your participation in the Kaos Conference?

D: I don't have a close relationship with the chaos elite, as much because of geography as other things. I'm not very good at joining a movement and carrying it through. I don't know why. I'm aware of geographical separation being a problem. I don't like thrashing across the country to join things, to take part and then having to drive back again. At present I'm looking for something more local.

These are people that I like to consider as friends. I enjoy their company when I am with them. The reason I am not more closely involved has nothing to do with inner feelings, or that I am critical of them; it just seem to have happened that way.

H: How do you think Kaodoxy is likely to develop over the next few years?

D: This is a question that foxes me. Possibly it's too close to home. I see a problem arising because we have moved into a time of public fascination with religion, which in a sense is the antithesis of the kaos spirit. I think there will be a call for something like... a kaos religion might be too blatant way of putting it, but people will be wanting something crystallised, something solid to take place of a religion - a kaos nation or something. I think this could be a bit of a crisis for the movement. I don't know quite how it would be handled.

The presentation that I gave at the Ukaos conference was to do with this very problem. I did it by pushing in the same direction: look, here is a kaos religious service, can we learn from this ? Can we learn to recognise the dangers and also see certain possibilities. Can we walk down the razor edge and survive?

H: There seems to be a tendency for kaos to abandon the lengthy and rigorous training methodologies of GD, OTO, shamanism etc, in favour of what virtually are just disposable slogans - which is fine for people like your good self who have already done the necessary work to philosophically justify such a standpoint, but what about the new-comer who has no background experiences or training? Doesn't this

make the philosophy very attractive for the lazy, but possibly leave its
bravado more than a little hollow in the long term?

D: I very much agree with the spirit of this question because -
although my best contribution to the occult is liberation, liberating
peoples ideas and things like that - I do, myself, recognise the need
and actually enjoy the times when I get my nose down to a bit of really regular practical ritual or occult practice. Almost the best summer
of my life was the summer of Abramelin the Mage - to be so focused
on what was apparently quite a simple set of practices. One of the
most rewarding magical experiences of my life was the slow and
painstaking making of the magical implements - the disc, the sword,
the cup and the wand, which was very difficult for me. It took a lot
of concentration. I took about a year over each one from the beginning of thinking about it - how I was going to do it - to actually making the thing in the end, but I found it was really satisfying and very
rewarding.

I think the reason I joined the OTO was I realised that in a sense
it was so formal I was quite the opposite of my own informal ways
and yet that was the very reason to join it because I thought "Here I
have got these freedom-loving ideas, if they cant survive in a formal
structure then in a sense they don't deserve to survive. How far can I
go into a structure and keep mine own integrity?" What I learnt from
the OTO was some very useful solid practice that I would not have
learned if I had not joined something as formal as that, something
very down to earth. It was quite wholesome for me - for other people it could be just what they don't need. They might need to be liberated from rigid ideas. For me it was actually quite good to hand my
own ideas on a rather rigid framework and see whether they could
survive that experience.

H: Given the disintegration of the OTO etc, and the expansion of
Kaos - through regular journals, conferences and the cults of personality - do you think that we are likely to see an Order of Kaos?

D: As I said before, I think there will be a call for something like an
Order of Kaos. Whether it happens or not I don't know, but I think
there is quite a hunger for something like that.

H: Why do you think Kaos majik is more about making things happen than other forces of majik?

D: I was very much aware when Pete's book first came out, that the previous current of magic was WE Butler inspired, where there was a lot of emphasis on psychological justification. It was possible to be in the occult, be into magic and really be practicing a form of advanced psychotherapy on yourself. You believed in the gods as inner archetypes and so on and so forth. Now that was a wholesome movement in a way, because it allowed magic to seep into the very materialistic world of the fifties where there was no room for real magic. Psychology was the ground it could survive on but the danger of that tendency was that magic became nothing but psychology - that the ritual you were doing was simply to activate your inner archetypes. People lost that outer thing that maybe we can really change the world because they had seen it so much in psychological terms. In a sense in SSOTBME I was trying to turn that tide by saying "look, our beliefs actually shape this world" - Austin Spare's point. What might seem to be mere psychology actually could be real magic.

I feel that Pete really took this up by turning the thing back to an area that had almost been discredited and that was "let's try and do spells, chaps, and make things happen". That theme came back in a big way with kaos magic and I thought it was a healthy thing.

H: Is it any more successful?

D: I don't think I can give a tidy answer to that. Possibly it's really the people who are successful or not, rather than the magical system.

H: What effects do you think your writing had/has/will have?

D: I've been shy about this question. I really like to think that I've opened peoples' eyes to different ways of looking at commonplace things. An analogy I think of is how people must have reacted to the first impressionist paintings after they were used to the formal academic styles. They may have looked at them and thought "my god these pictures are rubbish. The person has just thrown paint onto the paper." Then you go out an have a look at a poplar tree shimmering in the sun and wind and you look back at an impressionist painting and you think "my god, that really has captured the way it looks". Then you never see a poplar tree the same again. You see the world on terms of that movement of things.

I'd like to think that I'd put forward ideas like that where people will find an assumption that they had taken for granted, and almost given up thinking about, they will read it and they will say "hey, that's interesting, that's a whole new way of looking at it!" and, just as with an impressionist painting, its almost as if the world was reborn for you and becomes fresh again. Now, if I've done that, and that's really what I want to do, I'd feel very pleased - and I do get the impression from some peoples' response that in some measure that has happened.

I am aware also how things I wrote were very seminal for the kaos current. Even if that was only my increasing peoples' awareness of Austin Spare's ideas, I am aware of that.

H: What do you think it is about paradoxes and puzzles that generate so much thought and analysis even in entirely unrelated subjects?

D: Recently I find that I've been quoting that parable in the bible about some people that inherit a vineyard. They are told in the will that there is a great treasure buried there. This excites them enormously. They go out and dig the whole thing over trying to find this treasure and are furious when they don't find anything. However, as a result of their digging, they get a tremendous crop of grapes and really do make their fortune.

I really like that parable and I think it relates to what it is about parables and paradoxes that generate so much thought. Paradoxical wisdom intrigues the mind so that you work at it. The original thing may actually have been a load of rubbish but, if it makes you think, makes you work at it, it doesn't matter what the initial thing was because the activity that it generates is very wholesome and can be fruitful.

It's a bit like saying "what is it about a grain of sand that makes the oyster build a pearl around it?". The actual grain of sand is just a piece of rubbish, but something very marvellous can grow on that. Given a good paradox or puzzle, people sharpens their minds against it. The good result is often worth very much more than the initial impulse.

H: What is evil?

D: The slick answer is that this question is evil. There's a certain profundity in that slick answer, because in a sense evil is something you create by looking for it. In other words the very asking of that question generates evil.

This answer is a little too slick though. The strongest sense of evil that I have had is actually mine own reaction to something. Sometimes there is like a visual clue - just in everyday life I may look at something terribly wrong. It might be someone's face perhaps reflected in a mirror or a slightly distorted pane of glass, there is distortion in their face that makes it look like a horrific mask or something not even as tangible as that - because if it was tangible it wouldn't be so horrific. I see something, or miss-see something which is disturbingly wrong and I get a jolt in my stomach. I think that is the sensation of evil. The panic of something wrong with the world. This is probably the same sensation that a fundamentalist Christian who hears about Satanism may feel.

Now I would say that is actually a human reaction to something unfamiliar or what is perceived as a flaw in the world. Something that has gone wrong with the structure. A slip which may later turn out to be a revolutionary innovation, but the system - in this case oneself - has an initial flash of panic at finding the order has broken down and that gut sensation is what we call evil.

I think its possibly a mistake of people who, having felt this sensation - felt how real and vivid it is - that they then think there must be a real thing out there called evil to have generated such a real sensation; rather than looking and saying "why is it that I reacted in that way?".

H: Many of your articles refer to Jungian psychology. When I read Freudian and Jungian descriptions of the unconscious, they rather remind me of the 19th century descriptions of Africa. Most peoples' perceptions of Africa have changed quite considerably since the 19th century - Africans, on the whole are regarded as being quite civilised and there have been some steps towards recognising the extra ordinarily rich and complex structures of tribal societies. Why is it that the unconscious mind is still approached in an unrealistic and anachronistic manner?

D: I actually find this question very interesting: the proposal you make about changing views of Africa and the unconscious. I think you are quite right, this is one that I need to work on myself.

There is a tendency to talk about "primitive unconscious material". Now if I think what tends to happen - and you probably find it in the 19th century ideas about Africa - is that you tend to get two opposite extremes. You get the general view that this is primitive, uncouth, uncivilised, lesser, and then you also get a reaction which sees it as being sublime, noble, pure, better - and I think the same thing occurs with the unconscious. It's possible to flip when you first get interesting reactions from divination or interesting channelings, and suddenly the unconscious can do no wrong - if its an unconscious message it must be true and it is consciousness that is the wicked thing that invents lies and that sort of thing.

I think what you propose is very interesting because truth lies somewhere in between. As in the case of Africa: it is neither a grotty uncivilised animalistic place, nor is it supreme, the one repository of truth. It's in between: a real place full of real people. I think there is something to be learned about our attitudes to the unconscious by considering that analogy.

I like Jungian theory because, although I haven't actually ploughed through Jung's work to a great extent, some of the Jungian writers like Marie Louise von Franz I find very good to read. The sort of book where you read her psychological descriptions, then real life examples that really fit what she says jump in your mind. I think that basically she is just such a good observer that she would have somehow just observed these things in people anyway, even without Jungian psychology. There are a number of people like her - Liz Greene the astrologer who is very Jungian. I think his way of thinking hits it off with my way of thinking, we've got certain things in common, but also a lot of people that follow him write in a way that

I find very interesting. There are probably plenty more who don't - but I haven't bothered to read their books.

H: Nowadays, VR is viewed with the same wide-eyed optimism that science was viewed with in the forties, fifties and sixties - we are going to reach out, conquer and explore new planets, galaxies and universes, but science failed to deliver and somewhere between Apollo 13 and the Shuttle disaster most of the optimism seemed to dwindle. Now we have a new challenge - we are going to create and explore imaginary realities. How much more pathetic will we seem when we fail in this endeavour too?

D: The analogy that I see is that science in the fifties really was producing miraculous things. Our expectations rocketed sky high and it's relative to those unrealistic expectations that we have since been disappointed. What is happening out in space is actually pretty amazing, but it's not the Dan Dare stuff that we are predicting back then.

In this fashion cycle, science went out of fashion, people started wanting something more than the answers it was producing, but science has trudged on, technology has trudged on and in the eighties there was a slight rebirth of the fascination. Not as intense as the fifties: it really just was looking for toys, looking for novelty and the style thing of the yuppies. So there is a lot of talk now about "whoopee! next year virtual reality is going to be amazing" whereas in fact it isn't. It's people like myself who see the potential and the ideas, that are really fascinated by VR. Any man in the street who tries it, after an initial "gee whiz" will realise that actually it's nothing like reality.

I have faith that, when we have got over this and are disgusted by science, the technologists will continue plodding on. Memories are getting cheaper, RAM is getting cheaper, processors are getting cheaper and it will happen when we are no longer focusing on it, when people are in the throes of whatever is thrown up by this religious phase. When that begins to collapse the thing that ousts religion is always science, because science starts to deliver. I think that we will start to see the things that are now being gee whizzed about: they will be expensive, they won't be in in everyone's home, but you will be able to go to an arcade, pay a fortune and see the most amazing other realities with real time graphics on line. There will be a new fifties, with people just thinking "science! wow! look at this ... it really has got all the answers!". That in turn will go its course in about fifteen years or so and then people will begin to see that it isn't really what they are looking for and then they will turn back to magic.

H: What are you working on now?

D: Ah, myself, that's what I'm working on.

Well, in the short term the follow-up book to Blast your way to Megabuck$ - which again is essays that I've written sometime ago, but more recently than Blast your way to Megabuck$ - that needs it's final touches added. Its been edited and proof-read and everything but I've got to work out cover notes and what illustrations to put in so there is a certain amount of work on that. When I came writing the cover notes I realised that the book, although just collected bits, has a strong theme on morality and demonology, that is quite relevant to questions now being asked in society. It was meant to come out last November, but obviously its not kept to that deadline. I guess it will be out early this year. *(Editor's note: this rather pathetic reference is to the current volume, many years later).*

There is also another book which I wrote a couple of years ago, The Good, The Bad and The Funny about trinitarian thinking. Now that needs me to edit it and create some more illustrations because that book has got a lot of diagrams in it, which my previous books have not had. Another thing that needs work is the Hugo L'Estrange material - another guy I channel - that needs to be collected into a volume. All that is what I am physically doing right now. It is not what my mind is active on now.

I think at the moment I am trying to pin down rather more the ideas of kaos. Somewhere I made the analogy of science and technology, where magical theory is a bit like science, but society isn't actually impressed until you produce a technology that actually does something. I am looking at what actually does something. I am looking at what actually is happening, how are these things actually working out in the world. I am asking myself those sort of questions and I just today have had Mathematica software delivered because I realise that I actually was trained as a mathematician and I haven't pursued that one for so many years.

Last Christmas I did a Tarot spread. I don't often do them, but every time I did one the card "Science" keep turning up and - like in James Bond you know "the first time Mister Bond is happenstance, the second time is coincidence and the third time Mister Bond is enemy action" - when that card turned up for the third time, I thought "now what is it telling me?" and I realised that I had this mathematical education and, although I am aware of how its affected my thinking, because I think analytically and I reason analytically, I haven't actually followed that up. So, I'm going to look into some mathematical ideas over the next year or two and possibly scientific application of them just to see if that is a fruitful path to explore. I'll be experimenting with that.

FRAGMENTS

The joy of clearing the attics of my mind! In publishing these collected essays I have disposed of dozens of ideas that threatened to grow into dozens of books. Now, in these fragments, I weed out further thoughtlings before they in turn swell into essays.

It is time to sound a warning to mankind about the folly of all those New Age books and courses which foster creativity. What is needed as we approach the millennium is an Inner Child Abuse Workshop teaching us how to abort creativity in this over-cluttered world.

This is also the point where the intended chronological sequence of this compilation of essays finally breaks down.

TRADITION, OR CONVENTION

People are funny about tradition.

They speak, for example, of "a traditional marriage" when they mean a marriage in keeping with late twentieth century fashions.

My marriage was what I would call a traditional one: we met, we fell in love, we lived together and bore a child, we disagreed and went our separate ways. Surely the most traditional marriage of all, and a form that has survived through millions of years and countless cultures, crazes and conventions.

To be married inside a church is quite a novelty - until recent times it would have taken place largely outside the church rather than at the altar. A bride dressed in white or wearing a special dress for the occasion would be almost unheard of before twentieth century opulence. And to go on honeymoon abroad with tin cans hanging from your car is even more radical - such popular expectations belong to a tradition which cannot be older than the late fifties when cars and travel came within reach of nearly all.

It reminds me of a voluntary job I did helping in a camp for disabled children. One day we were going to Painswick Show and so a mountain of sandwiches had to be prepared and I was put in charge. To provide diversion for the sandwich workers under my care I said "let us finish by making the worst edible sandwich we can think of!" The resulting monstrous concoction of chocolate, fishpaste, cheese, sausage, vinegar and god knows what else was triumphantly produced after the picnic and people began spontaneously to collect money for whoever would be rash enough to consume the abomination without throwing up.

Next year I went on the camp and was again in charge of sandwiches for that day. Before I could begin a youngster took me by the arm and said "we've got a tradition in these camps that the sandwich makers make one horrible sandwich..."

Bearing in mind Goldfinger's famous speech to James Bond "the first time is happenstance, the second time coincidence, but the third time, Mr Bond, it is enemy action", I would have suggested that "the first time it is revolution, the second time is convention, but the third time, Mr Dukes, it becomes tradition". However, the above example would suggest this to be over-conservative.

In my teaching days I was asked by a school magazine to produce a nugget of wisdom for the young pupil. It was the late sixties and a time of teenage focus on long hair, clothing styles etc, so my advice went something like this:

"When you find some old fogey insisting that you bend to the fashionable whims of his own youth, calling them 'traditions', bear in mind that your refusal to conform could be the first signs of a growing inflexibility of which the old fogey is simply an advanced case. The precious gift of youth is surely the flexibility to adapt to even the most absurd institutions, and remain inwardly unscathed."

BLAST THE CAR

I stop my car on Salisbury Plain, walk a few paces from the roadside and sit on dry grass.

The day is warm. The engine silenced, I become aware of peace - and its boundaries.

Birds singing, insects buzzing and - almost negligible yet a persistent reminder - the very distant sound of traffic.

I want to recapture a childhood magic - lying on dry grass and contemplating wide open places as time drifted.

But the road annoys me. A car goes by.

The road was once a symbol of great potency - a Way from one Adventure to another.

I recall we used to sit and wait for country buses, discussing every vehicle that passed.

"Side-valve bike... You can tell by the note."

"Wow! He was shifting..."

Now each vehicle is a tiresome reminder. A reminder of what I stopped my car to escape.

If only I didn't know where the road went, or where it came from.

(A flashback to the Start Rite Shoe advert - children setting forth on the Path of Life.)

Another car. I focus on the driver's blank face.

It is not the face of someone setting out on the Path of Life. It is the far-away look of someone dashing to a destination - their mind is already there and impatiently waiting for the body in its clumsy machine to catch up.

One hundred years ago they would not have looked that way. The face would have been alert, eyes sparkling, senses tingling in the knowledge that their de Dion Bouton probably wouldn't make it.

The road would have been an adventure, and I would have leaped to my feet to follow the car.

Going should not be this easy.

The pilgrim shuffling on his knees to Mecca would be insulted at the offer of a lift - because the destination can be no more than reward for a journey worthily achieved.

The car has made roads trivial. Journeys a chore.

Still no magic in this place.

I return to my car, resolving to invest in a classic British two-stroke bike.

(Postscript, eleven years later: the bike is languishing in a garage, waiting for repair.)

RITUAL AS MACHINE

How lovely to go camping in the simple style: living close to nature and being free of all those gadgets which are designed to simplify life yet end up by dominating it.

Without modern conveniences the basic needs for heat, food and water occupy a large part of the day. Because it is a novelty I enjoy this focus on necessities - but would I tolerate it for the rest of my life without somehow re-introducing some gadgets to cope with common routines?

Aren't we lucky to be living in a society free of the stuffy conventions of previous centuries - free to speak our minds and be direct, natural and honest with each other?

Only yesterday I was chatting to this attractive woman and she felt free to say "come round any time!" And I have spent most of the rest of the day wondering what she was saying. She didn't have a ring on her finger, but that doesn't nowadays mean she is not "attached". How do I know if she fancies me as much as I fancy her? How long does "anytime" last?

With speculations such as these I am in danger of wasting the rest of the day. In other ages and cultures I would know all the answers. Apart from the ring as significator there might be a formal way to address a visiting card - the way it is presented bears a precise relationship to the donor's intention. There was a specific language of holding a fan which would distinguish "I fancy you but am not free" from "I fancy you and am available". In Victorian times a gift of flowers was so conventionalised as to carry a detailed message.

I have seen many business negotiations go wrong because of personality clashes and misunderstandings between executives who hold informal meetings over a meal or drink. Whereas in certain Middle Eastern cultures there are rules that, for example, one must always accept a first and second cup of coffee, but never a third. If a rule like that exists to take care of the mechanics of a first meeting, it allows one freedom to focus entirely on the content of the meeting.

It begins to seem as if a society with all the trappings of convention wastes about as much time on them as we waste fiddling with our labour saving gadgets. Conversely, those conventions save about as much time for other activities as our gadgets save for us.

I see one aspect of ritual is to be a machine. Most of today's great public ceremonies - such as a coronation of a monarch - are not so much originated in the distant mists of time as having been created within the last century. The Victorians were the great devisers of rituals - from social conventions, to public ceremonies, to masonic and occult ceremonial. They were also the great devisers of mechanical gadgets as any Patent Office collection will testify. Maybe these were two faces of the same impulse?

When faced with a difficult task - whether it is to interact with strangers, or to take over the government of a country, or to mark a growth in spiritual maturity, or to focus attention away from the everyday and onto some inner reality - do you leave the individual to the uncertainty of his or her own resources or do you invent a ritual procedure to mechanise those aspects of the task which lend themselves to mechanisation?

Is the brisk handshake and the meaningless "how d'you do?" a tiresome convention? Or is it a handy device to give you a moment to observe the stranger at close quarters?

Are the trappings of a funeral just an additional burden on the poor grievers? Or are they a welcome device to transport them across a period of time when the decision making faculties can be numbed?

Is the Golden Dawn neophyte ritual just a fossil of old-aeon tradition, or is it an inspired mnemonic device and spiritual teaching machine?

We all need to get back to nature... but only occasionally.

ELITISM

Did I hear someone speak of elitism as if it were a scourge?

How can that be? In England it is surely a bulwark against our greatest vice. Snobbery.

Am I alone in seeing a clear distinction? Put over-simply it is this: that the snob would take a Harrods Food Hall bag to shop in Sainsbury's, where the elitist would take a Marks & Spencer bag to shop in Fortnum & Masons.

In one case it is not what is in the bag that matters, so much as the recognition it brings. In the other, recognition is shunned as distraction from the joy of the purchase.

Both depend on a sense of excellence, but snobbery is founded on the one-dimensional tyranny of class. While elitism is infinite in its variety.

A Hell's Angel Chapter can be as elite as the Order of the Garter.

I take delight in special interest groups, in the knowledge that something (to me) as dull as train spotting or stamp collecting can generate its own heroes, create worlds where the man who started life as fireman for the Flying Scotsman is now Royalty.

To enter an elite is to become special. The focus is more on the qualities of the elite than on those excluded - whereas with snobbery the pleasure seems to be in forgetting those above you and delighting in the number that fall beneath your station.

Everyone should be special, each to his or her elite.

As I drive past endless dreary housing estates sometimes my only consolation is to think of all the manifold expertise, excellence and sheer eccentricity concealed behind those dull facades.

Lithops.

Living stones set to burst into flower.

The desert elite.

MESSAGE TO THE PRUDISH

Are you obsessive about cleanliness?

Does nothing give you greater pleasure than the sight of all that dirty water gurgling away after a thorough washing of clothes? Do you delight to see a good full dustpan being tipped into the bin after a thorough sweeping? Or of clouds of dust born away on the wind as you beat a laden duster out of the window?

If the answer was "yes", then you have thrice confessed that nothing gives you greater pleasure than the spectacle of dirt!

So also with the morally scrupulous: they will do anything for the sight of filth.

PREJUDICE

Another big topic of this year concerns the rise of neo-Nazi racist gangs as a symptom of a more general upsurge of softer forms of racism.

After all the previous talk of morality I feel like suggesting we give morality a rest and talk tactics for a while.

Imagine that you were Prime Minister of England and that you really wanted to declare war on France - how would you bring public opinion onto your side?

I suggest that the easy, but dangerous, way would be to start a big anti "European" campaign. It would be easy to trade on current fears about losing our identity in Europe, and recent anti Common Market feelings, and all this could be turned towards mobilising the country for a war on France.

The danger in this easy approach is that naming "Europe" as the initial enemy could in fact invoke the whole of Europe against us. Although it might be a bit harder to focus public rage on the land of claret, Boursin and Peugeot cars, at least it might be possible not to estrange other potential allies in the process. By naming "France", instead of Europe, as the enemy we might even get the rest of Europe onto our side.

Here is my analogy. I feel upset when I hear about violent racial attacks and I want to declare war on this activity. The temptation is to name the enemy as "prejudice" because everyone hates prejudice and will be quick to rally to the call. But I suspect that prejudice is actually a natural state, it is an almost universal quality. Indeed, is not the widespread criticism of prejudice anything less than a prejudice against prejudice? I do not believe the war can ever be won against such a large enemy, instead we need a more focussed campaign.

I wasn't too happy when the law was first changed to forbid landlords to advertise their rooms saying "no blacks". On the one hand I could feel the twinge of hurt that must be felt when anyone finds themselves excluded so crudely, but on the other hand I asked myself if it was not more painful to waste time negotiating with a landlord only to discover face to face from their body language and their evasion that they would rather let it to anyone but myself. Signs saying "whites only", like signs saying "no smokers" or "no scorpios", at least mean that the flat hunter can walk by and not waste further time.

In the face of childhood conditioning, media obsessions and personal misfortune, can we really expect people not to have these and other prejudices? Wouldn't it be more realistic to assume that *everyone* has their prejudices and to insist instead that the real test of life lies in how well people handle and rise above these prejudices?

When someone says to me that "for a public school Oxbridge type" I'm really not that bad, I feel rather proud that I have helped them become aware of me in the face of their obvious prejudice.

To me personally, physical deformity is every bit as ugly as prejudice, and yet I see people rising above this disgust and being nice to the halt and the lame. Might we not show the same consideration to prejudice as we do to any other aberration: seeing it as a handicap more than a sin? a reason to help someone rather than avoid them? And might not such an attitude in society bring the majority closer together and help to isolate the more particular factors that drive some people towards racial violence?

CENSORSHIP

I'm very keen on censorship.

In a world awash with too much information then most important art form must be censorship. There is so much emphasis on creativity nowadays - I can choose from dozens of workshops on encouraging my Inner Child and releasing my creativity, but not one on how to abort the Inner Child. Does no-one else but me suffer from the burning urge to create coming into conflict with other daily needs? Does no-one else resent the torrent of junk mail and newsletters that flood through the letterbox everyday?

So much art builds up material layer on layer in the manner of a painter or modeller. Censorship is more like sculpture, chipping away material until a small remnant of true beauty is revealed. This is such an exquisite and economical art form that I believe it needs our support. It needs to be defended.

Defended from rules. The decision to censor must come from an inner urge or revulsion. Once it is canonised into a set of rules - no mouth to mouth kisses, no erect members, no pubic hair - it dies as an art form and becomes an academic exercise.

Defended from monopoly. The idea that government can censor is as absurd as to suggested that only government can publish or paint. Art must be encouraged in the masses - censorship included. In a country of sixty million people I want not one censor but sixty million. Therefore I want no restriction on television, printing, radio, speech or any other medium. I want to be able to say 'no' for myself. I want to be able to reach for the Off switch and rediscover the silent music of John Cage for myself.

INTRODUCTION TO THUNDERSQUEAK

This piece was written on request from a German publisher who wanted to do a second German edition of Thundersqueak, and a first German edition of Words Made Flesh. As far as I recall, neither happened, so I've

included this introduction in the collection rather than waste it.
We are trained to stick up for our principles.

Not overtly: there is no school lesson and examination called "Sticking to Principles". The training is simply imbued in our culture in a deep belief that a "person of principle" is "better".

This is politically most convenient. If a government introduces some new measure, it helps the government if it can rely on all its opponents to come out onto the streets and protest. Because once they are on the streets they can be shot. Or, more realistically, once it has identified the opponents it can use that information to keep them gently out of power for ever more.

"Sticking up for your principles" is itself a principle. It could get you shot. What sort of an ally is that?

Thundersqueak says that principles are tyrants. They are the worst tyrants of all because they dwell in your own mind.

So don't stick up for principles - fuck them.

You then discover that the principles you have been sticking up for were not "your" principles, but those most convenient to other systems.

And you begin to feel quite principled about this discovery.

No! No! NO! Not this! Not that! I will not stick up for ANY of you!

The mud was washed and now the rock is being chipped away. It is slowly revealing something very empty in its flawlessness. Something very hard in its clarity. Something utterly precious.

Through refusing to stick up for anything you have begun to stick up for your Self.

Let it go.

The real value of a diamond lies not in its substance, but in the rainbow of colours revealed to all as light passes on its way.

MEDIA BLUR

There is a lot of talk about the "role of the media". Should they report so much horror in such detail? To which they reply by polarising the debate and saying "nothing but sweetness and light simply isn't *news*".

I cannot see what all the debate is about. In Words Made Flesh I suggested that any structure through which information flowed in a complex, highly parallel manner would show signs of rudimentary intelligence (examples being governments, societies, companies, professions and the human brain). So consider the media as a living, evolving entity and then consider the following.

Three imaginary islands. On one the media does all it can to present news in a pleasing, comforting manner so as to bring peace and happiness to society. On the next island the media decides to deliberately present news in the most vicious and disturbing manner in order to whip up anger and de-stabilise society with the intention of generating ever more vicious and disturbing news. On the third island the media believes deeply in "truth" and "the right of the people to know it", but what it actually does is to present news in the most vicious and disturbing manner so that it inadvertently whips up anger and de-stabilises society with the result that it generates ever more vicious and disturbing news.

Now think in terms of Darwinian selection. Which of the three media would become extinct and which would ultimately flourish?

If you cannot stand dogs that roll in crap, don't keep them.

WHY WE LOVE WAR

My most enjoyable car drive in recent years was when I set off for Birmingham in a blizzard, without hearing the weather forecast and all the police warnings for motorists to "stay at home". I careered joyously up the A34, with not another car in sight and with my driving enhanced by the pleasure of tobogganing on the unbroken sheet of snow beaten into ice.

After Oxford the road was more populated: I wove my way between abandoned cars, past queues of panicky motorists, and I even turned down the offer of help from the army who had been called out to rescue cars. What's more, I got there!

After all these years I was enjoying the sort of adventure only known before the days of MOT testing when we used to set out across country on a rickety old heap bought for a few quid; the thrill of getting there against all odds.

Last year my car was burgled, yesterday a neighbour's house. I now see two paths stretching out before me.

On one path is a sense of despair at the wicked ways of mankind; at the decline in public decency; at the collapse of law and order. Along that road I buy new locks for my house; I burglar-proof my car; I take care where I park it; I limit my walking to "safe times" and well lit places; I look anxiously over my shoulder and guard my possessions at all times; I am wary of strangers... and so on and so forth.

On the other path I say "hey! this is a bit of a lark!" Along this path I buy burglar alarms not in order to drive the burglars away to other houses, but for the fun of catching them. As I carefully park my car and warily survey strangers I am not thinking "no-where is safe in this modern day and age" so much as "secret agent Dukes 004 glanced up and down the street, coolly appraising the situation. He interpreted the young man's body language as benign, and smiled back, but he kept his hand within reach of his super-tanto Cold Steel clasp knife and checked that he boot was locked."

On this path Ramsey Dukes ends up just as heavily armed as on the other path, but he is enjoying every minute of it. But what happens if he actually is mugged and he uses his defensive might to wreak terrible reprisal? Will the British legal system step in and spoil the fun?

You, dear readers, be the jury. In solving this problem for himself, has Mr Dukes *become* the problem?

Yesterday a weasel emerged from a hole by my feet. I did not move, I just radiated adoration for its little twitching face and lithe upright body. It stared at me then bolted back into its hole.

It seemed to affirm that security just isn't *natural*. We have millions of years of self preservation against danger woven into the fabric of our DNA. When a civilisation briefly orders its world and pushes back those terrors out of sight, then the self preservation machinery is like a bored army. It runs riot and we create new terrors of our own. As I noted once before: if you tell New Yorkers that their town is lovely and you feel safe in its streets, they seem offended as if they treasured their reputation for violence. City dwellers feel guilty about living in Heaven, and they create Hell in recompense.

A personal note. Many of my friends went to progressive schools whereas I won a scholarship at an early age and was sent to a boy's boarding school. So I was educated to be a survivor in a pressure-cooker atmosphere of intense rivalry and viciousness. Although I was taught boxing, wrestling and rugby football, the non-physical viciousness and one-upmanship was far more striking - so much so that I have never met its equal since.

Now here's the irony: my progressively educated colleagues found that life was tougher than they'd been lead to believe, and they have been fighting their way ever since. They will tell me through gritted teeth that so-and-so is a real tough, hard-headed businessman - but when I meet him I see only a lovably insecure puppy yapping to gain space.

My education trained me for war, but not for life. After the jungle of my youth I have never come face to face with anyone I actually feel like fighting, they are all too disarmingly nice in my sight. The Big Enemy is always over the next hill, and when I get there I find a pussycat.

Maybe one day I'll get my war - and find my gun has grown rusty!

WHY WE LOVE SICKNESS

This is the essay I refuse to write.

Do it yourself: take the last essay and substitute illness for enemies, and the conclusion will be that there are two forms of hypochondria. The one is to be forever rushing from pill to potion to escape the marauding beast of sickness. The other is a joyful hunt through every byway of conventional and alternative medicine and therapy in search for the Holy Grail of Ultimate Health.

A WARNING TO THOSE WHO MIGHT CONSIDER BECOMING WHITE MAGICIANS

I remember one bleak Sunday morning long ago, in a far distant county waiting, shivering for a bus. A group of us, getting angrier and colder.

When one, very late, bus arrived and the conductor said he was not allowed to take on more passengers... we could have torn him to shreds. He protested at our wrath and said it was not fair: there was a bus strike on that day and he was one of the few who had opted to work because of his sense of public duty. All he had got for his pains was a tirade of abuse from angry passengers like us. Next time he would strike with the rest.

More recently I tried ringing the National coach service for information and - after endless engaged tones, numbers unobtainable, no answer and irritating recorded messages which simply put me through to another engaged tone - I eventually found a human answerer in an office in Scotland.

I said "before we start, I would like to say that I have tried about twenty offices before getting any reply..." He interrupted me to tell me that he knew what I was going to say, and please not to go on. I went on to say that I had no intention of taking it out on him because he was only doing his job, but I did want him to give me the name of someone I could write and complain to, because it was not fair that staff like him should have this pressure put on them while angering customers like me. I had obviously learnt something from that Sunday morning long ago

In response he was so relieved that he actually thanked me, and said he wished other people had the same attitude. It seems that the tendency to take it out on the most accessible person is the norm: that the world still tends to hit out at the minority who choose to serve it.

That appears to be a cosmic law; and it works like this. Let us say you are a city dweller who has just heard about the evils inflicted by human civilisation on the environment, and you decide that you will be no more part of it. So you sell your flat and set up an organic small-holding in the deepest countryside, determined to live your life in unexploitive harmony with Nature. Now I suspect that, deep in your heart, you somehow expect Nature to thank you for it: to shower you with her abundance; to make the sun shine on your endeavours; to make your seeds spring gratefully from the soil. In fact the opposite will happen: you must expect a lousy reception; the worst weather of the century; an epidemic of new crop blights, mad goat disease, poxy chickens and every calamity you can imagine plus a whole crowd more. Meanwhile the factory farmer over the hill reaps record profits and the value of city flats soars...

As with that bus conductor, those who decide it is time to *listen* to Nature must expect an earful of abuse. Those who fulfil their dream of going to a Third World country to tend the needy must expect to be broken on the wheel of politics. Those who decide to foster sensitivity in relationships are invoking hell from their partners. Those who wish to heal ideas will end up in hiding from them. Those who incarnate to save the world will be crucified.

Indeed anyone lead by curiosity and conscience to turn from the clamour of surface reality to listen to the voices of the wind, stars and spirit must not expect reward for their dedication. Instead they must be prepared to cope with the rage of the neglected.

NINETEEN NINETY FOUR

It is 1994 and I feel powerless.

Twenty five years ago I felt full of power, of ideas that could change the world.

I remember reading the story of the decline of the Irish railways, I remember laughing out loud at the description of decrepit steam engines too weak to pull their own weight, let alone any carriages, up an incline. Somehow all the years that my 1969 ideas never had the power to find an English publisher - let alone change the world - never seemed so hilarious!

Yet the reason I feel powerless is probably also because so many other people do now - I have a way of picking up society's moods. In SSOTBME I outlined a theory of cycles in which, for example, public fascination with science and technology tended to grow saturated and move on to fascination with magic; from there it moved on to fascination with art and style, and from there to religion and politics, after which it returned to science. After the techno-whizz typified by the 50s and by late Victorian times, people begin to turn inward and get excited about their own potential - a movement typified by the magical/mystical euphoria of the 60s and the beginning of this century. Personal exploration becomes personal promotion and style as in the 20s and the 80s - then guilt sets in. People set out to find their power, but have also found their limitations: so they turn outward again and want to find something bigger "out there". They feel individually powerless and want to be part of the bigger thing - whether it is a religion, a nation or a movement. This state was typified by the 30s and is being relived in the 90s. I guess it will last until the Millennium blows over, religion nosedives, and technology really starts to deliver the sort of wonders now being talked about. Techno-whizz will be the craze until the 2020s - when the coming of the astrological Age of Aquarius will again revive public fascination with magic.

Not that I ever felt that much personal power, it was just that these ideas felt powerful within me. I saw the tyranny of beliefs and how they infected minds, and was interested in releasing other beliefs whose infection would prove benign. In the 80s the computer world borrowed the biological idea of a "virus", and some of us immediately borrowed the idea back as a piece of information which could infect the human mind - see Andy Smith's "Satanic Viruses" for a fuller account. The characteristic of a mind virus is that it infects the host mind - becomes a passionate, self authenticating belief - and that the host then becomes an evangelical source for infecting others.

The enemy to this process appears to be "humanity" a.k.a. niceness, liberality etc. The most effective mind viruses kill doubt in the mind to make the carrier into a single-minded fanatic - the humanity is destroyed to create the evangelist.

I, however, attempted to create mind viruses that survived by *stimulating* humanity, beliefs that would convert Hitler into a woolly liberal, dogmas so undogmatic that they would spread on the wings of laughter, not preaching. I still honour the Thundersqueak principle that systems are the enemy and that it is nice, bumbling humanity that ultimately defeats the system. I still relish the concept of being such a total nonentity, such a useless drip that any movement I champion will automatically *lose* its glamour and begin to leak power. To be so blindingly mega-nice that both right and left wing extremists take one look at me and hurl themselves screaming out of the window.

In such terms I still (dateline 14/2/1994) see John Major as potential saviour of our nation. We know how strong government encourages a weak people and vice versa: I take this a stage further and argue that weak government means a strong people. Just give it time.

The punk movement defeated hippiedom by laughing at its ineffectiveness. Mrs Thatcher restored our faith in the influence of the 60s by claiming the opposite - that even after 14 years in power her government was still struggling to survive against "60s morality". And yet no-one has yet managed a true 60s revival because it needed the conditions of the 50s to launch it.

A cue for "back to basics"?

LEANER AND FITTER?

I pick up some business management magazine and skim through it. Every other article seems to be a profile of an exemplary captain of industry, and they all have one thing in common.

It appears that in order to qualify as an exemplary captain of industry in 1994 it is necessary to sack a large proportion of your workforce. This action is no longer recognised as a retreat or shrinkage of the organisation. Like the beaten generals who limp back from defeat shouting about their victory, by some miraculous alchemy of mass delusion our captains of industry applaud this action as a triumph. They boast that they have made their companies 'leaner and fitter'.

The phrase is normally used to describe a person who has reduced excess fat in order to become more nimble. This would hardly apply to a reduction in the workforce, because a company's staff are not fat, they are its muscle. So to lose employees is to lose muscle. Even if those employees were lying idle, they are still not fat, they are idle muscle - and a muscle's idleness is not its own fault.

I am not denying that it can be useful to lose muscle - a high jump champion would be hindered by an Arnold Schwarzenegger torso just as a gymnast on the rings would not want rugby thighs. I am only saying that there is something wrong with the head and nervous system - ie the board and management - if it not only fails to activate muscle but also compounds its folly by confusing muscle with fat.

Nor am I saying that a body does not need fat. Although fat cannot spring into action at the brain's command, it does serve as a vital source of energy. What is wrong is when the quantity of fat exceeds that necessary to fuel the body through emergencies, then the fat becomes a burden on the body.

The fat of a business is its shareholders. They are a vital source of energy as cash when a company needs to exert itself or survive a crisis, but they should not become a burden to the business. Making a small profit is healthy just as putting on a little weight is healthy, but large sustained profits lead to obesity.

` When I read that magazine I felt the urge to inflict drastic brain surgery on British business. But I have since moved with the times and come to accept the situation because, until someone finds a way of being industrially dynamic without ruining the loveliness of Nature in the process, then the best thing that could happen to any country is that its industry should be in decline.

PERSEPHONE

Praise be to Mother Teresa who descends to the poor and sick to bring them hope!

Praise be to the social worker who spends time with the homeless and outcast!

Praise be to the Salvation Army for their work among the unprivileged!

If Persephone is a hero for her brave descent into the underworld, how much more of a hero must be Hades who actually lives there?

If the rich man who donates his fortune for beggars is a hero, how much more so the beggar himself?

The lives of those who live on the street are a laboratory experiment at the leading edge of humanity's greatest final problem: finding out how little we really need to live on.

So who deserves the highest honour - those who offer them support or those who actually live that life?

Why are their no tramps and travellers on the honours list?

PRETENSION

A punk music critic dismisses psychedelic music as "pretentious"

I think "blimey, if you can't be pretentious when you are young, when can you be?"

My earliest definition of art was that it was "pretentious fun". It still seems as good a recipe as any for art - as long as you do not hold onto moralistic objections to pretension.

WHY DO WE DO IT?

A dear friend and critic of my lifestyle told me about a Circle Dance meeting I had missed. During the meeting a mutual friend suffered a fatal heart attack.

She told me of the shock, the activity, the rallying round and mutual support, the ambulance service and the possible police intervention which was happily not considered necessary because of several doctors being present.

She told me of the final acceptance of death, and the group's closing in a spirit of prayerful compassion and beauty. She explained how his death actually gave something to everyone present.

Alas for me: she went on to contrast the group's atmosphere - with its focus on positivity, love and light - with her altogether less favourable impression of my work with Thelemites, Chaoists, Satanists and those who would be described as "black" magicians. She asked me once again to explain what good such things do for them, because she has not been impressed by any such she has met.

I simply point out that these paths are not evangelical, so it is not my duty to speak for their defence and to praise them. People follow such paths, I explain, more because of a calling or inclination.

The truth is that I envy my friend sitting in her circle with candles, crystals and a shared experience that brings strangers so close. I envy her opportunity to be able to focus on love and such beautiful spiritual realities because I recognise that others contributed so much to the richness she enjoyed.

A family and friends suffered a loss which provided a gift.

An ambulance team came out at night and struggled with inadequate equipment and a malfunctioning de-febrilator, leaving others free to hold hands and offer comfort.

The police, had they been deemed necessary, would have shouldered the difficult task of questioning a group of shocked and high New Agers in order to extract the necessary details to satisfy the demands of conventional justice.

The doctors present bore the burden of guilt taken by healers when anyone dies in their presence.

An undertaker will bear the responsibility of carrying away a dead corpse.

And wicked black magicians like myself recognise, take on and attempt to integrate all these "negatives" as part of the rich matter of existence.

Included in those negatives is mine own envy that so much has to be done so that others can enjoy the freedom to dwell in love and light.

Recognising my envy, I keep my silence and do not spell all this out for my friend. That would be like the ambulance man turning to an onlooker and saying "hey you, take this pump and do a bit of work yourself". It is not my task to open drains while people are in their chosen state of bliss - because others can suffer disgust when faced with the sort of matter I deal with daily as part of my "black magic" role. You learn to cope with it yourself or share it with the select few who choose to buy this book.

My friend continues "as far as I can see all these pagans and black magicians get out of their stuff is a little boost to their egos. It makes them feel big to handle the heavy stuff".

Too true. I do not doubt that among those youngsters who join the police force there is a bit of an ego-thing about the uniform and the power. Others are a little seduced by the high esteem of the medical profession in society, and even the ambulance staff must have some sense of their role as knights charging to the rescue. Just as well that there are some ego benefits to encourage recruitment to difficult jobs - even the ego has its place in the order of things.

Do you demolish the ego? do you eliminate it? or deny it? or do you recognise its role and integrate it? Until such time as we all transcend the ego, I am glad that there are some who can at least use it for the benefit of society. No other encouragement is given to those who cope with the dark underside of life. Look down on us from your high places but, please, not with contempt.

If our mutual friend's death gave me any gift it was these thoughts to pass on to anyone who is ready to hear them.

Adieu, or adiable.

SHOCK HORROR

I recall a TV program in which a young man - probably a Guardian correspondent - publicly berated the tabloid press for its flagrant abuse of the gay community. He spoke to a tabloid reporter, a big, bearded man, about the unnecessary way he used derogatory terms like "poof", "woofter" and "pansy" at every opportunity, and how it merely served to reinforce public prejudice. The tabloid reporter argued that this was the language of the common people for whom he wrote, and why shouldn't he give them what they wanted?

It always amuses me to see the patronising and condescending attitudes of Anglo-Saxon intellectuals.

If you suggest that the Press should not be allowed to abuse people's privacy the way it does, there is a standard response. You will be told that a free press is the foundation of democracy and that any attempt to curb it is the first step toward totalitarian control.

There is a ridiculously simple answer to that, but it is one few people dare give. The answer is simply to restrict the freedom of the tabloid papers, and to let the broadsheets continue as before. Nobody should mind a government censor taking over The News Of The World - trash is trash whatever the source - as long as the Independent remains free.

Shock, horror. The reason no-one dare say this is because of a bizarre English delusion that the gutter press is in some sense "the voice of the people", and that it is elitism and snobbery not to praise it patronisingly at every opportunity!

This idea is firmly rooted in our nation's snobbish assumption of the toffs/proles duality. People really live that idea and keep it alive by feeding it with their blood. I went to public school and Cambridge (*yar, bleedin' stuck-up toff*) thanks to being a bright kid that was plucked from village school and sponsored by the welfare state and county scholarships (*oh my Gawd, a jumped-up prole*). And I noticed how people at public school can fall two ways: they can either play up their arf-arf superiority for all it's worth, or they can react by adopting mannerisms they consider to be prolish in order not to be recognised as public school pupils. The same thing happens in an intellectual setting: I have seen the most brilliant scholars adopt an attitude of "books are rubbish, culture is crap; fighting and fucking is what real people are all about" - and I know that if they look hard enough they are sure to find "real people" who prove them right, because their "real people" are those infected by the same prejudices as themselves. But there are also one hell of a lot of real people (without inverted commas) who would recognise such a posey attitude for what it really is.

Returning to the two people debating on television. The bearded tabloid reporter said that he was writing about homosexuals the way the people spoke of them - and that delusion shows how far out of touch he really was with his readers. The intense fascination with homosexuality was all his own: if anyone bothered to read his drivel it was probably because he was clever enough to express his prejudices amusingly.

Tabloid newspapers are not produced by illiterate proles, they are produced by college-educated journalists who may well have done a stint on a broadsheet. They show every symptom of being written by snobbish intellectuals who despise what they are doing and drown their revulsion with a big dose of fantasy about "the common man". I can just imagine that bearded tabloid reporter slavishly following his newspaper's style sheet listing all those daft words "poof, woofter, pansy..." as words supposed to be used by "them". It no doubt contains such chestnuts as "gor blimey, guv" listed as "correct dialect" for its readers, as opposed to "what-ho, old chap" which is strictly for Times readers.

Oh dear, oh dear. Tabloid journalists address their public like a bunch of naughty kids throwing turds at dogs and sniggering when they lap them up. They are in no way "the voice of the people", they are simply a rather nasty exudation dripping from the Anglo-Saxon intellectual wound and claiming to be life blood.

If there is any UK national paper which could call itself "the voice of the people", it could only be the Guardian. That is because we would be hard put to distinguish the people who write it from the people who read it. The same is true of a punk fanzine - but it certainly does not apply to any of the tabloids.

WHAT'S WRONG WITH NATIONALISM?

Somewhere I have written about my experiences teaching at Eton in the sixties, at a time when it was deeply unfashionable to be an Etonian. What struck me was the quality of many of my pupils - an observation which would not have surprised a snob, but which was surprising to one who did not believe in the innate excellence of British upper classes and their institutions.

My analysis of the situation was that it derived from a confluence of two factors. On the one hand it was deeply nourishing to sense that one's parents had sent one to what they arrogantly considered to be the best school in the world; on the other hand the knowledge of being so utterly unfashionable encouraged a pleasing modesty of demeanour.

What was interesting was that these two things did not seem to cancel out: however much the pupils embraced the 60s fashion and claimed to despise the school and all it stood for, nevertheless I still saw in most of them a sort of inner glow of confidence which almost certainly stemmed from their unadmitted and most likely unconscious recognition of their having what was, in the eyes of the world, a superior education. On its own this recognition could have encouraged an unpleasant arrogance and brashness as demonstrated by the 'Hooray Henries' of a later generation, instead it was tempered by 60s laid-backery to produce a demeanour which I can only describe as 'gentlemanly'.

Nearly twenty years later I found myself contemplating this memory in the light of remarks passed by a number of ex-colonials about my Englishness. "Go for it!" was the advice given by the Antipodeans, Americans and others who made it in the boom-time Britain of the 80s. "Don't be so bloody self-effacing and easy going! Let's see some chutzpah! some get-up-and-go! If you are the best, then say so! And if you are not, still say so!"

What such people seemed to have in common was the same inner confidence and certainty I had seen in my pupils. Some of them were outwardly as brash and arrogant as Hooray Henries, but most occupied an intermediate position - not as unassuming as the Etonians of the late 60s, they were noticeably louder without being totally nauseating.

Why, when I was so inspired by their example, did I find it so hard to act on their advice? What was the source of the inner glow shared by Etonians and ex-colonials, and why did I not have it to draw upon?

My conclusion was that I had not enjoyed the particular privileges of being brought up under a nationalist government. I did not have that unconscious inner belief in mine own superiority drummed into me. My childhood experience of a liberal, rural upbringing meant that I had never had the pleasure of meeting people inferior to myself. There were no Aboriginals, American Indians or Negroes to despise and feel better than. The nearest my family got to giving me a sense of superiority was when they condemned people who holidayed in motorboats as being inferior to those of who choose punts, skiffs or sailing boats - and that was hardly sufficient material on which to found a dominant world order in my unconscious mind.

Imagine instead the positive messages being imprinted on those who spent their 50s childhood in 'God's own country' as part of a superior white race.

Now, you might expect there to be a clash between liberal beliefs and a nationalist environment, just as I would have expected 60s fashion to negate Etonian superiority. But what actually happened was more like what I observed at Eton: the nationalist assumption of superiority layed down an unconscious inner confidence while the conscious rejection of these ideas tempered the outer manner to present a far more agreeable persona to the world. In fact, there could even be support for the inner glow: the liberal white South African of the 50s or the anti McCarthy American WASP child could not only have been imprinted with the privilege of racial superiority but also with the idea that they had an extra dose of moral superiority over other less liberal whites.

This could be the secret of today's liberal establishment in the States: they are all honorary Etonians in the best sense, in that they share that inner glow of their own superiority coupled with a pleasing modesty and openness of demeanour.

It could also be their downfall, because fashions have moved on. Since the 80s there has been greater reverence for the go-getter and less for the self-effacing easy-going gent. The liberal establishment is now derided for being 'soft'.

We Brits used to be able to despise the Germans, the Japanese and the Americans for their success, but we now are expected to revere that very quality. But what was the source of that dynamic thrusting success? For the Americans I am suggesting it was the childhood belief in American superiority. For the Germans and Japanese it would therefore be the fact that today's establishment spent their childhood education in an atmosphere of nationalistic and racial supremacy. But as those with Nazi education retire and are being replaced with a generation brought up in the strongly liberal climate of the post war years, I am not surprised to see the commercial dynamism of Germany and Japan beginning to lose its edge.

The trouble with nationalism is that the attitudes of humanity towards it are now in transition. On the one hand fashion now condones the dynamic thrusting assurance of those blessed with an inner sense of their own superiority. On the other hand it still distrusts the nationalistic processes which lay the foundation for such dynamism. In a family context this would be called 'giving mixed messages'.

Which way is the mood going? Will we learn to applaud the butchers of Vietnam and Yugoslavia and see their ethnic cleansing as the loving act of a parent wanting the very best for the next generation? Or will we return to a belief that industrial dynamism is really rather vulgar, the sort of thing indulged in by those with more money than sense?

Until someone finds a way of being industrially dynamic without ruining the loveliness of Nature in the process, I would rather champion the latter path.

PROACTIVITY

Looking back on that last piece I feel like approaching it from another angle.

Thing have moved on a bit and we Brits are beginning to feel that we ought to pull our fingers out. There are lots of books, courses and business gurus now telling us that we should become 'proactive' to survive in the business jungle of the 90s.

So when Ramsey feels a bit miserable in his dead-end job the message is "don't just sit there and wait for salvation! Go out and shout till you are heard! It's the PROACTIVE people that make it now!"

Then come all the stories: "there was this young graduate who had applied for a hundred interviews and not received a single response. But did he give up? No way! he stole a circus cannon, painted himself orange and fired himself through the boardroom window of a mega-corporation. He is now its CEO."

Wow.

A pause for the appreciation of the curious double message being given here.

You see, if today's successful people are really being proactive, then they don't need me to be so for them. A proactive company is not one which holds back recruitment until an orange graduate comes crashing through its boardroom window - it is instead one which goes out and actively hunts for its own staff. And if it is really proactive it would look beyond the queues in the job shops and mine the thinner seams by swooping on drug-sodden layabouts lounging in squats and just begging them to join the workforce.

I am buggered if I am going to waste any more time chasing publishers. If proactivity is the panacea they say it is, then let the successful publishers practice it. Let me be mobbed by publishers' talent spotters every time I step out of the door. I want to find my dustbins being rifled by crazed publishers looking for any signs of literary activity in my household. I want to read shock reports of primary school children being kidnapped by thugs from Penguin Books because they happened to get a star for their last school essay.

I see no evidence of this happening. The evidence is rather that people and organisations who are successful are not proactive at all: they are more like turtles in their shells.

In Britain we are all curled up in our shells crying out for someone to be proactive for us.

It's all to do with the millennium.

We are calling out to God to save us when we preach proactivity to others. Last time we did that he did not send a conquering hero, he sent a wimp who ended up being crucified.

So I'd like to introduce myself. My name is Ramsey Dukes and, right now, I feel crucified...

Pretty proactive, huh?

ABORTION

I recall a disagreement with my wife over sweets for our toddler.

My instinct was not to have sweets around the house, not increase their value by using them as a 'treat' or reward, and when they were around to hand them out one at a time and ration them in quantity and time - for example, none before a meal.

In fact everything that felt right for me had the effect of actively discouraging the eating of sweets, and my wife was furious: "I want him to grow up like a normal kid, not some screwed up son of a Victorian disciplinarian!"

Gulp. I never identified with Victorian values. That hurt.

But it did dawn on me that my roots were Protestant, and that I did have the instinct that pleasure is best deferred and savoured rather than gorged. So that sweets were a treasure best discovered later in life and enjoyed as an occasional bittermint with coffee, rather than being a childhood substitute for meals. That, in general, saying "no" was a form of love.

I suspect that the reason we disagreed so unpleasantly was that my wife came from the same tradition, but had rebelled against it. That lead to her seizing on the more extreme "instant gratification" as a rebellion against the Protestant in me (indeed, once we had separated such extremism evaporated).

In this black and white world there are two forces. A tight-lipped Protestant force of cruel, icy puritanism and repression, and a wanton, feckless Catholic force that breeds like rabbits and grabs everything it can at the price of a quick confession.

The second believes that the reason the world is so screwed up is because of the repression of the first. While the first believes that what is wrong with society today is that adults no longer know how to say "no" and discipline their young.

The fact that the "Catholic" tendency is in the ascendancy in an "instant gratification" consumerist society increases this anxiety in the Protestant mind, even as it succumbs to the social and advertising pressures.

For most Protestant adults now find it hard to say "no" to children - quite against their deeper instincts - and are over-reacting out of unease. I have heard lots of them reported as being more violently anti-abortion than any Catholic - the very idea they claim to be "unthinkable" and an act of "murder".

My inner Protestant proposes that it would be a better society if we insisted that no woman should be allowed to bear children until after submitting willingly to her first abortion - a process which would become recognised as a double initiation into both fertility and conscious responsibility for its results.

This would not only reduce the number of under-age mothers, it would also lay the foundation for a renewed recognition that the greatest love knows how to say "no" to children when conditions are judged not right. Abortion is love, when it means saying "no" to an unwanted child or saving one from entering an uncaring, distracted or inadequately resourced life.

So I am tempted to suggest this as an amendment to the constitution, but I won't.

Love must, after all, know when to say "no" to No.

PURITANISM

Having spoken on behalf of my Protestant ancestors, I now restore balance by taking up arms against their worst excess: namely puritanism.

A recent radio programme interviewed British people from different social classes about their attitude to food. The 'CD' classes interviewed came across as almost anti-food: it was something to spend as little time on as possible ("grab a ready-made pizza and chuck it in the oven") and then eat it with as much sensory distraction from the taste as possible - eg while watching television. On the other hand the 'AB' classes interviewed were much more "foodie" in their zeal for new and complicated cooking and dining experiences.

The programme makers expressed surprise at these differences and wondered where they originated, but to me it seemed so obviously to reflect the puritan traditions of our nation. Whether it goes back to Roundheads and Cavaliers, or to the Norman invasion even, the fundamental British assumption seems to be that an interest in the sensual pleasures of choosing, preparing and eating food is somehow "arty-farty", pretentious and unmanly. "I prefer simple, basic food" is said with pride, not shame in Britain.

The outcome of this repression of natural joy is to be expected: a large proportion of the population grow up equating eating with the tiresome need for a vehicle to stop at a garage and top up with fuel. Of those who escape this pattern, a large proportion do so merely by reaction against it: they therefore become its antithesis, taking on truly arty-farty foodie attitudes which leapfrog the sensual experience to the effect that eating becomes a fashion statement where the cost, complexity and rarity of a dish is more important than its taste. This apparent flight from puritan anti-sensuality is nothing more than its obverse manifestation: instead of enjoying food we enjoy the punishment it inflicts - the search to find an esoteric ingredient, its high cost and the difficulty in preparing the dish.

I, who love growing, preparing and eating delicious food, declare this puritan inheritance to be an abomination. I despise the puritan process in society and will justify my contempt with an analogy - followed by practical illustration.

First the metaphor. Imagine a mountain range. I am tempted to say "imagine a very beautiful mountain range" but that would be to begin with too much emotional bias. All I want you to imagine is a typical bit of mountain scenery: beautiful in some aspects, messy in others, nicely detailed here, a bit spoilt there, wild here, shaped by man there... just scenery. No more, no less.

Then someone announces that "there's gold in them thar hills", and the mining begins. What was once just scenery becomes a hive of human activity and, in a few years, several tons of pure, exquisite gold has been extracted and shaped into things of great beauty for a few very rich and successful people.

But what is left for the rest of us? Desolation: a ruined landscape of slag heaps, rusting mine machinery, ghost towns and a community scarred by the sudden introduction and then equally sudden withdrawal of wealth. A few tons of treasure to justify many millions of tons of ruin.

That is how the puritan process works, and I choose to illustrate it here with a deliberately unpopular example: namely paedophilia.

Paedophilia seems to me to be neither good nor bad. It means "love or endearment for children" and, as such, it is a complex and messy mix of parental pride, aesthetic appreciation, sensual pleasure, guilt, protective instincts, preservation of the species and a lot more. Neither good nor bad but simply a bit of human scenery - until the puritan process gets to work.

Let's begin with a woman who finds herself pregnant but does not feel "ready" for a child. That "not ready" feeling is a complex mix of selfishness, fear and genuine love that wishes better for her baby than she can give it in her present circumstances. So she decides on abortion. Then the puritan process begins. "Not 'ready' indeed! Typical 'me-first' modern attitude! She just wants her sex without the consequences. Her child has a right to life and, if she is not ready she has got nine months to get ready and re-shape her life for the parental responsibility she is morally obliged to bear."

A child is born. I recall the pleasure of holding my baby son in my arms - protective feelings mixed with sensual delight in this little warm bundle of exquisitely soft skin and tender flesh - so reminiscent of the perfect feel of young woman lover. The puritan process begins: "you dirty old man! When handed a baby, your role is to protect - not to enjoy sensual pleasure! Don't press the baby to your chest, hold it with the cool, detached distance of a surgeon. Don't let parents see you exchange warmth with their baby or you will become a pariah!"

A child grows older and I spend a long time seeking out a present, the sort of present I would like myself. Why? Again a complex mix of projection, self satisfaction plus the knowledge that the greatest value in a gift to a child might be the sense of shared pleasure as child and adult enjoy it together. "Typical! Using your kid as a surrogate for the toys you want for yourself!" sneers the puritan voice.

A little girl is flirting outrageously with me, and I am loving the experience. Her pre-sexual innocence means that she is utterly wanton and unrestrained with her coy glances, fluttering eyelashes and pouting seductiveness. I adore the sheer theatre of her actions, the over-the-top femininity which is at once laughable but also archetypally moving. I am seduced, though the feeling is not particularly sexual, and I long to applaud her performance. "Poor girl! People like you reinforcing these corny sexual stereotypes on her. Instead of encouragement, she needs a smack from her mother - and you at least should have the decency to look away and ignore such atrocious flaunting!"

A young athlete has just broken a school sporting record and is stretching and flexing in the sunshine before an adoring crowd of supporters. He looks so lithe and vigorous and I feel stirred by the memory that I too once possessed taught skin, firm muscles and a surging male competitive spirit. In contrast to the last example, there is more sexual feeling here: my own adolescent libido is resonating with this revelation of what I once was. As yang to yang, the urge is not to copulate with the youth, but I do feel briefly inclined to shag some woman brainless. Yet if I recall the feeling later and make love ecstatically with my partner... "you dirty old man, fantasising about youths!" In contrast with the previous example, puritanism allows one to applaud, but only as long as it is absolutely clear that the applause is for the achievement, and not for the body that achieved it.

What has happened? Examples from an endless series of mining operations from which is extracted a puritan ideal of perfect, selfless and self-sacrificial parental feeling towards children. A truly precious thing, for sure, and reason enough for those select few who believe they can afford such perfection to strut and preen themselves for their attainment.

But for the rest of us yet another area of the rich scenery of human interaction has been rendered desolate. At the cost of gaining exaggerated ideals of behaviour we have a society scarred by suspicion and fear of child abuse. I who was once a teacher have learnt to steer clear of children, not to gaze at them, certainly never to offer sweets, not to seem too friendly, nor even to attempt to discipline bad behaviour (in the spirit of fairness with which this argument began, I should admit that I was never that keen on kids, but all the same...).

Little wonder that no-one stopped those children dragging away the little boy who was killed on the railway track. The odds that ignoring them would lead to murder remain many million to one, whereas the odds that attempting to stop them would lead to accusations of molestation, criminal proceedings and social ostracism are now just tens to one.

Thus the vile process of puritanism continues to savage our human scenery for the adornment of the saintly few.

TECHNOLOGY FUTURE-SHOCK

I hear that television companies are gearing up to produce more programmes specifically designed for very young children.

Why?

Because the youngest children are spending more and more time in front of the television.

Why is that?

Because their parents are increasingly fearful of the dangers involved in letting their children out - dangers of kidnap, drugs, child molestation etc etc.

What makes parents think it is so dangerous?

Because they hear it on television...

Geddit?

Elsewhere I have suggested that very complex dynamical systems can evoke a measure of conscious intelligence, and that the most primitive need for such intelligence is usually to ensure its continued existence by any possible means.

The television industry is a sufficiently complex entity to have developed such rudimentary intelligence and, as the example suggests, it is doing what is necessary to propagate itself and evolve from diversion to necessity - even if it has to distort our worldview in order to do so.

Among the many ludicrous myths put about by technologies in their struggle for survival there is the following.

Information technology is creating absolutely unbelievable new possibilities for instantaneous communication, information retrieval and processing. The problem is that most people are too rigid in their thinking to grasp this incredible opportunity. The real hope lies with the next generation, because only children seem able to cope with this explosion in human potential.

What a load of old cobblers! The reason that most people resist computerisation and networked communications is not because it is so mind boggling but because it is such absolute and utterly useless crap. The fact that children (who know no better) can tolerate such rubbish, is wide open to alternative interpretations.

For years I worked as a copywriter on brochures selling network technology. Every company I wrote for insisted that I begin by explaining at length just what an advantage it would be for any organisation to be able to link its teams together "at a keystroke", and then go on to reveal that this miracle is now at last within our reach. That was despite all my attempts to explain that any businessman already knows such an intuitively obvious fact, and all they really want to be told is why the computer industry was so gormless as to create computers which could not be linked in the first place. The credibility gap derived from the IT industry's staggering ineptitude, not from their incredible technology (which, in any case, never could and still cannot connect people at a keystroke).

I have seen pictures of 'tomorrow's cities' in pre-war books: in them no-one travels by car, they all appear to fly to work in automatic autogyros or commute in electric monorail trains. Come the 1950s it was clear that the transport industry had let us down. It failed to deliver this desirable scenario.

In the 50s, meanwhile, we grew out of that dream and turned to Dan Dare in the Eagle comic strip who could speak to his wrist TV and be in immediate contact with any of his crew, anywhere. Far from gasping with incredulity at such mind boggling communications we grew up believing that instant walkie talkie video communications were coming any day. Forty years on we are still waiting. The IT industry has failed to deliver just as the aircraft industry did, and it is now generating these ludicrous myths about human resistance to novelty as a smokescreen to hide its own incompetence.

"Oh, but haven't you heard? They are already testing *wearable* computers at MIT research labs. A new age of *incredible* miniaturisation and *astonishing* communications is just about to explode!"

Bullshit. The same old promises we heard in 1960.

The IT industry is not the leading edge of human imagination. It is a tired old windbag. I propose bulldozing the entire mob of them into a mass grave with nothing on the headstone except their own inane epitaph of non-communication: "C: BAD COMMAND OR FILENAME".

Meanwhile our expectation turns to the genetic engineers. You see, I no longer *want* to wear a computer. Techno-goons are still chasing that old 1950s dream, while what I want is to be born with a small benign tumour in my brain, one which is a wireless link to a worldwide communications network. Not today's spastic Internet, thank you, but one with enough bandwidth to deliver the full sensory experience.

It is the year 2030 and I am walking in a park when I get a hunch that Bob wants to talk to me. I did not want to be disturbed but I trust that my unconscious personal assistant has measured the urgency of Bob's message against my reasons for wanting to be left alone, so I open to Bob a simple verbal window in my consciousness.

He explains the reason for calling an emergency meeting with me, Pierre and Fernando, and we agree to meet in virtual space. As Bob is enjoying gorgeous weather on a Californian beach, myself and Pierre accept his sensory input and find all four of us (as in a dream) embracing each other beneath the Californian sunshine and enjoying a cool drink as we discuss the problem. Fernando, however, does not enjoy hot weather, so he experiences all four of us as meeting over coffee cream on the verandah of his ski hotel. In each case the same conversation is enacted, the same decision is made (with the help of a quick browse in the British Museum Library) and we then return to our respective environments.

That vision might explain why, after merely two years and umpteen help line phone calls, I no longer waste my time trying to reach the Internet via CompuServe.

CRIPPLES

Can't stand cripples.

Woops! have I said something wrong?

Don't misunderstand me, I have nothing against the poor sportsman in plaster after a skiing accident, what really offends me is the slobbery spasticity of what they call 'handicapped people'.

Hey! come back! You've got me wrong!

Look, if I walk into a cafe and there's a table with a mongol child bellowing away, I'm much too sensitive to say "ugh! how disgusting , let's sit somewhere else". I'd simply say something like "there's a nice table over in that far corner", because I wouldn't want to hurt anybody's feelings.

What do you mean "That's even worse"? If you think an "honest expression of feelings" is infinitely preferable to "middle class uptightness", then why did you react so negatively to the honest expression of feelings in my opening sentence?

I came to you because you are wearing a badge which says "I SUPPORT THE HANDICAPPED" and I thought you might be someone who could support me.

I am handicapped by strong feelings of revulsion in the presence of severe physical and mental affliction. It tears me apart because I also realise that these are people who may have all the same human needs as myself - including the need for acceptance - and they might even need extra help and understanding because of their condition.

And yet when I revealed to you my own handicap you turned away in disgust as though I was less than human.

I am not proud of being handicapped - I have not resorted to the alchemy which turns a minority into an elite - but I do try to address it with sympathy. For example, I accept that there is an inherited animal disposition to cast out genetic abnormalities from the herd in order to increase its chances of survival. But I also recognise that, however useful in our ancestral past, this instinct has long since grown redundant - indeed the intense mental focus or challenge of physical handicap has even lead to great discoveries for the benefit of all mankind.

When I shun the company of cripples, then I am in one sense being unsympathetic. But can you be sympathetic enough to understand the sympathy that I am defending myself against?

The other day I was visited by a friend who had suddenly been crippled with pain from cancer running down the right leg. I ached with a desire to lift this burden of pain, and for nearly a month after I too was limping and suffering sleepless nights of pain in my right leg. As I look after elderly arthritic parents I find myself too growing slow and achey. When I offered sympathy to a depressed friend I became almost suicidal myself. As a student I helped out in Red Cross camps for handicapped children and I found myself suffering echoes of every form of mental and physical affliction in the process.

Sympathy seems to have its roots in the herd instinct, and those who feel it strongly need to be careful with whom they congregate. As my life becomes dominated with the care of the elderly, I find solace in Baywatch. TV Gladiators also present images of strapping physical health, but they are somewhat blurred by an unnecessary and tiresome competitive element, whereas the Baywatch cameras linger more affectionately on the bodies of the cast.

It is unlikely that Pamela Anderson will ever read these words, but that in no way reduces their comfort as prayer.

"Oh Pamela of the white sands, blue skies, azure ocean and scarlet swimsuit, I salute you. You for whom the surgeon's scalpel has invoked not disfigurement but even greater beauty, I salute you. For you are the priestess of not one but three faces of the Goddess -

Aphrodite of the Foam, Hygeia of the Surgery and Artemis of the Gym. I salute you and feel Health, Freedom and Beauty resonate in my being. Thus I bear my own wrinkles not as a scar but as a veil across the face of inner loveliness. I am healed and remain beautiful within as I wipe wrinkled old bottoms and trudge behind clumsy wheelchairs. Thank you, Pamela, for your triple blessings of inspiration, healing and hope. Humanity and the human form is exquisite."

INTOLERANCE

The Mayor of New York is advocating a different approach to policing, described as "zero tolerance". The idea is to crack down hard on petty crime and offensive behaviour in public in order to create an environment less conducive to more serious crime.

I find the idea of zero tolerance immensely distasteful. I loath the sort of person who advocates that sort of thing. It brings to mind some sort of police state... In short, I am experiencing a knee-jerk reaction against the suggestion.

It would be described as a liberal knee-jerk reaction, were that not a contradiction in terms. Better call it a "knee jerk reaction by an otherwise liberal person".

Liberalism likes feelings to be aired and judged in the light of reason - that is why it does not foster knee-jerk reactions. Something in me is insisting that zero tolerance is bad, so I ask the defendant to step into the witness box and explain itself.

The idea is to imagine that you live in a city street, and someone parks a car in your residents-only parking area - an offence, but one so common as to be hardly worth comment. The next day it is still there, and you notice that the windscreen has been cracked. Some kids are playing cricket in the street and they look mighty guilty as you walk past. The next time you see the car, the broken windscreen has been pushed in, and within a few hours someone has ripped out the car radio. You ought to tell the police. Next morning the car is not there, but its burnt out remains are found in a nearby park after joy riders have taken the car wrecked several flower beds and hedges by driving through them. The police now have a serious crime on their hands and everyone in the street feels threatened. Zero tolerance says don't wait for the big crime, crack down on the vandal. Crack down on those careless kids playing cricket in the street. And first of all crack down on the person parking where it was not permitted. No tolerance of minor offences discourages the sort of conditions that leads to greater crimes.

So far, this sounds rather good. If I put myself in the position of a normal citizen in a big city, then I would be jolly glad to have no litter in the gutters, no wrecked cars and broken glass, no noisy gangs swearing in the streets at night. It would be good to feel you could walk anywhere anytime without that uneasy feeling of threatening behaviour. Zero tolerance sounds great - so what does the prosecution have to say?

Zero tolerance would be OK as long as it didn't work. The awful thing about it is that it might work, then all those frightful "get tough" dogmatists would have something to crow about. If there is one thing worse than a total breakdown of civilisation reducing our inner cities to rubble, then it is surely the sight of some right wing prat saying "I told you so".

I suspect that zero tolerance might work because I remember my schooldays and the absurd way in which my contemporaries seemed to respect teachers who showed zero tolerance. I didn't respect such teachers, I hated them. It's probably their fault that I am now a revolutionary, a philosophical vandal, an ideas yob, a dangerous element in society, public enemy number... somewhere in the millions. The teachers I liked were the ones who could not keep order, and I liked them because they taught me more. They did not transfer as much academic information as the zero-tolerance teachers, but the drippy teachers created a far richer emotional environment in the class. Instead of a single one-dimensional relationship based on "respect", the poor teacher opened up a whole world of possibilities to explore: you could despise them, laugh at them, feel sorry for them or even like them. For this reason I oppose the 1980s desire to eliminate bad teachers from schools - any school dedicated to transcending mediocrity needs a proportion of bad teachers in order to raise pupils eyes beyond academic performance towards life and inspiration.

Anyway, I digress. I fear that my experience is that zero tolerance works - so much so that I even had to apply it myself as a teacher against mine own better judgement.

The fact that it works is bad. It reflects badly on mankind. Mankind is not as good as me, but I forgive it, because that is what is expected of superior people.

It is also wholesome to remind the Mayor of New York that zero policing tolerance is not the only effective alternative for making his city a safe place to walk in. Another solution would be to hand over control of the city to the Mafia. Although organised crime is immensely disruptive when involved in a struggle for power, once a gang gains total supremacy petty crime is outlawed, and life becomes sweet for the ordinary citizen. The safest place in America, I am told, used to be Las Vegas when it was controlled by the Mafia. Organised crime was organised, so much money as being made by black market crimes there was no room for petty freelance thievery. To mug someone on the street was to risk having your knees shot off.

The secret of the Mafia's success was zero tolerance. It was also the secret of the successful policing in Nazi Germany, Soviet Russia and all those totalitarian states which succeed in providing a secure and comfortable environment for citizens who are prepared to toe the party line.

That is the real danger in zero tolerance. It is not a threat to the average citizen, in fact it offers positive benefit. It is the ruling class that is at risk.

The first danger is that the almost inevitable success of the policy will generate smugness. Like the school which sacks its hopeless teachers and enjoys a boost in its exam results - the ruling class becomes so locked onto security and stability that it forgets the role of inspiration creativity and dynamism in society.

The other problem is that a whole lot of violent crimes are performed by young men who feel moved to prove how tough they are. At present the toughest options easily available include stealing cars and driving them dangerously, ram-raiding shops, taking drugs, raping women, mugging, breaking and entering. But in a zero-tolerance environment such career options would be curtailed and the toughest job around would be to become a zero tolerance policeman and go round beating up misfits.

Thus a zero tolerance police force - like the SS - tends to recruit the very people who would have been criminals in a more liberal society. In some ways this is a good place for them, but it creates a need for another layer of policing to prevent the police force from becoming as much of a menace as the criminal underworld it has displaced.

I have yet to hear the Mayor of New York speak on this subject. If he justifies zero tolerance in terms of necessary evil and the need for temporary measures to avert a crisis in the streets, then I could be firmly on his side. But if he claims it's a good way to run a city, then I am not.

THE IMPORTANCE OF FAITH

As the end of writing any book draws nigh I begin to imagine that someone might read it. That image evokes an upwelling of love in my heart for anyone who has persevered this far, which feeling in turn inspires a desire to pack my text with last-minute gifts, bonuses and extras by way of gratitude to my faithful reader.

What, then, could be more appropriate than to offer a few words of unsolicited advice on the running of New Age workshops?

One of the greatest disincentives to running a New Age workshop must be the fear that nothing might happen. You give everyone a crystal to hold while they close their eyes and breath deeply, or you bang a drum while they go on an inner journey to locate their power animals, or whatever... then you invite participants to 'share their experience' with the group.

Terror.

What if, having forked out a hundred quid for this load of rubbish, no-one has experienced anything? They all sit in embarrassed silence trying to avoid your gaze. What the hell do you do?

Simple.

You say "wow! that last exercise really generated absolutely incredible energy! We all need more time to assimilate it... so let's just sit and breath deeply for a minute then move straight into the next exercise".

Why does this work? I think it must be because everyone is so embarrassed. They feel like wallies for having paid so much, for having to do such daft things, for not having experienced anything, for fear that you will point to them like a school teacher in front of the class and demand 'well, Smith, what did YOU experience?'. There is also the dark cloud of uncertainty on the horizon - perhaps this whole New Age business is a load of tripe - a cloud that threatens lightning bolts of anger at having been duped as much as it threatens torrents of compassionate feeling for the poor person trying to scrape a living by holding these hopeless workshops.

Such embarrassment creates an electric atmosphere of tension, everyone wants to squirm. So when you mention 'incredible energy' people jump at that phrase because they would far rather believe that the feeling they are experiencing is a manifestation of awesome energies than recognise it as acute embarrassment. A moment's reflection allows them to adjust to this more comfortable interpretation, and the imposed silence also prevents them from comparing notes. Now they know they don't *have* to speak, and that there really are enormous energies about, the next exercise might actually produce some results - and if it does not you should perhaps consider putting psychedelic drugs in the chamomile tea.

It's a question of faith: in New Age workshops, as nowhere else, nothing happening is believed to be a sure sign of absolutely incredible energy.

After the workshop, faith becomes even more vital. Assuming that the objective is 'healing' - it usually is - what do you do when the person who followed your advice promptly catches a severe cold (or fever, or diorrhea or whatever)?

Simple. You say: "wonderful! That's the body's way of eliminating harmful waste! It shows that the treatment is really taking effect."

And when, on the following day, he sneezes so hard that he falls down the stairs and breaks a leg, then what do you say?

You say "already? That's wonderful! Your body is obviously confronting you with really deep issues - most of my clients last more than a week before they break a leg, or crash the car, or strangle their children... (*uh-oh! don't over-do it*). Tell me, what does a broken leg mean to you?"

If they reply that it means searing pain, loss of income or the like, you come back with "no, what does a broken leg *really* mean? Like, is it saying that you feel unacknowledged by your environment?"

With faith, everything that happens is inevitably part of the healing. And if they should die, remember only that you did not kill them: rather that you feel deeply humbled at having been privileged to help facilitate their death process.

Which is why it is wise to insist on pre-payment.

Now herein lies a temptation: perhaps you would like to prepare them by pointing out before you start that New Age 'healing' can manifest such a trail of disasters as to make one yearn to return to dear old familiar dis-ease. Don't be tempted! It would be utterly irresponsible to implant such negative expectations.

Remember also that their money becomes your money when handed over. Would you want to fill your bank account with bad karma? Only money given in hope and eager anticipation of wholeness can be relied upon to fill your coffers with shining light and love.

'Faith moves mountains'. It's been said before, but it needs to be repeated again and again in the unlikeliest of contexts.

My problem is that nowadays the moving of mountains constitutes ecological vandalism.

Four years on: I just wish instead that faith was capable of making the correct six numbered balls be picked out of forty nine.

WHAT DOES WOMAN REALLY WANT?

I keep seeing these men's magazines on the newsagent racks with variations on "what do women really want? Our survey reveals all" plastered across the cover.

Funny idea to buy a magazine to find the answer - why not simply ask some women? Note that I have sidestepped that objection in this essay because the title is not "what do women want" but "what does WOMAN want". You can ask women, but Woman is an archetypal essence that could prove less communicative.

Of course, the emphasis lies on that word "really". It suggests that - whatever any woman might say she wants - there lies behind it some deep unconscious hunger sensed by men but refusing to reveal itself.

This is supported by the fact that it appears to be an age old question. The myth of Sir Gawain and the Loathly Lady tells of the Black Knight's challenge to King Arthur that he has three days to find the answer to the question "what is it that women most desire?" Should he fail to find the answer by New Years Day, he will have to surrender his kingdom and his life... and poor Arthur didn't have the Christmas edition of Arena, Esquire or GQ to enlighten him.

If it can sell all those magazines, perhaps it will sell this book... Ramsey Dukes reveals all!

There was a recent TV program about one night stands, and it focussed on the life of one woman who sometimes went out clubbing to pick up some bloke or other for sex. The program voiceover asked her at one point if she ever wanted to extend the relationships she formed and she said not. When asked why not, the woman replied that she had tried it but she always found it unsatisfactory because - however good the relationship - she always ended up wanting more. "More what?" the voice asked. "More of everything" she replied.

I was struck by that answer. It reminded me of a feeling that I'd experienced towards the end of a number of relationships: that my partner seemed to have an inexhaustible need. Sometimes it was for more and more of one thing already offered in no small measure - like time or attention. More often it was expressed in polar opposites - for example someone loving me for being so exceptionally gentle then fretting that I was not more aggressive, or loving me for being so manly then fretting that I was not sufficiently sensitive.

Perhaps this is a universal pattern? Maybe a majority of men have experienced the feeling that their female partners have a need that is never clearly expressed, or expressible, but which is manifest as an eternal hunger for more than they can offer? If so, it would explain why the question "what do women really need" has such power to sell magazines.

Now it so happened that, at the time of the programme, I was reading a book I'd been given called "The Blind Watchmaker" by Richard Dawkins. In Chapter 8 the author describes an experiment where male long-tail widow birds were artificially fixed with even longer tails, and they attracted four times as many females as those with artificially shortened tails. He uses this to suggest that in this case natural selection is being driven by female sexual preference - every time a male is chosen for his long tail, genes for preferring long tails are also being chosen. This results in the female desire for long tails keeping ahead of the male's physical attributes, driving evolution for even longer tails.

Maybe this is a universal factor in the evolutionary process? That whatever direction evolution is moving in - males with longer tails, or bigger beaks, or greater aggression, or better singing voices - the female chooses the best she can aspire to and yet has a genetic drive for even more of that quality? And would not that genetic drive towards a future not yet manifest in flesh be sensed as a hunger for the infinite? And would not such a yearning be most likely to emerge in relationships where sex is the predominant driving force?

O man! you have always sensed this in a woman's infinite hunger, this evolutionary drive that ever taunts the male. Always more, more than you can ever give. The Goddess cries for blood, you are just an eddy in the river of life rushing into the fearful future of our species. Timid males stand giddy before the awful abyss of female desire! This is the jungle cry of a feral goddess. This is the vagina dentata. This is why men strive vainly to domesticate female sexuality. This is the hunger we sense in a lusty woman, the hunger that drives men to worship or to crime...

Incidentally, the Loathly Lady told Arthur that the secret was that "women most desire is to have their own way".

Whether true or not - it certainly sent the Black Knight packing. But perhaps he was the editor of GQ?

HELP THE AGED

On transcending half a century, Ramsey Dukes found the world growing fuzzy.

This was very great magic indeed - after years of campaigning against the reality of the material universe, was he now witnessing the cosmos' slow surrender to the juggernaut of his logic?

Or was it simply a manifestation of the long-sightedness attendant on old age?

Never ceasing in his quest for Truth, Ramsey went to an optician and was prescribed spectacles with Varilux lenses - a system like bifocals but without the bubble at the bottom of the lens. Instead, the focus gradually changes as you approach the bottom of the lens.

It takes only the slightest appreciation of optical principles to realise that this cannot be done - it amounts to cylindrical distortion of the spherical lens structure. But it works because the brain - after the first day or so when the optician warned that I might feel a little sea-sick - learns to adjust its processing of the distorted visual input and recreate a sharp visual environment. This is just a mild version of that curious experiment performed earlier in the century when a man was given spectacles which turned his vision completely upside down. After a few confusing days his vision had righted itself and, when the spectacles were removed, he again saw the world upside down until the brain adjusted back to normal.

Meanwhile something else had been brought into focus in Ramsey's awareness - the spectacle of old age. Suddenly sensitised to this issue he remembered hearing (yes, he still has a bit of that left) that the brain and nervous tissue retains its powers of recuperation long after other forms of flesh have chosen the downhill path. Thus stimulating cerebral exercises for the elderly actually help to keep their brains fit and working to full capacity.

In which case, forcing his brain to re-wire itself to the distorted input from Varilux lenses would not only restore his world to clarity, it should also help to keep his brain young and sprightly.

So here is a new form of therapy invented by Ramsey Dukes just in time to rescue the baby-boom wrinkly bulge of the coming decades: people over fifty will be fitted with a new pair of spectacles every year, and these spectacles will be designed with ever worse distortions and imperfections so that the brain will constantly be exercised to endure the visual assault course of a world turned upside down, inside out and round and round. This will keep us all young at heart.

There is a cheaper version of this prescription.

It is that everyone over fifty should read Ramsey Dukes.

BAD TEACHERS

I am a little concerned about recent attempts by successive governments to identify and remove bad teachers from our schools.

When I say that I owe so much of my education to bad teachers, this is not to deny that good teachers also have an important role. There will always be a place in any school for a number - even a majority - of teachers who can discipline their class into receptive rows for the efficient transmission of information and techniques necessary for qualification.

Yet such teachers take second place in my affection to those whose classes went awry. There can be few pedagogical experiences to match the intensity of a classroom revolution. My first serious lessons in politics, society and personal morality came at those times when I struggled to achieve some balance between involvement with my fellow classmates and feelings for the comparatively nice and well meaning person who was failing to keep us in order.

Agreement with a good teacher who is clearly right is the acceptance of a single option, whereas rebellion against the opinion of a bad teacher is the first step in an adventurous exploration of every opinion except the one being proposed.

I hope that pupils' memories of mine own teaching will not lose sight of its modest badness. I recall one class of bright yet rebellious pupils in my first term as a teacher: I was so unsure about the syllabus that I never dared ask for fear of the obvious question "what have you been teaching them up to now?" Instead I joined in their rebellion and we had an amusing time until exams drew near. They then realised how little they'd learnt and launched into a desperate couple of weeks of self education. My pupils achieved astonishingly good exam results, and I recalled that the same thing had happened when I was at school - a physics teacher whom we had mercilessly ribbed all year became a grades hero when the exam results were announced.

A school stripped of its bad teachers is a crammer. An educational system stripped of its bad teachers is a recipe for mediocrity.

Good.

Well into the second half of my life I reckon the pain of passing will be eased by the knowledge that I saw the world when it was at its best.

APE SHIT

In my Sex Myth essay I challenged the idea that a patriarchal age was founded when men used their greater physical strength and aggression to depose a pre-existing matriarchy. I argued that the warrior has a comfortable niche in matriarchal society, and that it was more in keeping with certain myths that the rise of the patriarchy was the rise of the little man, the rise of the priesthood and the ascendency of spirit over flesh. Thus women could be torn between the need for a civilised husband and a buried stratum of hunger for an alpha male.

That sort of theorising assumes that our animal past was driven by a genetic urge to mate with strong, aggressive partners in order to breed dominant and sexually successful children. I don't find that hard to believe in view of what we are taught about animal behaviour.

A friend, however, described a visit to a Dutch zoo where research was challenging the concept of the dominant alpha male. She described many examples where the obvious alpha male in a monkey colony was outwitted by a small and spirited male. In one case the female monkeys even ganged up against the alpha male in support of the little monkey. It was suggested that the 'alpha male' concept was an example of a patriarchal bias in science which caused Victorian researchers to misinterpret their observations in the light of male prejudice.

Naturally, as a symmettry-minded mathematician, I wondered to what extent today's researchers might be misinterpreting their own observations in the light of post feminist prejudices - but then I hit on an even sillier idea.

If, as suggested in the above mentioned essay, humanity was evolving upward from its patriarchal phase, then might not our nearest primate relatives be in the process of following in our prehistoric footsteps? Maybe the Victorians were correct in their observation of the alpha male, and today's researchers were equally correct in detecting the rise of the "little monkey of spirit" who is laying the foundation for a simian priesthood in future millennia!

Even better, what might such an evolutionary wind of change do to our institutions? I have argued endlessly that human organisations - from governments to professional bodies, from corporations to the media - are a form of artificial intelligence that has evolved to serve their own interests over that of the individuals within and around them. Thus a legal system which punishes a citizen for defending his house and family against criminal attack has evolved in order to further crime and thus generate an environment for its own prosperity - and that the common human mistake is to seek to expose the evil humans responsible for this conspiracy rather than to recognise that the legal system itself is the guilty party. Judging by the aggressive behaviour of these 'hive minds' - whether in nationalistic aggression or corporate takeover battles - they are entrenched in the most brutal phase of the early stage of evolution where a mother goddess presides over male slaughter (eg Mother Capitalism sending out Her warrior corporations to slay each other in Her name). So how might the revolution I described take place in our institutions?

According to the formula in my essay, it would need some non-aggressive institution to offer itself for sacrifice. My candidate for this revolution is Liberal Democracy, because it is the one prevalent system which would allow extremists to be voted into power and so destroy democracy itself. This happened in Germany in Hitler's time - and yet Liberal Democracy survived and is spreading in influence. I see it as the leading edge of a future priesthood among institutions.

Among nations, Tibet might qualify as a nation which sacrificed itself and has as a result grown in influence. But I wonder what sort of corporation or business could repeat this trick? Netscape which grew big by giving away its only product was a candidate, but it has not yet pulled off the Big Victory over alpha-Microsoft.

Some would insist that the aggressive behaviour in the world's markets is simply a multiplication of the aggressive nature of the males who operate those markets. I prefer to see the aggressive nature of world markets as primal: a nature that evolved in the struggle against communism, welfare state, and other competing ideas, and the struggle will no doubt continue against Islamic fundamentalism and future mutations of communism. As such the innate viciousness of world markets are independent of whether they are run by gentlemen, yuppies or female financiers - however they have evolved a culture of emulation which lures more aggressive individuals into their structure in order to pump up the corporate hormones.

So I believe it is necessary to civilise our institutions before we can civilise the way they are managed. We won't get decent government until a nation is prepared to dissolve itself for the sake of world peace. We won't get good management before a corporation offers to disband itself for the greater good of world trade. And the biggest challenge to religious fundamentalism lies in the New Age acceptance of 'doing ones own thing'.

However, it could be on account of such beliefs that I, one time brilliant scholar at a great university, have ended up as an impoverished and ineffectual writer, rather than a major player on the world stage.

So don't be too persuaded by this argument.

AN EXPERIMENT WITH TIME

In collating this material for self-publication I have detected a frantic note here and there reflecting times when I really thought the book was about to be published. There have been many false dawns, and in recent years I have felt desperate to the point where I would almost rather die than live another year with all this stuff still languishing on my hard disk.

Why do I never have enough time? Why does no-one else have time to help me or to look at this material and use it? The number of pitfalls and problems seems to pile up and jam the works even more. I sometimes feel that I have been singled out by the universe as the victim of a cruel experiment in frustration - except for the fact that I meet other people who feel just the same as I do. People whose schedules are cluttered and who are on the one hand pressured to perform and on the other unable to act because they cannot reach those whose co-operation is needed. Has the arrival of voice messaging made it any easier to do business?

So I deduce that it is not just that I am busy and trying to do more, but that I am caught up in a world wide web of stress. A global sense of too much to do and too little time to do it. Every day now feels like the last few days before Christmas - a time when there is pressure to complete jobs before the year end, and yet everyone is either on holiday, or at an office party or else also too busy trying to catch up to be obtainable.

That last analogy gave me the idea for my experiment with time. What I did was to meditate in my usual way for twenty minutes or so, but with one difference. Before the meditation I looked at the calendar and noted the date and month, and then during the meditation I held onto that day and month but visualised the calendar year as being 2002. The result was an unusual feeling of calm and a comforting reduction in pressure.

The theory is this: shared experiences like the last days of holidays, the end of school term, deadlines and the above-mentioned Christmas period all reinforce in us a feeling for the experience of *running out of time*. It is a pattern of pressure and response ingrained into us as individuals and into society as a whole because of times like Christmas when we are all running in synchronicity. Now the end of the millennium, no matter how much we may think it does not have any significance for us personally, is a major trigger in society for that pattern of response. Some of us - like the builders of the Millennium Dome or millennium bug consultants - really are dominated by the countdown to the year 2000. The rest of us are merely swept along in a general tide of media interest. And I am suggesting that there is also an element of telepathic group mindery operating at an unconscious level. Everyone feels a sense of pressure, frustration and information overload even though few of us directly relate it to the year 2000.

Now my subjective exploration of the feeling of 2002 was one of an open road ahead, a glorious relaxing feeling of there being plenty of time stretching before me. Nothing seemed so urgent. Was this the public mood that differentiated *fin de siecle* decadence from the long hot summers of the Edwardian era?

Confident that I will get this book out before 1999, I offer this meditation as a gift to my readers. If life seems frantic set aside a half hour, look at the calendar then picture that it is the same date a few years after 2000 - and see if you too enjoy the resulting feeling.

Maybe the next decade will see a balmy neo-Edwardian era of lazy summer outings and long cosy evenings to play with our VR machines and indulge in leisurely symposia on the web? Maybe there really will be long queues to visit the Millennium Dome?

A YAWNING GULF

A sense of deja vu: when I first set to editing these essays for publication all the talk was on the imminent crisis of war in the Gulf. Many years on I am editing for self publication and today's Radio 4 phone-in program is all about whether we should go to war against Saddam again.

The disturbing thing is that the whole business of war is being trivialised, because the entire discussion has focussed on the shallow issues of politics and morality rather than the true significance of war as a potential media event.

At every election it is recognised that it is the media which choose our politicians and get them elected. Yet when resulting political activity takes place, who bothers to ask what the media really need? People are quick to point out that it is the media that define today's morality, but when it comes to moral dilemmas, who bothers to ask to what end the media actually shapes our morals?

The death of Princess Diana has run and run, but this year will need a new story, and a Gulf war could fill the gap. The trouble is that last time it was ruined by the Iraqis who failed badly to live up to media promises. Plot-wise the Gulf War was a disaster: the enemy, promoted as the biggest threat to world peace since Hitler, simply caved in.

It has taken years of work for the media to rebuild Saddam's reputation as The Great Satan, but there are still gaps in the public credibility to be filled before we have at last generated a worthy heir to the late lamented Evil Empire of Soviet Communism (I dismiss the world Satanic conspiracy as a tabloid non-starter for the honour).

What is needed at this stage is not another badly scripted victory against the Iraqis, but rather a bungled operation leading to crushing defeat for the West. Even Princess Di revelations will knuckle under to a good scare story!

The main tenor of the radio discussion is that victory is impossible unless you have clear objectives, so we must wait. Meanwhile, however, constant media exposure is doing its best to cloud the waters and reduce the clarity of the objectives, while revelations of Saddam's evil are stoking public pressure that 'something must be done quickly'. This is surely laying a sound foundation on which to build an ill-considered military strike which has a decent chance of failing.

It may not be the perfect recipe for crushing defeat and the emergence of a new Satan, but I have respect for the English speaking media - the finest the world has ever known - and I trust them implicitly to direct our morals and politics towards the best possible outcome.

A LAST WORD ON THELEMIC MORALITY

Try this analogy for the three aeons described in the earlier essay.

In the beginning God saw humanity in confusion and so he presented them with a clock to mark the time of day.

As humanity became more conscious of time some began to ask "shouldn't we be doing something to maintain this clock?" whereupon the priests had them stoned for presuming to lay hands on God's property.

So eventually the clock ran slower and slower until it stopped. More and more people began to question whether it really was always six minutes to two, and the streets ran with the blood of those whom the priests had condemned to death for daring to question God's gift.

God heard their cries and decided on a new approach: he gave every person a solar powered quartz wristwatch. Now everyone had personal access to the correct time.

But even highly accurate quartz mechanisms are not absolutely perfect. As the years passed some began to notice discrepancies between different persons' times. This was hotly denied by the new priesthood (who had utter scorn for that old priesthood left staring at a stopped clock).

As general awareness about these irregularities spread, it was most furiously resisted by those people whose watches had strayed the furthest. These were the cult leaders - fanatics so sure of their rightness that they persuaded others to adjust their time to match their own.

Now the streets were running with the blood of battling sects. So God decided on a third plan.

A kind relative recently gave me a Junghams clock. It is another quartz clock, but with a difference. Several times a day it checks its accuracy against radio signals propagated from a central atomic clock. Although this means I have more accurate time than any of those earlier wristwatches, it also serves as a constant reminder that even this super-accurate time is no more than a local approximation that needs constant revision. And that in turn reminds me that even the atomic clock is no more than humanity's best yet attempt to measure the fourth dimension.

People fear moral relativity because they fear the removal of the prop of certainty that a "perfection" exists. They do not understand that a new, more demanding method is a necessary part of the package. They feel the same way that the fundamentalists must have felt when Jesus suggested that "love thy neighbour" could be called a "law".

SERIOUS FUN

Perhaps a last word from the OTTO?

Some occultists have really taken on board the need to have a sense of humour and not be too stuffy. I have attended some pagan ceremonies where there has been a delightful "woops! I forgot the consecration!" sort of atmosphere which makes a splendid contrast to the stuffy old ceremonial of the established church. But what did it do for the magic?

I recall Nietzsche's saying that the maturity of man is when he regains the seriousness of a child at play. One small problem with our informal and easy-going society is that it does not give us much incentive to be serious. One nice thing about ritual is that it can give us the excuse to be solemn and serious which ordinary life does not provide.

Like bittersweet flavours, solemnity and fun can be most delicious when brought into closest proximity. How do we do it?

There are two ways. The first I call the Christian formula: it is to have fun first, and then get serious. The Pagan formula is to be serious first, then have fun.

In the first approach you let rip on the sin, and then have a spiritual hangover and go for confession and absolution as befits a religion where the prodigal son gets greater love than his goody-goody brethren. (This may explain why the public experiences Christmas as a month long frolic which ends on the 25th of December, rather than a 12 day celebration beginning on the 25th.)

The second approach seems rather naughty in comparison: you begin with a solemn invitation for the Gods to join you, so that there presence will stimulate a rather better orgy to follow. Here the more solemn and moving the initial ritual, the more ecstatic can be the release - according to OTTO doctrine.

Whereas the winning formula in New Age workshops is that all deep feelings must be expressed as incoherently as possible in order to prove how deep they are and thus win applause - men must adopt an attitude of "I'm just an incoherent bloke aspiring to New Manhood" and women must be fluffy airheads dumbstruck with awe at the beautiful loving consciousness of everyone else present - a rather different mental approach is demanded in OTTO rituals. It is that "I am a reincarnation of Sir Charles Irving, the world's greatest ever Shakespearian actor, but fat chance of this crowd of nerds appreciating the fact unless I really lay it on thick".

Eleanor Bron won instant honourary adeptship for her superb portrayal of the mourning Isis in a scene in Ken Russel's film of Women In Love - essential viewing for OTTO aspirants needing to bone up on sweeping gestures and dramatic pauses.

So OTTO rituals allow tremendous scope for solemnity. In fact one of the most important disciplines practiced by OTTO initiates is "the look that kills" - at the least suggestion of a titter or smirk from anyone present, the ponderously gesticulating and intoning hierophant will turn and glare.

The ideal ritual thus begins with quiet dignity, then grows increasingly theatrical and over-played as each participant sacrifices inhibitions on the alter of ego inflation - seeing their own "performance" as sublime while everyone else is being utterly ridiculous. The resulting atmosphere develops the repressive intensity of a girls' school speech day when the headmistress' skirt splits as she reaches to shake hands with the mayor...

Such a ritual just has to end in a party.

THE LAST WORD ON TRADITIONAL FAMILY VALUES

Fred West.

A LAST WORD ON DEVIL WORSHIP

Out of respect for those who only bought this book because it mentions devils on the cover, I had better end on that theme.

A philosophy or creed seeks to attract members to its fold, so it beams out its message to the world. Those nearby see the message clearly as a guiding lighthouse, but for those further away it is just one point of light among many.

The appetite for recruitment may not be satisfied as a result, so new measures are taken. Sheepdogs are employed to go out and snap at the heels of distant browsers and drive them into the fold.

If Christ is your lighthouse then Satan is your sheepdog - and the fiercer you can breed him, and the louder his bark, the better he will drive the flock to you.

If Liberal Socialism is your lighthouse, then Right-Wing Thuggery is your sheepdog. If Capitalism is your lighthouse, then a creeping Communist Conspiracy. If Naziism, then World Jewry; if Traditional Values, then Sixties Decadence; if the Nation, then its evil neighbours; if Law and Order, then a festering criminal underworld...

In every case, the more vicious you can make the sheepdog, the more the public will shy away from it, and the faster the recruitment. The public no longer need to see the light, they are so pre-occupied with the demon dogs snapping at their heels and driving them towards it.

That is the problem.

Instead of the faithful walking towards your beacon with the light shining on their faces, they are now walking backwards towards it, staring into the shadows cast by that light and in awe of the snarling power unleashed there.

Those demon dogs are getting more attention than the light they are supposed to be serving. They attract more interest. The flock becomes fascinated by their power and reaches out offerings to please the beasts.

A young man from a liberal background puts on a Nazi armband, salutes, and feels excited as never before. The fundamentalist Christian's daughter takes out the tarot pack hidden under her mattress, and the cards almost burn her hands with their power...

Don't you feel some envy?

Find your anger and feed it the faggots of experience.
Onto this raging pyre cast every belief, prejudice, principle, certainty or truth...
There is always something that remains, a residuum of humanity that is actually quite nice.
Let it be your darkest secret. For you will by now have earned that most priceless of worldly assets – a reputation for extreme wickedness.

FINIS

AFTERWORD

This is what it was all about...

1. Ideas, beliefs, principles, assumptions... all these can be tyrants.

2. They can also be saviours. Thus one idea triumphs over another by liberating us until it too turns out to be a tyrant.

3. "Free will" is to dodge and duck as ideas do battle around and within us. In vain, while we are the battlefield.

4. It is necessary, therefore, to detach from ideas, beliefs, principles and assumptions. Step back and enjoy the struggle without becoming its victim.

5. This can be difficult and painful. It requires us to abandon our principles (provided that is "the one thing we refuse to do") and embrace relativity. It requires us to admit that even the most monstrous human beings have probably at times nurtured intentions every bit as benevolent as our own.

6. There is a precedent for this detachment: it was when mankind learnt to detach from Nature. This was progress: the bushman is in this one respect our inferior and we must therefore learn most carefully from them.

7. Detaching from Nature, from Mother Earth, was a phase of growing up. It was necessary for the development of Science.

8. Detaching from ideas is another stage of growing up. It is time to let go of Truth and discover our Selves. It is also necessary for the development of Magic.

9. Goodbye, Mother Earth. Goodbye, Father Sky.

10. A Great Adventure lies ahead.

www.ingramcontent.com/pod-product-compliance
Lightning Source LLC
Chambersburg PA
CBHW031914160426
42812CB00096B/399